"*This America of Ours* is a deeply subversive and patriotic book that inspires a coyote's howl. It is a brilliant rendering of what 'the open space of democracy' must be if we are to survive its present state of erosion. Nate Schweber possesses the ferocity of a journalist and the agility of a storyteller who animates the magnificent and mischievous spirit of Bernard DeVoto, one of the most astute writers of the American West and dogged defenders of public lands. Schweber also brings the forgotten intelligence of Avis DeVoto into her full light as a persuasive champion of wildness. This book reads like a thriller, with the twist and turns of history thoroughly charged by two active minds and the community that surrounded them. We learn how sharp-edged politics are transformed through bold, literary actions into public policies that protect sacred lands that not only have shaped the diversity of our character, but ignited our imaginations.

— Terry Tempest Williams, author of *The Hour of Land*

"*This America of Ours* is so many fantastic things all at the same time: the story of a complex marriage, the history of one of our most important historians, and a razor's-edge drama about a critical fight to preserve America's public lands—the wild places that define our nation's soul. And Schweber manages to tell all these stories in a thoroughly gripping narrative, a story whose pages I could not wait to turn."

— Michael Punke, author of *The Revenant, Ridgeline,* and *Last Stand*

"Americans have long recognized their debt of gratitude to farsighted individuals who created our system of public lands. Thanks to Nate Schweber's meticulous research and compelling narrative in *This America of Ours,* we can now take measure of our equal debt to Bernard and Avis DeVoto and others who saved those remarkable lands from destruction. A must-read for anyone who cares about conservation in America."

— Peter Stark, author of *Young Washington*

"*This America of Ours* is an intimate, compelling portrait of one of America's most consequential literary partnerships. Bernard and Avis DeVoto were magnetic intellectuals who spent their lives defending public lands and constitutional freedoms. Nate Schweber narrates their battles against McCarthyism and Congressional land grabs in vivid and witty prose. Using previously unpublished sources, Schweber illuminates the lives of both Bernard and Avis, and reveals the intensity of their friendships with luminaries like Julia Child and Robert Frost. *This America of Ours* is a must-read for anyone interested in the dramatic politics of conservation at America's mid-century—and anyone who enjoys a strong martini."

—Megan Kate Nelson, Pulitzer Prize finalist and author of *Saving Yellowstone*

"No question, Bernard DeVoto stands as one of America's great historians. But more than write history, he lived it and made it. Reading Nate Schweber's energetic and commanding account of DeVoto's impassioned career in defense of national parks and public lands, and his defiance of two of the country's most shameless bullies, Joseph McCarthy and Pat McCarran, the timeline of the despicable deeds that DeVoto risked his reputation and livelihood to thwart—it all feels an awful lot like NOW. *This America of Ours* is alarming, gripping, and gratifying. Herein justice is done—to the lives of DeVoto and his equally brave and brilliant wife, Avis, and to the better angels of our democracy. Welcome, if you please, two overdue inductees into the pantheon of environmental heroes."

—John Taliaferro, author of *Grinnell*

"*This America of Ours* chronicles the history of one of conservation's greatest power couples in their lifelong battle to save our wild public lands and oppose the destruction and privatization of open spaces. Schweber tells all in sturdy, vivid prose; the pulse of this book beats with a lust for life."

—Doug Peacock, author of *Grizzly Years* and *Was It Worth It?*

THE DEVOTOS' **AMERICAN WEST** AND
DINOSAUR NATIONAL MONUMENT, 1940s AND 1950s

OLYMPIC
NATIONAL PARK

FORT CLATSOP

WASHINGTON

Columbia R.

Walla
Walla

RED
CEDARS

Missoula

Great Falls

GLACIER
NATIONAL PARK

Bitterroot
Valley

MONTANA

Missouri R.

Yellowstone R.

Miles
City

GARRISON
DAM

THREE
AFFILIATED
TRIBES

NORTH
DAKOTA

OREGON

CRATER LAKE
NATIONAL PARK

LANDMARK
RANGER STATION

Boise

IDAHO

YELLOWSTONE
NATIONAL PARK

Buffalo

JOHNSON
COUNTY

GRAND
TETON
NATIONAL PARK

WYOMING

Black
Hills

Pierre

SOUTH
DAKOTA

Reno

McCARRAN RANCH

Carson City

Great
Salt Lake

Ogden

Salt Lake
City

Bonneville
Salt Flats

Rock Springs

NEBRASKA

DINOSAUR
NATIONAL
MONUMENT
(see inset)

ROCKY MOUNTAIN
NATIONAL PARK

YOSEMITE
NATIONAL
PARK

NEVADA

UTAH

COLORADO

KANSAS

CALIFORNIA

Las Vegas

HOOVER DAM

GRAND CANYON
NATIONAL PARK

MESA VERDE
NATIONAL PARK

Shiprock

N

ARIZONA

NEW MEXICO

OKLAHOMA

0   200   400 miles
0   200   400 kilometers

TEXAS

UTAH

COLORADO

SPLIT
MOUNTAIN
DAM
proposed
second phase

ECHO PARK DAM
Colorado River Storage Project proposed first phase

Green R.

Harpers
Corner

Yampa R.

DINOSAUR NATIONAL MONUMENT

0   5   10 miles
0   5   10 kilometers

THIS AMERICA OF OURS

Bernard and Avis DeVoto
and the Forgotten Fight to
Save the Wild

NATE SCHWEBER

MARINER BOOKS
New York   Boston

For Kristen, emphatically

THIS AMERICA OF OURS. Copyright © 2022 by Nate Schweber. All rights reserved. Printed in the United States of America. No part of this book may be used or reproduced in any manner whatsoever without written permission except in the case of brief quotations embodied in critical articles and reviews. For information, address HarperCollins Publishers, 195 Broadway, New York, NY 10007.

HarperCollins books may be purchased for educational, business, or sales promotional use. For information, please email the Special Markets Department at SPsales@harpercollins.com.

A hardcover edition of this book was published in 2022 by Mariner Books.

FIRST MARINER BOOKS PAPERBACK EDITION PUBLISHED 2023.

Designed by Greta D. Sibley

Library of Congress Cataloging-in-Publication Data has been applied for.

ISBN 978-0-06-326869-2

23 24 25 26 27 LBC 5 4 3 2 1

Where there is great love there are always miracles.

—Willa Cather

CONTENTS

PROLOGUE

March 3–July 8, 1948

THE YOUNG WOMAN CLUTCHES THE CYLINDER and rushes through New York City as it is swallowed by darkness and lacquered in sleet on Wednesday, March 3. The city is in a state of emergency because a postal employee has found an unmarked envelope with five hand-scribbled pages that say 150 bombs will explode at rush hour. Hundreds of law enforcement officers, fearing Russian attack, slop through Times Square, Pennsylvania Station, the Staten Island Ferry terminal. They stop cars, tear through baggage at Grand Central Terminal, trace rat paths through dank subway tunnels. After the young woman sloshes up the steps of the Beaux-Arts postal service building in Midtown Manhattan and slips through the Corinthian colonnade, FBI agents stop her.

"What have you got there, miss?"

"Powder," she replies.

In her trembling hands is the address for Bernard and Avis DeVoto, one of the most consequential couples of the twentieth century, whose business with whatever is in the cylinder alarms the agents. They detain

Jeanne-Marie Kranich and tear open her parcel, revealing a tin. Kranich pleads that she is only running an errand for her boss. Agents pop open the tin and from it wafts a savory-smelling ochre plume that no one can identify. A daring man touches finger to tongue, taps the substance, and darts it back. He grimaces, shakes his head like a dog, and suffers no ill effect. When rush hour ends without carnage, the letter is deemed a false alarm. Agents escort Kranich to have the parcel rewrapped at a stationery store and addressed to 8 Berkeley Street in Cambridge, Massachusetts, home of the DeVotos.

On March 5, Avis DeVoto fails to find the Vencatachellum Madras curry powder she asked for from her friend, a food writer who, with terrible timing, sent his secretary to the post office. Sometime after the curry was mailed, it was inexplicably removed from the package and replaced with one pound of peanuts, still shelled. An insomniac crime reporter puts the strange tale in the *New York Times* on May 22. "A Curry Mystery . . . Great Powder Disappearance Involves Seizure by FBI of Lovely Secretary" declares the headline. "There is a chance that J. Edgar Hoover of the Federal Bureau of Investigation has it."

The *Times* reporter is the first to postulate that the nation's foremost law enforcement officer is interested in the DeVotos.

Around the DeVoto breakfast table where eggs, newspapers, and Chesterfield cigarettes are devoured, the article delivers bombs of laughter. As a bonus, it is Avis's forty-fourth birthday. Having sent her foodie friend, Fletcher Pratt, a sarcastic thank-you for the peanuts, she mails the *Times* reporter, George Horne, a rollicking bravo. Bernard DeVoto, fifty-one, a writer, historian, and conservationist, tucks the article in his files. His crusading for public lands is dovetailing with his defense of the Bill of Rights, and he is collecting details about increasingly intrusive and opaque government investigations. He fears their potential co-option by land despoilers with intent to target, harass, smear, censor, and persecute.

A shared righteous sense of humor still draws the DeVotos together as it did when he was a misunderstood twenty-five-year-old who found in a radiant eighteen-year-old kindred spirit from Michigan's Upper Peninsula the "courage, faith, certainty" that quelled his thoughts of suicide.

Now, laugh lines and two sons testify to the longevity of their union, one fused by symbiosis — she loves to cook, he loves to eat, he loves to write, she loves to edit, he loves attention, she cherishes her privacy. As the marriage enters its climactic act, Avis remains in awe of her husband's Promethean mind. "He could surprise me to the day he died," she will say of Bernard, pronounced "BERN-ard," whom she dresses down at home as "DeVoto," "B.," and "damn genius." He holds scholarly accolades but she is more emotionally intelligent. An empath, Avis usually better interprets "overtones of a situation." But where she falters, he develops "intuitions and understandings quite beyond mine." Their intellects are as simpatico as their souls. They both feel the ramifications of the accusation from Wyoming.

On June 1 in the tiny, windy High Plains town of Douglas, some of the West's largest cattle ranchers, dressed in suits and Stetsons, discuss how to dispense with Bernard DeVoto. The elite Wyoming Stock Growers Association seethes because in *Harper's Magazine* Bernard exposed and thwarted a secret plot by its leaders to force the sell-off of as much as 230 million acres of America's public lands, including national parks, monuments, forests, and grasslands. The DeVotos uncovered the plot on an epic 1946 cross-country road trip, and in his 1947 blockbuster exposé "The West Against Itself," Bernard wrote (paraphrasing Woody Guthrie's fresh folk classic) "this is your land we are talking about." In retaliation, a Cheyenne newspaper printed the association's statement saying that Bernard "should have a hammer and sickle over his desk." Bernard joked that until reading that he had no idea he was a Communist. Hoover, missing the humor, keeps the quote underlined with an arrow pointing to it in the same classified Washington, DC, file where he stashes a synopsis about the curry.

Meanwhile in Cambridge, Bernard studies arcane congressional reports through the spring of 1948 and his blood chills when he sees that the National Park Service faces a new existential crisis. It is the scariest threat to the service's integrity since Congress created it in 1916 with a mandate to protect land "unimpaired for the enjoyment of future generations." Bernard discovers that the Bureau of Reclamation plans to dam an awesome, ancient sandstone chasm carved by the Green River inside Dinosaur National Monument. That wild canyon country, straddling the border of Colorado and his home state of Utah, is under the jurisdiction of the National Park Service. If the Bureau of Reclamation can smash down the legal barrier protecting Dinosaur National Monument, it will expose all national parks and level a path for plunderers of all public lands. Like guillotine blades, more dams will fall on national parks: Grand Canyon in Arizona, Yellowstone in Wyoming, Glacier in Montana, King's Canyon in California, Mammoth Cave in Kentucky. Ultimately, as many as 75 percent of the acres inside the nation's parks, monuments, forests, and grasslands could be thrown open to clear-cutting, livestock grazing, mining, real estate development—and closed to the public. Bernard considers this not only as a lover of pristine, open country, but as a social historian extrapolating how environmental devastation and monopolization of natural resource wealth in the West will spark factional war and threaten the union. He receives an alarming June 10 letter from National Park Service director Newton Drury confirming that the parks are "on very thin ice."

Most responsible is Patrick McCarran, Democratic senator from Nevada, whose paranoia is eclipsed only by his parliamentary genius. McCarran withholds appropriations from the National Park Service—"One can raise merry havoc with these departments by the control of their purse strings," he has boasted—and showers his favorite bureaus with money and power. One is the Bureau of Reclamation. Another is the Federal Bureau of Investigation. While nurturing Wisconsin Republican senator Joseph McCarthy, McCarran tacitly conscripts the FBI as the vigilante arm of the Wyoming Stock Growers Association.

Bernard works exhaustively to expose the malfeasance. The DeVotos fly to Boulder briefly in mid-June and Bernard gives an impassioned speech about conservation while accepting an honorary degree from the University of Colorado. It is a controversial accolade from his home region that he says "pleases me a damned sight more than the Pulitzer Prize did." They pause on June 30. The DeVotos cheer their silver wedding anniversary. Summer celebrations are time for Avis's favorite simple dish, chilled lobster bathed in hot butter paired with her husband's famous, icy "DeVoto Dry" martini (3.7 parts gin, 1 part dry vermouth, and a twist of lemon only). A quarter-century has accentuated the couple's Beauty and the Beast element. Avis has a femininely handsome face, luminous smile, high cheekbones, sapphire eyes that beam under arched brows, and wavy, chestnut hair. Her trademark cosmetic flourish is audaciously red lipstick, and her paycheck becomes fashionable dresses of ruby broadcloth and hyacinth blue chiffon that hug her trim waist and voluptuous bosom. Bernard, by contrast, is "far from a beauty," she tenderly admits. Nose, mashed; eyes, googly; lips, droopy; haircut, like iron shavings on an egg. He wrinkles his gray wool suits by slouching in odd shapes, adding a Quasimodo aura. His sense of humor about it is generally good. His advice to a man mistaken for him: sue.

Bernard has a sonorous baritone voice reminiscent of CBS newscaster Edward R. Murrow. In conversation with Avis he uses it like Gershwin scoring brass with woodwinds. A friend tells Avis that to share conversation with the DeVotos was to experience "such vitality that knowing you only for a few hours was equal to knowing most people for years." In this marital symphony, close friends detect Avis's part in Bernard's successes, like winning the previous year's Pulitzer Prize for History for his book about the Rocky Mountain fur trade, *Across the Wide Missouri*.

The DeVotos' great legacy is saving so many millions of acres of America's public lands, which in an unforeseen twist is about to make Avis best friends with a fellow aspiring gourmet, Julia Child, whose career Avis vows to launch. But the DeVotos' legacy will be undone if a dam is built in Dinosaur National Monument. That would set a precedent for the gutting of all national parks, monuments, forests, grasslands, battlefields, and other historical sites that the DeVotos thought they had saved. McCarran's muscled-up political weapon is accusing his adversaries of disloyalty to the country, which McCarthy is excitedly learning to repeat as the Second Red Scare dawns. The DeVotos will fight back, as always, with facts, humor, the Bill of Rights, and reminders of what unites all Americans—first and foremost the land. But McCarran and McCarthy's counteroffensive will enlist their ally, FBI director Hoover, who derives his power from collecting and strategically revealing secrets. He is boss of the agent who seized a curry tin addressed to the DeVotos, and another who arrived with questions at their Cambridge home months later.

On Thursday, July 8 at 8:30 a.m. the DeVotos' phone rings. It is an FBI agent saying he is coming in 30 minutes. He will not say why. Bernard is "half sick to boot, or more than half" from overwork, and Avis is worried. He wearily pulls on dark, baggy slacks and a rumpled sport shirt but neither rakes his gray stubble with his Rolls Razor nor pats his mottled cheeks with lilac vegetal aftershave nor spritzes his squat neck with Bay Rum cologne. At his door, Bernard greets a veteran agent, scrubbed and in a crisp suit and shiny shoes. He leads him past Avis's kitchen into his office boasting not a Soviet flag but 10,000 books. Expecting a "touchy interview," the agent flashes his badge and asks about a man who listed Bernard as a reference. Avis, something of an expert in investigations —her job is writing detective novel reviews for the *Boston Globe*—may have warned her husband the agent would take the opportunity to get information *from* him to collect information *about* him. Bernard cheerfully natters to the agent about his fiction publisher, Little, Brown and Company, with whom he is canceling his contract in protest because it publishes author Howard Fast (whom Bernard thinks is a hack and knows is a Communist). Bernard tells the agent little he does not already know, but by keeping the conversation going through midmorning, Bernard learns plenty. When the agent seems to realize he is being mined, he says no to coffee and leaves. There will be alarm in his report to Hoover that Bernard DeVoto has "an almost uncanny ability to realize what might already be in our files."

PART I

There can be no greater issue than that of conservation in this country.

—Theodore Roosevelt

That was a fine collection of sovereigns, that first Nevada legislature. They levied taxes to the amount of thirty or forty thousand dollars and ordered expenditures to the extent of about a million.

—Mark Twain, *Roughing It*

1

"Deep as the Roots of the Earth"

BEFORE THE DEVOTOS' LOVE BLOOMED, ancient trees swayed above carpets of wildflowers in Helen Avis MacVicar's hometown. Around Houghton, Michigan, on the Keweenaw Peninsula, a finger of land sheathed by the icy waters of Lake Superior, there were sugar maples, white pines, yellow birches, and hemlocks. At their bases among the maidenhair ferns flashed goldenrods, gaggles of black-eyed Susans, and hidden trilliums the color of porcelain.

According to Avis's family lore, the first member of her clan who traveled to North America from Scotland was a red-coated British Army enrollee who deserted to Canada during the Revolutionary War. Avis's grandfather ran a hotel in Walkerton, Ontario, near Lake Huron, before he walked out on his eight children. One of them, Walter, her father, immigrated to the United States and opened a dry goods store in Houghton, serving employees of the mining and logging companies busily turning an Eden into a hellscape.

In the 1600s, Jesuit missionaries to the Ojibwe tribe located a 1.5-ton boulder of cherry-colored copper on the banks of the Ontonagon River near Houghton. In the 1850s, as Indigenous societies were shattered, railroads came to haul away copper and iron. The devastation to the virgin forests of the upper Midwest was on par with the simultaneous slaughter of buffalo on the Great Plains and the extermination of the passenger pigeon. Grayling, cold-water fish whose oversize dorsal fins shimmer like oyster shells, were extirpated from Michigan as the earth was literally scorched. In 1871, slash piles left by cut-and-run loggers combusted and the conflagrations torched more than 2.5 million acres of Michigan and Wisconsin, killing as many as 2,400 people (eight times more than the Great Chicago Fire that year). By the turn of the twentieth century the upper Midwest's expanse of deforested land was half the size of Europe. When Avis was born in 1904, what around her had been revered as hallowed ground was being redubbed as "hollowed ground."

History swerved when Theodore Roosevelt, an imperialist and an ecological nationalist furious about the destruction of his country's natural heritage, intervened. By the time Roosevelt became president in 1901, he had ranched cattle in Dakota Territory, led daredevil Spanish-American War charges as an army colonel in Cuba, and authored more than a dozen books. The energetic and eccentric chief executive saw his nation's survival threatened by the Weyerhaeuser timber syndicate's progression from razing midwestern forests to amassing Far West landholdings rivaling the size of New England states. To check the syndicates and cattle kings seizing the West, Roosevelt created or enlarged 150 national forests. National forests curbed monopolization of water, the region's most precious natural resource. An irrigation obsessive, Roosevelt understood from his ranching days that in the dry West, mountain peaks rake precipitation out of thin air in the form of wintertime snow. This makes them equivalent to the gray-bellied clouds that hydrate the humid side of the country east of the Mississippi River. Conserving forests and grasslands is essential to shading, filtering, and regulating melting snow through blazing summers so clean water can consistently bathe downslope ranches, farms, and communities. Nothing but winning at war is more important, Roosevelt said.

"I am against the man who skins the land!" the barrel-chested, teeth-clacking Republican declared. Roosevelt knew that public lands managed scientifically and sustainably were the wellspring of his nation's permanent wealth. They would provide water, timber, grass, havens for wildlife, and peace of mind for humans. Passionate in equal amount about history and big-game hunting, Roosevelt wanted to cultivate patriotism in future generations by providing escapes from industrial pollution, opportunities to experience lonely, silent landscapes, and sanctuaries for awesome wildlife the likes of which the first Americans saw. He established the first fifty-five national wildlife refuges and used the 1906 Antiquities Act to create the first eighteen national monuments. "The forest reserves should be set apart forever for the use and benefit of our people as a whole and not sacrificed to the shortsighted greed of a few," Roosevelt told Congress. White Americans' extermination of Native peoples and theft of their lands for cultivation by enslaved Africans compromised the righteousness of his message. But as the nation evolved, all its citizens faced a challenge as old as life itself: how to source food, water, air, and materials for shelter without polluting or exhausting them. Enshrining public lands conservation as a nation's priority for the first time in world history marked an American political, philosophical, and moral revolution.

The environmental destruction epitomized in Avis's hometown inspired Roosevelt to protect the forests of the West, linking Avis to her future husband in the roots of conservation history. Bernard DeVoto sprung screaming into this world in Ogden, Utah, in 1897. When Bernard was a pugnacious, pudgy-lipped boy of ten, Roosevelt established the Wasatch National Forest, encompassing trees growing in striated belts on the mountains hulking over town: shaking aspen and Gambel oaks, spindly lodgepole pines, shaggy spruces, and alpine firs. In special places, there grew audacious fairy slipper orchids, like silver stockings wearing pink crowns.

The 40 acres of the West most sacred to Bernard was his maternal grandparents' fruit farm at the mouth of the Weber River, pouring from the national forest. His grandfather, Samuel Dye, had been a prosperous mechanic in drizzly Hertfordshire, England. Mormon missionaries converted him in 1852. He followed his faith to London, where he married a dressmaker, Rhoda. They immigrated 8,000 miles to Utah Territory where the church commanded them to farm a patch of remote alkali desert and make it bloom. Raising seven kids, they met that pioneer challenge so skillfully, courageously, and stoically that they earned the largest share of their literary grandson's familial admiration. Though young Bernard knew little about Roosevelt other than that his own eccentric father despised him, he remembered watching dust gales blow off unprotected Wasatch Range slopes, intuiting that they threatened his grandparents. It was Bernard's farm chore to rise at 3 a.m. and animate the irrigation works that channeled cold, clean mountain water to the fragrant, flowering trees fulfilling Bible prophecy. Bernard revered the climatographical, gravitational, biotic, and political miracle by which snow above timberline on 12,000-foot peaks — spectral in predawn moonlight — became fuzzy Elberta peaches that with a swipe of small palm from branch to chipmunk cheeks delivered a taste sweeter than heaven. It shaped how he would grow and love.

Helen Avis MacVicar was known to her kin as "Little Helen" and to her friends as "Scotty," and she disliked both nicknames. Observant from the moment she opened her eyes in 1904 and opinionated from the moment she could talk, this girl from the north country was fascinated by the people of Houghton. She connected to them through her lifelong passion, which she underscored in a teenage essay about her favorite youthful indulgences: "Next in order to sleep in my category of the delights of life, comes food. Food!"

She learned that breads and cakes baked in Houghton had a yellow tint because of good saffron, which was a favorite flavor of Cornish people who worked the mines. (She watched grime-covered miners emerge from the dark shafts of the Calumet and Hecla Mining Company to pucker cigarettes bought from her father's store.) Her favorite food was also Celtic: pasties, dough baked around meat, potato, and rutabaga, steaming hot and sold from baskets by peddlers at the train station at the terminus of a spur line of the booming Duluth, South Shore and Atlantic Railway. She also learned to make a hunter's stew called "booyaw," which was a dual French-Canadian and Native American concoction that was modified by immigrants from Sweden, Denmark, and Finland. Avis made hers with a mix of homegrown turnips, carrots, potatoes, onions, and jerked venison, which her father kept a crock of in the cellar of their house to keep the family in meat through winters made more severe by three sides of Lake Superior. "This is what I grew up on," she later wrote, still making pasties. "I am immovable about tradition."

She thought her "Pa" was adorable; quiet except for wry, deadpan observations inspired by rye whiskey. He was a union backer, a workers' rights man, and a rare Democrat. As for her "Ma," Avis was enraptured watching her bake brown breads and apple cakes, and turning into jams the handfuls of wild sour cherries and sweet thimbleberries that they picked beyond the smokestacks in the cutover woods on the edge of town. Unfortunately, that was the extent of their bond. Avis's talkativeness and constant questioning were at odds with her Presbyterian parents' innate taciturnity. Her estrangement accelerated after her baby sister died of disease. It left her parents' hearts calcified, in part, she detected, to her.

She escaped into reading. "I have always been addicted to it," she wrote as a teenager. Her favorite books included *Moby Dick* by Herman Melville and *Parnassus on Wheels* by Christopher Morley. She loved Lewis Carroll's *Alice's Adventures in Wonderland* so vigorously it "has four times been reduced to tatters in my hands." *The Damnation of Theron Ware* by Harold Frederic so shook her that after finishing it in the middle of the night she took a moonlit bike ride on country roads to pedal out her emotions.

She lived rambunctiously in what she called "the Copper Country, where so many delightful things happen." When a dam burst and flooded the town, she waded out until her galoshes were swamped (earning a spanking from her mother). To prove she was tougher than neighbor kids, she bounded backyard fences and raided peonies (more spankings). She loved watching pairs of lumberjacks in spiked shoes run atop giant white pine logs in the lake, spinning them "until the other fellow fell off his and perhaps drowned." Her favorite part about sledding was crashing. Sterner discipline threatened when her grandmother caught her with fingers inside colorful celluloid thimbles from the ten-cent store. Believing them stolen, she shut her granddaughter in a closet and ordered her to talk with God. She later asked how it went.

"He says I didn't take 'em."

As a teen Avis watched chugging ships carry stylish tourists to Chicago and she longed to follow. For high school she moved across the Upper Peninsula to the smoking pulp mill town of Escanaba where she was less affected by the outbreak of World War I than by her attack of hormones, which made her feel "steamed up." She blossomed to an average height and weight with a prominent bust, and her face refined to a mix of Tallulah Bankhead's pursed lips and Marlene Dietrich's dramatic cheekbones. She had a few boyfriends—"beaux," she called them. One was popular, athletic, and dull and she tolerated him because he had a car. She was drawn to a bookish young man who was an oddball, an outcast, rumored to be gay—a "pansy" in her Copper Country vernacular. She befriended him for life. She liked iconoclasts, underdogs, outcasts.

College offered a means of escape in the fall of 1922 and she always respected her parents for putting up no protest. At Northwestern University up the coast of Lake Michigan from Chicago, she fell in love with new things like journalism ("To me, a newspaper office is the most exhilarating place in the world") and junk food ("the jelly doughnut"). No sorority did she pledge because she found their rules too "iron bound." She lived in a tiny apartment with a roommate she threw slippers at for snoring, and once, for fun, they filled the bathtub with Jell-O. In English class —her favorite, for she had a way of speaking like the first lines of novels —she perched atop her desk, crossed legs sheathed in French nude stockings, book held to her face, eyes flickering over it.

She was a pioneer by fact of being a woman on campus, two years after the Nineteenth Amendment. Northwestern admitted co-ed undergrads in 1869, but it would take four more years before women would be admitted into the medical school. Though the effort she put into school made her tops in her class—"All I know how to do is work like the devil and hope for the best," she would say—the chauvinism she stared down would be trumpeted in a September 1927 article by an educator in *Harper's*. "How can a man teach with a room full of beautiful girls listening to him?" it began. "It could not be possible that such stunning girls would even pretend to take an interest in intellectual matters." That writer was her English teacher, Bernard DeVoto.

Under the snowy spires of the Wasatch Range on January 11, 1897, Bernard Augustine DeVoto was born a dark-eyed, olive-skinned boy so adorable that family lore has him winning a beauty contest. His mother, Rhoda, named after her mother, became a Jack Mormon after the bishop of Uinta appeared when she was a girl at her farmhouse door and announced she was to be his plural wife. Her father threatened to "shoot the hell out of" him. Rhoda married another scoundrel instead. He was a New Yorker who became county clerk in Rock Springs, Wyoming, and fled with stolen money to Mexico where he was rumored to be killed in a shoot-out. Rhoda remarried and had Bernard, who tenderly loved his scrappy and nurturing mother until she closed her haunted eyes a final time in 1919, a victim of the great influenza pandemic. The blow was softened by Rhoda's five younger sisters, who always shared in Bernard's maternal care, and shaped his worldview by modeling dignity, compassion, and community. (Further into that 1927 *Harper's* article, he admonished himself for sexism and went on to argue that colleges were wiser to invest in women's education than in football.)

Rhoda's second husband, Florian Bernard DeVoto, was born in Cairo, Illinois, the son of an army officer from Italy seeking political asylum. He earned five degrees at Notre Dame University, excelling at math, painting, and tuba playing. He kept a flapping mustache umbrellaed by a Roman nose. In the 1870s he moved to Salt Lake City to build a Catholic school, a beachhead in Mormondom. He lost his inherited fortune speculating on mines and became a land title abstractor for the Union Pacific Railroad in secularized Ogden. Officials throughout the West were in awe of Florian's ability to determine legal land ownership—a byzantine puzzle on a rugged frontier rife with fraud, with titles tracing back to grants from Spain, England, France, Mexico, and Russia; plus, after American purchases and wars of conquest, involving federal, state, territorial, county, and municipal governments, as well as Native American nations, railroads, timber and cattle companies, and individual homesteaders. Bernard learned public lands law by apprenticing for his father, one of the few people he ever called "genius."

That "genius" was also a bitter misanthrope who was despotic toward his only child. Bernard was not yet three, still a cherub in Victorian-era dresses, when he made a quantum leap from reciting doggerel from his mother about mittens and kittens to reading Homer. Florian drilled Greek, Latin, and Italian epics into him by the time he turned ten. Insisting Bernard's stunning mind be molded by Jesuits, Florian sent him to a girls' Catholic school (until nuns expelled him for leering at his classmates). Bernard would remember that Florian "bellowed at me through most of my childhood." Florian accused his son of "continual stubbornness." A neighbor remembered Florian forbade Bernard from venturing out from their house, where he might find playmates, or discover yeasty-smelling 25th Street leading from the train depot and teeming with drunks, beggars, and prostitutes. When Bernard did bust out, he acted awkward, angry, and got into fistfights. Attempting baseball, Bernard got his nose shattered by a bat so badly that multiple reconstructive surgeries left it without a point and with two porcine nostrils. He was taunted with the nickname "Barnyard Revolto" and was, the sister of a classmate remembered, "the ugliest, most disagreeable boy you ever saw."

As the boy whose initials spell "BAD" matured, Bernard developed a rebel charm and renegade humor that made girls take chances on him. He was searching for a dream girl, not a date but a partner, a Penelope to accompany his odysseys. He would think he found her in a shallow blonde daughter of the richest businessman in Ogden, whose turreted mansion he envied. She dropped him with the words "The Lord says that I must not let a Gentile kiss me any more."

He sought solace and focus by escaping into the Wasatch National

Forest. By his early teens he was sleeping alone atop Mount Ogden, approximating the experience of frontiersmen. He brought books of philosophy, poetry, religion, and American literature and history. They planted the seeds of his life's focus—"to explain America." Under swishing trees, crackling stars, and great gray owls, his independent spirit grew and he called himself "a maverick who may not run with the herd, unbranded." He freed himself from the maddening residues of both his inherited religions by rejecting all dogmas—"absolutes mean absolutism." He committed to thinking freely and living skeptically. He brought along his .32 automatic pistol and made himself an expert marksman (he said he dropped robins from the skies and ate them). He taught himself to do the same thing with bullets as with arguments: hit the bull's-eye. He comprehended his promise. "My mind is as good as there is."

Heroically, Bernard resolved to "pour that arresting, God-awful emulsion that is I" into writing the Great American Novel. In 1914 he enrolled at the University of Utah to study English, but his tenure was cut short by protest. Labor wars were rocking the state, Industrial Workers of the World songwriter Joe Hill would die by firing squad in Salt Lake City the following November. Mormon bishops demanded the university ban the Intercollegiate Socialist Society. Bernard enraged them by organizing the society himself, and then enraged its members by criticizing Karl Marx. No one would tell Bernard what to read or what to think. When the university bowed to pressure and fired his favorite English teacher, he dropped out in solidarity. "These people are not my people," he growled, "their God is not mine."

With a paternal aunt's financial help, he moved to Cambridge in 1915 and enrolled at Harvard University. Inside its red-brick Federal-style buildings among minds as fast as his, he felt like a freed antelope on open prairie. In 1917, when World War I worsened, he listened to Woodrow Wilson speechify about making the world safe for democracy and enlisted in the army. He proudly contemplated dying overseas; it roused him to begin his novel celebrating America. In uniform—puttees squeezing calves, epaulets weighing down shoulders—his whole 5 feet, 9 inches had to stand straight as a ponderosa pine to keep on his peaked cap with the golden eagle. But because he was such a good shot, the army sent Bernard to Camp Perry in Ohio to teach sharpshooting to draftees. He felt ashamed at this stroke of fortune—whoever heard of a soldier too good with guns for war? It left him wanting to serve his country some other way, to prove that he wasn't "a shavetail."

In 1920 the Jazz Age dawned, and the glitterati, the most dashing novelists of the era—Fitzgerald, Hemmingway, Dos Passos—migrated to Europe. Bernard returned to Harvard after eight months of military service, graduated seventh in his class with a degree in philosophy, and backslid to Ogden to bury his mother. Living in a pandemic-hollowed home with Florian, he fought with his novel and worked a string of jobs that went nowhere: Idaho sheep ranch hand, Ogden newspaper reporter, Union Pacific baggage handler. Trapped and hopeless, he fell into a deadly depression, "the thought of suicide not out of my mind, waking or sleeping, for a moment." Florian compounded his torture by telling him to improve at "suppression of your feelings."

His lifeline came in 1922 in an offer to teach at Northwestern. He came so close to killing himself on the train ride that on arriving on the elm-shaded streets of Evanston he saw a psychiatrist, despite the social stigma. It started his lifelong fascination with the subject. (He would develop theories about the relationship between mental turmoil and creativity that boiled down to his aphorism "Art is man determined to die sane.") Like many a great performer, Bernard taught so theatrically no one could guess his inner pain. "His classes were ever as galvanistic as the Evanston power plant," charged a campus paper. Outside the classroom, Bernard gave his time prodigiously to struggling students. In class he strutted, challenged, teased, engaged; perhaps—a little—showing off for an attentive brunette in the front row. When Bernard spouted about the novels he intended to pen, his enthusiasm jumped off him like sparks. "He was supposed to be teaching us about writing, not about America," a student remembered. "We all learned to love America more."

Avis and Bernard grew close in the fall of 1922. "I must have been in love with her from the first," Bernard would remember. The big complication was: he was her teacher and she was his student. A trove of graded papers from his freshman English class are surviving records of their courtship. He assigned weekly essays and his detailed, meticulous handwritten critiques often went longer than the pieces themselves. (When he was disappointed he was sardonic. "All this is probably my teaching," began his explanation of an essay he awarded a D minus.) Only Avis stepped up and challenged his critiques, addressing his concerns point by point and resubmitting them for his review.

"You write with ease and . . . welcome humor," he pencils. "Let me have more of it. Unless I tell you particularly to write on the assigned subject, you may henceforth choose your own."

"Thank you," she replies in red ink.

In essays about her childhood, Avis describes the vines that grew on Houghton's elm trees, the color of sunlight on her hardwood floor, the taste of russet apples, the sound of frogs, and the feel of summertime moonlight swims in Lake Superior.

"The first straight A I have given goes on this," Bernard writes. He ventures a question — is she also an aspiring novelist? He is realizing she can write better prose than he and has, he will jot in a personal letter, "the subtlest mind I have ever known."

Despite his private stirrings, he keeps the relationship strictly proper. He cuts her no slack. When she does not rise to her talent, he tells her "Too trite for you." He coaches her through a description of her home garden until it is so florid he can smell it. "Larkspur and California poppies, Sweet William and heliotrope" . . . "Good," he pencils . . . "pansies and the wild, unkempt clumps of my favorite marigolds" . . . again, "Good" . . . "Down there were chrysanthemums, white and yellow, the purple of asters, and marsh marigolds, more red-gold than in August."

"This is exquisite prose," he tells her. "Distinguished writing."

"I am eternally grateful," she replies. "I begin to believe."

A hint that she is interested comes when she writes of loving Christopher Morley's books and Bernard comments "rather full of sweetness and light, aren't they?"

"Do you speak from experience?" she asks.

In the same essay, she mentions *The Damnation of Theron Ware* and he pencils, "I've always wanted to read this." She does not miss a flirtatious beat.

"I'm surprised you haven't."

The joust opens him up enough to confess: "I am interested in the books you read."

Her next essay is over the top. Titled "DEVOTEES," it is a mock review of an imagined Bernard DeVoto memoir about being chased by a harem of incompatible women, and she infers herself in the role of heroine.

"Decidedly, we must <u>have more</u> of this young man," she gushes. "His is an amazing gift which should not be allowed to suffer from lack of appreciation."

"I must conclude that the paragraphs are adequate," he deadpans.

"Please ascribe the mechanical errors to the exigences of the moment," goes her red reply.

They began taking walks together alone, despite his consciousness of the teacher/student taboo. He fell for her. He could rationalize that, despite their seven-year age gap, they were technically both freshmen at Northwestern. They were compatible in humor, love of literature, curiosity about the world, and complex feelings about their hometowns. They had something else, that magic, romantic phenomenon called chemistry. Bernard realized she had changed his internal makeup because he stopped thinking about suicide. "It was because I was in love with her that I was able to pull through," he said.

His hesitation about marriage—the thing that would redeem the taboo—was that on a salary of $1,800 he could not care for her well enough. He could not buy her a diamond; he could barely afford his drafty, half-furnished bachelor pad and canned food. She had to wonder whether submitting to marriage was worth leaving college. But a marriage to him promised to brim with the things she wanted in life—writing, ideas, adventure, family, cooking, love, and support. "I never really <u>talked</u> to anyone except Benny," Avis would remember. "He was always there when I needed him and I worshipped his mind." He, in turn, proclaimed he wanted her as his true partner in life. "Whatever the future may be, if we are apart it will be empty," he wrote. "If we are together it will be depth-full of significance, of meanings as deep as the roots of the earth."

Spontaneously, she said yes on the first warm day of 1923, April 10, as they stood on a dock jutting into Lake Michigan watching the sunset. In the afterglow, three weeks later, she received a C minus for a subpar essay on Jonathan Swift. The worst grade she ever received underscored that not even for love would her freethinking fiancé budge from his code of honesty. Which made it all the more poignant when on June 30 in a quiet ceremony in Evanston he swore he would be hers until death did them part.

2

The Sagebrush Caesar

DEATH CAME FOR THEM sooner than they imagined because of land destruction accelerating in Utah. The event happened when Bernard took Avis west for the first time to meet her father-in-law, Florian.

It was high summer 1925 when they stepped off a smoking Union Pacific train into the Spanish colonial–style depot in downtown Ogden. The alkali air straightened Avis's curls and chapped her skin as she raised her eyes to the Wasatch Range, a sight nothing in her midwestern upbringing prepared her for.

Florian's home—half of a shabby duplex—was no place of refuge. His inclination to hate everyone yet give all his earnings to charity left him so destitute that Bernard began giving him money. Florian proudly addressed the couple as "Dear Children," and he corresponded with Avis about Bernard's "moods" and counseled that she needed courage to deal with them. He confided that he knew the source of all Bernard's accomplishments would be "your belief in him."

Bernard remained a hometown pariah, so he fled with Avis into the paradise of his youth, the mountain wilderness. When they arrived at their rented cabin in an alpine valley, Bernard was horrified. The trees and grass were almost gone and the babbling creek was the color of bile.

Utah was late in the stages of having its vegetative skin grafted off. To boost lumber, beef, and wool production in World War I, logging and grazing regulations were lifted in national forests but then never reinstated in peacetime. In the Roaring Twenties the federal government combined laissez-faire management with the spoils system during the Republican administration of Warren G. Harding. His interior secretary, Albert Fall, of Las Cruces, New Mexico, took bribes in exchange for dispensing oil-drilling leases on public lands. Governmental neglect and corruption denuded the land, and the number of animals the West could sustain plummeted. In 1900, Utah was able to support 3.8 million domestic sheep. By 1940 that number dropped to 2.3 million. As the savannas were turned to desert, the state's human population mushroomed, and desperate family ranchers in search of grass sprigs drove livestock high into the mountains just after snowmelt, so early that animals' teeth plucked grass shoots and their roots out of the moist soil. Come summer, it baked to hardtack. Bernard would write about parallels with the decline of the Spanish Empire, and the Middle East where an environmental warning was written in the Bible. "If Noah's flood occurred in Mesopotamia, as some have believed, overgrazing and overcutting were responsible for it."

Late one afternoon, on a day Bernard spent writing and Avis spent canning peaches and hunting rattlesnakes with a .22, humid air blew inland from the Gulf of Mexico, gained hurricane strength, and smashed into the Wasatch Range. Rain burst out at 8 inches per hour, six times the heaviest rate ever recorded in the rainforests of Olympic National Park. Such cloudbursts were normal. Abnormal was the lack of vegetation to soak it up.

The same thing had happened when another pair of newlyweds ventured into the Wasatch two years earlier. The husband and wife, expecting their first child, made camp in a high mountain valley in a meadow with young quaking aspen trees. Across the dappled way four Boy Scouts from

Salt Lake City also pitched tents. After the cloudburst, a pair of teamsters who had passed the meadow on their way to an uphill mine heard
rumbling and scrambled for their lives. A 30-foot wall of boulders and
quicksand crashed down the valley, smashed their wagons, and killed their
horses. When the flash flood exploded out of the canyon's mouth at the
bottom of the mountain, it carried boulders weighing hundreds of tons. It
spread wreckage over a square mile. On one edge of the disaster a young
woman sprinted to her home only to have the flood cut it in two and bury
her (terrified but rescuable). On another edge, a screaming family took refuge on the second floor of their home and watched mud and gravel rise to
the level of their window. A policeman charged into floodwater to reach
his daughter and suffered a fatal heart attack. Everywhere in the flood's
path houses and barns were obliterated, telephone and power lines toppled. The main north–south highway and railroad tracks beside it were
buried under 20 feet of detritus. Two farther sets of tracks were washed
away. Farms, similar to Bernard's grandfather's, were ruined.

The bodies of the four Boy Scouts were recovered in the debris. The
pair of newlyweds were found later, snagged in the mountains. The woman's head and legs were discovered separately. Her fetus was found ripped
from her body.

Like the teamsters had, the DeVotos rushed to higher ground when
the flash flood came at them. The cold lava almost tore down their cabin
and washed out the wooden bridge linking them to town. Floods like
these were not unique to Utah's Wasatch Range. Similar ones through
the 1920s devastated Silver City, New Mexico, Pueblo, Colorado, Escalante, Utah, and other western towns, all because of conservation failures. The sparking flood lit a fire in Bernard DeVoto's soul that would
grow until it put heat to every word he wrote. Bernard never got over his
anger and horror. Just when he had found the love of his life, the fight of
his life found him.

The sky over New York City darkened in the late morning of May 11,
1934, when Bernard was with an editor, pitching articles about the West.

The bright blue was swallowed by a sickly, acrid plume so dark that the city turned on streetlights. The editor asked what it was.

"It is for God's sake Kansas," Bernard snapped. "And maybe it will annoy you enough so that you'll let me write that piece about it."

It was the Dust Bowl. Like a plague out of Exodus, the worst erosion event in modern history proved that a western emergency was a national one. Enough soil to bury all 130 million Americans under 3 tons had billowed off the Great Plains, flown 15,000 feet into the air, and spread 1,800 miles north to south. It blanketed the Eastern Seaboard, dirtied ships in the Atlantic, even silted Europe. As the "Black Blizzard" hit Washington, DC, Oklahoma senator Thomas Gore called it "the most tragic, the most impressive lobbyist that [had] ever come to this Capitol." Over the next five years, hundreds of such storms raked the West and left 2.5 million coughing refugees bereft, their family farms destroyed.

The Senate was debating an emergency conservation act to curb the erosion—until Patrick McCarran interjected. McCarran, freshman from Nevada, an expensive suit squeezing his rotund 5-foot, 7-inch, 235-pound body, his cowlick of silver hair shining above eyebrows V-shaped as a water wake, rose to say he would oppose it "so long as I have vitality sufficient to resist."

Pat McCarran and Bernard DeVoto had much in common. Both were the only children of overbearing Catholic fathers, both educated themselves with books in western mountains, both married outspoken women. Both had intense ambitions that drove them to the Northeast, where they earned reputations for being outsiders. Both considered themselves populists. They even hailed from the same extreme western subregion, the Great Basin, 200,000 square miles from the tips of the Sierra Nevada to the tops of the Wasatch Range, across California, Nevada, Utah, Oregon, Idaho, and Wyoming. The Great Basin encompasses the world's oldest living organism (bristlecone pine), biggest trout (Lahontan cutthroat), and the largest salt lake in the Western Hemisphere. From the Great Basin rises the highest peak in the contiguous United States, Mount Whitney, 14,505 feet above sea level. It looks down on the lowest point in North America, Death Valley, 282 feet below sea level. Pat Mc-Carran and Bernard DeVoto epitomized the same extremes.

McCarran was the son of an Irish immigrant, Patrick McCarran Sr., who became a private in the Second Cavalry Regiment and was sent to Nevada in 1862 to quell the Paiute War near Pyramid Lake. Patrick Sr. deserted, started a sheep ranch east of Reno along the Truckee River, and threatened to shoot all trespassers. His Irish bride gave birth to their only child in 1876. The elder Patrick's attempt to pass along the family business ended when McCarran allowed his merinos to wander onto the Union Pacific tracks and a speeding locomotive exploded them. Sued repeatedly for failure to pay his ranch hands, and barred by absentee landlords from grazing the state's most fertile valleys, Patrick Sr. was forced to sell away his ranch piecemeal.

In public school, McCarran was laughed at for his overalls. He never graduated from college but passed Nevada's oral bar exam in 1905. Nevada was nicknamed "the Rotten Borough" for its extravagant corruption. It was effectively run by owners of the billion-dollar Comstock Mine, most of whom lived in San Francisco. In the 1880s Nevada's state legislators pulled off one of the most brazen public land heists in western history, seizing for themselves more than 2 million irrigable acres in what is the union's driest state. By 1900 fewer than one hundred wealthy individuals owned 75 percent of the state's remaining private land. The land and water monopolization so squeezed ranchers like Patrick Sr. that by the 1930s, 70 percent of agricultural producers had been forced to take predatory loans from the state's biggest bank. With his father's rage, McCarran hated the bankers who grew more powerful with every foreclosure. "The gang on the corner," he spat, referring to their second-floor office in the ornamented, Classical Revival–style Reno National Bank at the intersection of First and Virginia Streets. To fight back, McCarran ran for Senate in 1916 and 1926 as a pro-union Democrat. The gang on the corner made sure he lost.

Norman Biltz ran the gang and was McCarran's enemy. Biltz, a Republican, was nicknamed "the Duke of Nevada" and "Mr. Big" as he seized power of the state's political machine. Born in Connecticut, Biltz moved west to build a real estate empire. He dreamed of making Nevada a millionaire's haven, and he kept a list of the two hundred richest Americans, eighty of whom he boasted he sold property to. Biltz would almost single-handedly stop an attempt to make a Lake Tahoe National Park by developing 27 miles of its shoreline for a $500,000 investment (less than $10 million in 2021 dollars). Working for the bank, Biltz repackaged and resold 90 percent of Nevada's foreclosed-on ranches, often as tax shelters for nonresidents. He would sell a giant ranch near Elko to crooner Bing Crosby, who loved it so much he bought six more. Biltz embodied everything McCarran purported to despise.

When the Great Depression struck, Biltz's bank went under and McCarran saw his chance to climb above. McCarran won his senate seat by declaring himself a steadfast ally of Franklin Roosevelt, who won the presidency in 1932 by a landslide. In Washington, DC, on inauguration day, as Roosevelt's words about fearing nothing but fear itself hung in the air, McCarran, fifty-six, stepped into an elevator and his life's trajectory changed. He came nose to nose with Biltz. Before the elevator doors opened, McCarran couldn't resist a gloat.

"I fooled you and the rest of your gang on the corner, didn't I?"

"You certainly did, Senator," Biltz said, lifting his broad lips into an amiable smile.

It was the beginning of a lifelong friendship.

Biltz gauzed McCarran in comforts and flattery — three-piece suits, meals, hotel rooms; mortgage forgiveness, gasoline for his Cadillac coupe; introductions to Tahoe aristocrats who proffered luxury cruises and campaign cash. As he grew jowly and demagogic, McCarran was such an openly corrupt politician he would purr to Biltz, "I wonder if you know that the greatest happiness I could have would be to do something for you."

McCarran turned against Roosevelt so violently it baffled him. "I don't know why Senator McCarran and I don't get along, but we don't," the president said. For the first part of McCarran's career he was relatively unknown outside Nevada, which at the time had the smallest population of any state, and the obscurity helped him. Eventually he would be called "the Sagebrush Caesar" and "the Democrat as Autocrat." No senator more quickly amassed power — or abused it. For a decade he ran the Senate's Western Bloc and installed himself on key appropriations committees. In the 1930s, McCarran boasted that he made the federal government spend $1,150 on each Nevadan. In the 1940s Nevada had the nation's biggest discrepancy between federal taxes paid and expenditures received: $41 million out, $175 million in, including for McCarran Airport in Las Vegas. McCarran's largesse flowed disproportionately to his friends, like water projects for properties owned by Biltz ("Greatest senator Nevada could possibly have," Biltz complimented). McCarran was called a "political hog" who ran a "patronage pigsty." "McCarran is a son of a bitch from practically every point of view," Roosevelt's interior secretary, Harold Ickes, said. President Harry Truman would observe "he is always for something when he can get his hand in the money barrel."

The conservation measure McCarran opposed in that Dust Bowl summer of 1934 was the Taylor Grazing Act. Its intent was to stop erosion on the final 170 million contiguous acres of the public domain, the former homelands of Indigenous nations, including the Sioux, Cheyenne, Arikara, Crow, Cree, Pawnee, and Blackfeet, to name but a few, that had become, by way of Thomas Jefferson's Northwest Ordinance of 1787, the responsibility of the US federal government. Minor reforms to homestead laws in the early twentieth century followed by a World War I wheat bubble caused mass plowing on the dry Great Plains. Displaced herdsmen, seeking the last of the deep-rooted native grasses, waged bloody range wars on public land where no farmer had dared stake claim: the driest and most remote prairies, deserts, and canyonlands, of which Nevada has more than any other state. The Taylor Act —which passed despite McCarran's opposition—effectively stopped dryland homesteading and range wars. It organized the public domain into districts that were managed by a new federal conservation agency, the Grazing Service. Its employees, trained in the emerging field of scientific range management, cooperated with district advisory boards made up of elected area ranchers.

Like water against stone, amendment by amendment, McCarran

eroded the Grazing Service. It was the dawn of the corporate ranch, and of the cattle *and real estate* company. McCarran set electoral eligibility standards favoring the biggest ranchers; he empowered boards to set their own grazing lease fees at far below fair market rates; he added regulatory loopholes for ranches controlled by banks; and he agitated for board members to buy their districts outright. His efforts were a boon for plunderers like Norman "the Duke of Nevada" Biltz with profit motive to mine grass, sell hobby ranches, and pamper politicians. McCarran was building his own Tammany Hall in the sage.

As McCarran grew more powerful as the decade progressed, Roosevelt responded by pushing for reforms to the boards, specifically that they represent small ranchers. This was a declaration of war to McCarran. He announced he would lead a "real investigation" that would go into "even the smallest detail" on "every public lands question." It was the first post-Taylor investigation of public lands. More important for the culture, it set a playbook for all McCarran investigations—and for those he would inspire.

McCarran held his line and, in a duplicitous attempt to appear interested in public opinion, curated a series of meetings throughout the rural West for citizens to air their grievances. His assistant, George Storck, screened and organized them according to McCarran's caste hierarchy: large ranchers over small ranchers (except if the former was Native American), and all ranchers over everyone else—farmers, hunters, municipal water users, hikers. Storck's correspondence shows the unequal treatment that went into the preproduction of the McCarran Hearings. Storck allowed the West's largest livestock associations to dictate topics and schedule the order of speakers. Consequently, small ranchers and other concerned citizens saw McCarran brush aside their issues: flash floods, as the DeVotos experienced; the Dust Bowl, as all Americans experienced; lack of public access, as outdoor recreators experienced; and range monopolization by local oligarchs and absentee owners, which small ranchers acutely experienced.

Still, they cried their appeals to McCarran. Mary Whitehall of Deming, New Mexico, wrote McCarran that boards were "trafficking in public lands" and that the situation was "a vital matter to the numerous cattle-men who have a small ranch." A. Phillip Foremaster of St. George, Utah, wrote that he was terrified about "the sale of land to individuals," which would drive him off range his family had ranched since the 1880s. "It almost makes one wonder whether the ones who become leeches aren't the best off after all." Mrs. Charles Ellis, of Carbon County, Wyoming, wrote that she was being menaced to stay away from the hearings by the Wyoming Stock Growers Association. "It is almost an impossibility for small outfits to stay in business." Theirs were the "smallest details" that McCarran shrugged off as he amplified voices he wanted to hear, silenced those he did not, and reveled in his power becoming absolute.

Future president Lyndon Johnson, who would be terrified by McCarran but would also study how he wielded power, remembered diplomatically that "Pat McCarran was an earth-shaking force. He lived in the midst of great controversy. And he himself was one of the controversial figures around which the storm raged." What else could be said about a senator from a desert state who stood in the Dust Bowl and took its side?

3

"The Blueprint Plans of Creation"

BERNARD EMERGED FROM THE DEVOTOS' NEAR-DEATH EXPERIENCE in the Wasatch Range still cocksure that he would leave his stamp on America by writing great novels. In Evanston, the DeVotos became a literary cottage industry. Every word Bernard wrote, Avis edited. Bernard kept his teaching job as he toiled away on novels. He also became the assigning book review editor of the Evanston *News-Index* and made Avis his go-to hire. In late 1925, they swapped roles. For extra money, Bernard submitted short stories to popular magazines, which he called "the big slicks." When he received his first acceptance letter, from the *Saturday Evening Post*, the biggest and best-paying magazine in the country (and a check equal to a third of his teaching salary), he remarked, "We have arrived."

They moved into a less humble apartment on Orrington Avenue. Instead of quitting teaching, Bernard took on more: three classes per day, four days a week at Northwestern; night classes twice a week at the Illinois School of Commerce. Avis tutored children of immigrants. She was

a metabolic furnace of activity, writing, editing, reading, cooking, dec-
orating. Her correspondence with Florian so melted his curmudgeonly
heart that he never left home without her letters in his pockets. When
there was money to spare, the DeVotos threw parties, which became local
legends. Alone, Avis peeled off all her clothes and sashayed seductively
past Bernard on her way to the roof to sunbathe. When he could break
from writing, he tore his clothes off to join her.

In January 1927 Bernard wrote in a *Harper's* essay that the trend of
business executives running colleges to prioritize athletics over academia
was turning higher education into a "con-game." The reaction was ferocious. A Northwestern football fan took to a campus paper to argue
a counterfactual: Bernard's face looked like it had been run over with a
wagon wheel. In what felt like an attempt to push him out, the president
summoned Bernard to answer a rumor that he served liquor to students
(Avis said that they were too poor to waste good alcohol on amateurs).
The episode encapsulated much of what attracted Avis to Bernard: stat-
ing the unpopular, demanding institutional integrity, drama, controversy,
intrigue. "He has strong likes and dislikes, and a splendid absence of
tact," she would say approvingly. Though it broke the hearts of his students, Bernard quit in the summer. He and Avis moved to Massachusetts,
where she would live for the next seven decades.

Bernard could afford to write full-time because he had a patron saint:
H. L. Mencken, the corpulent, cigar-chomping Oscar Wilde of Baltimore
whose rakish prose Bernard could ventriloquize. Mencken was thrilled
to publish Bernard in his magazine, the *American Mercury.* Mencken also
bestowed on Bernard a nom de plume, John August. Bernard began a
two-track literary career. To express himself and rise in stature, Bernard
DeVoto wrote novels, essays, and criticism. To make good money, John
August wrote "tripe" stories for the big slicks. Mencken offered to cover
if anyone suspected. "I'll have my staff perjurer make all the necessary
affidavits. He is a clergyman and hence talented." A wise-eyed young
writer, Wallace Stegner, first saw the name Bernard DeVoto in a *Mercury* issue hurled in anger out of an office door at the University of Utah.
When Bernard-as-Mencken wrote essays on Mormons (accusing them

of "smugness" and "self-righteousness"), police at the Ogden jail burned copies lest they "injure the delicate mentality of the prisoners."

The DeVotos made a similarly brash impression when they settled at 64 Oxford Street in Cambridge. When Avis, in cocktail dress, made her formal debuts, she revealed herself a cuss artist. She painted with the pastels of "bastard," "goddamn," "sonofabitch," "hell," and "ass." She remembered it was a habit she "picked up from DeVoto, who is reasonably profane." To intellectual leftists, Bernard raised his arms and blew his nose so they could see *Saturday Evening Post* checks peeking from his coat pocket. He bought a camera, and his favorite subject—aside from western scenery—was Avis, who posed for artistic nudes which, to the DeVotos' amusement, were swiped by a moonstruck young woman at a party. The DeVotos mellowed hard feelings about their eye-opening modernity by running liquor. They made a connection at a Vermont farm that touched the Canadian border, and imperial pints traveled a shadowy forested path from a topcoat's pockets to their used Ford's chassis. "My own first notion of DeVoto, as I watched him in our driveway unloading bottles from the trunk of his car," remembered historian Arthur Schlesinger Jr., "was that he must be the family bootlegger."

Yet Bernard's attempts at literature underwhelmed, and it tore him up. After a rejected first novel, he wrote four more in succession. They sold poorly and earned mixed reviews. His printed debut, *The Crooked Mile*, pillorying a fictionalized, post-frontier Ogden, was panned as cynical and "adolescent." His follow-up, *The Chariot of Fire*, about the Mormon exodus, was called "overlong." Bernard's third printed novel, *The House of Sun-Goes-Down*, about a defeated Confederate soldier who drifts west, was ripped for its "self-conscious manner" and "verbal virtuosity." Bernard tried shifting regions by setting his next novel, *We Accept with Pleasure*, in Boston during the Sacco and Vanzetti trial. It was called a contender for "disappointment of the year." Though Avis judged he was improving, one of Bernard's revered Harvard English teachers spoke his greatest fear: that he might not have a great novel in him.

The West and Bernard DeVoto's concern for its land pointed a way through. He would later admit that starting out he was a "young ass of intense ambition and an even intenser inferiority complex." In tone, his novels were flat, out of tune because of envy. His cultural criticism was sharp, shrilled by ego. But in one genre, his sound was honest, pitch-perfect, original, and true: western nonfiction.

The May 1927 *American Mercury* ran a deeply researched essay about the Oregon Trail under Bernard's byline and written not in Mencken's voice, but in his own. When Bernard hit that note, it resonated. "You have put into words a belief I have long held close in my mind," wrote a woman from Chinook, Montana. Wallace Stegner would observe that the essay forecast Bernard's lifetime song "of love for the country and contempt for the people who abused or gutted or colonized it." Susan Bowling, an elderly woman in Pryor, Oklahoma, with no formal education, shared the effect of Bernard's writing in personal terms. It gave her "goose bumps of delight . . . in somewhat the same way beautiful music does."

Bernard followed up with an article in the November 1927 *Harper's* titled "Footnote on the West," written with the Wasatch Range breaking in his mind through New England fog: "No other life is quite so rich in colors or perfumes, and none is so intimately aware of the basic rhythm of the earth, the blueprint plans of creation. In the West we say that when a man has once lived in the desert he will come back to it again. He will."

Like Melville gone inland to write about the sea, DeVoto went east to write about the West.

In 1929, as his dream of writing great novels faltered, Bernard took a tutoring job at Harvard to stay in the realm of literature while supplementing his unsteady income as a freelance writer. Dungeoned in a dreary office furnished with dusty chairs inside the Victorian five-story Holyoke House, he made a monstrous impression. Wet-palmed freshmen sat across his desk, blinking at the ugliest man they had ever seen rock in his chair, snort, whoop, and fire questions about what they had read. *Plymouth Plantation? Jefferson's Notes on Virginia? Hawthorne? Emerson? Thoreau? Melville? Henry Adams? EMILY DICKINSON? MARK TWAIN?* "He was roaring now," remembered a straight-A student, whose negative answers decrescendoed as he feared lightning from his tutor's eyes would burn the building down. "Well what in the name of God Almighty do we have here? An over-educated Harvard esthete, who knows all the minor Elizabethans and Victorians and not a thing about what has been done or said in his own country."

The catalyst for Bernard taking the job was a frightening bout of writer's block. In one week he wrote and threw out 30,000 words, and Avis became afraid to leave him alone with his guns. He developed a new dream: being a tenured professor. "Of course I belong at Harvard," he would say. With Avis as his Annie Oakley, he cultivated a western wild man persona that—as at Northwestern—alternately thrilled and appalled his colleagues. He infused Harvard with his zest for traditional American writers, like Willa Cather, Ellen Glasgow, and Carl Sandburg. It pitted him against other faculty aspirants who favored modernists like the expatriates Henry James and T. S. Eliot. Though the battle was on an intellectual field, the stakes were high—Bernard would need his colleagues' support to get tenure.

In 1930 Avis gave birth to the couple's first son, Gordon, a skinny and shy baby nicknamed "Bunny" who is shown in pictures wrapped in both his parents' arms and playing games with his mother, like blowing bubbles. The DeVotos tried to have another child, but Avis miscarried. In 1932 they moved into a Federal-style home on Weston Street in nearby Lincoln, Massachusetts, that had seventeen rooms, five bathrooms, eight fireplaces, acres of land, a swimming pool, and a toboggan run. Because of the stock market crash, the rent was $100 per month. The DeVotos hired a young Irish maid named Hannah to keep her off the streets of Boston. Florian lived with them until his death in 1935. That year, *Collier's* magazine bought a ten-part John August serial for $20,000. The more money he made, the more dependents he took on. Bernard began sending money to Avis's parents, which helped them move to a retirement community in sunny Florida.

Avis remembered the Lincoln years as the best of her life. "Goodness we had fun!" She began collecting cookbooks and experimenting in the kitchen, which she loved. She hosted and catered fantastic parties that became a mainstay of the DeVotos' existence. Every Sunday afternoon, the DeVotos invited their best friends over for cocktails, conversation, and food. The weekly gatherings became a motivator for Bernard, his reward for a week spent teaching and straining cataleptically alone in his office trying to make his Eastbrook fountain pen bleed saleable words. Like Eleanor Roosevelt, Avis knew her husband was a ladies' man whose mood lit up around pretty girls. The gatherings included a smattering of "toothsome young virgins." Also, a high percentage of psychiatrists, with whom Bernard cultivated professional and personal relationships. Avis loved it when Bernard turned on, and she lived for the parties too. "When he's in the mood to expound he speaks with the tongues of angels and I am awed and reverent and uplifted and thank God I got him." Student George Homans, a descendant of John Quincy Adams, remembered revealing he did not drink and Bernard asking him, "What do you do to smell like a man?" He was introduced to the DeVoto Dry martini, and the elixir enhanced the joy of the music Avis played by ear. "Our main business was drinking, rationalized only by our singing of what I suppose should be called American folk songs, while Avis played the piano. The gallons of whiskey that got spilled over that piano!"

The bellowing bunch of bright students, social shrinks, and witty beauties was exactly what Bernard always wanted but never found in Utah: a circle of friends. They adopted a name for themselves in honor of the man they revolved around—the Tribe of Benny.

Benny continued to write best about the West. In 1932 he published his first critically acclaimed book, *Mark Twain's America*, his study of how the western frontier shaped his literary hero. Because of it, Bernard would be named literary executor of Twain's estate, responsible for reading and editing his unpublished works for posthumous publication. Bernard discovered Twain's first story, and scenes cut from *Huckleberry Finn*. "Those 20 pages have been a glorious experience."

In August 1934 Bernard published "The West: A Plundered Province" in *Harper's*. He described how the wealth of the West's natural resources had been systematically siphoned to the East. And how—contrary to popular myth—it was western settlers who learned to work together who halted the liquidation. Westerners figuring out the realities of their natural environment for the benefit of all and bucking the manipulations of the self-interested would become Bernard's greatest and most controversial theme.

Harper's was so impressed that it gave Bernard DeVoto the sword he would use to wage his life's most important battles. He was hired in 1935 to write the magazine's monthly "Easy Chair" column. Founded in 1851, the "Easy Chair" is the oldest feature in American journalism. That gravitas, coupled with *Harper's* influential readership, gave Bernard power, prestige, and authority. The terms of the deal were that he would write whatever he chose. That was worth more to him than the paltry pay, $200 for each 2,650-word essay. Bernard could choose the issues he cared about, and America had to pay attention. He reveled about being able to start "bellowing from a platform" and giving the public "the inestimable privilege of my literary views once a month." He would make dauntless use of the "Easy Chair."

Staid Harvard was not impressed. Bernard's most cutting antagonist there was F. O. Matthiessen, the thin, sandy-haired chairman of the undergraduate programs of literature and history. Matthiessen, who identified as a "Christian Socialist," was one of the leftist "young intellectuals" Bernard blew his nose at. He said he was sure that Matthiessen thought he was "subsidizing fascists." "Hates my guts and always has." While Harvard president James Conant warmed to Bernard's appeal for tenure track—allowing him to advance to full-time English professor—Matthiessen chilled the prospect.

In early 1936, Conant turned Bernard down for tenure, which dropped his spirit "lower than a snake's ass hole." That summer the family left their beloved Lincoln house and relocated across state lines into an unremarkable replacement near a golf course in suburban White Plains, New York. Bernard had been offered a job editing the *Saturday Review of Literature*, which forced him to commute 27 miles south to smoggy New York City, a place he detested, thought was a petri dish of artifice, hucksters, con men. He suffered it as he reached his fortieth year because he saw opportunity to use the platform to praise his favorite American authors. He also broadened the bullpen of writers to include voices from outside the cloistered Northeast. He gave work to Stewart Holbrook, a logger in Oregon, and Edith Mirrielees, a teacher raised in Big Timber, Montana.

Most of the reviews Bernard wrote were positive. Novelist Sinclair Lewis judged him the best literary critic in the business. But it was Bernard's negative reviews that became legends. In a piece titled "Genius Is Not Enough," Bernard broke the scoop that hot novelist Thomas Wolfe's books were actually assembled by his editor, Maxwell Perkins. Bernard hammered on the Lost Generation and popular works that expressed ennui, contempt, and cynicism. "They turned their backs on America."

No ideas laundered in print did Bernard DeVoto bash more than those of Karl Marx, whom he panned as boring, ignorant of history, and an intellectual lightweight. Marxism, Bernard wrote, came from an "imbecile delusion." Though American politics had swung dramatically to the left, Bernard charged Depression Marxists with "monumental credulity" for buying into a critical system whose conclusions were "settled in advance of the facts." Bernard leveled the most insulting words he could: fools, liars, smug. His acidity became news itself. "Writing in a prose style so vehement it sometimes seemed apoplectic, Editor DeVoto raged at U.S. intellectuals accusing them en masse of 'misrepresenting' the country," *Time* wrote in 1938. "His critical haymakers included swings at Thomas Wolfe, William Faulkner, Marx."

The progressive magazine *The Nation* hit back that Bernard was a "fascist." Writer Edmund Wilson dismissed him as a "spokesman for the literary right." The *Saturday Review of Literature* received anonymous threats of violence. The *New Masses,* an American communist newspaper, panned him for being a "snob." "Like most conservatives, Mr. DeVoto recoils from writers who heartily believe in something." Actual Soviets cut deeper. The Russia State House of Foreign Literature would accuse Bernard of propagating "the bestial ideology of American imperialism."

Saturday Review subscriptions lagged, and Bernard was laid off after sixteen months. John August rode to the financial rescue and sold another serial to *Collier's.* But the *Saturday Review* experience gave Bernard another orientation point toward his true calling. When an article he commissioned for the December 5, 1936, issue did not come, he, on deadline, improvised his own unorthodox seasonal replacement. He wrote about the Lewis and Clark expedition in 1804 celebrating Christmas farther westward than any other Americans. He described Sacajawea giving weasel tails to William Clark. That his nonfiction resonated broadly was clear in the amount of fan mail it generated. One female fan from Utah, of all places, sent him a gift of weasel tails.

The DeVotos fled New York to rejoin their tribe; Bernard said he couldn't wait to get back to America. By 1938, both Bernard and Avis had settled into new phases of their respective careers. Bernard had forged a national (and international) reputation as an outspoken cultural patriot and belligerent anti-Communist and, most enduringly, found his voice writing nonfiction about the West. Avis, in addition to editing her husband's increasingly pointed work, discovered her own passion for cookbooks.

She wrote a chapter about the folk cuisine of northern Michigan for a book published by W. W. Norton & Co. in 1940 called *America Cooks*. After Bernard was let go from Harvard, Avis returned to her hometown for the first time in fifteen years. She rediscovered the joys of the foods of her youth. Especially pasties, sold piping hot out of baskets at the train station. She wrote, "Last week when I was in Houghton with my husband and child we took a picnic of pasties out. Nothing has tasted so good in years." It was her first foray into cookbook creation, and she was excited to share recipes for pasties, booyaw, thimbleberry jam, and other delicacies from her girlhood.

The DeVotos resettled in Cambridge, where an unexpected love affair threatened their union.

4

A World on Fire

BY 1938, having won three-quarters of his lifetime's Pulitzer Prizes, Robert Lee Frost was recognized as America's greatest living poet. According to the eminent critic Bernard DeVoto, he was also the greatest living American.

Frost had rapped on Bernard's door underneath palm trees on January 16, 1935, when they were both lecturers at the University of Miami's Winter Institute of Literature. Frost bore something unusual: a compliment. He loved a *Harper's* essay Bernard had written about independent New England farmers, capturing their fiery flintiness and stoic Yankee work ethic. They were the same values Frost translated, through verses about wooded paths, birch boughs, and changing seasons, into revelations about love, fidelity, labor, and regret. Bernard loved Frost's writing because it was economic, exacting, and in tactile contact with American soil. Beholding the big, magnetic, strong-shouldered bard with the broad forehead, tousled silver hair, and eyebrows like curled-up Siberian huskies, Bernard was astounded at how alike their minds were. Same with Frost. "I can't get over my not having realized you were on earth," Frost would tell Bernard.

Like Bernard's life, Frost's life spanned the country. Born in San Francisco, Frost spent his adolescence on his grandfather's farm north of Boston before starting his own in New Hampshire. In 1905 he married Elinor Miriam White, a thin-faced teacher, and together they had five children. For twenty years he farmed and wrote his poems in relative obscurity until Ezra Pound (born in Idaho, expatriated to Italy) publicized him. As success, money, and accolades poured in, Frost resisted budging from the roots of what inspired him. "They would not find me changed from him they knew/Only more sure of all I thought was true."

In the figure of Frost, Bernard saw the father he had always wished he had, encouraging, complimentary, supportive, ambitious. "You don't know your own power," Frost would say. "No one else has your natural sensible and at the same time embracing thoughts about life and America." Frost intuited that Bernard DeVoto wrote with his whole body, like an archer, not like a pistol shooter. As Bernard worked with psychiatrists to temper his nervous tortures, he could look at Frost and know that what he wanted to be was attainable. Frost was sane, decent, genius. "I go tearful whenever I talk about him," Bernard said.

If Bernard could see his fantasy father in Frost, Frost could see his actual mother in Avis, who shared his Scottish heritage. Frost was enraptured with Avis's wit, empathy, knowledge, fearlessness, and style. Bernard liked to take pictures of the two people on whom his sanity most depended interacting. One photo shows Avis and Frost seated side by side on a porch. He talks at his palms cupped in his white-trousered lap like he is cradling a profound spherical idea, his face exudes vulnerability. Avis leans slightly toward him in an open-necked summer dress, roped braids of hair hugging her temples, feet dangling, smoking, listening. In another photo they are on a dirt path, she in a relaxed short-sleeve shirt and skirt with her hair in a kerchief, him in a suit jacket appearing to admire her. Both eat wild blackberries. Avis's term whenever she got along with somebody was "easy," and with Frost she was obviously easy. So much so that she would later be asked by a girlfriend if she found him physically attractive.

The DeVotos proudly introduced the Frosts to their social circle in Cambridge; he was more impressive than bootleg liquor. In 1936 the Frosts needed temporary lodging and the DeVotos found them a home on Mason Street, next door to the Morrisons, their first neighbors and best friends. Theodore Morrison was a trim, fit Harvard lecturer with good posture and an angular jaw. He directed the Bread Loaf Writers' Conference each summer at the foot of the Green Mountains at Middlebury College in Vermont, where the DeVotos were martini- and advice-dispensing mainstays and Frost was a guest star. Kathleen Morrison worked as a copy editor at the Atlantic Monthly Press, and she looked like Avis's big sister. She was also of Scottish heritage, and she wore sumptuous white muslin dresses, spoke in a soft voice, and made hard eye contact. When Frost lectured at Harvard in 1936, the DeVotos arranged for the Morrisons to host his worshipful afterparties.

The three couples were so easy they would be called "a family of sorts." But their mix of intimacy, sympathy, insularity, and intelligence, spiked with Bernard's ambition and Frost's fame, was ripe for drama. In 1937 Frost published his third Pulitzer-winning book, *A Further Range*, which *The Nation* trashed as too conservative. That set Bernard flying with one of his most exasperated attacks, that *The Nation*'s review was so idiotic "the monkeys would have to tap typewriters throughout eternity to surpass it." Frost was delighted, and he relished the publicity. Some began to suspect that Frost was using his influence over Bernard to manipulate him, grooming him not to write about the West, but instead to write his biography.

In March 1938, Elinor Frost, suffering from breast cancer, died of heart failure. Frost was devastated. He acted out in his grief until friends feared he was having a breakdown. At that summer's clubby Bread Loaf conference, Frost heckled one visiting poet until Bernard told him to quiet down. Frost made a savage comment and left. Both DeVotos rushed to talk to Frost, and they went on so long that Bernard fell asleep, leaving Avis alone with the poet. In the following months, Bernard told Frost that his actions were changing for the worse. It made Frost respond with a letter containing a psychological switchblade. "Who cares whether they were for the worse or not. You may as a serious student of my works. But Avis and I don't give a sigh."

Those words—*Avis and I*—slashed at Bernard's conceptions of love, loyalty, and art. Frost made it known that he and Avis were in alliance, and Bernard was cut out.

In the midst of this tumult, Frost began an affair with Kathleen Morrison, still married to Theodore Morrison. While Frost tried to cleave Bernard and Avis, he succeeded in driving a wedge between the Morrisons and the DeVotos. It pained their community of friends as they kept the affair secret (the Morrisons stayed married). Frost was not finished. He disparaged Bernard behind his back for seeing psychiatrists, portraying the seriousness with which Bernard took his mental health as weakness, and proof that Frost had broken him. "I am too strong for him," Frost boasted.

Bernard realized that Frost had a "demon," and it tore up his heart. Frost had become a father figure to Bernard because of their shared faith in America and a spiritual love for the land. Bernard could read the conservation ideal in Frost's poetry of yeomen returning to the soil in love what they took from it in sustenance, an allegory for patriotism at its best. Frost's demon made Bernard reassess and mature. He realized he could no longer look to any idol to model that great art, sanity, and belief in America were compatible. If Bernard wanted proof, he would need to find it in himself, with strength from his family. Though they would stay publicly cordial, Bernard disowned Frost with a private handshake and eleven sharp syllables. "You're a good poet, Robert. But you're a bad man."

While Bernard's relations with Frost ended in ice, with Avis they ended in fire. In the aftermath of the Frost/Morrison affair, she promised that everything would all come out eventually. "He was a devil in his day, after Elinor died, and he knows it and a lot of people know it." Bernard credited his wife for helping him both resist Frost's manipulations, and also to get through his disillusionment. Frost had "reached for Avis and me" but failed because "Avis is too tough." Independent of him, Avis wrote down what she thought of Frost, a sentiment in rhyme with her reaction when asked about his attractiveness. Frost was "such a bastard."

The fallout ensured that Bernard would write more nonfiction about the West, not hagiography of Frost, and with Avis's complete backing. But as the bonds of the DeVotos' marriage seemed to strengthen, Bernard was simultaneously opening his heart to another woman.

Her name was Katharine Sterne. Two years younger than Avis, she had a pedigree to impress a wordsmith: graduate of Wellesley, art critic at the *New York Times*. In 1932 she was twenty-six, in the bloom of her life, when tuberculosis felled her to a living coffin. She lay in an iron lung, and within its sighing confines she spent her days in a corner of a musty, malodorous sanitorium filled with the moans of her polio-stricken companions on the outskirts of Poughkeepsie, New York. Sterne sent Bernard a fan letter from there, and an impassioned correspondence ensued.

Her plight—her first letter arrived as she prepared to have eleven ribs amputated and her right lung collapsed—touched Bernard deeply. She was poignantly funny about being a "female zombie" living in a "den of horrors." Reading was her only relief, so Bernard showered her with words. Sterne confessed they did "a hell of a lot to save the day." Bernard and Sterne never met in person, but they swapped more than eight hundred intimate letters.

Sterne was a member of the Tribe of Benny in absentia, but she and Bernard became especially close. Bernard's habit was to write all day and into the evening, and then at night, after pouring whiskey for himself, pour his mind out to Sterne. Part of her pathos was that she was beautiful, sharing facial features with another Katharine—Hepburn. She sent a photograph of a model clipped from a magazine along with the note "This is what people say I look like." For as much compassion as Bernard showed by his letters, they also reveal that he and Sterne had chemistry.

Avis betrayed no jealousy at the amount of mental time her husband spent with another woman, only astonishment. "Instead of writing a journal, after a long day writing for a living, he wrote to Kate Sterne." After the frights Avis endured during Bernard's depressions, she objected to nothing he did to moderate his mood. Sterne was respectful of Avis and complimented her book reviews. Avis agreed that if she had a daughter she would name her after her husband's "witty, restrained, cultivated, cool" pen pal. Aside from the physical boundary between Bernard and Sterne, Avis watched them mind the romantic one. "She kept her distance. He kept his."

But both DeVotos were concerned with how the Sterne friendship might be perceived by outsiders. Bernard mused to Sterne about their relationship and his emotions. "It's a very deep and warm and tender feeling, my dear, however complex and whatever the faculty might make of it. The obvious thing is that I certainly never would have written to a man as I have to you, that you have represented some blend of wife-daughter mother to this odd soul, and that you have got yourself seriously tangled in its oddities."

Sterne was the most dramatic example of a pattern in Bernard DeVoto's life of developing mutually fulfilling friendships with women. Bernard aggressively hired women who excelled at their jobs, like reviewer Edith Mirrielees and literary agent Helen Everitt. He was also a generous champion of, and mentor to, talented women like Pulitzer-winning novelist Julia Peterkin and historian Catherine Drinker Bowen. Famously, Bowen beseeched Bernard for career guidance after a professor put her down for being too "romantic" about American history. "Sure you're romantic about American history," he counseled the future John Adams biographer and National Book Award winner. "It's the most romantic of all histories." (Bowen treasured that letter for life.)

In 1944 Sterne died. A friend of hers delivered to the DeVotos' door all the letters he had written her, which she had carefully saved in their original envelopes. The friend said they extended her life. Sterne lived long enough to see Bernard dedicate his book *The Year of Decision: 1846* to her for being "a very gallant woman." "You shouldn't have sprung that dedication on me in my, er, weakened condition," Sterne wrote. "I bawled for an hour. God knows I don't deserve it, but I am very honored & very very proud. I do thank you, Benny, from the bottom of my heart."

The Year of Decision became the first in a great trilogy of western non-fiction that came to define Bernard DeVoto's career. He would, years later, dedicate a single book also to Avis. Though it would be heartfelt, it was a squib—minor work compared with the one in which he celebrated Sterne. It was an example of how Bernard, despite his generosities, could be oblivious about receiving more from some of his relationships than he acknowledged. Women chefs kept him fed. Women editors rescued his words. Avis, who did both, compensated for the emotional labor he did not invest in his family. Bernard the patriarch was a consummate financial provider—which Avis credited him for—but he could be self-centered, overbearing, and distant. Avis would admit that he "wasn't always the most comfortable man to be married to." The worst that can be said of the DeVotos' marriage is that he could take Avis for granted, and she could, even in an era of less frequent divorce, be too tolerant.

Nevertheless, as the DeVotos approached their seventeenth wedding anniversary in 1940, the birth of their second child—a boy, named for another of Bernard's great loves, Mark Twain—proved the longevity of their attraction to each other. They disproved Tolstoy's adage—their happy family was not like others. It had unique variances and private contours, but it worked for them, and their causes.

The DeVotos' bond held despite distance between them. In the spring of 1940, Bernard went west for book research while Avis remained in Cambridge. But when Bernard reached the epicenter of the Dust Bowl, he needed her steady support to help him endure what he saw. The sky an hour outside Dodge City, Kansas, was blasted with blowing soil stretching to every horizon. Drifts like Saharan dunes clawed 2 feet high on the western exterior walls of sagging farm shacks with windows blown out, and 1 foot high on their eastern interiors. Downwind of wooden fence posts—which had been gnawed at by starving livestock—V shapes were blown in the particulate that gave Great Plains farmers black lung dis-

ease at rates like those of Appalachian coal miners. Eight-inch mummi-
fied wheat stalks that had managed to sprout years earlier had the soil
blown away, leaving them teeming in the wind atop 8-inch-high roots
that looked like pinworms. Bernard nearly had another nervous breakdown. Everywhere he looked was death; dead crops, dead animals, dying
clapboard towns, cemeteries of dead people under toppled headstones
—Bernard felt he was seeing Western civilization end in a human-made
wasteland. "That part of Kansas has been killed," he said. For as badly as
he had wanted to see the tragedy, he underestimated how much it would
scar his psyche. It was his Utah flood horror in horizontal form.

Bernard felt so lonely and "practically pathological" he drove like a
fiend until he saw a sign for a telephone. He called Avis long distance to
hear the soothing sound of her voice, and to "assure myself that people
still lived on this earth." Her tough love response: Nuts—keep going.
Eventually he saw an uplifting sight: workers from the Soil Conservation Service, a division within the Department of Agriculture, reseeding
swaths of moonscape. They were trying, he reported, to "bring the land
back, very brave and hopeful."

He continued farther into the West. His purpose was to travel the
Oregon and Santa Fe Trails. His companion was Arthur Schlesinger
Jr., now a round-faced historian with a fondness for bow ties who had
taken Harvard classes from the man he once assumed was his bootlegger.
Schlesinger would remember that behind Bernard's "public irascibility"
was "a lovely man" who gave him "an opportunity no young student of
American history could resist."

In the Arkansas River valley on US Highway 350 near the town of
La Junta, Colorado, Schlesinger saw clouds glow pink at sunset and
said, "Storm coming up." No, Bernard replied, amused that the green-
horn made the same mistake recorded in trapper journals, "the Spanish Peaks," the snowfields atop the twin blades of volcanic rock lifting
high out of a subrange of the Sangre de Cristo Mountains. Bernard
sped southwest toward a belt of the Rocky Mountains inside the San
Isabel National Forest. In the foothills and the high country, stands of
junipers, pinyons, lodgepole pines, aspen, box elders, spruces, firs, and

ponderosas swayed above wind-tussled thatches of blue grama and western wheatgrass, some grown to lengths not seen since before World War I. Snowmelt bound for family farms and ranches chattered clear through creekbeds below handsome, sturdy stone bridges grasping freshly graded roads. Across the land grew new state parks, town swimming pools, rural hydroelectric dams, roadside picnic areas, national forest trails, national parks campgrounds, and stout buildings made of native materials. From the buildings poured energetic federal workers who pressed saplings into stump lands and sprinkled grass seed on cow-burned meadows.

The environmental triage Bernard saw was the work of Franklin Roosevelt, who was doing more for conservation than even his fifth cousin, Theodore. "A nation that destroys its soil destroys itself," Franklin Roosevelt would say. "We must all dedicate ourselves for our own self-protection to the cause of true conservation." Among Franklin Roosevelt's legal achievements were establishing or increasing the size of 133 national forests and designating 29 new national monuments and parks—doubling the acreage inside the national park system. When Roosevelt was elected there were 67 national wildlife refuges. By the time Bernard went west there were 252. Despite the horror Bernard witnessed in Kansas, he conceded that "the West is a better country than it was in my time. Better, even, than when I saw it last fifteen years ago."

Roosevelt's most consequential conservation achievement was social. In one of the first acts of the New Deal, he created the Civilian Conservation Corps. Though overwhelmingly male, and racially segregated, it put 3.5 million jobless young Americans to work on the land. The CCC fought soil erosion on 154 million square miles of farmland, restored grass on 814,000 acres of rangeland, and planted 3 billion trees. The CCC introduced people from urban areas to rural areas and Easterners to Westerners—all united in a crusade to restore their country's natural resource wealth. Bernard DeVoto—who quipped that he supported the New Deal on Election Day and criticized it every other day—was forced to admit that, in the West, "I'm afraid you get a pretty genuine respect for New Deal accomplishments."

On average, each CCC worker gained 11 pounds of muscle, which gave great advantage when one in six were drafted to serve in the country's next crucible—World War II. As Bernard's and Schlesinger's eyes bulged in wonder at western scenery, terrifying news hit from Europe. Hitler ordered his Wehrmacht into France, Belgium, Holland, and Luxembourg. The radio in Bernard's Buick crackled out nightmarish reports about Nazis toppling Rotterdam and Brussels, and of the English military's desperate escape from Dunkirk. It was from a *Salt Lake Tribune* purchased in Idaho Falls that Bernard learned about the fall of Paris. "The world is on fire," he said. He and Schlesinger gave interviews to skeptical newspapermen and said the United States needed to fight Hitler. They were treated like "prophets of disaster." That September the isolationist America First Committee rose up to oppose the war. It would hold a huge 1941 rally at Chicago's Soldier Field where its marquee speaker, Charles Lindbergh, would be upstaged by Pat McCarran.

Conversations with individual Westerners steeled Bernard's spirit; a burly Idaho rancher told him he was in the last war and was "ready to get into this one too"; an outspoken woman pumping gas in Wyoming asked, "Has Roosevelt declared war on them yet?" On May 26 Bernard pulled over on a dusty road at twilight near Trinidad, Colorado, where, above the sound of crickets, his radio blasted Roosevelt's fireside chat about preparedness, national defense, and "those who would not admit the possibility of the approaching storm." A Mexican family materialized from out of an adobe hut and leaned on the car to listen. "I guess maybe America declare war pretty soon now," a man said.

As Schlesinger prepared to return home to Cambridge, Bernard wanted to cut short his trip to throw himself somehow into war preparation. "Avis dissuaded him over the telephone," Schlesinger remembered. "What could he do in Cambridge to stop Hitler?" Avis reminded Bernard that he could do more ultimate good if he stayed and worked on his true calling, writing about the West.

She rode the train to Ogden in mid-June to be with him and relieve his anxieties. She brought their son Gordon, who was nine (baby Mark was left with a nanny). The DeVotos drove north to Jackson Hole, Wyoming, and took what was to be their last vacation for years. They stayed in a rustic CCC cabin, surrounded by lupine, larkspur, Indian paintbrush, and wild roses, on the banks of chattering Cottonwood Creek, under the trident of the Grand Tetons. "Always the loveliest place in a beautiful country," Bernard said. For the first time since Hitler's rampage, Avis could sleep without Nembutal. She fantasized about building her own cabin and never leaving.

They continued through Yellowstone National Park, marveling at steaming geysers, roaring canyons, bears nosing up to their car. "More grandeur than anyone can ever know in its entirety," Bernard said. Then to Glacier National Park—Avis's favorite—where they zigzagged their Buick past fjord-like lakes on vertiginous Going-to-the-Sun Road, shimmering with wildflowers and rainbows in the spray of waterfalls. They crossed the Continental Divide in the clouds at Logan Pass and plunged eastward until the northern Great Plains hove up to meet them on the Blackfeet Indian Reservation. "Buffalo country, immensely big and immensely green," Bernard said. He was exhilarated and Avis felt entranced. She forgot she had extracted a promise from him not to drive faster than 50 miles an hour, and on Montana's long threads of prairie highway above the Missouri River she balled the Buick over 75. In the backseat, in Gordon germinated what would be a lifelong love of road tripping. The air rushing through the family's hair buoyed their spirits. The pair in the front seats conversed nonstop and it bonded them.

This "fine trip, while the world died," guided Bernard's work for the rest of his life. On that stretch of the Lewis and Clark Trail, he talked about how the explorers' mapping of a route to the Pacific forged the way that millions of American settlers followed. Being there, and listening to the lessons of the Missouri River, gave Bernard an epiphany. The western land the explorers found was filled with species adapted to drought: sagebrush, prickly pear cacti, tens of millions of buffalo. In the 1800s the North and the South raced to add western states in a battle for dominance in Congress. The future of slavery hung in the balance. But the land of the West settled the question—it did not have enough rain for a cotton economy, which meant that the slave system was bound by climate and geography and, therefore, politically doomed. Lewis and Clark proved that all waters—meaning all trade routes that the people who occupied the land would follow—pulled together from the tops of the Appalachians to the tips of the Rockies toward the Mississippi River; there was no inland sea or central mountain belt that could divide two nations, one slave, one free. So when Abraham Lincoln, explaining his decision to wage war on secessionists, said "We cannot separate," he spoke not opinion but literal truth from the land.

Bernard DeVoto meditated on how the centripetal force of rivers forced unity on the American mind—the idea of E pluribus unum. But as the nation expanded, exterminating and assimilating the Indigenous people of the West, another untruth about the land almost as pernicious as the Mason–Dixon line—"rain follows the plow"—brought the country again to the brink of ruin. The political expediency and commercial propaganda that thwarted reforms to homestead laws led to the plow-up of the dry Great Plains in the early 1900s. The Dust Bowl followed and threatened to hollow out the middle of the nation at the same time that Hitler was ascendant. While Pat McCarran obstructed the fight against both the Dust Bowl and Hitler, Bernard grasped that it was conservation that was saving the West and giving America the world's best hope (the responsibility, he would argue) to stop fascist Germany, Italy, and Imperial Japan. Bernard could trace the epiphany from Lewis and Clark through Lincoln to Franklin Roosevelt, who pledged "the great arsenal of democracy"—America's natural resources—to the fight for freedom.

The DeVotos stopped at the Range Rider's Café in the ranching town of Miles City, Montana, and fell in love with its 3-inch-thick steaks. They continued east to Houghton and feasted on pasties (*America Cooks* was published that year). They followed the shore of Lake Superior and the St. Lawrence River through Canada until they were home. The Buick had made it through 9,255 miles. The DeVotos made it too. Their family was bigger, and their love was stronger. They passed the bumps of Frost and Sterne. They figured out the unique machinery that made their marriage work. Bernard discovered his path as a writer and Avis kept him on it. She became his traveling partner. As World War II and a major manuscript deadline loomed, Bernard DeVoto finally knew the historical perspective through which he would write his first great nonfiction book about the West.

5

Years of Decision

IN THE STORMY SPRING OF 1941 Bernard put 10 percent down on a $5,000 three-story Victorian at 8 Berkeley Street, a few blocks from Harvard University. In a year when fewer than half of all Americans made $1,000, John August sold another serial to *Collier's* for $20,000 (which also got the DeVotos a new Buick Special sedan). The big, distinguished home sold for half its assessed value. It was built by Theodore Roosevelt's friend and biographer, William Roscoe Thayer. A heavy sliding door to the left of an entrance hall opened to a large library whose bookshelves brushed the high ceilings on eight walls. In the middle stood a giant, mahogany work table and beneath it spread enough oak parquet floor for Bernard to lay out his maps to crawl around on. "For the first time in my life I'll have enough space to work in," he said. The house would be a de facto western embassy.

Across the hall was an equally huge twin living room, for which Avis bought sofas, chairs, and more cookbooks. It would be the family room, the party room, the baby-grand-piano room, and the gallery for framed photos of dear friends. Upstairs were separate bedrooms for the DeVotos, as was customary, and which suited his habit of insomniac reading. Around "Villa DeVoto" rolled a large yard with ivy twisting up its perimeter fence and a loamy garden big enough for all of Avis's homegrown vegetables and flowers. American elm, honey locust, and sycamore trees sprouted from the property, which backed up to a Gothic-style seminary school. Eight Berkeley Street was where Bernard and Avis would live out their married days; the home where their boys would grow into men; the stately permanent headquarters for the DeVotos' literary cottage industry. Between editing Bernard's words, Avis prolifically reviewed detective novels for her "Thrills and Chills" column in the *Boston Globe*. As Mark made melodious first sounds, Avis told a friend, "I'm a happy woman. I have everything I could want."

The bombs that slammed into Pearl Harbor hit just as hard in Bernard's mind. He rushed to join the war effort and registered for the draft (though he aged out of eligibility when he turned forty-five in January 1942). The army put Bernard to work stateside giving educational speeches. He studied Nazi propaganda, which Joseph Goebbels had begun broadcasting to wage psychological warfare. Bernard talked to community groups and taught them to identify the characteristics of enemy propaganda: it sowed distrust, emphasized division, and exaggerated antagonisms between classes and races. Its lies weakened America from within by pitting citizens against each other. "The swagger of the Nazi mind openly boasts that it is not concerned with the truth of anything but only with its effectiveness," Bernard told a women's club in 1942.

Bernard took classes in dressing battle wounds and volunteered for shifts watching Boston Harbor for the expected attack from German U-boats. Most of all, he begged of his friends in the Office of War Information to enlist his pen. The federal government was hiring journalists and writers to disseminate war information and inspire patriotism. Bernard was not the only one who thought he would be a perfect fit. A high-ranking official in the War Department Bureau of Public Relations talked about giving Bernard the reserve rank of marine brigadier general and deploying him to North Africa or Guadalcanal to write official battle histories. The prospect, which would bury Bernard's disappointment about his service in World War I, made him feel "giddy."

When his orders did not come quickly, Bernard signed on to lecture at Indiana University. He brought the West and conservation into his motivational speechifying by lecturing about one of his heroes, the explorer, ethnographer, and geologist John Wesley Powell. After having his right arm sheared off while fighting for the Union at Shiloh, Powell in 1869 became the first Anglo to explore and map the Grand Canyon. Studying his meticulously recorded data about western climate, Powell innovated ideas about public lands, reservoir sites, grazing regulations, and national forests and parks. With implacable scholarship and integrity, Powell birthed the conservation policies that would make living in the West possible for tens of millions. That America could produce such a person, Bernard told bemused and isolationist audiences, made it worth fighting for.

Public lands contributed to the war in ways farsighted Powell could have imagined. Clean water springing from national parks and forests propelled downstream hydroelectric dams that powered aircraft, ship, and munitions factories in cities such as Seattle, Portland, Denver, and Henderson, Nevada (accordingly, the combined populations of California, Oregon, and Washington jumped by 15 million). The Grand Coulee Dam, which Franklin Roosevelt had ordered built on the Columbia River in Washington, powered the Hanford Site of the Manhattan Project. Waters from the Sierra Nevada and the Colorado Rockies had allowed the growth of cities such as San Francisco, Los Angeles, and San Diego, which bulwarked against serious Japanese attack on the US mainland. Meanwhile, soldiers trained in Mount Rainier National Park in Washington and the future Denali National Park in Alaska, and they relaxed in Yosemite, Sequoia, Carlsbad Caverns, and the Grand Canyon. Of the fewer than 7 million Americans who visited a national park in 1943, 1.6 million were soldiers.

In 1943 the Bernard DeVoto literary comet took off. He published his first western nonfiction masterwork, *The Year of Decision: 1846*. It was a cinematic portrayal of world-shaping events on the western frontier that was as rigorously researched as an academic history but written in an authoritative, colloquial, and heroic style to appeal to the masses. It depicted the grit of soldiers fighting the Mexican–American War, the flight of persecuted Mormons, and the never-say-die Donner Party, the dozens of California-bound emigrants stuck through winter atop the Sierra Nevada in 1846–1847 who survived by cannibalism. It showcased Bernard's style of telling American history through synecdoche, as stories of individuals that synthesize into a greater whole. The book ends with the discovery of gold in California and the Wilmot Proviso, which would ban slavery in new western territory, setting the stage for the Civil War. As always, the praise that meant the most to Bernard came from the West, like the rancher from Goleta, California, who thanked him for a book he could share with his son.

The book's smash-hit status was assured when it was made a Book of the Month pick at the nadir of World War II—MacArthur's suffering army trapped at Bataan; Percival surrendered at Singapore; Japan commanding Guam, Wake Island, and Hong Kong; horrific fighting at Guadalcanal; a thousand US sailors killed by Germans in a single month; Chelmno opening, Auschwitz-Birkenau, more. The message of Bernard DeVoto's book was that Americans had passed through unimaginable trials in faraway places in the past, and they had it in their DNA to do it again. In 2000, historian Stephen Ambrose wrote that DeVoto used the book to make every reader "feel proud to be an American and certain that the United States and its allies were going to win the war."

Avis put as much effort into the book as Bernard did. She edited, fact-checked, researched, indexed, answered correspondence, and proofread until her eyes gave out. "I have gone blind proof reading DeVoto," she would exclaim. She also kept him sane, fed, in a livable home, and with sons parented while he sweated in his office, chain-smoking and writing.

The expectant marine brigadier general did not bask in his accolades, he awaited his orders.

The McCarran Hearings that smoldered in 1940 burst into hot flame during World War II. So did McCarran's hunger for power. Less than

two weeks after Pearl Harbor, McCarran strategized how he could exploit the crisis to "raise merry havoc" on conservation agencies by re-
channeling appropriations. McCarran's wily investigator, George Storck,
worked himself to exhaustion selecting and curating McCarran Hearings
speakers. But Storck and McCarran fell out over the investigator's insistence on driving himself across the West to call on recruits, rather than
evading gas and rubber rationing by commandeering rides from Interior Department employees. Storck thought it would look improper. Mc-
Carran fired him (an event celebrated on an office document with a
handwritten "Hah-ha!").

He replaced Storck with Earl Haskell, a man with fewer years and
scruples. Haskell leaned on the membership of the Wyoming Stock
Growers Association to "go to town" lobbying the leader of the full
Senate Committee on Public Lands and Surveys to appropriate more
money to McCarran. In return, Haskell made house calls to coach ranchers through what McCarran wanted said at his hearings. When a small
sheep rancher spoke in opposition to range monopolization in Wyoming,
McCarran allowed a representative from the state's largest woolgrowers
association to interrupt and take over. (Leaders of the big Wyoming associations alternately praised McCarran for being "unbiased" and "the
fairest.") When members of the Navajo tribe spoke, McCarran required
that they be translated only by white men, so they would not come across
sympathetically. At the same time, he wrote amendments to outlaw Native Americans from buying land or water rights. Civil rights advocates
protested McCarran making Native Americans, the ethnic group with the
highest per capita war service, the only group so discriminated against;
Haskell tipped the FBI that there could be a Communist among them.

McCarran commandeered federal conservation workers to chauffeur him on personal trips. When a Washington, DC, reporter found out,
it broke through war news and became a minor national scandal. Mc-
Carran responded by increasing his abuse. He ordered Forest Service
and Grazing Service officials not to speak at his hearings, while giving,
one witness observed, "every consideration to the land users who had
grievances." Haskell encouraged Westerners not to talk to conservation

workers out on the ranges, warning that it could make them government targets. He painted McCarran as the only one who would protect them against "reprisals." The fearmongering made the McCarran Hearings rattle with pent-up fury and distrust. Haskell explained he wanted to affect the conservation workers "psychologically," to make them "color up around the ears." And to put on "quite a show."

One woman continually shut out was Virginia Graham of Silverton, Colorado. Her father was a busted small rancher turned busted small miner. Graham wanted to share data she collected about the relationship between domestic sheep overgrazing in the San Juan National Forest and the pollution of her town's water. Haskell privately called Graham's letters a "headache" and informed her that none could be read aloud at any hearing. These were McCarran's hearings, and he abused his power to make sure only those voices that served his goal were heard. Fuming with paranoia and rage, McCarran throttled through Salt Lake City, Las Vegas, Boise, Reno, Denver, Albuquerque; Fredonia, Arizona; Ely, Nevada; Burns, Oregon; Glenwood Springs, Colorado; Lander, Wyoming; Vernal, Utah.

As World War II ground on, rumors swirled through the West that some of the biggest ranchers were withholding beef from American consumers and soldiers, in order to give McCarran leverage in his fight against Roosevelt's conservation policies. The hard evidence for this shadowy strike was that, despite the need to feed the war effort, supply was suspiciously above demand; the number of cattle in America grew by more than fifteen million during the war years. Leaders of big stock growers associations became nervous about their reputations. ("The whole business is very much hush-hush out here," a Montana tipster would write Bernard DeVoto.) The spokesman for the Wyoming Woolgrowers Association discreetly asked for the identification of anyone claiming "that stockmen were hoarding livestock." However, he was undercut by an associate conceding "a large percentage of these are in the West." Other ranchers—even in Nevada—were so disappointed at McCarran's apparent war profiteering that they told him to stand down. "Nevada stockmen and Western stockmen as a whole, I believe, are particularly sensitive to the fact that it is necessary to pay for and win the present war," Walter Gilmer, president of the Nevada State Cattle Association, scolded Mc-Carran on January 14, 1943. Two weeks later, H. Stanley Coffin of the Coffin Sheep Company in Yakima, Washington, added, "We do not want anyone to question our patriotism."

McCarran did not care—until Nevada's voters did, threatening his absolute power. On the night of the 1944 primary election, McCarran was despondent, silver hair all disheveled. He could count on winning general elections, because partisan Democrats supported his affiliation, partisan Republicans supported his positions, and Independents supported his federal dollars. But in the Democratic primary he trailed by hundreds of votes. He followed returns in Reno with the power behind the throne, Norman Biltz.

"We have no chance in Clark County," McCarran sulked, knowing that his poll tax support motivated Las Vegas's growing Black population to vote against him.

"Well, Patsy, let's wait and see," the Duke of Nevada said, confidently.

McCarran squeaked to victory. Afterward, President Roosevelt received a report that late on Election Day, Las Vegas gamblers and transients were paid $40 each to vote for McCarran. The brush with political death changed McCarran. No longer did he view anyone who would speak out or vote against him as a fellow patriotic citizen with a different point of view. Now his nonsupporters were traitors, worthy of being dealt with like enemy combatants, all complicit in a plot so extreme he struggled to make it out. McCarran swore he had been targeted by Communists and that an invisible army against him was being led by a single, shadowy figure. His conspiracies became so grandiose that Biltz could only humor him as he droned, "Norm, I can't get through the cloud. I can't find that person. But I feel his influence all over Washington."

"Patsy told me many, many times," Biltz remembered. "That was the thing he worked on and dreamed of day and night."

The trees budded on Berkeley Street in spring 1944 as Bernard DeVoto blinked at his orders from the Office of War Information. He was being shipped to North Africa, and the allied campaign there was to be the subject of his next great history book. Finally, his pen was enlisted.

The orders came so late because Bernard fell at odds with the office. He objected to censorship intended to cleanse the war experience. In barrages of letters to friends working for the OWI—among them Schlesinger and the director, Elmer Davis—Bernard argued that not only could Americans take straight news about the war, they needed to have it. "The way to get an informed public opinion," he said, "is to inform the public."

To get a sense of how Bernard would operate, the Office of Naval Intelligence conducted an investigation to augment the personal history questionnaire he filled out in Washington in late 1943 (among his admissions: he was John August). The ONI was alarmed to learn from Utah sources that Bernard was an "intellectual revolutionary" who "prized very highly" his copy of *Das Kapital* (certainly he prized criticizing it).

Despite the tardiness of the orders, Bernard was glad for them. He needed money again. In January 1944, *Collier's* ran the final John August serial, *The Woman in the Picture*. It was a tale about a man and a woman racing through the West to stop a presidential candidate whose fascism was being whitewashed by a media mogul. Bernard was so uninspired writing it (and annoyed that August's name was popular in England while his own remained unknown) that he retired his literary alter ego to focus on nonfiction.

He packed his bag and got his shots. He lined up a team of assistants and booked a hotel room in Washington, DC, from where he would depart. The military then amended its terms. Bernard DeVoto would be barred from reading official battle reports and other confidential papers for the book that would bear his name. The restriction threw him into agony. He was being manipulated to write propaganda. His yearning to serve was pitted against his duty to tell the truth. He sought counsel from a naval historian friend who advised *don't go unless they will open it all up for you.*

That weighed on his mind, but on his heart weighed his regret at never going overseas to fight in World War I. Bernard considered Avis.

She had suffered all year from insomnia and infections. Since Mark's birth, she had become anemic, which meat rationing did not help. Avis grew so weak that Bernard even began changing diapers and cleaning house.

Four hours before his train's departure for Washington, Bernard buckled under the weight of his options. He touched eyes with Avis and said, "I don't think I'd better go." She replied, "I don't think you'd better," and burst into tears. He picked up his phone and told OWI, sealing his fate to never leave the North American continent. Censorship made up his mind, Avis made up his heart.

On April 4, 1944, a Cambridge police sergeant and three inspectors dressed in suits and fedoras burst into the claustrophobically cluttered University Law Book Exchange. They asked the owner, a slight, bow-tied man standing under a Harvard pennant and a US flag on his wall, about a tip. Was he selling Lillian Smith's *Strange Fruit*, a novel depicting a romance between a white man and a Black woman (which borrowed its title from Billie Holiday's song)?

"Well, will you wait," Abraham Isenstadt told the lawmen, "the fellow who is going to buy it will be here in a few minutes."

Bernard DeVoto walked in wearing a three-piece suit and hat and handed a $5 bill to Isenstadt, who gave him a hardback copy and $2.25 in change. After that, they were both arrested. The book was banned. The New England Watch and Ward Society said it would corrupt the morals of youth. Bernard bought it as a public protest against censorship. A photograph of him taking the book from Isenstadt with scowling officers about to pounce ran in that day's *Boston Traveler*. Bernard understood he could spend more than two years in jail, and might open himself up to further prosecution for owning other banned books. "If they were to hold me on it, I would be looking at my wife and children through prison bars for the rest of my natural life," he told a journalist in 1945.

Free speech became the battle Bernard raised up as World War II wound down. Angry about his experience with the Office of War Information, Bernard proclaimed that any group that would deny access to falsehood would also deny access to truth. "The place to fight censorship is whatever place it appears in," he said.

Bernard's stridency got him his first gig as an advisor to a presidential candidate. Wendell Willkie, the Republican who had lost to Franklin Roosevelt in 1940 and ran again in the 1944 primary, was also so alarmed by creeping censorship that he reached out to Bernard. They met on a train, and Bernard penned words that Willkie used in stump speeches throughout the rainy Midwest.

"Mr. DeVoto points out that as a people we have done well with our war efforts, from the miracle of production which we have wrought to the good humored endurance of dislocated and regimented lives," Willkie said, his cleft jaw swinging. "But he finds among us today a new and growing fear. I quote him: 'The fear is that, terrible as the war is, the coming peace will make these war years seem to have been a time of quiet, order and optimism.'"

As Bernard went to trial for buying *Strange Fruit*, an unexpected supporter came and stood by him, F. O. Matthiessen, his Harvard nemesis, the self-described Socialist who never missed an opportunity to bash him in public or private. Despite everything that separated them, Bernard and Matthiessen shared a commitment to free speech. With Bernard by his side, Matthiessen addressed a gaggle of reporters. "To those who believe that the fight against fascism must begin at home, here is an opportunity to rally public opinion in order to prevent the recurrence of such an unjustifiable violation of freedom of the press." Bernard looked over admiringly. When he was down—when other friends who fancied themselves hard-fighting liberals scurried away—Matthiessen stepped up.

Ultimately, the charges were dropped after an officer falsely testified that Bernard planned to sell the book to students. (Bookseller Isenstadt was fined $200.) The Massachusetts Civil Liberties Union parlayed momentum from the case to get censorship laws nullified by the state's legislature and higher courts. Bernard teased Matthiessen that being falsely charged finally made him feel at home with Russia. "It was perfect and I want a summary of the incident carved on my tomb," he said.

Bernard threw himself into the spotlight resisting censorship, the wicked thread connecting war propaganda to banning books to the Mc-Carran Hearings. Lillian Smith publicly thanked Bernard for his "courageous defense" of her book. But the private, racist hate mail came to Avis personally. One anonymous letter even threatened to traffic their son. "Dear Avis: Wouldn't it be interesting to get Bunny's reaction to 'Strange Fruit' . . . Oh boy, wouldn't it be fun to fuck a little nigger girl."

That poison-pen writer knew a truth about the DeVotos: the most venomous way to hurt Bernard was to attack Avis and the family. She learned—better than he realized—that she could take it. "I'm tougher than he was," she would remember.

As the war entered its climactic phase, Bernard proved himself so independent that he could stand for the Bill of Rights alongside a Republican party nominee for president and a Socialist. He showed he could loyally support the war effort while opposing antidemocratic forces that undermined America's sacrifices. When an opportunity to finally serve his country abroad became compromised, at a time Avis needed him, he stayed behind and helped her. When a sacred domestic right was threatened, she supported him risking his freedom.

Their marriage was a steel fuselage and their literary partnership was a jet engine. In between his war lecturing, "Easy Chair" writing, and helping with homemaking, Bernard started his next great book, *Across the Wide Missouri*. In between her prolifically reviewing mystery novels for the *Boston Globe*'s "Thrills and Chills" column, as well as parenting and homemaking, Avis edited and read proof. *Across the Wide Missouri* worked backward from *The Year of Decision: 1846* to the heyday of the Rocky Mountain fur trade in the 1830s. With prose thundering like a buffalo stampede, Bernard wrote the lives of Jim Bridger, Kit Carson, Joe Meek, James Beckwourth, Hugh Glass, Osborne Russell, John Colter, and Jedediah Smith. His narrative innovation was writing *Wide Missouri* as a corporate drama where the American Fur Company, the Rocky Mountain Fur Company, the Hudson's Bay Company, and a cast of eastern interlopers and speculators battled for control of the West. As well as different Native American tribes (Bernard deeply researched and wrote about more than fifty of them) by turns using and getting used by the corporations. The inspiration for the book was an art collector's discovery of some of the earliest known paintings of the West, done by Alfred Jacob Miller. Bernard believed the dramas of that era were as riveting as anything by Shakespeare or the Ancient Greeks, all set before the backdrop of the most magnificent scenery on Earth. This DeVoto and DeVoto production—the most accessible of their best work —would win numerous awards.

Working back through history meant that the next book the DeVotos would tackle, *The Course of Empire*, would feature Lewis and Clark, whose trail to the Pacific the DeVotos intended to trace with their Buick as soon as wartime rationing ended. What the DeVoto Corps of Discovery would find would also profoundly alter the western landscape, and American history, but leave one explorer partnerless.

PART II

I sat wondering at the contagious powers of Rumor.
Here, through this voiceless land, this desert, this
vacuum, it had spread like a change of weather.

—Owen Wister, *The Virginian*

6

The Landgrab

THE ORIGINAL CORPS OF DISCOVERY left St. Louis in a 55-foot keelboat on May 14, 1804. The DeVoto Corps of Discovery left Cambridge in a six-year-old Buick Special on June 9, 1946. Strapped on the roof was a topper the size of a child's wading pool. Joggled inside were Bernard's necessities: portable western library, maps, notebooks, pencils, Speed Graphic camera, Chesterfield cigarettes, rye whiskey. He allowed the other three members only two suitcases. "I think he's got nerve," Avis would say. She packed denim dresses, nylon underwear, shoes, sleeping pills, a bathing suit, riding pants, a sewing kit, and all the clothes that Gordon, fifteen, and Mark, six, would need for three months. Bernard took the wheel. Avis rode shotgun wearing her tailored frontier pants. Gordon excitedly awaited more driving time in the backseat. Beside him, Mark fell carsick and began vomiting.

They drove through the leafy Berkshire Mountains in Massachusetts and on through the Catskills in New York. They took a ferry across Lake Erie from Buffalo to Detroit, and another across Lake Michigan from

Ludington to Manitowoc, Wisconsin. Bernard was indignant about being served processed cheese in a Wisconsin restaurant; he could not understand how such a beautifully bucolic state had such lousy food. Mark oohed and aahed at freight trains. Onward through Minnesota cornfields to South Dakota, where the prairie grasses shortened, the horizon opened, and the straight highways seduced Bernard to drive 80 miles an hour.

An estimated one-third of Americans hit the road again in 1946. Jackie Robinson stole out of California to start his professional baseball career. John Wayne rolled into Monument Valley, Arizona, with director John Ford to make another Western. Norma Jeane Dougherty traveled to a Los Angeles modeling agency to begin a new career under the name Marilyn Monroe. Julia McWilliams, a tall woman intrigued by cooking, and her sort-of-fiancé, Paul Child, traveled the DeVotos' route in an identical Buick going the opposite direction. Drivers pushed pairs of newly minted Roosevelt dimes into coin-operated pumps for each gallon of gas. Musician Bobby Troup, driving from Pennsylvania to California, wrote a road trip anthem that jazzman Nat King Cole would make a hit by the year's end.

> If you ever plan to motor west
> Travel my way, take the highway that is best
> Get your kicks on Route 66

The DeVotos joined the Lewis and Clark Trail at the Missouri River town of Pierre. It was there they also crossed the Hundredth Meridian, the eastern border of the 40 percent of the contiguous United States, stretching west to the tops of the Sierra–Cascade massif, that Bernard loved the most. The Far West was home to the public lands that made him ecstatic—thrusting, snowcapped mountains; burnt sienna deserts blooming with cacti; dramatic rivers pouring through sculpted canyons; sage-tufted prairies stretching to all horizons under a rotunda of blue. Bernard planned in advance to write a single "Easy Chair" column about "my old groove," the status of natural resource conservation and public lands. Based on how improved he had seen the West on his 1940 trip, he expected it to be a hopeful column.

But his internal alarm started to whoop. He visited state historians, chatted with residents, and read local newspapers. Everywhere was chatter about a giant dam being built upstream on the Missouri River, soon to be the fifth largest in the United States. The Garrison Dam in North Dakota would be 2.5 miles long, 210 feet high, and made of 25 times more landfill than the largest Great Pyramid in Egypt. All around, Bernard saw rampant land speculation; dry acres bought for pennies in anticipation of flipping them for small fortunes once the projected $136 million dam brought irrigation. Bernard felt astonished to be seeing "a genuine blown in the bottle Western boom," like the historic rushes on gold, furs, timber, oil, and grazing land. He knew that the greatest land frauds in US history went hand in hand with such resource grabs. He "began to pick up hints" of another.

The hints turned tragic after the DeVotos crossed the river west in South Dakota, passed Wall Drug, drove through Custer State Park, and coursed north through shamrock-colored grasses on the Standing Rock Indian Reservation. They arrived by the edge of the Fort Berthold Reservation, home of the Three Affiliated Tribes: the Arikara, Hidatsa, and Mandan Nations. The vast river bottom cupped some of the most fertile agricultural land in the state. It was given to the tribes, reportedly, in gratitude for the kindness the Mandans showed in introducing Lewis and Clark to Sacajawea, the young Lemhi Shoshoni mother who helped guide the Corps of Discovery to the Pacific. Though the Three Affiliated Tribes had not consented to the Garrison Dam, Bernard watched crews haul in abandoned homesteader shacks and metal corn cribs to house the workers who would build it. The peoples' anguish at the fait accompli would be immortalized in a 1948 event with George Gillette, a tribal attorney. With his hair clipped short and his body clad in a neat suit to match the more than a dozen white men representing the federal Bureau of Reclamation, Gillette broke down in tears as the under-construction dam was officially authorized. It was flooding 150,000 acres of the tribes' land, including 94 percent of its cattle-grazing pastures, and 80 percent of its people's homes. In a cruel encapsulation of federal dealings with sovereign tribes, developers planned to name the artificial lake for Sacajawea, but tribal members would not be allowed to fish there.

Standing in the wind with such barbarous injustice playing on his round glasses made Bernard DeVoto feel like he was witnessing the ugliest parts of western history repeating. As a historian, he was personally offended that the dam would transform the landscape around Fort Clark, once a fur trappers' rendezvous. George Catlin had painted some of the world's first images of Plains Indians at the fort in 1832. A century later, in recognition of history's role in binding together a diverse nation, Franklin Roosevelt reorganized the National Park Service to protect historic sites such as the fort. But here it was, condemned to be channelized and plowed, the Park Service as powerless as the Three Affiliated Tribes.

As he wondered what else was surely happening, Bernard sought solace, as he always did, in a good meal. He went wanting in the town of Minot. In a greasy restaurant near the family's hotel, he gnawed a terrible steak "pan-fried to parfleche," paired with beer whose taste was little changed on its way out. He could not stop thinking about the antecedents to what he was witnessing.

As the DeVotos saw the twentieth-century West through their windshield, Bernard pictured the nineteenth century in his mind. The violent murders of James Averell and Kate Watson came to hold great significance for him. The couple homesteaded a small ranch near the Oregon Trail in Wyoming Territory in 1889. Averell was a college graduate from the Northeast who opened a saloon that catered to Sweetwater Valley homesteaders. He wrote for Natrona County newspapers and denounced the monopolization of the public domain by cattle barons, which violated federal homestead law. He and his wife, the saloon's cook, who was so adept on the ranch her nickname became "Cattle Kate," were hanged from a cottonwood tree by "stranglers" on horseback. An owner of a competitor ranch whose foreman led the vigilante posse wrote that Cattle Kate "died game" while Averell begged for mercy. The investor called the terroristic killings "in many ways indefensible and yet" necessary for business. After the extermination of the buffalo, about a hundred cattle kings—sons of wealthy Easterners, titled European gentry, and Scottish and English businessmen—freely ran two million cows on the territory's open public domain with no competition, and would kill to go back to that time.

The social elite kept a list of newcomers whom they marked for death by calling them "rustlers," meaning cattle thieves. They had founded the Wyoming Stock Growers Association, and it operated from a block of Victorian mansions in Cheyenne known as "Millionaires' Row." In 1892, two years after statehood, association members financed a fifty-man posse of former Texas Rangers and other gunmen to hunt down the top alleged rustler, a settler with the heroic name of Nate Champion (who poetically rode a white horse). Champion was in Johnson County, where residents had formed a rival stock association. He single-handedly held off the vigilantes until they set his shack on fire and shot him twenty-eight times. More than three hundred allies had formed a counter-militia by the time Champion was killed. Panicked acting governor Amos Barber, a wealthy Philadelphian, woke President Benjamin Harrison and had the US Army's Sixth Cavalry sent in to stop the "insurrection." It was an example of the same class that had damned the federal government for giving homesteads to small ranchers now eager to take federal help to violently put them down. The mess became known as the Johnson County War.

J. Elmer Brock was then a flinty, brown-eyed boy living in Johnson County. Brock's father farmed a tenancy on an enormous ranch run by a member of the British parliament, Sir Horace Curzon Plunkett. The Brocks were allowed one milk cow, but all its calves had to go to Plunkett to keep them from competing on the rapidly denuding public domain. Despite growing up in this oppressive feudal system, Brock romanticized the vigilantes who enforced it. "The outlaws of 50 years ago were a different breed—hard, cold, quick on the draw, and often ruthless, but somehow clean, like the western air they breathed," he wrote in 1949. "And their crimes were usually big, like the country they lived and worked and sinned in!"

Brock, who was president of the Wyoming Stock Growers Association in the early 1930s, shared a literary obsession with Bernard DeVoto:

Owen Wister's 1902 novel *The Virginian*. Wister, a Philadelphia-born Harvard graduate, had been inspired by visiting Wyoming in the 1880s and jawing in leather armchairs with his friends on Millionaires' Row. He saw Oregon Trail emigrants and dismissed them as "a miserable population." Wister wrote *The Virginian*'s eponymous main character as a handsome, chivalrous cowboy who in a key scene murders his former best friend, on behalf of a ranch boss, for rustling a cow. The book made range war the fundamental plot device for a new storytelling genre, the Western.

If Brock could valorize freebooting mercenaries who killed the Champions of the West, Bernard DeVoto could have seen his grandfather, and perhaps himself and Avis, in their victims. Bernard thought that *The Virginian* and all its hackneyed spawn about white hats versus invading black hats (or feather bonnets) used range war to moralize about caste war: that the plunderers of Millionaires' Row, and those who identified with them, symbolized by the mythical, heroic cowboy, were always righteous and just. And that those they killed were innately bad, deserving of punishment, an inferior caste. Brock's take was more personal: he searched for years for the actual Virginian, as though he felt a kinship.

The methods of vigilantism shifted from the open plains to the halls of Congress as McCarran seized power. Brock welcomed the McCarran Hearings to "get us what is ours," and he cooperated closely. Brock, who ascended to the presidency of the American National Livestock Association (the Wyoming association's lobbying arm), co-wrote, at McCarran's invitation, a list of grievances. Its language appeared nearly verbatim in a resolution McCarran submitted to Congress, suggesting it was Brock's pen that wrote McCarran's public lands bills.

After curating six thousand pages of testimony that was cooked before it was collected, McCarran used his hearings as justification for slashing the budget for the Grazing Service by 60 percent. The agency the Roosevelt administration created to protect public lands was already so impoverished by McCarran that each employee was responsible for supervising a half-million acres. By the process of discrediting, defaming, and defunding, McCarran kept his Dust Bowl promise: he cut the Grazing Service so deep it could not recover. Bernard DeVoto would call it "a classic demonstration on how to assassinate a federal agency."

In a move that the majority of Americans neither knew nor cared about, in early summer 1946 President Truman quietly folded the remnants of the Grazing Service into the moribund, historically corrupt General Land Office to create a new federal agency: the Bureau of Land Management. It might more accurately have been called the Bureau of Pat McCarran. The senator was secretly at work on the next phase of his plan when the DeVotos awoke from troubled sleep in North Dakota and pointed their Buick farther west in search of answers.

The morning heavens blue as forget-me-not petals and winds rippling to every horizon steadied Bernard DeVoto's mood. He pitied anyone who did not see loveliness in North Dakota, its carpets of yellow sunflowers and blue grama, its vast prairies that shrink the ego and free the imagination. Avis jotted down how much she loved the unrolling land. "Beautiful. Ripe wheat, vast skies."

Theodore Roosevelt—whose Badlands ranch beyond the horizon on the driver's side was about to be turned into a national park—said it was where "the romance of my life began." The DeVotos drove west through a cradle of American conservation. Theodore Roosevelt National Park would host reintroduced populations of elk and buffalo, the latter the animal that first brought its namesake into the Far West as a hunter in 1883 and radicalized him as a conservationist. Around the tiny oil-drilling town of Williston were four-legged emissaries of Roosevelt's legacy that could keep pace with the DeVotos' Buick. Pronghorn antelope—faster than cheetahs over long distances—were bounding back after their population in North Dakota was blasted down to just 225 in the 1920s.

Above the DeVotos swooped Canada geese, migrating whooping cranes, and bald eagles: all three species had nearly gone extinct but were pulled back from the brink because Roosevelt—Franklin this time—created an astounding fifty national wildlife refuges in North Dakota. Waterfowl across the nation had rebounded from thirty million to a hundred million during the second Roosevelt presidency. Ear-flapping families of whitetail and mule deer saw their numbers rise from one million to three million.

The wealth in wildlife symbolized the Roosevelts' conservation achievements, and a moment in the spring of 1946 symbolized a transference of their guardianship. The conservation pioneer who connected both Roosevelts was Gifford Pinchot, who co-created the National Forest Service with Theodore Roosevelt and gave Franklin Roosevelt the model for the Civilian Conservation Corps. The conservation philosophy was, Pinchot explained, "the greatest good to the greatest number for the longest time," and public lands were "to help the small man make a living rather than the big man make a profit." Shortly before departing for the West, Bernard DeVoto shook the hand of the elderly, patrician Republican in Washington, DC, in what would turn out to be one of the last months of his life. While Bernard's plan had been to write one "Easy Chair" about the Roosevelt/Pinchot conservation legacy, his suspicion that "something important was being cooked up" made him decide to write more. Some stories, he would say, "require you to commit yourself, to stick your neck out."

Avis no doubt could tell he was starting to pant like a hound on the hunt. She would have felt excited to be a part of it. Bernard was, she boasted, the "most articulate spokesman" for conservation and public lands, which, she would hastily add, were "a great interest of mine too." On the big, wide-open prairie underneath the Canadian border they visited Fort Union, the historic steamboat stop where the Missouri and Yellowstone Rivers meet. Emotions welled up in Bernard when they crossed the state line into Montana and the land began to buck. The plateaued bluffs and twisting badlands reminded him of his dreams about his childhood in Utah. Irrigated alfalfa fields and cottonwood trees brought back memories of his grandfather's farm. "The high Montana plains, which exhilarated me," made Bernard reembrace his "Western roots." He hit the brakes often to read each highway historical sign—Montana had the nation's best—all written by Bob Fletcher, lyricist of the song "Don't Fence Me In." Bernard loved the signs so much that in rolling hills he posed his family beside one for a photo. Little Mark wears a toy Indian headdress. Gordon slouches with a wry smile and the cuffs of his jeans rolled up. Avis, in trim black slacks and a stylish black sweater pulled over a collared shirt, hugs herself, grinning and eyes twinkling, as if keeping a secret.

The DeVotos relished their roadside meals in Montana. "Even the crossroad hamlets had good restaurants," Bernard would rave. "Wherever you are you are not likely to be eating at restaurants as good." They could taste the fresh-baked German brown breads, potato pancakes, crisp garden salads, and, for dessert, pies bursting with sweet fruit. A blind man eating his way cross-country would know when he reached Montana, Bernard wrote, because it was where "you begin to encounter good pies in restaurants." What the DeVotos wanted most, however, after years of rations and road parfleche, was great steak. They could not wait to get back to the Range Rider's Café—their favorite restaurant from their 1940 trip—where platter-sized prime cuts sizzled to juicy perfection awaited them for $1.50 in downtown Miles City.

Miles City was established just after George Custer and his Seventh Cavalry were decimated by the Sioux, Cheyenne, and Arapaho, and would become famous for its saddlery, cowboy parades, and rodeos; in the 1880s, Theodore Roosevelt called it a "raw, thriving frontier town." In 1928 it became the most progressive in the West. A collective of struggling ranchers and agriculture experts founded the first regulated public domain grazing district on 108,000 Custer County acres around the grassy junction of Mizpah and Pumpkin Creeks. It inspired Franklin Roosevelt to sign the Taylor Act and create the Grazing Service. The history of public lands conservation swung in Miles City.

It swung again as the DeVotos strode into the Range Rider's Café on Main Street. The place was packed. The DeVotos shuffled up a staircase leading from a long, dark, wooden bar tended by a man in a crisp, white shirt with his back to a wall-length mirror and a battery of whiskey bottles. In front of him pressed a crowd of boisterous cowboys clinking foamy glasses of Pabst. The family took seats in the upstairs dining area. One cowboy could be heard bellowing below louder than all the others.

"I could have avoided listening only by going outside," Bernard remembered. Eavesdropping on this "very loud and very drunk cattleman,"
Bernard got confirmation of what he had been suspecting since South
Dakota. The man boasted that there was to be an attack on the Forest
Service and the National Park Service. The methods McCarran used on
the Grazing Service would be used again: deciding whose voices count,
demonizing opponents, discrediting agencies, and destroying them via
defunding. It would be the culmination of the natural resource plunder-
ing Bernard had picked up on in Pierre.

To write the story that would expose the plot, Bernard knew he needed
more details. Fortunately, the DeVotos had a friend in Great Falls, Montana, who would help.

Joseph Kinsey Howard was a man the DeVotos had never met but bonded
with via letters. They had their road mail forwarded to the small apartment Howard shared with his beloved mother in Great Falls. Howard
had a square build, a high forehead, thick, dark eyebrows, and a lamp-
shade mustache that cut the glare of his resting frown.

Overworked and underpaid, by day he reported for the *Great Falls Tribune*, by night he wrote books, and on weekends he traveled the vast expanses of Montana promoting art programs in rural communities. Three
years prior, his book *Montana: High, Wide, and Handsome* became an in-
stant and controversial Treasure State classic. It celebrated Montanans
while detailing the state's history of being plundered by outsiders, and a
few insiders. Howard so aggravated the monopolistic Anaconda Copper
Mining Company, which controlled every newspaper in the state save the
Tribune, that his book was banned in stores. But bars in the mining city of
Butte sold it under the counter. Bernard DeVoto called Howard a "born
fighter, an instinctive member of minorities, and a champion of the exploited and the oppressed." The two underdogs were kindred spirits.

From Miles City, the DeVotos drove to the newly designated Custer
Battlefield National Monument. They continued through Forsyth and
Lewistown until they arrived in Great Falls. They went to Dempsey's,
a spacious bar and restaurant overlooking smoking factories and hy-

droelectric dams clogging the waterfalls on the Missouri River where the Lewis and Clark expedition portaged their canoes and fought grizzlies, and where Private Silas Goodrich founded the Montana church of fly-fishing for cutthroat trout. Bernard so loved Dempsey's "tenderloins and T-bones, thick and tender, and decently hung and broiled in an anteroom of paradise," he recommended that New Yorkers drive 2,200 miles to try someplace decent.

However, Bernard's introduction to Bruno, the burly horseman tending bar, whose overlarge fists could stop and start fights as business required, almost went bad. When Bernard ordered a nice gin martini with a pretty twist of lemon, Bruno advised him to try again and, this time, "smile, stranger." In walked Howard, whose usual Bruno knew: a 45-cent Barclays Scotch. Avis, bright eyes and mind, read the dynamic and went over and talked to Bruno to keep him from looming over Bernard while he shared what he learned with Howard. Though Howard did not know about the public lands plot, its outline would have sounded familiar — more powerful interests monopolizing the West's natural resource wealth. He knew ranchers Bernard could interview. Meanwhile, Bruno became so enchanted with Avis that he bought the house a round of 70-cent Old Overholt rye. Howard had never seen Bruno like that. "Avis was really the one who charmed him," he remembered.

The DeVotos spent three days in Great Falls, where Avis made more fast friends while Bernard interviewed his way through the surrounding countryside. Bernard discovered that big ranchers were excited about something, while small operators "bitterly resented the intention of the national associations." It was important context, but unfortunately nobody from either group knew any specific details. At some point — plausibly when Howard was venturing more investigative suggestions — Avis blurted that he was a western "neurotic." Howard was taken aback until she explained that it made her feel right at home. "Discerning, that woman," he told Bernard wistfully. "You people were good for me; I had a hell of a good time with you."

Armed with more of Howard's contacts, the DeVotos motored southwest on the Lewis and Clark Trail, following the Missouri River to Three Forks, and then up the Jefferson and Beaverhead Rivers. They crossed into eastern Idaho via Lemhi Pass and rumbled north through the tawny hills of Sacajawea's homeland, talking to ranchers and peeking at the Salmon River about to rage down a rugged canyon. They climbed the clouded, lodgepole pine–staked switchbacks of Lost Trail Pass, their highest mountain-crossing yet. Bernard's eyes stayed on the cliff beside the Buick's tires, Mark kept his fixed on the altimeter. Each time it counted another 200 feet, he squealed. At the 7,000-foot summit Mark yelled, "Gosh, I wish the West was in the East." He made Gordon the target of what he found so joyous: June snowballs.

They descended back into Montana, following the river shimmying north underneath Bernard's favorite mountains pleating the sky, the Bitterroots. Eleven feet of snow on their craggy summits prohibited any view of Lolo Pass, Lewis and Clark's hardest crossing. The DeVotos stayed in elegant comfort in Missoula at the new Art Moderne–style Florence Hotel whose seven ivory stories dominated the downtown skyline above the Clark Fork River. As they relaxed into their favorite lodging west of Berkeley Street, a letter came from Howard paying tribute to Avis. "Echoes of your passage through our town continue to turn up. I ran into Bruno," he wrote. Bruno now mixed a first-rate DeVoto Dry martini and raved about Avis, "She was a nice bunch of folks."

Like Lewis and Clark riding dugout canoes down the Clearwater to the Snake, the DeVotos' journey toward the Pacific was expeditious — though at Lewiston, Idaho, Bernard yearned to double back to Lolo Pass. His mood dimmed in Washington's Walla Walla Valley when he chatted with red wheat farmers driving Cadillacs who had clouds of topsoil billowing off their fields. "Let it blow, there's no end to it," they said. Bernard would ruefully write, "There has never been an end of anything in the West till the end came." They watched salmon try to ascend the Bonneville Dam on the tamed Columbia. Sea gusts heralding great accomplishment met them on their misty approach to Fort Clatsop in Oregon where at their first glimpse of the Pacific they exclaimed "Ocean in view!" Bernard taught the quote to Avis — which she always remembered — in William Clark's original 1805 spelling, "Ocian in view! Oh! The joy!"

At the end of the Lewis and Clark Trail the DeVotos' road trip transformed into a freewheeling national parks project. Bernard's book advance had paid to get the family out West; he would write parks stories for magazines to finance their return. After spending July 4 in Portland and visiting the 620-foot roaring ribbon of Multnomah Falls, the family headed south. They dropped off Gordon, who would be sixteen in August, in a national forest for a job with a logging crew, arranged by Bernard's friend Stewart Holbrook (Gordon would have preferred staying with his family; Mark thought his brother's $1-per-hour salary was astronomical). Three DeVotos gained altitude through the Umpqua National Forest until, buttressed in giant hemlocks, at the top they found the ancient volcano's mouth filled deeper with water than any other body in America. Crater Lake was a cerulean iris in a sclera of snow.

Next: Yosemite. Great coastal forests of giant trees beckoned the DeVotos on their drive from Oregon to California, but they were dismayed to pass gray hills stubbled with stumps. The clear-cuts were reminders of the Oregon Land Fraud from the turn of the century. Interconnected swindles — from members of Congress down to timber companies paying itinerant sailors the price of a beer to file fraudulent land claims — had privatized enormous swaths of public lands. "The shabbiest chapter in our history," Bernard would call it. More than 90 percent of the venerated redwoods, *Sequoia sempervirens*, the tallest living organisms on Earth, and found nowhere else on it, had been splintered into shingles by the same model of chummy scams, which McCarran's Grazing Service "advisory boards" had updated.

At the base of thrusting granite in the Yosemite Valley, where John Muir had met Ralph Waldo Emerson in 1871, the DeVotos were greeted by the next person who would help them uncover the public lands plot: Ansel Adams. Adams, in his mid-forties, was an intense man with dark, wide-set eyes, a triangular face, and a small mouth he kept surrounded by whiskers. Born in San Francisco, he had been a professional pianist before picking up a camera. Like Bernard DeVoto, he was a workaholic who relaxed by drinking and socializing; he even shared Bernard's badly broken nose, suffered in the aftershock of the 1906 earthquake. Adams's office was the outdoors, where he would spend consecutive 18-hour days in the mountains, lashed by wind and rain, waiting for slivers of sunlight to give him his perfect images. The stark, black-and-white minimalism of his western prints conveyed majesty and power. Franklin Roosevelt designated Kings Canyon National Park after seeing Adams's photographs. "There has never been a photographer in your class," Bernard told him.

Adams invited the DeVotos into his photography studio. They examined boxy cameras he had used during the war to capture the American landscape, to give soldiers "an emotional presentation of what we are fighting for." He took the DeVotos on a tour of the giant sequoias with knotted trunks lofting into the sky in the Mariposa Grove. He turned their gaze farther heavenward to the highest rock faces in North America: the granite monoliths of Half Dome and El Capitan, sculptures from the last ice age. Adams taught the DeVotos to see public lands through his eyes. Bernard aimed his newspaperman's camera on Adams and took a photo of him proudly marveling at the scenery. Someone — possibly the famous photographer himself — turned the camera on Bernard and caught him with a delighted grin. Mark remembered Adams showing the DeVotos the Yosemite Firefall, an evening spectacle when burning coals were poured 3,000 feet off Glacier Point, creating a cascade of glowing orange.

Adams agreed to help illustrate a Bernard DeVoto national parks article for *Fortune* magazine. He knew no details about McCarran's plot, but he gave the DeVotos a critical tip to get them to the next person they needed to talk to, a Forest Service ranger in Bernard's hometown of Ogden. In the 800 miles between the Yosemite Valley and the Wasatch Range was the entire width of the Great Basin, most of it encompassed by McCarran's fiery fiefdom, Nevada. It was high summer, air conditioning existed only in the most expensive cars, and Bernard worried about how to safely transport his wife and son across the scorching desert. Adams told the DeVotos his trick: "Drive it at night."

• • •

The most frightening and dramatic drives of the DeVotos' lives began when they wheeled out above the Yosemite Valley. The Tuolumne Meadows laughed with yellow sierra butterweed, pink shooting stars, purple meadow penstemons. Higher they went, into atmosphere thin with oxygen and thick with gray domes of rock. At the woozy apex, 9,943-foot-high Tioga Pass, Bernard "stopped above eternity to smoke a cigarette."

The descent down 3,000 feet of elevation was "the most hair-raising drive of my trip," Bernard remembered. The family rested in Carson City, Nevada, in the Du-Lux Motor Apartments. Bernard made a pilgrimage to Virginia City, to see Samuel Clemens's house from his days reporting for the local newspaper about the hurly-burly of the Comstock Mine.

The DeVotos departed at dusk on July 14 and reached neon lights shimmering in a broad basin beneath the Virginia Mountains, where a sign between clanging casinos spelled out in white: "RENO: The Biggest Little City in the World." They arced east past the six-story, red-brick Riverside Hotel, whose corner bar was McCarran and Biltz's de facto office. They entered a bleak canyon between the Pine Nut Mountains and the Pah Rah Range that in daylight would have appeared as beige bluffs stubbled with gray saltbrush. Lurking down where the Truckee River slowed and browned was the old McCarran homestead, the clapboard house with a shamrock nailed above the door. The DeVotos gave Mark Nembutal to sleep. They each swallowed white amphetamine pills washed down with coffee. Bernard described their speedy conversations as about "those subterranean notions of great importance and little meaning."

They passed the wheel back and forth every 50 miles. Each gas station they stopped at had sleepy, all-night card dealers at green felt tables throwing Jokers at insomniacs. They passed spectral hitchhikers; families of homeless war veterans holding their infants toward headlights to appear harmless, dozens of miles from any shelter. Occasional highway signs advertised guest ranches far off the road. The Buick swung between road-killed jackrabbits. In the distance, Bernard could scent the petrichor of the Humboldt River. Silvery volcanic mountains alternately sheathed and revealed the full moon, creating a spectacle of continual moonrises. It was so ethereal that Bernard wondered if he could sell a magazine story about driving in the dark. Avis corrected his perspective. "It's moonlight and moonlight is not the dark."

As dawn approached they descended from Nevada's last blackbrush into the crystal-crusted Bonneville Salt Flats in Utah. "We were as exhausted as if we walked a week without sleep," Bernard remembered. He was too faded to drive so Avis pulled a double shift. His head lolled and his bloodshot eyes took in the psychedelic show of sunrise. Spokes of light rotated through salt cyclones throwing off rainbows. "Chaos may have been such an interflow of color before Creation," he thought. With the sun came oppressive heat and it squeezed his pulped mind out to the fragments of the Donner Party's wagons mummifying in the distance. Suddenly, two blasts like gunshots sounded and the car careened. Both back tires exploded. It was the era before seat belts when, Bernard would say, Westerners were not injured in car accidents, they were killed. Avis kept the car under control. "I am an absolutely superb driver—never had an accident," she would boast. Because of her, after repairs in Salt Lake City, they reached Ogden safely. "I pay due tribute to the endurance of women," Bernard would write in his moonlight drive story for the August 1947 issue of *Woman's Day*.

Approaching Ogden, the DeVotos passed glistening irrigation ditches striping fields of leafy fruit trees and cows lowing in the shade of box elders. Familiar, fecund land calmed Bernard's psyche, but he was impatient to find the details of the public lands plot. Beneath the Wasatch Range's spires the DeVotos checked into the downtown Washington Motel, no doubt greeting Black families who knew about the oasis from the Green Book. A few blocks uphill toward Bernard's childhood home, above the humming bars and brothels of 25th Street, rose a four-story Art Deco–style building ornamented with chevrons and built of brown bricks that progressively lightened as they ascended. It was one of the first structures built by the Works Progress Administration, the largest New Deal agency. It housed the US Forest Service regional office. Inside worked the man the DeVotos came to see.

Chester J. "Chet" Olsen was a tall, stout forester with a fleshy, round face and deep-set eyes, a trowel chin, and lips that rested in a slight smile. Born on a Utah ranch in 1896, he grew up learning the wonders of the trees. Olsen worked among Earth's largest, densest organism, 40,000 naturally cloned aspen trees in Utah's Fillmore (Fishlake) National Forest. He went on to manage fire-resistant ponderosas in the Kaibab National Forest around the Grand Canyon, followed by the cottonwoods and cacti of the Humboldt National Forest around Elko. He was transferred to Ogden in 1936, where he planted a vegetable garden at his new home and volunteered for the Boy Scouts, the Red Cross, and the Ogden Kiwanis Club. His boss gave him a civic mission more colossal: stop the floods crashing down from the Wasatch Range, destroying farms, killing families. Based on the DeVotos' terrifying experience with a Wasatch flood in 1925, they monitored Olsen's works from afar.

Olsen spent the late 1930s leading hundreds of CCC workers high into the Wasatch National Forest. He liked to ride a chestnut horse with a star on its face, but his charges used bulldozers, horse-drawn plows, and hand shovels to dig contour terraces into the cutover and overgrazed slopes so that the inclines resembled staircases going up to 9,000 feet. Atop each terrace, the CCC replanted vegetation. (Utah had an astounding 10,000 young men working out of 116 CCC camps; together they planted 3.2 million trees.) Olsen's crew of 200 built upward of a thousand miles of terracing, which functioned as organic catch basins for rainwater. The high-stakes test of whether it would work would come with the cloudbursts of the 1940s.

The result was stark: outside of Olsen's areas was disaster—flooded farmland, roads, homes. But in the watersheds Olsen healed, the creeks ran high but clear and not a single one overflowed its banks. Bernard DeVoto trumpeted it as "the most spectacular job of restoring damaged land the West has ever seen." Bernard had a hunch that Olsen knew something about McCarran. It's plausible he treated Olsen to a meal at the Valley House, a red-brick, twin-gabled restaurant 12 miles east of

Ogden whose fried chicken, trout, and biscuits he would rave about in
Harper's. It would have caused dismay to Avis, who hinted at the meal
when she left posterity's best description of Olsen: "A darling. A Mormon, completely unintellectual, very shrewd and sweet and capable and
innocent and natively intelligent and uncomplicated and shy and the kind
of honest good Democrat that is the backbone of the party. His food
tastes are exactly like B's, worse luck."

As Bernard guessed, Olsen had information on McCarran. What
DeVoto didn't know was that it overlapped with an existing FBI investigation that had expanded to political corruption from murder.

After World War II, mobsters relocating to Las Vegas became a new
wave of western emigrants, and none was more flashy, flamboyant, and
deadly than Benjamin "Bugsy" Siegel. Born in Brooklyn, Siegel (whose
nickname meant "crazy") led the National Crime Syndicate's enforcement arm that the press dubbed "Murder Inc." The FBI suspected Siegel
in thirty killings. Siegel ran from his East Coast enemies to Hollywood,
where his bad guy authenticity and radiating handsomeness pulled like
gravity on famous new friends Gary Cooper, Clark Gable, Cary Grant,
and his brother in sapphire eye color, Frank Sinatra. In 1946, as hydroelectricity from the Hoover Dam transformed Las Vegas from a dirt-road
hamlet to a city of fifty thousand, Siegel had a vision to build the first luxury lodging on the strip. His Flamingo Hotel was to have 105 rooms en-
sconced behind a guarded 40-acre perimeter wall, ornamental trees, an
interior of rare wood, and an escape chute beneath the bulletproof glass
of the Presidential Suite leading to a getaway limousine. The Flamingo
would be more glamorous than the soon-to-be built Horseshoe, whose
owner, Benny Binion, a convicted murderer from Texas, could be seen
strutting the burgeoning strip in alligator boots, western-cut suits, and a
ten-gallon white Stetson. It would be more modern than the city's first
skyscraper, The Desert Inn — three stories tall — which broke ground in
1946 and would be owned by Morris Dalitz, formerly a midwestern bootlegger. Siegel would be a more fashionable ambassador for Las Vegas
than Gus Greenbaum, a former Al Capone associate who owned the
dowdy Spanish Ranch–style El Cortez. Siegel's problem was that, as he

fell further into debt with the mob, he compensated by trying to sprawl the Flamingo beyond its original blueprint. Which was illegal.

A specific facet of Siegel's activity seized the FBI's attention. He was issued a stop work order from the Truman administration, which mandated that all available construction materials first go to house twelve million veterans to alleviate pervasive homelessness among returning troops. FBI agents planted listening devices — conveniently called "bugs" — in Siegel's room in the Last Frontier Hotel, where he stayed during the Flamingo's limbo. The agents heard Siegel discuss dispensing cash to woo influential Nevadans. In the shouting style of FBI memos, agents wrote that Siegel "said that Senator MC CARRAN is already cooperating" — specifically, to get him permits and a fraudulent loan through the federal Reconstruction Finance Corporation. As an FBI agent summarized it, "funds made available to Senator McCarran were in the nature of a bribe probably originating from Siegel." The third in command at the FBI, Cartha DeLoach, thought the Siegel investigators hit jackpot. "They were in the middle of a gold mine, picking up nuggets every hour." In the spirit of Capone going to jail for tax evasion, agents began building a case against the leader of Murder Inc. for conspiracy to defraud the government alongside McCarran.

The strongest evidence the FBI would collect dovetailed with what Olsen told Bernard DeVoto. The Civilian Production Administration scheduled hearings about the Flamingo for August 13 to 15 in San Francisco. They would be at 1355 Market Street, and Siegel booked a room (which the FBI bugged) less than a mile away among the Nob Hill mansions at the St. Francis Hotel. A tipster let the FBI know that McCarran would be in the city too, "in case he was needed by the individuals building the Flamingo." Agents had heard Siegel say that McCarran would "pound the table with his fists" to get the Flamingo permitted.

Olsen told Bernard where McCarran was going next: directly to the opulent Hotel Utah in Salt Lake City for a meeting on August 16 and 17 between the American National Livestock Association and the National Woolgrowers Association. It was a seamless weaving of one strand of McCarran's corruption with another. After McCarran's opening speech,

Wyoming Stock Growers Association boss J. Elmer Brock would preside over an unadvertised meeting of a select ten-member Joint Livestock Committee on Public Lands. It would codify their agenda for Congress. All the answers to the questions the DeVotos had hunted for from Pierre through the Montana plains, over Idaho's mountains and down the Columbia to the Pacific, around Crater Lake and over Yosemite, then across the Great Basin to Bernard DeVoto's hometown would be revealed then and there.

Olsen's boss, regional forester William B. Rice, was going to the meeting in Salt Lake. Of the 150 large stock growers expected, Rice would be the sole federal conservation representative — a pro forma invitation. Rice was acclimated to being in such situations: during the war he suffered the indignity of being a forced McCarran chauffeur. Bernard and Olsen set a plan to meet in Boise with Rice after that meeting. Any information Rice could learn, he would share. That settled, the DeVotos could continue their national parks tour, but with a new marital caveat that signified how heavy the situation had become for Bernard: he would ask Avis that if he should die, or be killed, to burn his sensitive correspondence with Olsen. It would protect them all.

Everything hinged on the meeting in Boise. The DeVotos' route to it began in the Grand Tetons, looking even more luminescent than before thanks to the viewshed across the benched Snake River plain, preserved in 1943 with Franklin Roosevelt's proclamation of Jackson Hole National Monument. Bernard could have spent the summer where the expanded Grand Teton National Park would meet Yellowstone, gazing at the deep, dramatic Lewis River Canyon, a geological wonder so often overlooked it reveals the region's maximal splendor. Curving around the cutthroat trout haven of Yellowstone Lake, the DeVotos left the park via the vaulting mountains of the Northeast Entrance and swished down burnt sienna canyons to the tan plateau country of Cody, Wyoming. They dropped Mark off at a dude ranch and arced southeast across the length of the state to dip into Colorado. They visited Rocky Mountain National Park, then ricocheted north through Wyoming's Red Desert up to Glacier National Park in Montana. Bernard DeVoto proclaimed there that taking his family to see their nation, their history, and their public lands—despite the tension of knowing it was all imperiled—was "the best thing I ever did in my life."

They went south, past the mountain-cradled freshwater sea of Flathead Lake, and west into Idaho, singing with the scent of pines. They saved their worst drive for last: a dirt road into the Sawtooth Mountains so terrifying—hemming cliff edges, hanging above deep creek canyons—that it made the descent from Tioga Pass seem like a playground slide. "Thirty-nine miles of suicide," Bernard called it. Avis "nearly went mad" during the ten days they "rested" at the Landmark Ranger Station in another CCC production. "I know what cabin fever is now and I never want it again." She devoured her only book, *Letters of Lady Mary Wortley Montague*, and wished she'd brought cookbooks. Mark, whom they fetched in Wyoming, watched exhausted Chinook salmon flopping in fern-shrouded freshets at the end of their incredible journey. Bernard clacked on his black, portable Smith Corona typewriter and rushed out with Forest Service crews to watch firefighters parachute from planes to battle blazes in the Boise National Forest.

Olsen and Rice kept their promise and met them in the city of Boise. Bernard was excited, astonished, and amused at their story. Rice was an easygoing middle-aged man with unassuming body language who had joined the Forest Service with Olsen in 1919. He did in Salt Lake what Bernard had done in Miles City: he listened. "Some of the big shots are indiscrete talkers. What they say gets around," Bernard wrote privately. From the information Rice gleaned from "loud talk in a hotel lobby"—likely McCarran's Hotel Utah—he located a transcript that the Joint Livestock Committee made of its secret meeting. Everything Brock expected of McCarran was revealed. It was investigative journalism gold; it was, Bernard grasped, "the heart of the matter." Rice entrusted it to Bernard, who for the rest of his life publicly revealed nothing about his source except a statement nearly ten years later that scrupulously avoided names.

"Every newspaperman knows quite positively that if plans are being kept secret, the plot includes at least one conspirator who is captive, who opposes it but goes along because he is forced to. As a reporter, all I had to do was to find this man, and I found him."

To go along with Bernard DeVoto's reading of the transcript—no doubt punctuated by his exasperated whoops and grunts—came a revealing story about its radical inception. McCarran, after kicking off the Salt Lake City meeting with a stemwinder to the stock growers against grazing fees and "the swivel-chair oligarchy," blew up at Brock. The pair had been in full agreement about transferring nearly 146 million Bureau of Land Management acres from the Interior Department to states to put them up for sale. But McCarran stormed out in a huff as Brock demanded that sales begin immediately. McCarran feared the public backlash would thwart the next phase of his plan, which was to implement his "advisory board" system in the national forests. Board-approved crews would resurvey the forests.

In this resurveying lay McCarran's scythe. All land with grass—lush slopes, alpine meadows, technically any vegetated area between tree trunks—would be reclassified as "grazing land." The grazing land would be transferred out of the Agriculture Department to the Interior Department and thence to states for sale. The Joint Livestock Committee hoped that as many as 80 million additional acres (out of the Forest Service's 136 million acres total) could be sold—while simultaneously, an unspecified number of acres in national parks and monuments, such as around the Tetons, would be transferred to the Forest Service and put in the pipeline. Bernard would explain to his readers:

"The plan is to get rid of public lands altogether, turning them over to the States, which can be coerced as the federal government cannot be, and eventually to private ownership.

"This is your land we are talking about."

The fury inside Bernard DeVoto rivaled the Yellowstone caldera. Most enraging were the program's intended buyers. Sale lands would be offered first to those to whom the advisory boards had granted grazing permits (especially themselves). They would have thirty years to pay at 10 percent down and 1.5 percent interest. The land was to be appraised only for its worth for livestock grazing, so per-acre prices were estimated from $2.28 to $.09 — which was six pennies more than what Jefferson paid in 1803. It was a tidy move that would filter the 21,600 public lands ranchers in thirteen western states into two categories: those with easy access to credit, capital, and connections, and those who would lose their livelihoods.

Municipal water systems, irrigation farmers, hunters, anglers, hikers, and wildlife would also lose out in the fantasy of legislating a return to before the Johnson County War, when a privileged caste controlled grass with no competition. What the Joint Livestock Committee lacked in originality it made up for in audacity. The total acreage at stake could top 230 million: far bigger than Texas, nearly double the size of California, an area approximately equal to everything Theodore Roosevelt protected. It would undo a half-century of conservation in America. "The West committing suicide," Bernard fumed. His natural conservatism erupted when he read the transcript. He called the ideas, pejoratively, "revolutionary." The program was a "landgrab."* Out of all the public domain scams in history, this one's ultimate aims, he spouted, were "incomparably the biggest."

With forest fires licking the skies behind them, the DeVotos began their race east at the end of August. They rendezvoused with Gordon, who was happy to ride in the car again. He had not excelled at his forest job (the start of a fraught dynamic with his father). Cornstalks and bad meals met them again in the Midwest. Bernard considered — as deciduous forests and commuter trains returned to view — how his life was about to change. He had not expected the landgrab scoop when he went west, but his sense of his vocation compelled him to it. Because it was political malfeasance, he knew that exposing it would be seen as a political act, and therefore, to the exposed, he would become the enemy. But it was of such public importance he could have ignored it no more than war. Some functions of

---

*Terminology note: in articles and correspondence, DeVoto wrote the term both as "land grab" and "landgrab"; he referred to the men behind it as "land-grabbers."

journalism demanded risk. He felt a moral obligation to go on to advocacy; and Avis knew what he would write would come from the heart. He was something new in the annals of conservation. Unlike others who had moral awakenings in the West—from the Roosevelts to Pinchot to Powell to Muir—Bernard did not visit from the East: he was a born Westerner. After this homecoming, for the rest of his life he would call himself not just a historian, but a historian *and conservationist*.

The next time the DeVotos could say "Ocian in view!" was early September when Boston's Back Bay sluiced before their eyes. The trip ended at 8 Berkeley Street after 13,580 miles. Bernard's "best thing I ever did in my life" came in his twenty-third year of marriage, and it was a shared family experience (albeit with varying degrees of pleasure). As partners, the DeVotos showed they could cross the Lewis and Clark Trail and take a zooming tour of six national parks. Avis proved herself remarkable at winning friends. Something ossified in them both, in their partnership, in the West. Hard trips strain even the best relationships; the DeVotos became stronger, like bone.

There was a specific change inside Bernard after he saw the devastation wrought by the Garrison Dam on the Three Affiliated Tribes. He recognized that the special interest groups that had historically dispossessed the most Indigenous land in the West had expanded their acquisitiveness to all federal lands—public and tribal. Because Bernard had chronicled western settlement with no great sympathy for Indigenous people, he was and would remain accused of racism (particularly in urban and academic enclaves). But he evolved. He would soon sponsor the American Indian College Fund, write articles celebrating Indigenous contributions to English, and advocate for national monuments to preserve Indigenous history. While he would never be called a friend to Indigenous people, his transformation into a committed conservationist remade him as their enemies' new enemy.

As a first matter of work, Bernard had to choose the precise time to run his story in *Harper's*. If he ran it too soon, the landgrabbers could moderate their program just enough to still make most of it law. If he waited too long, he would get scooped and it would be too late. He had to time his story to maximally exploit the program's shamelessness, which he (and McCarran) recognized was its greatest weakness.

He gamed out the chess moves by which it could become law. The suite of bills constituting the landgrab would be introduced to Congress at the last moment, probably March 1947. Republicans would have taken over the branch for the first time in fourteen years (aided by the Republican vote Bernard intended to cast that November in Massachusetts). Bipartisan members of McCarran's Western Bloc would pressure colleagues who knew little about the West and had insufficient time to study the bills. Truman would likely issue vetoes. But at that point—proximity to victory making bygones with Brock—McCarran could work his dark magic. No senator would prove more skilled at ramming heinous legislation over Truman than McCarran.

Bernard considered how to present his scoop in *Harper's*. He opted not to write it in an "Easy Chair," but instead as a double-length feature article. He placed it in the context of history by giving a scorched-earth chronology of the successive resource raids that marked the chapters of western conquest: trapping, mining, drilling, grazing, logging. He detailed the economic and political systems that until the 1900s allowed easterners to siphon away wealth and leave behind dead land. It was a restating of his "plundered province" thesis from the 1930s. But his update offered a crucial coda: through the Dust Bowl years, Westerners en masse, like successful settlers of the past, learned new ways of cooperating, and had worked with Rooseveltian systems. Square Deal and New Deal reforms provided the greatest amount of government investment in the West: roads, irrigation, parks, public forests and grazing ranges, conservation professionals.

Bernard broke down the selfishness and greed behind this historic moment in stark terms. He described Westerners who suffer from what he called a "psychic split." Native born or transplanted, they identified with cowboy mythology, which made them sympathize with an ethos of plunder imported from the East—a sort of high lonesome Stockholm syndrome. McCarran was the embodiment of "the Western mind stripped to its basic split." He furiously denounced the federal government and just as furiously lapped from its treasury. He warped Rooseveltian reforms, made to share natural resources broadly, to shower the wealth only on a specific privileged caste. Such Cadillac men demanded the 1800s *and* the 1900s, laissez-faire capitalism *with* socialism, ownership rights *without* responsibility, investment *but not* regulation. "It shakes down to a platform," Bernard wrote, "get out and give us more money."

Hence the article's title: "The West Against Itself." McCarran was not the only bad actor. Bernard called out a rogue's gallery: the leaders of the biggest stock growers associations, Wyoming's congressional delegation. But the one he savaged was McCarran. What Bernard wrote about him in *Harper's* was sulfuric.

"Senator McCarran has been the ablest representative of cattle and sheep interests in Washington, against the West and the people of the United States."

Bernard knew what he was writing would infuriate McCarran, and he wanted to make sure Olsen and Rice were protected in case McCarran launched an investigation of the Forest Service. Bernard would write Joseph Kinsey Howard and ask if he could name him as "where my dope comes from" if he were subpoenaed. Howard told Bernard: absolutely.

Avis was the first to pore over the story. After it met her approval it went to Frederick Allen, the editor of *Harper's*, who turned giddy. He called it a "magnificent job" for the "interplay of enthusiasm and condemnation" burning through it. "It strikes us as one of the best pieces of writing we have had in here for an age."

Bernard teased his scoop by writing a series of "Easy Chair"s about the West through the fall of 1946. Because he wanted "The West Against Itself" on newsstands in early December, he put it in the January 1947 issue. The big cattle and sheep associations would be holding Christmas-time conventions. Members of Congress would be readying to return to work. The article hit the same month as the Jimmy Stewart movie *It's a Wonderful Life*, which initially flopped. "The West Against Itself," by contrast, was a direct hit. Bernard remembered later, "My article fused an explosion."

7

A New Word for "Rustler"

"THE WEST AGAINST ITSELF" stopped the landgrab. By exposing the Joint Livestock Committee's program and rendering it too radioactive for Congress to touch, Bernard DeVoto did for America's public lands the same as catching an unsupervised child falling off a balcony.

Dusty western ranchers and bookish college professors cheered; lovers of wild, western outdoors and queens of Washington's social parlors huzzahed; precocious teens and reactionary legislators clapped, crusader journalists and big-game hunters shouted in unison.

"Let no man think that the issue is a Western affair," said Aldo Leopold, the pioneering ecologist who read Bernard DeVoto while developing his "land ethic" philosophy. "Disrupt the public domain, and the national forests will follow; disrupt the national forests and the national parks will follow."

It galvanized a legion of new DeVoto fans, admirers, and begrudging appreciators.

"Faithful Old Cowboy," wrote rancher Harry Sever, of Whitman County, Washington. "You are a <u>man</u> and a writer and a '<u>righter</u>' after <u>my</u> own heart."

With "The West Against Itself," the Tribe of Benny became DeVoto Nation.

"You are just as right as the Gospel," praised Horace Albright, the second director of the National Park Service.

Wyoming's former governor, Leslie Miller, came around to "thinking exactly along the same lines as Mr. DeVoto." Stephen Kaufman, a tenth-grader in New York City, said he discussed with his class "how the West can save itself from Eastern absentee ownership." Rancher C. F. Latham in Arizona did the same with much "discussing and cussing" among his brethren. "Many so-called private owners are more like overseers for some loan company or bank." (The January 1947 *Harper's* itself was sharked: its price during the National Woolgrowers Association meeting in San Francisco was raised from 50 cents to $5—and it still sold out.)

From Silverton, Colorado, Virginia Graham, whom McCarran had brushed off like dandruff during his hearings, sang a hallelujah that Bernard DeVoto was a protector with a pen. "Do fight for us and do <u>write more</u>." On behalf of the bighorn sheep on the Desert Game Range in Nevada, wildlife biologist Albert Van S. Pulling gave praise. R. D. Farnsworth, owner of the Colonial Motel in Boise, punctuated "Amen!"

Gifford Pinchot's widow, Cornelia, cheered DeVoto (as did, for good measure, Theodore Roosevelt's oldest daughter, Alice). *Oregonian* reporter and future senator Richard Neuberger wrote, "I believe no article has stirred forest people and conservationists so much in recent years."

Academia registered its appreciations. Jack Holmes, government and citizenship professor at the University of New Mexico, complimented DeVoto's efforts to "pull the teeth and expose the backsides of the men and groups who are trying to pull off the last big land grab." Bennett Weaver, English teacher at the University of Michigan, cheered, "Keep your wrath! It's glorious." Paul Frieder, English professor at Montana State University, predicted "you deserve more thanks than you will get."

Hosannas flew in like red-winged blackbirds from outdoorsmen in the domestic animal and wildlife trades alike. Cattleman C. E. Dougherty of Shawnee, Oklahoma, would nod at DeVoto, "Your last article in *Harper's* about the Great Western Land Grab was good stuff." Ornithologist William Vogt wrote precisely, "If I have ever read a better article on conservation than yours in January *Harper's*, on the West, I cannot recollect it." Rancher Henry Seidel of Oakesdale, Washington, ballyhooed that it "blew a gratifying breeze across the hot air coming down from the men in the socalled 'KNOW.' My sincere thanks for doing such a wonderful job."

The Idaho legislature adopted a memorial to Congress warning it not to make America into Europe, and declaring that "private ownership of the remaining public lands would result in a feudal ownership and restriction of human liberties." The editor of Wyoming's *Laramie Republican-Boomerang*, E. H. Linford, compared reading "West Against" to waking up from sleep. "I have found the 'awakening' very stimulating and disturbing." The *Colorado Granger* editorialized, "You will agree that [Bernard DeVoto] is correct." From Montana, Joseph Kinsey Howard sent word that people stopped him and muttered, "Well, you sure impressed that guy DeVoto, anyway."

No one took more fulsome joy in the accomplishment than the one who did the second most for it. "I am so proud of my old man for the part he has had in this fight," Avis would say. "I truly believe he changed history."

She was paid a tribute by Rhoda Hanson, of Miles City, Montana, the town where the DeVotos got their first solid clue. Hanson, who wrote about the sheep industry for the *Denver Post*, shared a tip that rumors were spreading that when the DeVotos were in town they had talked to "reds." With cowgirl colloquialism, Hanson offered to bodyguard the president and first lady of DeVoto Nation.

"Having met you and your wife, and bein an admirer of yours, I have read all, but ALL, I would say of what you have said [about]the public lands . . . Give my best regards to your wife, and I do hope you will come out this way again. I should deem it an honor to have you—and gladly will I beat off the stockmen and defend you to the death, suh."

• • •

McCarran suffered a heart attack precisely when "West Against" appeared, though there is no evidence that the correlation was causation. McCarran was so clearly affected that all winter he cried that he had been made the victim of a "campaign of vituperation." The target of a "vitriolic attack" and "inflammatory phrases" made by a source he cagily did not identify except to say, "I think it would not be difficult to put a finger on that source." It was someone, he hinted, who would dare "attack me personally, impinge my motives, and depreciate my good faith." He was a Theodore Roosevelt man, he told seven hundred conservationists at an Izaak Walton League convention in Chicago in early 1947. He looked gaunt and moved with difficulty, but he wanted it known that what he midwifed was "not a land grab, no matter how many times it may be so characterized."

As McCarran nursed his wounds, he could relax about the FBI's Bugsy Siegel investigation. Director J. Edgar Hoover inexplicably ordered it dropped. Hoover's lieutenants could not understand, nor could the ten investigators in Las Vegas. "Agents were stunned," one senior FBI official remembered. Speculation simmered as to what made up Hoover's mind. Certainly it was difficult to win a conspiracy conviction, and mob investigations were notorious for putting agents in morally compromising situations that image-conscious Hoover abhorred. Hoover had to consider politics too. Senate Judiciary Committee chairman McCarran set the FBI's budget. Throughout the Siegel investigation, Hoover seemed sensitive to protect the man who controlled his money. "The inquiries relating to the alleged participation of Senator McCarran," Hoover ordered, "should be handled on a discrete basis."

That made for a stark juxtaposition. It was January 1947 when Hoover dropped the Siegel/McCarran investigation. In February came a situation involving Bernard DeVoto that Hoover refused to let go, and did not handle discretely. Bernard's phone rang at his home in Cambridge. It was a panicked secretary for the Massachusetts Civil Liberties Union. The Boston City Council voted to censor a speech by a woman named Hilde

Eisler, wife of Gerhart Eisler, a Communist with whom McCarran was obsessed because he refused to testify to the House Un-American Activities Committee. Though Bernard had never met or corresponded with either Eisler, the CLU asked him to rush to Boston City Hall because free speech was being violated. With the same urgency that made him get arrested buying the banned book *Strange Fruit*, and on the same principle that made him an advisor to Republican presidential candidate Wendell Willkie, Bernard launched himself at the mayor and explained that the council had violated both the Massachusetts and the United States Constitutions. The mayor agreed and issued a veto. Overall, the incident was so minor and quickly forgotten that it merited only a few short newspaper stories. However, one, with a telltale clue inside it, made it to Hoover's attention. Eventually it would have McCarran's too.

Topics up for discussion by the banks of the North Platte River in the town of Douglas at the Wyoming Stock Growers Association's annual meeting in July 1948 included: whether to call public lands hunters "uninformed persons" or "radical agitators"; the urgency of building a 2,000-mile border fence to keep out Mexicans because they could carry hoof-and-mouth disease, a serious cattle ailment; and dispensing with Bernard DeVoto.

"Attacker of our greatest basic industry," yawped Charley Meyers, the association's publicist. "Malignant."

"Slapped you fellows around," agreed Farrington Carpenter, a trim Connecticut native who had done honorable work as the first leader of the US Grazing Service but had dwindled into a freelance association spokesman.

"We have been lambasted and belabored by such professional critics as Bernard DeVoto," confirmed Senator Edward Robertson.

In response to Bernard's landmark piece, the association had moved quickly to relaunch the McCarran Hearings and target the Forest Service in 1947. But with the hearings' namesake ailing, the leadership fell to Wyoming representative Frank Barrett, a sheep baron and corporate lawyer. Barrett would stand in hearings and superciliously shout and shake until his voice broke and his face became a ripe tomato. But as practiced as he was at theatrical rage, he was not as suave a planner as McCarran. Barrett blanched at his second hearing, in Billings, Montana, on August 30, when the gallery filled with the pluralism of DeVoto Nation: foresters, farmers, small ranchers, hunters, anglers, veterans, municipal water suppliers, Native American representatives, trade unionists. Governor Sam C. Ford, a fellow Republican, let Barrett know he had his constituents' backs.

Barrett and his partner, Colorado representative Robert Rockwell, a jocular Republican rancher who served on the corporate boards of department stores in his native New York, overcorrected. In Rawlins, Wyoming, and Grand Junction, Colorado, stock growers associations packed the galleries with their membership, and the congressmen gave them the best speaking slots, encouraged invective, silenced Forest Service officials and their defenders. In Rawlings, rancher Charles Moore rose to dissent. "I want to file a protest against the treatment accorded the conservationists." A Farmer's Union representative felt so disrespected that he wired the speaker of the house to complain about the "firing squad hearings." Struthers Burt, proprietor of the Three Rivers Ranch in Jackson and a member of the Wyoming Stock Growers Association, informed Bernard DeVoto, "If it wasn't for congressional immunity they would get their goddamned asses kicked . . . McCarran, and the rest of their leaders, are as bright as weasels and with just as much fore-sight and patriotism."

Bernard followed the hearings in real time because, like the national desk of a big newspaper, he developed a network of stringers in the field to report back to him. In Wyoming he had Moore and Burt as well as naturalists Olaus and Mardy Murie. In California, Ansel Adams. In Colorado, big-game hunter Arthur Carhart. In Montana, Joseph Kinsey Howard. In Idaho, forester James Vessey. In Oregon, Richard Neuberger. In Utah, Chet Olsen. In Washington, DC, Horace Albright. Bernard said he was "boiling" and "out for blood" and wanted names of "all the big bastards, all the little sons of bitches" in on the landgrab.

In twenty-six months he wrote eight explosive articles for *Harper's* that so acutely explain conservation issues that they could run in tomorrow's paper. "The West Against Itself" and "The West" (January 1947), "The Western Land Grab" (June 1947), "U.S. Forest Service and the Western Land Grab" (January 1948), "Gifford Pinchot's *'Breaking New Ground'*" (May 1948), "Sacred Cows and Public Lands" (July 1948), "Statesmen on the Lam" (July 1948), and "National Park Service" (March 1949). They resonated from Okanogan, Washington—"You started your exposure of the conspiracy to grab the public lands of the West and we still humbly followed the trail you broke," the Double J Ranch wrote—to the *Washington Post*—"Honors for the finest piece though, go to the chunk of honest, explosive prose by Bernard DeVoto in defense of conservation," went a column by publisher Katharine Graham.

Because of Bernard DeVoto's national journalism, local journalists stepped up as they had not done during the McCarran Hearings. The *Grand Junction Daily Sentinel* reported that Barrett was "weighted in favor of one side" and missed "no opportunity to denounce the other party in the dispute, which was given limited time to present its case." A *Denver Post* editorial unflatteringly conjured up Buffalo Bill's hokey artifice by nicknaming the hearings "Stockman Barrett's Wild West Show." Bernard could only marvel. "The surge of public opinion was like that which had followed exposure of the land-grab scheme earlier in the year."

As public attention turned to the hearings, voices against selling off public lands rose. Barrett tried to obfuscate, but J. Elmer Brock, attached to his side, sternly insisted that "acquiring ownership" was indeed the goal. Barrett canceled the meeting in Phoenix when he learned conservationists planned to attend. At the hearing in Lake Crescent, Washington, inside Olympic National Park, a Nebraska representative revealed he could not distinguish a burned, dead pine from a live one. The hearings wheezed to an end in Ely, Nevada, on October 4, with another galley packed with small ranchers, irrigators, sportsmen, miners, and municipal water officials objecting to the sale of Forest Service lands, a final democratic renunciation of McCarran and his tactics.

But the triumph was upstaged. Immediately after the Barrett Hearings came the House Un-American Activities Committee's sensational investigation of the Hollywood Ten. "Hollywood Crawling with Reds" blared the *Des Moines Register.* "Communists Plot to Run Movies" shouted the *Minneapolis Star.* "Bare Grip of Reds on Film Industry" howled the *Chicago Tribune.* It heralded the arrival of the Second Red Scare.

The Hollywood Ten were a group of screenwriters and directors, all found to be past or current members of the Communist Party, whose ensuing martyrdom made more societal impact than any of the films into which they were accused of inserting pro-Russia messaging. The moral high ground claimed by the investigators—which included two future presidents, Representative Richard Nixon and actor Ronald Reagan— disintegrated when the committee's chairman, New Jersey Republican J. Parnell Thomas, went to prison for corruption. The paranoid committee had operated on the fringes of government until 1938 when its chairman, Texas Democrat Martin Dies, made it powerful by sanctioning the use of "prescriptive publicity." The idea behind prescriptive publicity was to administer punishment via damning rumors and shady allegations, trusting that communities would ostracize and employers would blacklist anyone inferred to be somehow "un-American." J. Edgar Hoover approved and leaked raw, unverified data from the FBI. "Extend *every* assistance to the committee," he ordered in flagrant disregard for the separation of powers. It was an official swap of due process for a form of vigilantism. There was rich symbolism in Gary Cooper, who played the Virginian in a 1929 film adaptation of the novel by that name, testifying against the Ten.

Bernard DeVoto had been blasted throughout the Barrett Hearings as a "dude ranch historian." But following the Hollywood Ten investigation, statements about him from the Wyoming Stock Growers Association two-stepped toward libel. Brock called him a "pink pen pusher." Brock's son-in-law wrote in the association's journal, *Cow Country*, that journalists of Bernard DeVoto's "ilk" deployed "the most used weapons of the Communists," telling lies about America. DeVoto compatriot Arthur Carhart demanded a retraction. The association's secretary joked that they both had their little feelings hurt. After the association apologized but did not retract the statement, Bernard mused in *Harper's* about suing the association for a half-million dollars and starting a program to teach literacy in Wyoming.

Avis could be her usual proud, amused, and mischievous self when it came to the innuendos. She would wisecrack about "one of the stock lobbyists in Wyoming the other day who described B. as a renegade Westerner who teaches history at Harvard and drinks pink tea with his little finger stuck out. Boy, I'd like to watch this guy's face first time he gets a load of DeVoto. What is pink tea, anyway?"

Before the summer 1948 meeting in Douglas, association publicist Charley Meyers had put in the *Wyoming Eagle* something he understood Brock would use to start "bedeviling" Bernard DeVoto. The Cheyenne newspaper printed that Bernard "should have a hammer and sickle over his desk, or it might just be better for the U.S. if he moved to Russia."

Brock thought it was information that Hoover should know. The association figured out its new word for "rustler": "Communist."

Not all of Brock's truculent campaign against Bernard DeVoto involved skullduggery (one trade publication simply ran a photo of Bernard from the rear, emphasizing his rump). Brock submitted Charley Meyers's *Eagle* article to *Harper's*. After it was rejected for its libelous insinuation that the "Easy Chair" was written by a Communist, Brock demanded that *Harper's* print some counterpoint to "oily" Bernard DeVoto. (Brock was accustomed to such behavior garnering respect; stock growers meeting transcripts show members thrilling to his curt comments, delivered with a cold stare.) Editor Frederick Allen said he would be pleased to publish a rebuttal in the interest of open debate. But it would have to be fact-checked.

Brock sent Allen a manifesto that was the latest incarnation of one he rewrote repeatedly throughout his life. Brock's sincerest point was that no one knew western ranges better than the ranchers who worked them and earned their livings on them. They loved the land, Brock said, and anything that would harm the land would harm their livelihoods. Therefore, they should be made private owners of the land because it would incentivize them to personally take utmost care of the grass, and he gave true examples of ranchers rehabilitating ruined farmland through careful grazing. The bureaucratic system of "multiple use" on public lands was damaging because it outsourced land rehabilitation while tacitly fostering zero-sum competition for resources, a tragedy of the commons.

Brock diluted these points in lakes of invective, looping logic, historical untruth, scientific fiction, economic theorizing, constitutional fallacy, and radical politics—along with blatant mistakes he might have hoped would spread alarm among his fellow ranchers. Brock would claim that the Forest Service wanted to seize an additional 150 billion acres of land (on a planet with 37 billion). He would demand that federal lands be "returned" to western states, although—except for scraps bought for watershed protection and wildlife habitat—the lands had never belonged to the states. He would argue that the Constitution forbade the federal government from owning any more than 10 square miles of land, which pertained specifically to Washington, DC. On the issue of forests, he claimed that they harmed watersheds. On the issue of water, he proclaimed that beef was more valuable. On the issue of erosion, he dizzyingly argued that ranchers had never significantly caused it, but erosion redistributes fertile soil, meaning that flash floods and dust storms have benefits, and erosion made the Grand Canyon, so any government effort to slow erosion would "involve costs out of all proportion to the benefits derived." Brock insisted that overgrazing in a capitalist system was "an <u>economic</u> impossibility"—which led to his climactic point: "We are tired of being bossed around by a bunch of communist-minded bureaucrats. We don't want to be like a slice of Russia."

Bernard read the manifesto. "J. Elmer Brock is one of the most fantastic minds I have ever encountered and he fascinates me." Allen asked Brock to condense, revise, and fix his mistakes. Arrogantly, Brock refused and excoriated *Harper's*, "Ye blind guides which strain at a gnat and swallow a camel."

Brock shopped his manifesto to different magazines, which made Bernard wear himself out attempting to fight the spread of disinformation, which, like censorship, he believed needed to be confronted wherever it was found. Bernard carried on a lengthy, withering exchange with staff at the *Land Letter*, a publication that in June 1948 ran a Brock screed without scrutiny. Its editor heard that "you are in the dilemma of presenting yourself as either not knowing what your contributors are talking about or else not giving a damn." Bernard was so concerned that he contacted Ben Hibbs, editor of the biggest-circulation magazine in America, the *Saturday Evening Post*, and offered his services as a fact-checker in case Brock came peddling. To his relief, they were not needed. "Brock is the prize sonofabitch of them all," Bernard said.

Upon learning of Bernard's exhaustion and exasperation, Brock decided that was a better victory than persuasion—a prescient insight.

"I have been enjoying myself a lot in goading DeVoto," Brock confided to J. Byron Wilson, secretary of the Wyoming Woolgrowers Association. "It seems to me that in his last *Harper's* article he just about burst a blood vessel."

"Like you I take a good deal of pleasure in needling DeVoto," Wilson agreed. He suggested making DeVoto "a little madder."

Brock spread rumor that the Forest Service was bribing Bernard to write about conservation, and that Bernard was a fabulist and a plagiarist.

For all their animosity, there was a wary respect between Bernard and Brock. Bernard appreciated Brock for being his industry's unfiltered id, confessing to what other leaders denied (the beef strike, the landgrab). "I hope he may live forever," Bernard said. As a literary device, Bernard created a composite character based on Brock and McCarran named "Two-Gun Desmond." While Brock, in turn, appreciated nothing Bernard said, he acknowledged his power. Brock referred to Bernard as "the bull"—appropriate for its connotations of an angry charging bovine as well as its excrement. He would warn Wilson when a new Bernard DeVoto conservation column was loosed: "Brace yourself for here comes the bull."

The rivals shared a mutual western-centric frustration with big-slick magazine editors in New York. Bernard wanted to publish a story about conservation in national forests, about the photosynthetic miracle of sunlight becoming wood, oxygen, a regional economy, and springs of water. Brock wanted the same but for cows, which were grass alchemically transformed into beef. Both men pitched their respective ideas. Editors told them they were too boring.

But Brock had a stroke of genius about how to get around fact-checkers. It would make the Wyoming Stock Growers Association even more elite and powerful (by 1947, 333 association members ran nearly 68,000 cattle on national forests, versus 324 non-association members who ran fewer than 34,000 cattle combined). It would allow Brock to get his message to audiences Bernard could not touch. In the direct aftermath of "West Against," Brock ordered the Wyoming Stock Growers Association to start a public relations committee (with Charley Meyers as its first leader). In 1948, the Colorado Stock Growers Association followed. Within three years the Wyoming association doubled its annual fees from $5 to $10, and the Colorado association doubled the price it took per animal sent to the Denver stockyards.

Serving on their mutual lobbying arm, the American National Livestock Association, Brock used the money to hire a Madison Avenue advertising firm to launch the first nationwide beef campaign. Brock's entire public lands philosophy, his every rebuttal to Bernard DeVoto, became digested down into three simple mass-produced words: "Eat More Beef."

Finally in 1948 the Wyoming Stock Growers Association caught Bernard DeVoto in an act of journalistic malfeasance. It was a factual error so egregious, they argued, that it negated every conclusion he had ever reached. His January 1948 "Easy Chair" attributed to Wyoming representative Barrett an anti–Forest Service bill actually written by Alaska representative (E. L.) Bartlett.

Bernard was ashamed and annoyed. In 1945 he commemorated his first decade of writing the "Easy Chair" by boasting that "every time a factual statement of mine has been challenged it has stood up. Is this a brag? You're damned right it is." Upon learning that his error-free streak was over, he issued a public correction and apologized for the "injustice" he did Barrett. "I cannot understand how I made such a mistake in material fully familiar to me and make no effort to justify it." His private reasons for the two misplaced letters were that his eyesight was deteriorating, and he was delirious from overwork. Avis also missed the "howler." She was by turns aggravated and philosophical. "If you proof it fifteen times you won't get every error," she lamented. "There are just no books at all, bar the Bible and Webster's Dictionary, that are free of howlers, and I'll bet there are a few subtle ones."

As Barrett contacted a Philadelphia attorney about suing for libel, the association played the DeVotos' blunder to the maximum. It pressured every newspaper within its sphere of influence to run stories about it — giving readers "both sides" of the story meant giving the DeVotos' mistake as much coverage as the Barrett Hearings. The timing was particularly embarrassing for Bernard because *Across the Wide Missouri* had just been awarded the Pulitzer Prize in History, as well as the inaugural Bancroft Prize. All across the country, newspapers ran reams of stories about the glories of *Wide Missouri* and *A Streetcar Named Desire* (which won the Pulitzer for drama). But that news was embargoed across Wyoming and Colorado, where for months papers breathlessly covered *l'affaire* DeVoto. "Barrett Rips At Article In Magazine," hissed Cheyenne's *State Tribune Leader*. Four months later the *Denver Post* was still blasting on its front page, top fold, "Bernard DeVoto, Ranchers' Critic, Offers Apology." (Which was not fully accepted: the association's secretary insisted that it was "merely incidental" and that what Bernard really needed to atone for was his "sharp criticism.")

The association's influence had circled ever closer around Bernard after a stranger appeared at the DeVotos' door in Cambridge in late 1947. Walter Scott was a shifty, sickly, middle-aged character. He had just left his job with the Soil Conservation Service in Craig, Colorado, where he worked closely with some of Bernard's fiercest critics, to seek treatments at Johns Hopkins University. Scott wanted to send a message to Bernard personally regarding the landgrab. With characteristic hospitality, Bernard invited Scott inside, spread out maps on his floor, got down on all fours, and, like a bear, pawed at national forests and grunted out arguments about erosion control and watershed protection. Scott listened closely and offered to set up a meeting in New York City with Barrett (though would be forced to telegram Bernard, "I'M AFRAID HE IS SOME WHAT FRIGHTENED IN ANY CASE HE WILL NOT BE ABLE TO COME").

Scott puzzled Bernard. In psychiatrist mode, he steered the conversation until Scott confessed that his dream was buying his own private western Colorado ranch with a view of Mount Sneffels. Scott suggested Bernard "compromise" on public land sales so as to not ruin his shot. He portrayed it as best for them both. "Such intemperate language as you choose to use will provoke reciprocal hostility."

Bernard's bemusement burned off when he got a tip from his western network that Scott was sent by Brock. By that point, early 1948, Bernard was at work on his first double-length conservation feature for *Harper's* since "West Against." Avis was fully engaged too. She was making conservation speeches to women's groups, writing letters to editors, and hounding academics. "There are now three classes of Harvard professors," Bernard said in May 1948. "Those who have joined Avis' crusade, the dead, and a few in headlong flight whom she will axe before the weekend."

Scott's hopes of Bernard tempering his words, or of Avis editing the spice out of them, were dashed. The DeVoto and DeVoto literary team had been fired up by the Barrett/Bartlett embarrassment; as Avis liked to say, they had only begun to fight. Back in bear mode, Bernard growled at Scott that instead of compromising, he intended "to defeat the bastards in toto." His roaring exposé in July 1948, "Sacred Cows and Public Lands," about Barrett's "investigation" of the Forest Service, used a direct comparison to clarify the role the congressman played. "When the Grazing Service was marked for destruction . . . Senator McCarran of Nevada obliged."

After "West Against" threw cold water on the landgrab, "Sacred Cows" soaked its coals. In response came strange, angry letters from Scott, now in Orlando, Florida, intimating to Bernard and his editors that he was talking to security officials. The next stranger to appear at the DeVotos' door was an FBI agent.

8

"Due Notice to the FBI"

THE FBI AGENT who left without staying for coffee (or curry) came at a transitional time in the landgrab movement's trajectory. It was a move that Bernard's friend and trusted source, Morris Llewellyn Cooke, knew better than anyone. Cooke, an elderly gentleman who wore pince-nez, had helped Theodore Roosevelt enact Square Deal conservation reforms and went on to help Franklin Roosevelt with the New Deal. He understood how the "Deals" could be corrupted to the extent that a part of them was now threatening the national parks.

Cooke was a member of Friends of the Land, the environmental organization whose journal, the *Land Letter*, had published Brock unedited. Before his dressing down of the journal's editor (printing "avowed extremists" without "factual analysis" was "recklessly irresponsible"), Bernard pounded out an angry seven-page critique for Cooke: "Brock is making an ass of himself" . . . "altitudinous absurdity" . . . "His constitutional, historical, and legal arguments are utter nonsense—in fact that word dignifies them, they are idiotic." Cooke was so astonished he asked if he could circulate the letter. Bernard, recognizing that he should substitute his linguistic habaneros before public consumption, told Cooke that he would rewrite it, and he did. There is a possibility the FBI agent noticed this among the papers, books, and Chesterfield boxes that Bernard always had splayed across his desk.

Cooke was an expert on dams, the clean-energy-generating, salmon-killing structures that are among the most complex and controversial conservation issues. Cooke had been Franklin Roosevelt's director of the Rural Electrification Administration, which used dams to bring hydroelectricity to the most neglected corners of America. In praise of Cooke's leadership, Arthur Schlesinger Jr. wrote that no other New Deal agency "so visibly transformed lives and expanded opportunities for so many people." When Cooke started at the REA in 1935, fewer than 11 percent of isolated farms had power; by 1947 the number was nearly 60 percent (and in 1952 it would be 90 percent). Cooke believed in distributing America's natural resource wealth equitably, which had been the ideal behind the Bureau of Reclamation's founding under the first Roosevelt and its expansion under the second.

Unfortunately, a brutal law of diminishing returns applies to reclamation dams, and in the desert Southwest, which in the main has only the Colorado River system, politics muddied the waters. In 1922, states in the Lower Colorado River Basin—California, Arizona, and Nevada —negotiated a compact with states in the Upper Basin—Utah, Colorado, New Mexico, and Wyoming.* The Bureau of Reclamation would build a series of dams allowing the Upper Basin and the Lower Basin to evenly split all of the Colorado River's water. The Lower Basin was developed first. The Hoover Dam begat the explosive growth of Los Angeles and Las Vegas as well as mass, nationally vital agriculture in the fertile valleys of southern California. When in the late 1940s the Bureau of Reclamation drafted plans for dams in the less-fertile Upper Basin, population pressures in the Lower Basin and national crop surpluses made for

---

*Arizona did not sign the compact until 1944.

tension. The downstream dams served more people; the upstream dams were guaranteed by compact.

Plans still went forward, Bernard learned by reading congressional reports in the spring of 1948, to overbuild dams in the Upper Basin. Bernard would see the continuation of his conservation fight in a proposal being developed by federal engineers called the Colorado River Storage Project. Once Congress approved the project, it would entitle the bloating Bureau of Reclamation to build six major dam units: one dam on the Colorado River at Glen Canyon in Arizona, another dam on the San Juan River in New Mexico, a reservoir cluster in western Colorado, a dam on the Green River at Flaming Gorge in Utah, and two dams on the Green River inside Dinosaur National Monument. Bernard realized that dams constructed in Dinosaur National Monument would deconstruct the National Park Service. Franklin Roosevelt had enlarged Dinosaur National Monument in 1938 so the National Park Service could preserve the colorful, mountainous, deep sandstone canyon country straddling the border of Utah and Colorado. If dams were clamped down in it, the National Park Service would be supplanted by the Bureau of "Wreck"-lamation.

According to the proposed Colorado River Storage Project, the first dam to be built inside Dinosaur National Monument would flood an area called Echo Park. The Echo Park Dam resurrected a controversy that was supposed to have been settled for all time thirty-three years earlier when another dam flooded the Hetch Hetchy Valley in Yosemite National Park. Hetch Hetchy was inundated to give San Francisco a new reservoir after the earthquake of 1906. The compromise was that in 1916 the National Park Service was founded to make sure nothing like Hetch Hetchy happened again. The National Park Service was given a congressional mandate to protect natural resources, "unimpaired for the enjoyment of future generations." That mandate never faced a more pivotal test — Bernard realized — than the Echo Park Dam.

Bernard became horrified to learn that the Echo Park Dam was a precedent-setter, a first domino. Many of the last remaining canyons where dams *could* be built were inside national parks. Anticipating Dinosaur National Monument's fall, the highly educated staffs of the Bureau of Reclamation and its rival agency, the US Army Corps of Engineers, would plan dams for inside, or close enough to flood significant portions of other national park units, including: the Grand Canyon in Arizona, Yellowstone in Wyoming, Glacier in Montana, King's Canyon in California, Mammoth Cave in Kentucky, and Fort Donelson National Battlefield in Tennessee.

More dominoes would fall to more extractive industries from there. They included Olympic National Park in Washington and Lassen Volcanic National Park in California, where logging companies wanted to shave old-growth Sitka spruce and red firs. Theodore Roosevelt National Park in North Dakota, which oil drillers wanted to penetrate with pumpjacks. Shenandoah National Park in Virginia and Isle Royale National Park in Michigan, coveted by miners. Everglades National Park in Florida, craved by real estate developers. And Yosemite National Park in California and Jackson Hole National Monument in Wyoming, hungered for by ranchers who, in the latter case, intended to segregate it from Grand Teton National Park. As the parks faced plunder, national forests and Bureau of Land Management lands would be ravaged—how could the federal government protect public lands at the extremities if it could not protect the heart?

At first glance, the attack on national parks seemed distinct from the landgrab because its advance guard was not the Wyoming Stock Growers Association or any other group outside the federal government; the parks were targeted from the top down. Yet Bernard DeVoto could see how this inside job was an evolution. In the landgrab, a western caste had demanded to be given disproportionate natural resource wealth. With the Colorado River Storage Project, the Bureau of Reclamation—empowered by McCarran—was engineering the giving. Both were examples of Square Deal and New Deal conservation being twisted to siphon spoils to a politically connected few.

Morris Llewellyn Cooke understood how Bureau of Reclamation dams were abused. Born in Pennsylvania (the state with the most waterways), he had learned conservation from his old boss, Gifford Pinchot, and *his* boss. "I do recall the struggle in Teddy Roosevelt's days to get control of grazing out of the hands of soil despoilers," Cooke would tell Bernard DeVoto. In 1948 President Truman, in a magnanimous bipartisan move, appointed former president Herbert Hoover to lead a commission to cut federal spending. Cooke helped Hoover investigate water projects, for which the federal government was preparing to spend $12 billion, a budget exceeded only by the military's. No politician better leveraged that pork than McCarran, master of the hydraulic force of the federal spigot. By serving on the Interior Department's Appropriations Committee, and commanding the Western Bloc in the Senate, McCarran presided in the late 1940s over the National Park Service's budget being set at a paltry $13 million while the federal dam-building agencies were flooded with an overpowering two-thirds of a billion. McCarran exploited the Red Scare to get more for his cronies. Bureau of Reclamation commissioner Michael Straus took a stand that a portion of the notoriously ill-conceived Central Arizona Project was financially indefensible. Sensing money evaporating, McCarran threatened to have Straus's security file made public, which would have embarrassingly revealed the FBI investigation of an anonymous tip: that in 1942 Straus's wife lunched with reporters for a Communist newspaper.

As happened conspicuously often to those who stepped between McCarran and money, Cooke fell under suspicion too. The FBI, zealous in its contact tracing of Communists, marked Cooke as exposed. Cooke continued to speak out against wasteful dams. His gadabout lifestyle also earned him a minor distinction in pop culture. In September 1947 he visited a dilapidated nineteenth-century house in Georgetown rented by a short, stocky artist who asked Cooke if he could list him as a job reference. The man's tall, elegant, apple-cheeked wife cooked dinner: making Cooke, a friend of Paul Child, among the first to enjoy a meal prepared by Julia Child. The DeVotos could not foresee how the three would play roles in the climax of their coming battle for the national parks.

Bernard knew what he had to do next. He would synthesize information from Cooke and other experts, combine it with his own knowledge about the West, and write another blockbuster. The threat the Echo Park Dam posed to Dinosaur National Monument and all the national parks was so serious he wanted it to run in a bigger magazine than *Harper's*—he wanted the *Saturday Evening Post*.

But before he could do that, he learned of another western conservation investigation—of sorts—that spurred him to write the most notorious *Harper's* column of his career. If the Echo Park Dam represented the surface of the evolving landgrab, news out of Montana educated Bernard about what lurked below.

"What finally sparked me to write that piece was my anger and disgust at a loyalty investigation in the Department of Agriculture," Bernard DeVoto explained privately in October 1949, the same month that *Harper's* carried his thunderbolt "Easy Chair," "Due Notice to the FBI."

The question of whom Bernard alluded to would burn for decades, both inside and outside the FBI. The clue trail runs through his intricate writing process. He composed first drafts longhand with a fountain pen dipped in ink. Avis would edit and help him type his second and third drafts during the fact-checking and rewriting process. "He checked and checked and rewrote so much," she remembered. "The third draft was what made his stuff real DeVoto—it pulled the structure together, put in the polish and warmth and movement." They would mail his "Easy Chair"s to *Harper's* at 49 East 33rd Street in New York City about two months in advance of publication. Whatever was on his mind while composing a particular column can be discerned from his private correspondence from three months before.

In June 1949 his mail lit up with the plight of Roald Peterson, who worked on cattle grazing ranges in Montana for the Forest Service.

Bernard had much to say about Peterson's ordeal, which served as the paramount example of why he took such exceptional pains to protect his Forest Service sources. To make his points, Bernard had to write under deep, deep cover. He began "Due Notice to the FBI" like John August fiction. A man answers his door to an IRS agent. The agent has personal questions about a neighbor: how much he makes, where his three kids go to school, how much he drinks, if he eats French food, how he affords his parties, if he reads the *New Republic*, if he swims nude, if he ever criticized the income tax, if he ever socializes with people who call for abolishing it, if he gave his secretary sexy nylon stockings? When the agent is told it is none of his business, he appeals to patriotic trust. "Of course the evaluators know that most of the stuff sent in is mixed, idle, or untrue — they simply go through the vast chaff in order to find an occasional grain of wheat," Bernard writes. The unconvinced man then watches the agent knock on another door and collect a dubious story that the neighbor is a mob associate and having an affair with his secretary.

It was funny fantasy, but within it were real details Bernard culled from government security investigations. In early 1947, Truman issued Executive Order 9835 creating a loyalty program for federal employees. He had been under intense pressure from McCarran, and though he feared it could become a tool for a "witch hunt," the late 1940s saw the Second Red Scare escalate. Mao Zedong conquered China, Russia detonated its first atomic bomb. There were certainly Communists in government; historians would estimate that in the late 1930s there were as many as 75 (out of approximately a half-million federal employees). Some — like Julius Rosenberg, who leaked atomic secrets to Russia — harmed America badly. But the hunt for them did different harm, ultimately greater. In an era when the number of Communists was highest, America still made it through the hardest trials of the twentieth century, the Great Depression and World War II. By the late 1940s the number of Communists both in and out of government was its lowest in a decade — the fallout of the Hitler–Stalin pact, an improving economy, and Truman's executive order. But as Communists dwindled, the fear of them blew sky high. In the hysterical atmosphere, those accused of being Communists, Socialists, spies, disloyal, un-American, or nonconformist were subject to the most stigmatizing scrutiny — while the motives of those doing the accusing were hardly questioned. Bernard DeVoto pulled back one veil partway through "Due Notice" and said he put those questions in the mouth of a fictional IRS agent because everybody knew that agency did not go door to door collecting hearsay about Americans' private lives.

There was, Bernard wrote straightforwardly, "an avalanching danger to our society," allowing the FBI, shielded by anonymity and immunity, to "put at the disposal of this or that body a hash of gossip, rumor, slander, backbiting, malice and drunken invention which, when it makes the headlines, shatters the reputations of innocent and harmless people and of people who our laws say are innocent until someone proves them guilty in court."

"We are dividing into the hunted and the hunters," he continued. "There is loose in the United States today the same evil that once split Salem Village."

Bernard admitted in "Due Notice" that he had been visited by the FBI and that he had spoken willingly. He declared he was through with that. He implored all Americans to join him in his new constitutional condition: he would give information only if subpoenaed in open court where the person whom he was to speak about was there represented by an attorney. "I like a country where no college-trained flat-feet collect memoranda about us and ask judicial protection for them. We had that kind of a country only a little while ago and I'm for getting it back."

Buried so far inside "Due Notice" that it was undetectable was Bernard fighting his best against a clandestine smear campaign targeting Forest Service employees. Thwarted in the landgrab, some Wyoming Stock Growers Association members responded by pressing for transfers and firings of incorruptible range regulators. Subsequent *Denver Post* headlines spoke to this campaign: "Rancher's Target Moved from Job" (a Colorado range and wildlife manager); "U.S. Shifts Second Top Forest Man" (the supervisor of the Bighorn National Forest, Brock country).

Roald Peterson was one of them. Raised on a western North Dakota homestead, Peterson studied conserving prairie grasslands, the least-protected biome on Earth. In 1940, after graduating college, he worked with the Louisiana Farmers' Union helping sharecroppers. He married a woman from greater New Orleans and served stateside in Texas in the Army Air Force in World War II training pilots in meteorology. In 1945 he moved to Montana to work as a range conservationist for the Forest

Service, combining his twin life's passions of helping small agricultural-
ists and conserving grasslands. The Petersons had two daughters and a
son, and they put down roots in Missoula, Montana. "Pete" was appreciated and respected by ranchers across the state, and he loved the life he
built for his family. It started to fly apart when he was anonymously accused of being a threat to his country.

In June 1949 Peterson was hauled before a five-man Agriculture Department loyalty review board in Missoula. Under Truman's order, federal department heads appointed investigators to staff the boards, which
worked symbiotically with the FBI (i.e., tips from boards triggered FBI investigations, tips from the FBI triggered board investigations). The FBI let
the board know that two anonymous informants claimed they personally
knew Peterson to have been a Communist in 1940. The board provided
no accounting of its sources, nor clues about the informants' motives, nor
any other details that Peterson could use to defend himself from the as-
persion. Witnesses thought the hearing was a sham, a means of intimi-
dation, a setup tied to a pressure group demanding Forest Service spoils.
"Accusers did not appear to be identified and cross questioned," cried a
letter to Bernard DeVoto from Leon Hurtt, a Forest Service range and
research consultant who was among more than twenty Montanans who
testified in Peterson's defense. "Democratic processes were trampled."

Based on the tenor of the letters that reached Bernard, the ordeal was
more grueling for Peterson's friends than it was for the stoic man himself.
Fortunately for them, under Truman's parameters the allegations were
too flimsy and Peterson was cleared. But his life would never be the same.
"Due Notice" hit back at Peterson's persecutors at a time when Gallup
showed 78 percent of Americans thought J. Edgar Hoover was doing a
"good job." The article was a shockingly maverick defense of due process, but hidden between its lines was just as fulsome a defense of science. It said that public agencies that allowed scientists to be ramrodded
for running afoul of special interests no longer served the public. The response from the swelling ranks of DeVoto Nation was roaring.

• • •

Avis loved being a part of Bernard writing anything "sassy" to J. Edgar Hoover. Her enthusiasm was shared by a new faction that joined DeVoto Nation's coalition of conservationists, history lovers, Communist haters, wilderness buffs, small ranchers, obsessive academics, artists, and journeymen journalists: civil libertarians.

Ralph Jacobs of Verona, Wisconsin, thanked Bernard for "decrying our sheep-like acceptance of all manner of infringements of our civil rights and privacy . . . Our ancestors kept a loaded rifle over the door to enforce their determination."

From Lakewood, Colorado, W. F. Henze, a seventy-two-year-old father of two soldiers, wrote despite self-consciousness about his grammar. "I want to thank you for your splendid article an will now go down get myself a Snort to think I had Guts even to write you a letter . . . Some of your Western stuff realy ads up."

Hollywood actress Florence Eldridge, who had gossip about her revealed via the FBI, grabbed Bernard in a mental hug. "There are so few voices crying in this wilderness that one tends to draw close to others for comfort." Claire Cochran of Silver Spring, Maryland, chimed in, "You are so right. They were around here again yesterday, asking if we thought one of our neighbors was 'of average intelligence'—when we scarcely knew the man." From New York City Jack O'Brien would write, "If, in the future, college-bred investigators should inquire of me whether friends, neighbors, relatives, house-guests, cocktail companions, etc. have read Bernard DeVoto's <u>Due Notice to the FBI</u>, I shall merely tell them, 'I hope so!' But this is <u>all</u>."

"Best wishes to Mr. and Mrs. DeVoto in their hell-raising activities," Chas Sauers of River Forest, Illinois, concluded. Bernard replied with American Gothic humor. "I am glad you liked my piece and I will destroy your letter lest the Gestapo find it when they come to ship me to Indiana."

"Due Notice" also showed Bernard DeVoto's foreboding prescience about Senator Joe McCarthy, who at that date was a relatively unknown and ineffectual politician, a congressional backbencher who showed little promise of rising to prominence. (In fact, in 1949 the best-known American named Joe McCarthy was the manager of the Boston Red Sox.)

The freshman senator from Wisconsin was in a slump. A former boxer and judge born on a chicken farm in Grand Chute, McCarthy had called himself "Tail-Gunner Joe" and, campaigning vigorously as a marine hero, beat lackluster incumbent Robert LaFollette Jr. in 1946. When newspapers revealed that Tail-Gunner grossly exaggerated his war record, he called them Communist. But his mania was not all-consuming. He lost himself in gambling, womanizing, gobbling well-done steaks, and chugging bourbon. In speeches, he had a salesman's addiction to superlatives like "incredible," "fantastic," and "unbelievable." His fantastic scandal was getting caught taking a $20,000 loan from a sugar lobbyist, which earned him a hated nickname, "the Pepsi-Cola Kid" (he loathed it like his other one, "Joe Frump"). His unbelievable act was excoriating US Army investigators who found that in 1944 Nazis had massacred some five hundred surrendered American soldiers and Belgian civilians at Malmedy. McCarthy's backers chalked it up to his antagonism toward established authority, which was what they loved about him. They also assured that his obsessively reading *Mein Kampf* was just to learn rhetorical techniques. "That's the way to do it," he exclaimed. Pundits predicted that unless the hazy-eyed slugger with the black, peninsular widow's peak offered voters more than hedonism and fascistic posturing, he would strike out of public life in the 1952 election.

Initially, McCarthy clashed with McCarran, but became so enamored he started to play him like a character actor stepping into a role. Their colleagues became shocked to hear McCarthy mouthing McCarran's big lie that Communists were overtaking the country. McCarran, 1944: "This plan and this program are so big as to stagger the imagination." McCarthy, 1951: "A conspiracy on a scale so immense as to dwarf any previous venture in the history of man." The young Republican flattered the old Democrat in the sincerest way, by imitation. "McCarthy had made a determined effort to win McCarran's favor," wrote McCarthy biographer David M. Oshinsky. McCarran was using his paranoid hunt for his shadow figure to funnel wealth to his cronies, and he saw in McCarthy someone just as uncaring about the collateral damage. McCarran: "If I throw up a hundred false balloons, if I make a hundred efforts that fail, if I make a hundred mistakes and do eventually find that one, I will have served my country well." McCarthy: "If a fowl looks like a duck, walks like a duck, swims like a duck and quacks like a duck, then we can safely assume that it is a duck."

During his hearings on public lands, McCarran had diminished the voices of his dissenters; now he welcomed help demonizing them as disloyal to America. McCarran needed a messenger, and his acolyte with the honest taste for dishonest publicity needed a message.

Bernard DeVoto took one of the earliest, subtlest, and most grammatically precise national swings at McCarthy in "Due Notice."

"From now on any representative from the government, properly identified, can count on a drink and perhaps informed talk about the Red (but non-communist) Sox at my house. But if he wants any information from me about anyone whomsoever, no soap."

"A surprising number of people have expressed themselves to me in favor of it and this is heartening," Bernard DeVoto wrote in November 1949 in response to more praise for "Due Notice to the FBI." "There is one conspicuous exception, Mr. J. Edgar Hoover."

Bernard had not made the FBI look good, and no one was more fastidious about appearances than its haughty director with the searchlight eyes. From working with Hollywood scriptwriters to portray G-men in movies as superheroes to having the large, leather chair in his office set regally atop a 6-inch dais to enhance his height, Hoover was an expert image manipulator. He had done magnificent work catching murderers and kidnappers, and he had built his bureau into an awesome force in part by inspiring such a sense of institutional love and duty that it defined the FBI's very culture. But the loyalty investigations ballooned his power and wilted his accountability. On September 7, 1949, when he received a memo from an agent in Butte, Montana, that Bernard DeVoto wrote something "rather obscene" about the FBI, Hoover was furious.

From his fifth-floor balconied office in the Department of Justice

Building, he fired orders to the FBI headquarters in every state plus the territories of Hawaii, Alaska, and Puerto Rico. "This article reflects the necessity of constantly being on the alert." He sent an angry but vaguely worded letter for publication in *Harper's*. "I do not care to dignify Mr. DeVoto's compilation of half-truths, inaccuracies, distortions, and misstatements with a denial or an explanation."

Hoover compared citizens giving information to FBI agents to testifying before grand juries. Bernard responded in an accompanying editor's note that he was astonished that Hoover did not understand the difference between a police force and an empaneled group of citizens. The exchange gave Bernard a new goal: to debate Hoover in public, to get him on record specifying what types of private information the FBI was collecting and how it was being used.

It was Avis who nudged the showdown toward reality. In October 1949 she went to a cocktail party and was introduced to Fowler Harper, a law professor at Yale University. In the course of their "both slightly tight" chat, Harper told Avis that Hoover was scheduled to appear at Yale and would take questions from a panel. Avis—no doubt picturing the look on Hoover's face the first time he got "a load of DeVoto"—immediately volunteered her husband for it.

Meanwhile, Bernard made Hoover hang his insistence that "Due Notice" was all wrong on one specific fact: that investigators had asked if subjects read the *New Republic*. Bernard's claim that he could prove they did drove Hoover wild. He ordered forty agents assembled at 6:30 a.m. one November day to scour documents dealing with 708 Harvard affiliates. Knowing Bernard cared about the National Park Service, Hoover additionally had all 303 loyalty board investigations in the Department of the Interior combed for any *New Republic* reference. (Had he better understood conservation history he would have known that Theodore Roosevelt removed Bernard's sources from a corrupt Interior Department by placing the Forest Service in Agriculture.) Hoover even polled all supervisors of the FBI's loyalty section. "Like a dog worrying a bone, Hoover could not let go of it, nor could he bury it," intelligence community historian Sigmund Diamond would write in 1992. "Indeed, the amount of energy the FBI devoted to the matter was astonishing." Hoover finally felt confident in proclaiming Bernard a liar after a 1947 bureau bulletin was brought to his attention. Reflecting Hoover's fear of the FBI becoming seen as partisan, the bulletin ordered agents to respect the difference "between true Liberalism and Communism" and never ask "questions such as, 'Do you read the *New Republic*?'"

Bernard showed one of his cards: a leaked loyalty review board interrogatory that asked, "Have you ever subscribed to or regularly read any of the following: '*In Fact*'; '*New Republic*'; '*Russia Today*.'" Because Hoover refused to talk with Bernard directly, Bernard sent his response privately through a liaison, Daniel Mebane, editor of the *New Republic*, whom Hoover contacted to assure that "Due Notice" was untrue. Bernard gave Mebane another message: "You may tell Mr. Hoover that I have others."

Hoover responded savagely that the FBI was not culpable for anything a loyalty review board did, and he ordered them monitored to make sure they "don't try to pass the buck to us." Rather than deal straightforwardly with the concerns Bernard raised in "Due Notice," Hoover went on an angry, dirt-gathering spree. The agent who interviewed Bernard in 1948 was questioned (he denied having asked about the *New Republic*), and he provided a detailed description of Bernard's clothing, mannerisms, attitude, disposition, forthrightness, and hygiene. Hoover ordered Bernard placed under more intense investigation. Into his FBI file went hate letters, a memo about Avis's curry, Bernard's Office of Naval Intelligence documents, and newsclips about the "Due Notice" feud, including a misleading one from the Communist Party newspaper the *Daily Worker* praising Bernard's defiance of "Hoover's Blacklist." All five people whose "Due Notice" letters were printed in *Harper's* got investigated; anyone being investigated who mentioned "Due Notice" got put on a list. Moles inside the magazine and at Harvard were squeezed for more information. In response to Bernard's criticism about using unscrupulous investigative tactics, Hoover used more unscrupulous investigative tactics.

It climaxed with Hoover taking a dozen pages of information from the most biased source: J. Elmer Brock, McCarran's landgrab partner. An unseen hand went through Brock's documents and drew a dramatic black arrow to an underlined passage about how Bernard DeVoto ought to work under a hammer and sickle (from the *Wyoming Eagle* article that Brock promised to use in his "bedeviling" of Bernard). Attached to one of Brock's own manifestos is a letter on his livestock company's stationary cheering Hoover. "As far as the sentiments of the Stockmen in the West, we would like to see Bernard hanging from a Cottonwood limb." The sentiment earned Brock obsequious praise from the nation's top detective. "I am grateful for the thoughts which prompted your communication, and I hope that the work of the FBI will always be deserving of your complete approval." By accepting the first published claim that DeVoto was a Communist—one that was self-interested, vindictive, and false—Hoover blurred the line between law enforcement and vigilantism.

Through Mebane, Bernard revealed what he would ask Hoover at Yale. He wanted an explanation about how the FBI collected and assessed raw data. Bernard proposed examining data unveiled in the trial of Judith Coplon, a young Justice Department analyst whose two spying convictions were overturned because she was arrested without a warrant and the FBI lied about wiretapping her lawyer. Data she gave to her Russian boyfriend included gossip about Hollywood actors and a university president; hearsay about the sex life of a government employee's spouse; an allegation that a Bronx man walked around his apartment naked; and references to the *New Republic:* all details that tracked with "Due Notice." The files were all public. If there were additional documents that refuted the charges of privacy invasion and thought policing in "Due Notice," Bernard would urge Hoover to show them—if they existed.

To further make Hoover feel secure, the debate would be moderated by student William F. Buckley Jr., an erudite conservative who turned patronizing into art. Buckley would write his own response to Bernard DeVoto in the *Yale Daily News*, headlined "Hats Off to the F.B.I."—never revealing that he was secretly a Hoover informant.

Hoover still refused to take questions from Bernard. Both DeVotos were disappointed to learn from Fowler Harper that after Buckley broached the idea of Bernard joining the panel, Hoover "blackballed" him. Hoover declined to even debate Bernard in print. "I learned long ago not to enter into a wrestling match with skunks."

It still was not the end. Hoover put Bernard on the FBI's punitive "Do Not Contact" list, a catalog of "enemy" journalists to whom the bureau would extend no courtesies of scoops, tips, information, or fact-checks. Hoover ordered that no one, without his express approval, was to have any interaction with the DeVotos. It was cunning of Hoover to pile his files with dirt from Bernard's enemies; it was craven to hide inside his institutional fortress. Hoover's walls might have held were it not for simple human nature. From Bernard, Hoover would learn that even his best agents could make dumb mistakes.

November 5, 1950, should have been a good morning for intelligence gathering in Cambridge. Most of the city's eclectic blue bloods would be home reading Sunday papers fat with midterm election news. For days, slippery rains had soaked the streets and humid winds boxed the soggy last leaves drooping from elm branches. Gloomy clouds grounded most of the 1,200 planes scheduled to shoot through northeastern skies that weekend as part of a training for more than six thousand volunteers to spot incoming Russian squadrons. The fog finally lifted that afternoon, by which time a young FBI agent—in flagrant disregard for Hoover's orders —had spoken with Bernard DeVoto.

The agent's mind had been fixated on tweedy Harvard European history professor William Langer, whose appointment as a State Department consultant had triggered a loyalty investigation. Langer lived in a house on the same street as the DeVotos. According to his file, Langer fell under House Un-American Activities Committee suspicion for joining three hundred others in criticism of Spanish dictator Francisco Franco. In World War II, Langer's Office of Strategic Services commander praised his "devotion" to democracy and an army brigadier general said he was of "unquestioned loyalty to this country." But the FBI peered into Langer's amicable 1941 divorce. Details easily explained as a man falling in love again—the manager of the apartment Langer lived in post-separation told the FBI that on four occasions she spied a female guest emerge at dawn "'with hat down low shielding the face as much as possible'" —sounded treasonous to the investigators. On Berkeley Street, the FBI heard from a grudgeful neighbor that Langer's second wife showed "a very superior attitude," and that they were a "peculiar" couple because they "entertained profusely." This salacious speculation about someone's personal life, with commentary from biased sources, was precisely the untrustworthy data collection Bernard DeVoto warned about. (Had the FBI asked Avis about the Langers, she would have said that they threw fantastic parties and that Mark DeVoto was best friends with their young son, George.)

Suppressed shame heaves through the confession the erring agent immediately wrote to Hoover after speaking with Bernard. In the process of canvasing the houses around the Langers' at 1 Berkeley Street, he absentmindedly rang the bell at 8 Berkeley and recognized instantly the slouchy man who answered the door with a withering smile. The agent understood that he literally missed the memo ordering him not to visit the DeVotos' house.

Despite being treated with "extreme cordiality," the agent warned Hoover that he was fearful Bernard would publicize the accident to bring more "embarrassment" to the FBI. Hoover demanded to know how this had happened and he admonished the Boston bureau's special agent in charge for not being more "alert."

Avis would say Bernard "could surprise me until the day he died," and this would have been an example. He never mentioned it. He certainly could have used it to embarrass the FBI, but he had to know that the only substantive new information it would have given the public was that on that particular day the FBI's bungling left one of its own exposed. Bernard kept his fights with generals, not foot soldiers; misleaders, not the misled. He had to understand too that knowing an embarrassing secret about the FBI gave him leverage over Hoover, who had run to McCarran, and opened his files to Joe McCarthy, putting the DeVotos and their now conjoined causes of civil liberties and conservation in the most dire trouble yet.

9

"Shall We Let Them Ruin
Our National Parks?"

"NOBODY ASKED THE AMERICAN PEOPLE whether they want their sovereign rights, and those of their descendants, in their own publicly reserved beauty spots wiped out," Bernard DeVoto began his blockbuster anti-dam article, his dogfight with the FBI still hot in his mind. He at last got his shot to write about conservation in the *Saturday Evening Post*. He gave his article in the July 22, 1950, issue a headline so attention-grabbing it become timeless: "Shall We Let Them Ruin Our National Parks?"

Bernard revealed to the nation the battle to save Dinosaur National Monument. This was the first great test of the sanctity of the National Park Service and its 1916 mandate to protect land "unimpaired for the enjoyment of future generations." Bernard introduced all the arguments that in the ensuing years a mass movement would use to fight the Echo Park Dam. A good deal of his information came from Morris Lewellyn Cooke's reports to Presidents Hoover and Truman showing that batteries of proposed Bureau of Reclamation dams were environmentally destructive wastes of taxpayer dollars. But suggesting compromise, Bernard presented calculations that all the water-storage benefits of the Echo Park Dam could be had by modifying other dams in the emerging Colorado River Storage Project. There was a pleasant historical echo in that the name of the army engineer he cited was Ulysses S. Grant III, whose grandfather in 1872 signed the act making Yellowstone the world's first national park.

By the end of the year *Reader's Digest* would republish the article, bringing the call to action to an even vaster audience. "The parks do not belong to any bureau, any group of planners or engineers, any state or section. They belong to all of us. Do we want them? Will our grandchildren want them?"

Bernard's source network roared in praise. Horace Albright called it one of "the finest national-park articles." Ansel Adams, president of the Dinosaur National Monument Council, agreed. Arthur Carhart thanked Bernard for spotlighting the West's greatest environmental "crisis situation." Former Wyoming governor Leslie Miller wrote in hearty appreciation of Bernard calling out "those who vote the pork-barrel appropriations." A future key ally, California alpinist David Brower, on his way to becoming the Sierra Club's first executive director, called the article "noble."

But the article did not initially hit as hard as Bernard wanted it to. When a fan in New Jersey asked if Bernard thought the Echo Park Dam could be stopped, he flatly said no. Even to Bernard, by now a veteran of conservation battles, the dam was a different beast. Stopping the land-grab had been a clear case of identifying bad outside actors conspiring with a few bought senators on a vastly unpopular plot. Dams were far more complex: the balance of environmental harm versus economic benefit was convoluted, the most powerful proponents were engineers working for the federal government, and a new climate of fear was spreading across America.

Breaking news from abroad curbed the reach of "Shall We Let Them Ruin Our National Parks?" and complicated Bernard's stance against the Echo Park Dam. With Soviet tanks at the vanguard, ninety thousand North Korean soldiers stormed south of the 38th parallel. A Gallup poll showed most Americans expected that next would come nuclear war with Russia. The Atomic Energy Commission insisted that the Korean War made the Colorado River Storage Project essential to send hydroelectricity to the Nevada Test Site in order to upgrade World War II's atom bomb into the thermonuclear bomb. McCarran was delighted. Vegas casinos would make decadent shows of the test blasts visible from 65 miles away, serving "atomic cocktails" to tourists mingling with showgirls dressed skimpily in mushroom cloud costumes.

Meanwhile, small ranchers—the poor "downwinders"—would protest not only proximate range and aquifer destruction but radioactive fallout across expanses of Nevada, Utah, and Arizona, where dangerous isotopes would contaminate all types of mammalian milk, where human thyroids would malfunction and leukemias would appear with abnormal frequency. It was more pork for McCarran. His political fortunes boomed when Truman, on June 27, somberly approved the Echo Park Dam. That same day he committed US troops to Korea, where the breakout of violence made him tell his daughter, "It looks like World War III is here."

The conflict in Korea, officially called a "police action," which would claim nearly thirty-seven thousand American lives, would become personal for the DeVotos. Their shy, skinny twenty-year-old son Gordon struggled in college and lost a series of odd jobs. He loved his family ferociously, but was generally brusque and awkward. Though he had a good mind for math and English grammar, he favored science fiction books and tinkering with cars and guns over school. His father sent him to psychiatrists; Avis always wished Bernard gave him more of his own time. She compensated by doting on Gordon, making sure he had his favorite foods, roast beef, pasties, lime pies. She would be especially worried, therefore, as Gordon would decide to drop out of Boston University, join the army like his father, and go to Korea and fight the Communists. He would be there as McCarthy came around to suspecting the DeVotos were on their side.

· · ·

On February 9, 1950, Senator Joe McCarthy burst into the Hotel Mc-Clure in the stout downtown of Wheeling, West Virginia, to give what would be the most important speech of his life. The context was that two days earlier, Hoover had given shocking testimony to McCarran's appropriations subcommittee that set the Justice Department's budget. Hoover claimed that there were more than a half-million Communists and sympathizers already embedded across America; an invading army already here. Hoover explained that there were 53,000 definite Communists and that they were radicalizing ten times as many fellow-travelers. With this claim coming just months after the robust public reaction to "Due Notice to the FBI," it is possible that Bernard DeVoto influenced the ratio Hoover gave McCarran. Hoover did not need to convince McCarran that the crisis demanded a new national detention law. But how to make the American people feel as urgent about it as McCarran did? McCarthy bustled beneath a crystalline chandelier and into a ballroom filled with 275 permed and jeweled members of the Ohio County Women's Republican Club. Theatrically, he waved a piece of paper in the air. He said there were Communists and spies in the State Department. "I have here in my hand a list of 205." McCarthy did not specify how he arrived at his number, but a fuse was lit.

Also in the ballroom was a stringer for the Associated Press whose 110-word story powered the decade's biggest news explosion. Communists were taking over government, McCarthy implied, but who were they exactly? A gaggle of reporters met McCarthy on a tarmac in Denver the next day and asked to see his list. He said he forgot it on the plane. That night in Salt Lake City he modified his claim: there were actually 57 "card-carrying" Communists in the State Department. Reporters immediately suspected McCarthy was bluffing. But within the rules of straight, objective news, journalists knew they could not write their personal judgments. "How do you say in the middle of your story, 'This is a lie?'" a newsman asked. "The press is supposedly neutral. You write what the man says."

The next night, in Reno, two veteran reporters used to similar antics from McCarran confronted McCarthy atop the Mapes Hotel where he had just whipped four hundred listeners into a frenzy. Everything in the speech, remembered Ed Olsen of the Associated Press, had been "inference, allusion, never a concrete statement of fact." McCarthy was in the Sky Room Bar, gulping bourbon. The reporters asked him to stand and deliver: show the list. McCarthy agreed, jammed his fist into his pocket, and pulled out lint. He bellowed that the reporters had stolen his list (keeping to himself his magician's secret: "Hell, there ain't no list"). The bar manager had to come over and say that if McCarthy did not quiet down he needed to leave. There was poetic dimension when McCarthy, nine bourbons deep, finally stumbled out at 3 a.m. into cold Nevada air reborn as a mega-McCarran.

That the ideology became known as "McCarthyism" and not "Mc-Carranism" was due to McCarthy's more sensational talent at attracting attention. His power mushroomed as his name appeared in newspapers with a frequency eclipsed only by that of the president. "My forum is page one," he crowed. A May 1950 poll showed that 40 percent of Americans thought McCarthy's charges were "a good thing for the country," while only 28 percent thought they "did harm" or were false. McCarthy would soon be voted the fourth most admired man on the planet. The FBI swooped in and gave McCarthy linguistic tips for staying plausible. An assistant FBI director taught McCarthy to mind his clever alliteration and swap concrete statements like "card-carrying Communist" for vaguer ones like "sympathizer" and "loyalty risk," which he could substantiate by showing that someone read certain magazines.

The addict's problem McCarthy faced is that he had to say increasingly outrageous things to sustain the same attention high. His accusations began to land on people the DeVotos knew personally. McCarthy never missed a chance to bring up Alger Hiss, the former State Department official sent to prison for perjury in January 1950 after a bizarre trial that hinged on whether he gave secrets in the 1930s to then-Communist Whittaker Chambers. In the late 1920s Bernard had been "pals" with Hiss, then a Harvard law student (Avis remembered him as a "prig"). In March 1950 McCarthy came out with his most sensational claim yet: he found McCarran's man, "the top Russian espionage agent in this country." After building suspense for weeks (one of McCarran's tricks), McCarthy un-masked the man inside a three hundred–capacity Washington conference room sardined with an additional four hundred anxious spectators.

It was Owen Lattimore. The owlish Johns Hopkins University profes-sor had served as a civilian advisor in China during World War II. Accord-ing to McCarthy's pat theory, the State Department had the power to stop Communists from winning China's two-decade civil war, but Lattimore, by maliciously editing a quarterly journal from the Institute of Pacific Re-lations, successfully lobbied it not to. ("Pure moonshine," Lattimore re-sponded.) To the DeVotos, it was preposterous to think that nothing in China's history or domestic politics affected it more than an obscure En-glish-language journal edited by their laughable friend Lattimore. When Lattimore had come to the Bread Loaf Writers' Conference as a student, a pungently foul odor filled the air. Bernard thought a rat had died in the fireplace. It was Lattimore puffing a special tobacco from Mongolia, which was camel dung. "Positive as it's possible to be that Owen never fol-lowed the party line, but he was undeniably foolish on many occasions," Avis remembered. "Oh God I wish this madness would subside."

As Lattimore's long persecution by McCarran began, the DeVotos felt sorry. Lattimore was a prime example of prescriptive publicity; of politicians scoring points by scapegoating subordinates. His career was destroyed. However, he fared better than another one of the DeVotos' friends, Bernard's onetime Harvard nemesis F. O. Matthiessen. A cruel smear campaign against Matthiessen came in tandem with McCarthy's liftoff, and it made the DeVotos furious. "I doubt if there are better schol-ars in the field of American Literature," Bernard pushed back in a March 1950 letter. The rumors correlated with McCarthy conflating commu-nism with homosexuality. That spring McCarthy proclaimed that he was exposing all "communists and queers," and he bleated that anyone who opposed him was "either a Communist or a cocksucker." In early April, Bernard fired off another irate letter to the editor of the *Boston Herald* defending Matthiessen against McCarthy's insinuations. Sternly, Ber-nard reminded his community that Matthiessen promoted his progres-sive ideas — like free speech in the *Strange Fruit* case — within the rules laid out in the Constitution. But it was too late. On April 1, Matthiessen, forty-eight, had plunged from the twelfth floor of Boston's Hotel Manger, leaving behind a note saying that he was "depressed over world conditions," and three thousand letters between himself and the man he had been in a romantic relationship with for twenty years.*

By December, McCarthy's attacks turned physical. He stalked Washington, DC, gadfly columnist Drew Pearson and smashed him to the ground in a coatroom of the Sulgrave Club (remembered Richard Nixon, "If I hadn't pulled McCarthy away, he might have killed Pearson"). McCarthy was abominable; most politicians knew it. But to partisans who hated Truman, McCarthy's idiocy was useful. As the DeVotos tried to wrest public attention to the threats to national parks, McCarthy worked to silence them, and McCarran resolved to leave his most important national legacy since killing the Grazing Service.

"Why Has Washington Gone Crazy?" asked a headline in the *Saturday Evening Post* one week after Bernard's "Shall We Let Them Ruin Our National Parks?" The accompanying article was written by Stewart Alsop and his dapper brother, Joseph, a former student of Bernard's at Harvard.

McCarthy responded to the Alsopses' article—about the paranoia he and McCarran spread across the nation—with a letter to the editor with information between its lines. McCarthy threatened to "publicly discuss any of [Joseph's] mental or physical aberrations" that he saw fit. Only later would Joseph translate to Stewart: "I have been an incurable homosexual since boyhood." (The secret was in Hoover's files.) The Alsops never wrote anything more about McCarran or McCarthy for America's most widely read magazine.

Bernard suffered a more extreme setback. With McCarthy menacing the magazine, the negative fallout from "Shall We Let Them Ruin" spooked the *Post*'s moderate Republican editor, Ben Hibbs. At the National Park Service, director Newton Drury, a fellow moderate Republican, was demoted and then resigned. Though no official reason was

---

*Painter Russell Cheney.

given, an editorial in Salt Lake City's *Deseret News* said it was because "he fathered the DeVoto falsification of the facts about the Utah-Colorado dams." Hibbs, who was working to modulate his magazine's crusader notes into harmony with Norman Rockwell's cover paintings, had no choice but to press pause on Bernard's byline. His assistant told Bernard, "We are hoping that the storm will presently subside."

When it didn't, Bernard was blacklisted. He was barred from writing anything more for the *Post* about conservation or the West, which, at this stage in his life, effectively became an all-out ban. *Reader's Digest* followed suit, temporarily barring his byline. Despite Bernard receiving less punishing treatment than the Hollywood Ten, his blacklistings show more of McCarran and McCarthy's effects on the environment: Bernard had his microphone cut right as he addressed his largest audience about conservation.

It was also a serious financial blow for the DeVoto family. Bernard never had a harder time writing anything than his next western book, in which he decided to place Lewis and Clark in the historical context of the hunt for the Northwest Passage dating back to Columbus. Struggling to synthesize so much world history, he spent his $12,000 advance. Losing such high-paid markets as the *Post* and *Reader's Digest* meant that both DeVotos needed to work together like never before to keep afloat. At the same time, McCarran fathered a law with the power to shackle the DeVotos to a fate far worse than bankruptcy.

North Dakota senator William Langer (no relation to the DeVotos' neighbor) wheezed at his lamplit desk in the Capitol building for three of the first hours of September 23, 1950, as part of a twenty-four-hour filibuster against what was known as the McCarran Act. Decrying the most extreme measure McCarran maneuvered into his act, the gangly, putty-faced Republican known as "Wild Bill" gasped out words until he collapsed on the floor and had to be rushed to Bethesda Naval Hospital. "For the first time in the history of America we hear about concentration camps in America."

If any doubts lingered as to what McCarran could have done despite a Truman veto if Bernard DeVoto had not thwarted the landgrab in 1947, the McCarran Act (officially the Internal Security Act of 1950) erased them. McCarran biographer Michael Ybarra called the McCarran Act "almost the perfect expression of McCarthyism: the greatest peacetime sedition law in the country's history." Truman called it "totalitarian" and issued the veto Langer fell trying valiantly to uphold.

McCarran introduced his omnibus bill on August 10, 1950. It liberalized deportations, restricted speech, and allowed for the federal government, if the president declared a national emergency, to lock Americans in concentration camps. McCarran's vision for this "preventative detention" was like Japanese internment during World War II, only based not on race but on political belief. The McCarran Hearings had given McCarran the taste of power to dismiss his opponents; his appetite swelled to also wanting them detained. The McCarran Act would create a subversive activities control board whose members would decide which Americans got rounded up—a remarkable move for a country that only five years earlier had liberated Nazi death camps. McCarran won votes by preying on politicians' fears of looking weak and then dragged his law over Truman's veto. No one was more anguished than Illinois senator Paul Douglas, a disabled World War II marine veteran who tried and failed to insert civil liberties protections into the act. The Democrat stepped over Langer's body to join the doomed filibuster. He called McCarran "an evil man."

A measure of how radical the Senate tipped in the fall of 1950 was that Bernard DeVoto again zigged when he might have zagged. With the same anti-revolutionary fervor he put into "The West Against Itself," he rushed out an "Easy Chair" that was a defense of Congress wrapped around a challenge for citizens. In "But Sometimes They Vote Right Too," he wrote that although McCarthy showed "the symptoms of paranoia in any standard textbook," and McCarran worked only for "a small private fief of big stock companies, big industrial corporations and big gamblers," the US government still perfectly represented the wisdom of the American people. "Sure the people are stupid: the human race is stupid. Sure Congress is an inefficient instrument of government. But the people are not stupid enough to abandon representative government."

Democracy was not a pathway to the stars, he would say, but articles of war. (DeVoto Nation was conspicuously quiet.)

The McCarran Act had a sequel. The McCarran–Walter Act in 1952* would set immigration quotas to align with ethnic percentages of the US population in 1920 in order to welcome Christians from western Europe and keep away Jewish refugees in eastern Europe. McCarran would ram his bill past another veto by Truman ("a pissant in human form," McCarran said) by pitting factions of Americans against each other: in exchange for the law's rank anti-Semitism, McCarran would grant naturalization to Asians. Joe McCarthy would applaud, "Pat is one of the greatest senators we've ever had."

Obsessed with immigration and conspiracies about Jewish Bolshevism, McCarran doubtlessly imagined his camps populated by the people he quietly derided as being "of one blood, one race, one religion." His top aide added that the McCarran Act was also to be of tremendous use investigating educators and "who writes for a particular magazine." So it seemed that the gates would likewise open to writers of DeVoto's "ilk," and potentially to any American who opposed McCarran. He made remarks indicating that, with the prospect of his camps filling, his authoritarian prejudices were swelling to horrifying proportions. When his daughter asked if she should visit Israel, his response conflated aggrieved and dreamy racism with public lands conservation: "Under the Taylor Grazing Act all grazing rights have been allotted to the Jews and all the Arabs can do is tend camp for the kikes so what's the use."

Blacklisted by two of America's most-read journals, under FBI investigation, with old friends falling to ruin, his own imprisonment in a concentration camp suddenly legally feasible, and still trying to make his fellow citizens care about conservation and the Bill of Rights, Bernard DeVoto took his penultimate *Saturday Evening Post* paycheck ($1,500) and gave Avis a gift. Since they married, she had wanted to visit Scotland, her ancestral

---

*Officially the Immigration and Nationality Act of 1952.

homeland, and England, setting for her favorite novels, and Paris. Her soul hungered to try the food.

In June 1950 she boarded her first transatlantic flight. In Edinburgh, she thought L'Aperitif and The Cafe Royal were wonderful. For a month she stayed at Whitehall Court in London and sampled the fine restaurants Savoy, Le Caprice, and Simpson's. She preferred the battered fish served casually on Lower Belgrave Street. For a week she visited the countryside, and in the Cotswolds her inn served fresh vegetables and homegrown chickens. She explored Oxford, Salisbury, Winchester, and the original Cambridge. She felt liberated to be in a country where people loved John August but did not know Bernard DeVoto. Taxi and bus drivers talked down their noses at her and she was endeared. "I insist that under all that surface calm they are boiling and seething. That's the way I like it."

Paris, still piled with war rubble, smelled of burned wood, old plaster, human sweat, and fresh vegetables. The food stole her heart. Her favorite was a dish of eggs, cream, and tarragon that she tasted at Bossu on the Quai Bourbon. She visited "some very strange dives," including a "little hole in the wall" restaurant beside a nightclub where she ate Basque pipérade. "One more never to be forgotten egg dish." She stayed at the Hotel du Quai Voltaire, tried using a bidet, and wondered if she could bring it home to America. There was a bustling market a fifteen-minute walk away on Rue de Bourgogne that thumped with three-wheeled carts piled with turnips, potatoes, brussels sprouts, artichokes, purple garlic, and a forest's carpet of mushrooms. Vegetables Avis could not find in America abounded: zesty shallots, leafy chard, leeks, truffles, celery root, sweet orange squash blossoms. There were giant peaches, and strawberries, which Avis consumed "compulsively," along with her coffee, cheese, and blanc de blanc champagne. A regular at the market was Julia Child, whom—as in Montana in 1946—Avis just missed.

Though she wished he would have, Bernard did not accompany her. "I am perfectly positive I will never get DeVoto abroad—he has never been and never wants to go. Terribly provincial of him. But as he always remarks, 'Well, I've never been to El Paso, or Independence, or the lower Green River.' And he would go there first. Maddening."

The month before Avis left for Europe, Bernard returned west ("like a homing pigeon," she would say) to the buffalo country around Fort Peck, Montana. Ostensibly, he went to study proposed Bureau of Reclamation and Army Corps of Engineers dams in the Missouri River watershed. But he arranged to spend three days in blissful freedom, "just like my boys Lewis and Clark," floating into North Dakota atop a 20-foot flat-bottomed boat with A. B. Guthrie Jr., the Montana novelist who won that year's Pulitzer for *The Way West*. Between chalky cliffs they slogged through tea-colored water and dragged their aluminum pirogue over sandbars and driftwood snags. Guthrie was charmed when the man who wrote *Across the Wide Missouri* hollered to a lone boy bobber-fishing off a bluff.

"Say, son, can you tell us where we are?"

"Mister, you're on the Missouri River."

The two historians mentally traveled back in time, and whenever a Black Angus cow reminded them which century they were in, they pretended it was a buffalo. And there were lots of buffalo. Panic that Korea would escalate into war with Russia made beef spike to its highest price point ever, $243 per hundredweight, almost $100 more than during the price guarantees of World War I. With McCarran's gelding of regulations, cattle kings were limited in the amount of money they could make only by how quickly they could fill the ranges. Bernard's 1947 warning in *Harper's* about how overgrazing would cause floods and drowning deaths in Kansas City was never heeded. What was on the minds of community leaders there came straight from McCarran and McCarthy. K. L. Peterson, a livestock buyer in the city's legendary stockyards, shot a letter to Missouri senator James Kem urging that "the Government issue firearms to responsible American men and women everywhere" as the only way to prevent "wanton wholesale massacre" by hidden Communists. The sheriff of Kansas City ordered nearby quarries inspected for use as mass graves.

The beef bubble coincided with a Kansas drought that ended dramatically in May 1951, 750 miles due south from where Bernard and Guthrie had disembarked. Fat raindrops whacked the denuded ranges of Gove

County (location then of both the geographic and geodetic centers of the United States*). Rivulets of silty water poured into Big Creek, which jumped its banks and churned toward the Missouri faster than a speeding car. The flood killed three of four teenagers driving 50 miles to the east near the small town of WaKeeney. Police whooped through the streets of Hays at midnight, evacuating half the town's eight thousand residents. Water swallowed Fort Hays State University. A gas pipe exploded. A wall collapsed in a home and killed a teenager. An elderly philosophy professor died trying to save his books. A young bride held her husband's hand as she reached for her coat in a flooding basement when a tree crashed into the house and let in a wave that swept her to her death.

The Republican River became engorged near Junction City and drowned another person. The Kansas River to the east flooded the barracks at Fort Riley. More water from the Big Blue River charged through two hundred residential blocks of Manhattan and forced out two thousand people. Kansas State University became an enormous refugee camp. The water buckled sidewalks and shattered glass storefronts; it punched holes through red brick and caused one building to collapse. A patch of pavement beside City Hall caved into a 15-foot-deep sinkhole. Less than a mile away a drenched army captain struggling past the Riley County Courthouse died of a heart attack. A sixty-year-old woman was killed when her stone house caved in. Lawrence flooded and its railroad tracks became tangles of ribbons. A levee broke in Topeka and damaged seven thousand buildings. An oil fire raged and 24,000 more people were evacuated. Every phone was down. Anywhere a radio worked, shivering, shell-shocked people huddled around. CBS radio newsman Jim Burke reported, "To those of you who have never witnessed a flood and its resultant effects, let me tell you, it's a sickening sight."

The structural damage was extensive. The flood breached the 35-foot-high Army Corps of Engineers walls around the low-lying, triangular district at the junction of the Kansas and Missouri Rivers. Twenty-foot waves

*This would move to Butte County, South Dakota, on the admittance of Hawaii and Alaska to the union.

crashed through the Kansas City Stockyards, seventeen major bridges washed away, including one holding locomotives, bobbing oil tanks exploded. For five days the worst fire in Kansas City's history raged, leaving every structure across seven city blocks blackened, gutted, and ruined.

By the time it was over, forty-four people were dead and more than a half-million were refugees. The flood damaged or wrecked more than 45,000 homes and buildings, closed 3,000 businesses, and damaged 10,000 farms. Losses were estimated at $2.5 billion—the costliest single-event natural disaster to its date in US history. Two million acres—a little more in Kansas, a little less in Missouri—were rendered fetid and dismal, buried under an astringent silt that dried to powder and took to the sky at any touch. All summer the entire region was festooned in an acrid, yellowish-gray pall. Everywhere was trash; tires hanging from the roots of downed trees, garbage strewn from telephone wires like unkempt clotheslines, toppled lamp poles, shredded windsocks, bowed parking meters. The air stank of dust and mold. Heart-weary people mucked festering pools of glop out of ruined homes, schools, and churches. The Fairfax Airport was so damaged that construction crews broke ground on a new Kansas City International Airport—in Missouri. The Kansas City Stockyards were abandoned.

On July 17, 1951, Harry Truman, who was raised not far away in Independence, Missouri, visited. "It's the worst thing I have ever seen," said the first president to use a nuclear bomb. He returned to Washington to hear Congress cry for more money for flood-control dams.

As Truman left Missouri, Bernard DeVoto circled back to Montana as a favor to his trusted friend Joseph Kinsey Howard. In early August, Howard put together a "Bread Loaf West" writer's conference at the University of Montana, nestled in Missoula at the base of a bulbous, tan mountain with an amulet of white rocks making an "M." It was a culmination of Howard's indefatigable work to make his sparsely populated state the arts capitol of the West, though it aged him so much he resembled the rough roads he traveled. Howard, forty-five, had turned thin and gray with a deeply rutted face. But he remained the perfect person for Bernard to strategize with about the Echo Park Dam. "The Bureau knows damn well the dam won't pay for itself," Howard wrote.

In Howard, Bernard could see what his life might have been like had he stayed in the West. Howard crusaded for education, fought land despoilers, scrabbled for money, and faced his own smears when he spoke out against natural resource wealth being funneled to a privileged few. After Howard applied for a Guggenheim Fellowship, he learned the Anaconda Copper Mining Company had tried to sabotage him by mailing the foundation a $500 check it had made out to him to write propaganda, but not his return letter rejecting it. When Bernard found out about the company's deception, he immediately let the foundation know Howard "is absolutely uncorruptable and as a practicing journalist has fought Anaconda for years in every way he could." When Howard won the fellowship, he let Bernard know he felt "delighted and proud and more grateful for your help than I can tell you." He used the Guggenheim money to work on his next book, *Strange Empire,* an epic history of the Métis, people of dual French and Native American heritage fighting for recognition in the western United States and Canada. As further evidence of the mindmeld with Howard, Bernard's in-progress book was titled *The Course of Empire.*

It was fire season in the Rocky Mountains, when the forests were baked dry and lighting threw down blazes, so the scent of smoke wafted through classroom windows as Howard and Bernard took turns standing at a lectern. When Howard was up, Bernard perched impatiently on a chair behind him, folded angularly, eyeglasses flashing, inhaling cigarettes. As soon as class let out, Bernard raced to the airport west of town where crews of Forest Service firefighters climbed in small prop planes to parachute into burning country. Soon, Bernard's pals stuffed him in a flight suit and strapped him to a parachute so he too could pile inside silver fuselage and watch their leaps into hazy skies. Buzzing over infernos made Bernard, fifty-four, feel considerably loftier than his deskbound journalistic competitors. He celebrated the Forest Service again in the November 1951 *Harper's* with a feature story titled "The Smoke Jumpers."

The "summit of human enjoyment" he had was riding with Howard to the top of Lolo Pass in the Bitterroot Mountains to finally see what had been the hardest stretch of the trail for Lewis and Clark. Reaching the mountaintop, which had been buried in snow in June 1946, made Bernard weep tears of joy. Just on the Idaho side of the divide there was an ancient grove of red cedars—the biggest tree species east of the Pacific coast, called "the tree of life" by Native Americans. They towered over giant ferns and little, exquisite, pink fairy slipper orchids on the banks of Crooked Creek, drumming clearly on down to the nearby Lochsa River. Bernard's guide to his paradise up the skinny, dead-end, dirt logging road was Forest Service veteran Elers Koch, one of Gifford Pinchot's first recruits, who learned the mountains in 1910 from fighting the 3-million-acre hellfire called, factually, "the Big Burn." Koch enjoyed the special pleasure of tracing historic footsteps with men "who also appreciated and understood." Wordsmith Bernard sat on a boulder beneath the cedars, and the only line he could think to express his feelings was from Hamlet: "Rest, perturbed spirit!"

"I temporarily recovered my sanity," he remembered of his ten days exploring the trail with Howard, in a country gone so politically mad it was on the verge of ruining its national parks and throwing its citizens in concentration camps. Bernard was home in Cambridge for one week when came the shattering news that Howard had died of a heart attack. His ashes were scattered on the Rocky Mountain Front above the little writing cabin where he had nearly completed *Strange Empire*. Bernard, in final tribute to his friend, finished the book and gave his fee to Howard's impoverished mother, Josephine, alone in Great Falls.

Bernard felt such grief, anger, and frustration that his *Empire* might have fallen away too were it not for Avis. Losing Howard was devastating, and his harried death by workaholism was a warning for Bernard, nearly a decade his senior. Bernard was accelerating in every direction simultaneously: brawling with the Bureau of Reclamation, the FBI, McCarran, McCarthy, the Wyoming Stock Growers Association, all while hitting his monthly *Harper's* deadlines, preparing to send his older son to Korea, and bracing for more financial pain from blacklistings. He was also adrift on the sea of writer's block with his "God-damnedest fool" of a book, a draft of which he judged "the dullest broth of watery, uremic, and flatulent prose ever compounded."

Avis prodded him to focus, stick to his thesis about how the myth of the Northwest Passage gave way to the truth of the Missouri River, and build the story to Lewis and Clark. She reminded him the lesson he gave his students: *run it through the typewriter again.* She absorbed a measure of his psychic strain by typing notes, line editing, proofreading, and checking every research citation. "It's a hell of a job. The footnotes and bibliography especially, which have some horrifying items in illiterate 16th century French, Spanish and so on. I am losing my mind." With her sharp help, Bernard's confidence grew until he got "over the hump" and his book became sculpted, powerful, and clear. All Avis had to do, she would say, was "crack the whip."

Friends with insight into the DeVotos' marriage recognized it. "All of us know how much you contributed to his brilliant productivity," Elizabeth Wecter Pike, wife of writer Dixon Wecter, would say. The DeVotos had traveled separately and their reunion was marred by grief and worry. But under pressure, they made a diamond—*The Course of Empire* would win the National Book Award in 1953. As the conservation crisis deepened, Avis's collaborator role grew more pronounced, and that brought unexpected and charismatic new allies into their lives.

10

New Friends

BERNARD RECEIVED A SURPRISE TELEPHONE CALL a few days after Joseph Kinsey Howard's death. It was Wyoming senator Lester Hunt. Previously, as Wyoming's governor, Hunt had supported the landgrab, and Bernard publicly rebuked him. Now, Hunt was on his way to becoming Bernard's friend and most powerful ally in the fight against the Echo Park Dam.

Though Hunt was a Democrat in a highly Republican state, he had worked as the dentist in the small town of Lander, and people throughout Wyoming appreciated him for traveling vast distances to heal toothaches. After becoming governor in 1942, Hunt kept taxes low, fixed highways, and launched programs to care for veterans, the elderly, and the disabled. He made Wyoming iconography history by choosing the art for the state's emblem: the silhouetted rider on a bucking bronco (which had the immediate effect of making the Cowboy State's license plates the nation's most stolen per capita).

Hunt had followed the lead of Wyoming's biggest livestock associations and wrote a letter in support of the landgrab in 1947. This "pimping for the stockmen" is what Bernard addressed first. "On his far from guilt-less head I heaped every kind of reproach and insult I could devise."

Hunt called because he had heard that Bernard was writing a book about Lewis and Clark. Since Hunt was elected to the Senate in 1948, he kept in his Washington, DC, office a large collection of Sacajawea memorabilia. A (dubious, unfortunately) tombstone for the magnificently brave woman rises from a small tribal cemetery in the foothills of the Wind River Range a few miles north of Lander. As Bernard remembered the exchange, "for the glory of Wyoming and American womanhood I must appear there and go over it at my earliest opportunity."

Hunt had evolved into a statesman Bernard respected. It started with the serious way Hunt conducted himself in 1949 on the Senate Armed Services subcommittee that investigated the Malmedy massacre oppo-site Joe McCarthy's contrarian grandstanding. While McCarthy spread the false rumor that American prosecutors coerced Nazi confessions with torture, Hunt sailed to Germany, toured the killing ground, and took tes-timony from witnesses. Hunt admonished McCarthy for "hitting below the belt." Bernard appreciated that Hunt showed the courage early on to rebuke McCarthy and his tactics.

What most impressed Bernard was Hunt's evolution on public lands. After Bernard exposed the landgrab, Hunt dropped it completely. Hunt went on to fight in the Senate for more funding for the National Park Service, and he became a critic of the Bureau of Reclamation. With his instinct for centrism, Hunt put himself at the fulcrum of an unlikely yet astonishingly powerful conservation coalition. He forged middle ground with Bernard, for the sake of national park preservation. And with Wyo-ming Republicans, for the sake of keeping government small. And with landgrabbers, for the sake of not flooding grassy valleys. They could stand together against the Bureau of Reclamation. As the Truman ad-ministration began exploring alternatives to damming Dinosaur National Monument, Hunt's coalition proved so popular even McCarran muscled into it. He told a constituent in 1952 that he was well aware of "a dam which, when completed, will destroy Dinosaur Monument," and promised "I will do everything possible to prevent the destruction of this great monument."

Because Hunt lived in a state that would be directly affected by the Echo Park Dam, he was its most powerful barrier. Bernard wrote Hunt regular letters, including a dream of how Dinosaur National Monument might be permanently saved through rebranding. The name "Dinosaur" did not reflect Franklin Roosevelt's 200,000-acre expansion to protect the geological melodrama of its fractured, rainbowed, craggy canyons. Nor did it reflect the awesome wildlife habitat for bighorn sheep, mule deer, black bears, cougars, bobcats, foxes, golden eagles, falcons, pinyon jays, mountain chickadees, giant pikeminnows, and rare suckerfish. Or its flora: ponderosas, Douglas firs, pinyons, junipers, cottonwoods, box elders, mountain mahogany, serviceberry, shadscale, greasewood, and yucca blooming like porcupines (which also lived there). It did not encapsulate the land's amazing silence or the shooting-star shows above. Or the traces of human history, from the Fremont people's petroglyphs, to the Utes' buffalo hunting range, to Mormon pioneers' homesteads, to Butch Cassidy's hideout. The national monument's imperfect name came from an 80-acre fossil quarry of the largest known collection of Jurassic-period dinosaurs, more than four hundred giant species. "One couldn't have prayed for anything better," pioneering paleontologist Earl Douglass had shouted in 1909.

Woodrow Wilson created Dinosaur National Monument in 1915 by using the Antiquities Act, which Roosevelt used again to expand it in 1938. But most Americans did not understand the imperative of preserving national monuments the same way as national parks. With the Antiquities Act of 1906, Congress, in recognition that its deliberative process could be too slow to protect imperiled, extraordinary landscapes, gave the president power to create national monuments to safekeep places of great scenic, scientific, and cultural value. Congress reserved the right to amend national monuments, most often by elevating them to national parks. Therefore, Bernard told Hunt he wanted Congress to redesignate Dinosaur National Monument: "Green River Canyons National Park."

A bill would be introduced by California Republican representative Leroy Johnson. Hunt—who had helped amalgamate Jackson Hole National Monument into Grand Teton National Park—would tell Bernard, "I have had considerable correspondence from Wyoming people with reference to Johnson's bill creating a national park out of Dinosaur National Monument and shall be very happy to support this."

But first, Hunt had to make an emergency save. In April 1952, Utah Republican senator Arthur Watkins introduced the Colorado River Storage Project to Congress, which, as per the Bureau of Reclamation's plan, would build the Echo Park Dam immediately. Watkins tersely told Hunt, "For your information, I shall introduce a bill in the Senate today authorizing this project." Hunt brushed him back. "The great majority of my people in Wyoming are so intent on economy and reduction of governmental expenditures that they do not at this time favor legislation proposing new irrigation projects."

Hunt's fast action saved Dinosaur National Monument in 1952 and made him Bernard's most important foe-turned-friend since the late F. O. Matthiessen.

Bernard DeVoto and Lester Hunt also shared a unique bond as fathers of sons who needed serious medical care. In a parallel to how Gordon DeVoto received psychiatric treatment, when Senator Hunt's son was four, he fractured his right femur so severely that doctors recommended amputation. For the sake of his son, Lester Hunt Jr., nicknamed "Buddy," Hunt underwent numerous painful operations. Three times doctors tried to graft bone from Hunt's leg onto Buddy's. On the fourth attempt, it worked. Hunt saved Buddy's ability to walk. Buddy grew into a curious and compassionate young man who wanted to join the clergy. Divine intervention literally brought the Hunts and the DeVotos together: Buddy enrolled at the Episcopal Theological School in Cambridge. Its campus ran directly up to the DeVotos' back property line. Buddy and the DeVotos passed each other countless times. But as Bernard and Senator Hunt bonded over their sons and strategized to save Dinosaur National Monument, McCarthy allies probed for any way to make Hunt flip on the Echo Park Dam. They would soon cast their beady eyes on Buddy.

• • •

While Senator Hunt was excited to read what Bernard DeVoto would write next, more high-powered editors were not. By the end of 1951 a third major magazine effectively blacklisted Bernard under the pervasive atmosphere of McCarthyism. He wrote a story for the April issue of *Fortune* based on an idea from Avis: why American stainless-steel kitchen knives would not stay sharp. It should not have been too controversial a subject for an award-winning writer at the peak of his career, but the stigma of the smears against him attracted ever more sophistic accusations. *Fortune*'s editor received a letter from an officer at a national advertising organization implying that criticism of an American-made product was communistic. The letter reminded *Fortune* that a report by the House Un-American Activities Committee listed Bernard "as being associated with some others who are definitely known as Leftists." Never again did the magazine accept another Bernard DeVoto story.

Better fortune came as an unintended consequence of one of Bernard's lifelong female friendships. Mabel Souvaine was an exceptionally dynamic editor who saw no reason why her *Woman's Day* readers would not be equally fascinated with national forests as casserole recipes. She loved publishing Bernard's conservation writings and wanted to help his family more by giving him opportunity to write extra (at $750 per story) by taking on another nom de plume: Cady Hewes.

"Hewes" columns were written from the point of view of a fictional husband and father who is constantly exasperated by his witty wife — who is a brilliant cook — and their two bratty children. The autobiographical spoofs were the prototype of many a future television sitcom, and they were a complete DeVoto collaboration. Avis remembered "talking out" all the ideas, themes, and plotlines with her husband. The work made Avis deeply grateful to Souvaine, who printed one Hewes story in 1949, another in 1950, three in 1951 alone, and eight more through the rest of the McCarthy era. Avis praised *Woman's Day* as "a magazine that helps support us and to which we feel deeply bound."

Receptive like never before to Avis's ideas, and recognizing that false advertisers were growing rich by targeting housewives, Bernard unsheathed the knife idea again in his November 1951 "Easy Chair." It was titled "Crusade Resumed," in reference to a column he wrote in 1939 suggesting improvements to consumer goods. Bernard joked he was returning to "the only mission I have ever set for myself, that of trying to get for the American housewife a kitchen knife she can cut something with." With a wry joust at *Fortune,* he added, "I direct the attention of the Un-American Activities Committee to the manufacturers of kitchen knives and the advertisers they subsidize."

The same executive contacted the business manager at *Harper's* and suggested that they had "a Communist or fellow traveler" in their employ. "He was saying: we are in a position to control a lot of advertising contracts, better watch out what your columnist does," Bernard wrote. The executive learned he would have an easier time drawing blood from a stone with one of his knives than getting *Harper's* (or *Woman's Day*) to censor the DeVotos.

The column brought new fans; letters from housewives rapturously laughing and amateur chefs who finally felt understood flew in from around the globe. Avis juggled blearily to keep up. "I do all my husband's secretarial stuff, all the typing, take dictation from a tape recorder, and handle a lot of his routine mail on my own. The house is big and the children need me a lot. Plus all this I am now correcting proofs on the new book."

She lingered over a March 8, 1952, letter from a California woman living in Paris. It read: "Your able diatribe against the beautiful-beautiful-rust-proof-edge-proof American kitchen knife so went to my heart that I cannot refrain from sending you this nice little French model as a token of my appreciation."

With the enclosed paring knife, Bernard thin-sliced the lemon peel for a martini and was duly impressed. On April 3, a beam of light hit the DeVotos in their darkest and most worrisome time. Avis sat down and formally began the most important friendship of her life with the words "Dear Mrs. Child."

11

Potent Mixtures

AVIS BEGAN HER CORRESPONDENCE WITH JULIA CHILD as she did with everyone she met; she let out her mind and heart in letters that so reflected,
as one friend phrased it, "the charming DeVoto conversational collaboration," that it made them collectors' items. ("Dear Mrs. DeVoto," one
fan wrote in 1951, "I shall treasure your note along with, in particular, the
one received from General Eisenhower. But for totally different reasons.")

Quickly it dawned on Avis that her transatlantic correspondence
with Julia was special. "Well, it is very relaxing writing to you," she typed
on May 30, 1952. Over the next nearly forty years Avis and Julia would
share more than four hundred letters, many thousands of pages' worth;
Avis would continue relaxing by communicating with Julia literally up to
her dying day. When Julia revealed in her letter to Bernard that she had
studied French cooking, Avis could practically be seen licking her red
lips. She wrote back a reminiscence about Paris; tasting one dish of eggs,
cream, and fresh tarragon, and another of veal in cream sauce with vermouth and more tarragon (her favorite herb). Julia, the ingenue, sent

back recipes for "Scrambled Eggs, French": cook for less time, under lower heat, stirring constantly and then mixing with tarragon-infused butter. Also "Veau a la Crème, a l'Estragon (a method)": heat butter in a pan until it foams and turns blonde; sauté veal for 2 minutes on each side, sprinkle with salt, pepper, and minced shallots; add brandy and set on fire for 30 seconds before covering the pan and adding a splash of dry white wine and "some good reduced meat stock"; sprinkle in chopped tarragon and stew for 5 minutes; uncover the pan to let the sauce reduce and add heavy cream; add more chopped tarragon and serve. "All of this shouldn't take more than 15 minutes," Julia explained helpfully.

Soon, Julia sent a fish-filleting knife and shallots. The women began swapping recipes, gifts of herbs and spices, and personal details. Julia's self-portrait: "6 ft. plus, weight 150 to 160. Bosom not as copious as she would wish, but has noticed that Botticelli bosoms are not big either. Legs OK, according to husband. Freckles." Avis wrote, "well, dear, I am no lady and I argue loudly and I lose my temper and it's disgraceful." Julia described Paul Child in Renaissance terms. "He really can do just about anything, including making a French type omelette. Carpenter, cabinet-builder, intellectual, wine-bibbler, wrestler. A most interesting man, and a lovely husband. You'd like him very much." Before mailing a requested photo of Bernard, Avis prepared Julia that he had "a rough-hewn face, they say charitably."

The liftoff of the friendship can be seen in Avis's addresses. In April, May, and September she writes "Dear Mrs. Child." On Christmas Day she writes "Dear Julia." In January it is "Julia my pet!" and come February: "Dear Julish." In her first "Dear Mrs. DeVoto" letter, Julia had ventured a pinch of politics, explaining that when she talked to people who "think McCarthy is doing a fine thing" it "makes digestion even more difficult." Avis knew she had found her soul sister.

Julia McWilliams was born in Pasadena, and from her late mother, for whom she was named, she had inherited her elongated vocal cords, which gave her voice a slide-whistle quality. Her overbearing father, John McWilliams, sold real estate and cattle and Julia grew up knowing little of

Bernard DeVoto, of Ogden, Utah, and Avis, of Houghton, Michigan,
were a shocking, outspoken, and stylish couple in the Harvard University
community in Cambridge, Massachusetts, in the late 1920s and 1930s.

All photos courtesy of the Department of Special Collections, Stanford University Libraries and
Mark DeVoto unless otherwise noted.

Splayed notebooks, a Chesterfield carton, the glower of ten thousand books; an FBI agent's view of Bernard at his home office in Cambridge. (*Below left*) Elegant, cool, adventurous; Avis on Jenny Lake in Grand Teton National Park in 1953. (*Below right*) Poet Robert Frost tried—and failed—to come between Bernard and Avis.

In 1946, Bernard eavesdropped in Miles City, Montana — near this roadside history marker where Avis, Gordon, and Mark posed — and got his first real tip about a potential 230-million-acre landgrab. (*Below left*) Bernard walked across an overgrazed range in Colorado. (*Below right*) Regional Forester Chet Olsen of Ogden quietly found Bernard's landgrab details.

Wyoming rancher and lobbyist J. Elmer
Brock was the principal landgrab architect and FBI informant regarding Bernard
DeVoto. (*Top left*) His collaborator, Nevada
Senator Pat McCarran, curated hearings
during World War II to promote selling
public lands. (*Below*) McCarran inspired
red-baiting Wisconsin Senator Joe McCarthy,
who, in this 1952 speech, attacked "Richard
Dee Voto." *The University of Texas at Arlington
Library Special Collections*

*Photograph by Harris & Ewing.
Courtesy of Library of Congress*

Photo by Francis Miller / The LIFE Picture Collection © Time, Inc.

Bernard's 1950 *Saturday Evening Post* article "Shall We Let Them Ruin Our National Parks?" fought to keep the Echo Park Dam out of Dinosaur National Monument and launched a "whitewater navy" of rafters on Utah's Green River. *National Park Service*

Wyoming Senator Lester Hunt. *Courtesy of United States Congress*

Forest Service range conservationist Roald Peterson. *Courtesy of Sarah Shomion*

Presidential candidate Adlai Stevenson, center, asked Bernard for a conservation field lesson in 1954 inside Idaho and Montana's Bitterroot Mountains. (*Below*) Bernard, front row, right, served on the National Parks Advisory Board, and in 1950 he recruited his friend and compatriot, publisher Alfred Knopf, seated behind his right shoulder.

Sympatico in body language, the DeVotos listen to a forest service official in New England circa 1954. (*Below*) The DeVotos, photographed in Denver in 1953, in what was Avis's final favorite portrait of herself and her husband.

After Bernard's death, Julia and Paul Child rushed Avis a ticket to Europe in 1956. Avis honored her literary partnership with Bernard by assisting Julia. *Photo by Paul Child © Schlesinger Library, Harvard Radcliffe Institute.* (*Below*) Mark DeVoto escorted his mother to the DeVoto Memorial Cedar Grove dedication in the Bitterroot Mountains in 1962. He eventually scattered her ashes there.

food other than the steaks and potatoes made by the family maid. Julia attended her mother's alma matter, Smith College, in Northampton, Massachusetts. In World War II she joined the Office of Strategic Services (the forerunner of the Central Intelligence Agency) to serve her country, see the world, and flee her father's house. She worked as a clerk handling some of the government's most highly classified communications about agents in China, Burma, India, and Washington. When she was sent to Ceylon in 1944, she met Paul Child.

Paul was a multitalented artist. Born in New Jersey, he grew up playing cello. He studied woodcarving and sculpture in Paris, and went on to teach photography at Avon Old Farms School, an elite academy for boys in Connecticut. There, he met a painter, a mother of a student, named Ethyl Kennedy and they were together for seventeen years until she died of cancer in 1942. That year, the OSS asked Paul to teach judo and build war rooms.

As Paul emerged from mourning, he was attracted to Julia, eleven years his junior and 5 inches his taller. He found her strikingly beautiful and infused with a "pleasantly crazy sense of humor." Julia found Paul captivating. She loved the way he absorbed culture, read widely, and talked about art and architecture. When they were transferred together to Kunming, China, in early 1945, Paul whisked Julia away from the bland American mess hall to sample savory Yunnanese food in restaurants hidden off the medieval city's crowded main streets. It was her introduction to world cuisine. She loved it. Paul found in Julia a dining companion as fearless (and as unbothered by the inevitable dysentery) as he. This is how they fell in love. They commandeered a jeep and toured mud villages in the countryside, they watched clouds smoothing over distant mountains carved with ancient temples, and they drank mulberry wine next to a sculpted red sandstone bridge in a rice paddy. Paul began visiting Julia's quarters at night to read his poems to her. "Over the 18 months or more that I have known McWilliams I have become extremely fond of her," he wrote his twin brother. Gossipy colleagues twittered when they saw him with books about sex. Yet as the couple tried becoming lovers, Paul found only his spirit willing. He clarified to his brother that he was only "exhausted." Julia, however, was left to wonder in her diary about the tenderly underwhelming experience of losing her virginity. "Perhaps it is his artisticness that makes him seem to lack a male drive."

After the war, Julia and Paul were shipped separately back to America. Paul went to Washington, DC, to live with his brother and hunt for work. Julia returned to her father's house in Pasadena and wrote Paul passionate love letters. To entice him to visit with the promise of a home-cooked gourmet meal, she enrolled at the Hillcliff School of Cookery in Beverly Hills and learned something about herself that would change the world: "I do love to cook."

Paul followed his yearnings to Union Station in Los Angeles on July 7, 1946, and found Julia nervously pacing the train platform. She introduced Paul to her stern, underwhelmed father. He looked disapprovingly down on the short, bald man in European clothes who wanted to talk about philosophy and architecture rather than the stock market; they were incompatible personalities. After a few days, the couple could no longer stand the tension and decided to flee in Julia's Buick. Their destination was Paul's brother's cabin on the edge of Acadia National Park in Maine. Paul said the purpose of the long drive was to test for "operational proof" that their romantic chemistry was the same outside the laboratory of war.

"We may have passed each other on the road," Avis would exclaim when she learned their route. Their paths overlapped in groves of California redwoods (which Paul cheered had been saved from "rapacious lumber interests"), at Crater Lake ("dramatic"), and by the Bitterroots, which reminded Paul of Tibet and made Julia love "that high silent country, and that lovely smell." Paul fell for Julia's "deep-seated charm and human warmth which I have been fascinated to see at work on people of all sorts, from the sophisticates of San Francisco to the mining and cattle folk of the Northwest." She smuggled along eight bottles of her father's best whiskey as an aphrodisiac. By the town of Deer Lodge in Montana, the state they spent the most nights in, it was working well.

Paul proposed at the beginning of August on a stony beach circled by white gulls and shrouded in tuckamores of red spruce and hemlock trees on the edge of Acadia. "I love her dearly," Paul told his brother. The newlyweds moved to Washington, DC, and Paul worked an uninspiring desk job for the State Department. In 1948 he was hired by the US Information Agency to help build libraries in Europe, as part of a postwar effort to fight Soviet expansionism by promoting the American ideals of freedom of thought and expression. The Childs moved to Paris and in October 1949 Julia began classes at Le Cordon Bleu, the renowned chefs' school, which she paid for with the GI Bill. By November, she was transformed. "I feel it in my hands, my stomach, my soul." Paul agreed. "If you could see Julie stuffing pepper and lard up the asshole of a dead pigeon, you'd realize how profoundly affected she's been already by the Cordon Bleu."

The Childs studied the DeVotos' literary partnership because they wanted to duplicate it (with gender roles reversed). Julia revealed to Avis that she dreamed of becoming a cookbook author. Julia taught cooking classes in her small upstairs kitchen inside the Childs' bohemian Left Bank apartment. Julia and her two French partners, Simone "Simca" Beck and Louisette Bertholle, called their endeavor L'École des Trois Gourmandes ("The School of the Three Hearty Eaters"). The trio were struggling to write a book of French recipes for an American audience. Julia was doing most of the writing, and her vision was for the cookbook to be encyclopedic and precise. Simca's was for it to be better than the short flop *What's Cooking in France*, which she co-wrote in 1949 for the independent American publishing company Ives Washburn. Determined to try again in partnership with an American, Simca had introduced herself to Julia at a party in 1951. However, Julia worried that Simca had morally bound her future projects to little Ives Washburn. The cookbook Julia dreamed of putting her name on deserved, she thought, a bigger publisher. "I immodestly think that this could become a classic on French cooking," Julia confided to Avis.

Avis took the quandary straight to Bernard and reported back what he said: "no such thing as a moral obligation to a publisher." With that, the DeVotos integrated themselves into Julia's burgeoning literary career at the same time they were fighting to protect the national parks and de-

fend the Bill of Rights. For Bernard, it was an act of professional courtesy for a fellow writer with initiative. For Avis, it was an act of love for
her new best friend.

As Avis and Julia's friendship deepened, Paul and Bernard became
friendly. Paul's introduction came by writing his reaction to the shortest,
most outlier book of Bernard's career. In late 1951, Bernard published a
stopgap squib called *The Hour: A Cocktail Manifesto*. It compiled his recent
essays laying out his strident philosophies about alcohol. *The Hour* was
marketed as a gift wives could put in their husbands' Christmas stockings. Bernard wrote with such an entertaining mix of 1950s swagger and
patriarchal affection that the book became a best seller, would be reis-
sued in 2010, and became the internet's most frequent find for "Bernard
DeVoto" in the early twenty-first century.

It reveals magnitudes that Bernard dedicated *The Hour* to Avis, the
one time he so honored her.* *The Hour* is Bernard's love letter to the finest
spirits; ones poured from bottles, others in human form. Bernard's peroration is that no man can have a truly perfect cocktail hour without the
woman he finds most charming, most attractive, and most lovely—without his Avis.

Reading *The Hour*, Paul laughed at Bernard's proclamation that America's three greatest contributions to the world were rye, bourbon, and
"art's sunburst of imagined delight"—the DeVoto Dry martini: 3.7 parts
gin to 1 part dry vermouth, stirred with ice and poured with a lemon twist
only. "Nothing can be done with people who put olives in martinis, presumably because in some desolate childhood hour someone refused them
a dill pickle and so they go through life lusting for the taste of brine," Bernard wrote. He specified the difference between "slugs" and "slops." A
slug—whiskey neat or iced—was permissible. Slops contained sweeten-
ers and were "all pestilential, all gangrenous, and all vile."

Paul saw his entrée. With the same mock-heroic tone, Paul teased
Bernard about endorsing vermouth and listed, from *Les Vignobles et Les*

---

*Inexplicably, the 2010 reprint omits the dedication.

Vins, an 1891 text on French wine, all its saccharine ingredients. "Heresiarch! You add vermouth to gin, deliberately opposing yourself to your own doctrinal standards, thereby promoting schism."

Bernard's response honored the glory of his martini and his marriage. "Be not so Protestant in your absolutes; allow for the occasional miracle that the good Lord vouchsafes his Church. Mixed drinks are an abomination, true, and yet nature has 92 disparate elements and yet combined them in my wife, so all the things you list go into vermouth, vermouth goes into gin, and lo, transfiguration."

The DeVotos' determination to make Julia Child a success in addition to their crusade to save national parks had an unforeseen common antagonist. Tall and lanky, Patrick Hurley was a preening former US ambassador to China. Hurley was born and raised in Oklahoma Territory, where he learned his favorite war whoop from hunting with the Choctaw Nation: "Ya-hoo!" After serving with distinction in World War I, Hurley, a Republican, became Herbert Hoover's secretary of war. In 1932 Hurley led US troops in attacking veterans camped in front of the White House for back pay (two were shot dead). Franklin Roosevelt sent Hurley to China in 1944 hoping his mettle might unite the country's two warring factions to help America fight Japan. Nationalist leader Chiang Kai-shek and Communist leader Mao Zedong found Hurley easy to manipulate. Hurley mispronounced their names, bellowed "Ya-hoo" at official dinners, and got so blind drunk he mistook a female journalist for his wife. To compensate for Hurley's stubborn ignorance, Paul Child built picture props so he could communicate with Chiang. Paul and Julia both wrote that Hurley was a "fool."

Rather than accept blame for his failures, Hurley hunted for scapegoats. In late 1945 Hurley returned to America and claimed he was the victim of a treacherous plot. He blamed "disloyal" State Department employees and "weakness in American foreign policy and the communist conspiracy." Hurley became a central figure in a hawkish group known as the "China Lobby." The Lobby believed, after Chiang lost the Chinese Civil War, and Mao's Communists took Beijing, that the outcome had

been, in Hurley's word, "engineered." The Lobby pushed for an immediate segue from World War II into open-ended war in Asia. President Truman rejected it for being too complex and costly for the weary American
public to support. The conviction that China was purposefully "lost" was
a McCarran mania and a tenet of McCarthyism.

In June 1949, Hurley formed an alliance with McCarran after they
met at a China Lobby dinner. McCarran took money from nationalist
Chinese donors and introduced legislation to send another $1.5 billion in
US aid to Chiang. Hurley reinvented himself as a New Mexico uranium
mining magnate and embarked on the first of three unsuccessful bids
for Senate campaigning to sell off public lands. Hurley and McCarran
fed each other's paranoias, and their lust for vengeance would eventually
swoop up the DeVotos and the Childs.

In September 1949, Paul Child's office was put on alert that McCarran was on his way to Paris as part of an investigation. Officially, McCarran sailed to Europe to see former Nazi concentration camps where some
400,000 skeletal "displaced persons" still shivered in diseased squalor.
The House passed and Truman endorsed a bill that would admit 134,000
refugees to America. "The floodgates of this nation are being pried open
for the entrance of millions of aliens," cried McCarran, who had apoca-
lyptically warned that the bill was a "Trojan Horse." McCarran sat on it
in his judiciary committee for eighteen months, and his final delay tactic
was to take his wife for ten weeks on a European "investigation."

They toured the French Riviera, Italy, and Switzerland. "We are having a wonderful time," McCarran's wife wrote. McCarran visited his
mother's birthplace in Ireland. In Rome, he forced an awkward meeting with Pope Pius XII, three years from giving his encyclical pleading
for help for the world's refugee children. McCarran kissed his High Ho-
liness's ring and asked for favors for two of his daughters (both nuns). "It
was grand," McCarran marveled. The McCarrans spent nine days in
Spain meeting the portly, bespangled Generalissimo Francisco Franco (to
whom the "Ambassador from Nevada" would send $100 million in US
taxpayer dollars). "A very tolerant humane man," McCarran called the
dictator whose coup was aided by Hitler. Finally, McCarran visited Funk

Kaserne Emigration and Repatriation Camp outside Munich and complained that almost 90 percent of its occupants were Jewish. With thinly veiled anti-Semitism, McCarran cabled his findings back to Congress. "My investigation indicates need to tighten existing law."

As the refugee bill languished, national journalists besides Bernard DeVoto noticed McCarran. The *Washington Post* called him "a one-man monkey-wrench to the legislative process." Meanwhile, a Ukrainian father of two hung himself in a resettlement zone near Frankfurt after the fear of revocation of his family's approved immigration to America became unbearable. "We had not realized the extent of the emotional strain our DPs were laboring under," an official with the International Refugee Organization in Germany reported.

McCarran suffered emotional strain too. In late September he checked into the palatial Hôtel de Crillon, its neoclassical columns facing the Place de la Concorde, Paris's largest public square, gliding out to the banks of the Seine at the eastern end of the broad, leafy Champs-Élysées. One direction led to the vaulting Arc de Triomphe, the other direction to the elaborate Louvre Museum. Considering his belief that the "loss" of China had been "engineered," McCarran might have been tortured by his proximity to the Childs, whose worldview and experience he considered highly suspicious. An easy fifteen-minute stroll would have taken him past the square's 75-foot-high, 3,300-year-old hieroglyphic-covered obelisk gifted from Egypt, over the arched Pont de la Concord, to the townhouse with the rickety elevator that climbed two stories to a musky apartment with wobbly furniture where Julia diced fresh vegetables with a big French window view of the twin spires of the Basilique Sainte-Clotilde Catholic church. "I couldn't get over how gorgeous everything looked, the beauty of the buildings and the Seine and the bridges and the monuments—the majesty of it all." McCarran was so stricken with contempt he just sulked in his suite. "I wouldn't give one block of Reno for this whole city."

Back in America, McCarran would ratchet up the hunt for anyone who betrayed Hurley in China by expanding the criteria by which State Department employees could be investigated. McCarran's enlarged criteria would include associations with conservationists. Unfortunately for the Childs, there were secret government security files linking them with Morris Llewellyn Cooke. The former Rural Electrification Administration leader who educated Bernard DeVoto about wasteful dams had been a job reference for both Childs. McCarran would make listing Cooke as a reference come back to haunt both families.

While McCarran and Hurley's fusion had put the Childs' future at a risk, it had a profound and immediate political impact on Bernard DeVoto. It made him register with a political party for the first time in his life, and it made him a friend and advisor to Adlai Stevenson.

Illinois governor Stevenson, a Democrat, had haunted eyes, thick lips, and a long nose below a dome of flesh that got him the derisive nickname "Egghead." But he was eloquent like his hero, Abraham Lincoln, and had a similarly quick and subtle sense of humor. He fought corruption without rest (a necessity in Illinois), raised educational and physical standards for police officers, cleaned up graft in the departments of agriculture and commerce, improved schools and hospitals, and modernized roads. Stevenson did it while reducing the per capita cost of government. "Our aim has been a better job with fewer employees," said Stevenson, who made personal responsibility a motif of his speeches. He was a terrifically able executive and a fine orator; his biggest handicap as a candidate was thoughtlessness about his appearance. He was photographed in shoes he had worn holes in on the trail. Fewer pundits saw that as proof of his frugality and work ethic than that he was shabby. Stevenson had personal baggage too. He had divorced in 1949; and when he was twelve he had demonstrated a drill move with a loaded rifle and accidentally killed a sixteen-year-old girl, his cousin. Despite his personal problems, Stevenson governed with such competence, care, and compassion that Truman handpicked him to be his successor.

McCarran's prosecutorial paranoia led directly to Bernard and Stevenson's introduction. In fall 1951, McCarran subpoenaed Henry Wallace, Franklin Roosevelt's former vice president, to testify before the "McCarran Committee" (officially the Senate Internal Security Subcommittee, another creation of the McCarran Act). Wallace was represented by Chicago attorney George Ball, who had been Bernard's student at Northwestern. Throughout Wallace's humiliating ordeal, Ball was in contact with Arthur Schlesinger Jr., another DeVoto alum. Schlesinger and Ball wondered if, in the spirit of trying to change the tenor of government, their old teacher might like to travel to Springfield, Illinois, and meet the governor, a fan.

Bernard was flattered and slightly bewildered to be asked to shadow Stevenson for a few days and give his opinion on the potential presidential run. In Springfield, Bernard concluded that Stevenson was neurotic and should certainly go for it, "for there hadn't been a neurotic in the White House since the first Roosevelt, and what a hell of a lot of fun that was." Stevenson, whose goal was to build a "brain trust" better than Franklin Roosevelt's, asked Bernard to advise him on public lands and conservation. It made Bernard heady about getting his ideas turned into policy (the Echo Park Dam would not stand a chance). He wrote his endorsement in the April "Easy Chair," titled "Stevenson and the Independent Voter," and thus scored another scoop for *Harper's*: he introduced America to the 1952 Democratic candidate for president.

The platform the Democrats would adopt at their bunting-festooned convention in Chicago that summer contained 982 words about natural resources that clearly had Bernard's imprint. It put forth a vision of public land conservation to "preserve the sources of priceless water" for the benefit of "new, small family-sized farms." Its preamble sang that America was "blessed with the richest natural resources of any nation on earth," and it continued, "in our highly complex civilization, outdoor recreation has become essential to the health and happiness of our people." It ended with a commitment: "To the 28,000,000 of our citizens who annually purchase fishing and hunting licenses, we pledge continued efforts to improve."

In the Republicans' platform, the 380-word natural resources section contained a plank to sell off public lands ("opportunity for ownership"). In *Harper's*, Bernard railed at what a radical departure that was from the party of Theodore Roosevelt and Gifford Pinchot. What enraged him most was whom the party empowered to insert that plank: Patrick Hurley, the paranoid pariah hunting scapegoats for his failures in China. The fact that the Republicans would give such a serious job to a disgraced conspiracist drove Bernard to synesthesia. "One wonders why the rest of the platform drafters, highly practical men all, allowed General Hurley to stick them with so loud a smell."

Though Bernard wrote that Dwight Eisenhower was a "great man, great leader, and a living symbol of courage," he was disappointed by his timidity against the bad actors in his own party (unlike Truman with McCarran). Bernard was faintly nauseated that, while giving surrogates, like his running mate Richard Nixon, free reign to mudsling, Eisenhower, the president of Columbia University, who had a bald head, thin, low-slung lips, and wide-spaced eyes, scrubbed his image by hiring Madison Avenue advertising executives. They wrote slogans including that he would "Sweep Out The Mess" in Washington. They also wrote Eisenhower's own version of the Wyoming Stock Growers Association's "Eat More Beef" slogan: "I Like Ike." Bernard appreciated that Eisenhower and Stevenson were internationalists, but not their domestic divergences. Rather than reform, Eisenhower spoke of wanting to form government "partnerships" with businesses. That had frightening spoils implications with regard to issues like the Echo Park Dam.

Bernard had true affinity for Stevenson, but that was not what changed the former Republican advisor and avowed independent. It was the Republican Party becoming immunocompromised to cranks and bullies and indifferent to the environment. Though Bernard would continue to vote for Republican candidates in local elections, so long as the national party was committed to selling off public lands, he announced he would never again support any of its candidates. Bernard readied for the 1952 campaign torn between his heart, which felt Stevenson would be a great president, and his head. He knew that Hoover's snooping combined with McCarran and McCarthy's red-baiting would make it the dirtiest election of his lifetime.

• • •

Meanwhile, over in Paris, a ritual began in the little kitchen with the window looking at the green and white church spires. As chef Julia laid out fresh ingredients on her soapstone counter (she was writing about fish cooked in bouillabaisse sauce), sommelier Paul would uncork wine (he collected Bordeaux but knew his wife loved Chablis). He would read aloud the "Easy Chair" in *Harper's*. Julia soon called Bernard "my hero," and told Avis, "I want to know what Benny thinks about everything." In times of vexation she would ask herself, "What does Benny say?"

It flowed naturally that she became interested in conservation or, as she phrased it, "the public lands business." She asked Avis if there was anything she could do for the cause, like make a donation. "Good God no, don't send money. This battle is purely and simply a political thing now." But Avis repeated, in her stream-of-consciousness asides, about wishing Bernard could somehow feel "less harried," because he was working "damn near all the time," writing not only conservation articles, but also speeches for Stevenson and dossiers for Democratic Party officials.

Julia sent recipes she knew Bernard would like. And Avis's responses proved she was right.

"B. said it was the best pork he has ever eaten. Juicy, tender, and with a divine flavor."

"We are going to have poached salmon with beurre blanc for dinner. Honest to God, Julia, you have brought a revolution into this household."

"B says the best yet. He loves it."

As Julia slyly shared her passion with Bernard, she became outspoken about his. "We've just gotten the new *Harper's* with DeVotos article on the Public Lands," she would announce. "My, what a terrible problem . . . I can't see how people are not aware of the consequences." After reading an article about politicians threatening national parks, Julia would write, "What's the country coming to, with those irresponsible meat-balls in control!" Her concern, combined with McCarthy dyspepsia, made her perspicacious and partisan. "Maybe the Republicans find that by rousing the country to all these circus affairs the other things they are doing may pass unnoticed, such as moving in on the public lands."

12

Richard DeVoto's Ordeal

AT THE BEGINNING OF OCTOBER 1952, Avis dashed a letter to Julia to thank her for an eggs pipérade recipe that she made three times. "My family thanks you too." Avis felt she needed to apologize for sounding frenetic. All of Bernard's work for Adlai Stevenson, she explained, spilled over on her. "With the boss going out to Springfield and helping with other speeches here, I have to swing quite a lot of his affairs myself."

But she was glad for it. She told Julia how much she backed Stevenson, from the moment she saw him on her black-and-white television (the first she ever owned). "This is a completely new kind of man in politics. I think he is going to be bigger than Roosevelt."

All through the fall, Stevenson barnstormed the West — Seattle, Phoenix, Albuquerque — giving Bernard DeVoto–written speeches about conservation. As Stevenson gained on Eisenhower, who campaigned in September through Wisconsin with McCarthy, Bernard advised his man to speak forcefully. "Drive a bulldozer through the Republican planks on natural resources, conservation and public lands."

Avis lost her appetite and her health suffered because she, like every-one else she knew, was "perfectly hysterical about the campaign." She signed off to Julia with a pair of implorations. "Blessings. And Vote."

Just after Avis mailed that letter, out in Salt Lake City, McCarran touched off a smear-campaign landslide that by the end of the month would en-gulf the DeVotos and their crusade. He did it by contacting Harvey Matusow, a plump, logorrheic, ex-Communist actor from the Bronx. McCarran paid Matusow's fare to Salt Lake City to give testimony that would send a union leader to prison for allegedly falsifying a government loyalty affidavit. McCarran summoned the actor to his suite in the Hotel Utah with another job request. "I was elated at the thought of McCar-ran's coming to me for help and was over-eager," Matusow recalled. Mc-Carran wanted the 1952 election to climax with attacks on journalists.

McCarran dispatched Matusow to Las Vegas to spread false rumors about Hank Greenspun, the colorful and pugnacious editor of the tab-loid *Las Vegas Sun*. A mob associate who ran arms to Israel, Greenspun was the only writer in Nevada who regularly attacked McCarthy "and his twin brother in the ranks of bigotry, Senator Pat McCarran." Green-spun published a sordid affidavit from a man who claimed he and Mc-Carthy were lovers. Greenspun called his yellow journalism "fighting the devil with fire," because McCarthy "was as much a homosexual as the hundred homosexuals he said worked in the State Department, which he never produced." The scoop earned Greenspun a new subscriber, Avis DeVoto. She told Julia, "Greenspun apparently is pretty much of a thug, as who isn't in Las Vegas, but he seems to be extremely useful."

McCarthy traveled to Las Vegas, picked up McCarran's theme of smearing critics in the press, and amplified it. Shouting on the micro-phone-stacked rostrum in the crowded Las Vegas War Memorial Audi-torium on October 13, McCarthy emphasized Greenspun's Jewishness, and that he had smeared "a man I love dearly, Senator Pat McCarran." Greenspun, with a ferocious stare, charged at McCarthy shouting, "De-bate me, if you're not afraid of the truth." McCarthy grabbed his hat, hurtled over the footlights, and dashed out a side door.

On October 27, McCarthy whirled into Chicago. He strutted into the ballroom at the large, elegant Palmer House Hotel for an event unprecedented in American political history: he was to give a nationally televised speech as a surrogate for a presidential candidate, Eisenhower. A group of businessmen called the "McCarthy Broadcast Dinner Committee" raised $78,000 in part by selling floor seats for $50 to the event, whose expected attendance was announced in a *New York Times* headline: "1,500 to Hail McCarthy." There was enormous anticipation about what he would say.

The stakes could not have been higher. McCarthy wanted to say Stevenson was gay, because Hoover had fed the rumor to him, and he teased it by calling Democrats the party of "pinks, pansies and punks." But Democratic officials telegraphed an ultimatum: if McCarthy tried, Eisenhower's alleged mistress, Kay Summersby, would find herself in the middle of the campaign. It was a week before Election Day and the last Gallup polling showed the race nearly deadlocked, with the likeable Ike stalling and the egalitarian Egghead surging.

As both McCarran and McCarthy conspired to ensure Stevenson was beaten, clues to how McCarthy composed his speech ran — again — through Hoover.

Among the things Hoover gave McCarthy was Don Surine, his top investigator. In 1950, Surine, a ten-year FBI veteran, was fired for misconduct after he was caught falsifying records, and additionally, while investigating human trafficking in Baltimore, having sex with a victim. Despite his fall from grace, the 6-foot, 4-inch Surine maintained such close friendships within the FBI that Hoover got him his soft landing. Surine became a conduit through which information passed among Hoover, McCarthy, and McCarran (to whom he was regularly loaned for special assignments). Surine had a particular penchant for manipulating media and intimidating journalists, and he parroted McCarthy's standard of proof. "If it walks like a duck, talks like a duck, and acts like a duck, then, goddamit, it *is* a duck." Bernard DeVoto would hear that a man matching

Surine's description had sleuthed for days around Boston "trying to dig up dirt" on him.

Bernard's FBI file has more clues. The file was opened and thoroughly studied on September 16, 1952 — forty-one days before McCarthy arrived in Chicago, forty-eight days before the election. Markings that might indicate by whom are redacted, but an invisible hand (undoubtedly known by Hoover) typed a summarizing "addendum" of the most sensational parts — as if for campaign opposition research.

Details from the top paragraphs in the addendum aligned with what came out of McCarthy's mouth. Instead of attacking Stevenson's sexuality, McCarthy smeared his closest advisors. The speech played on a crackling radio on Stevenson's eastbound chugging campaign train. It was so full of falsehoods, and McCarthy was so enthusiastically cheered, that Stevenson would remember the night as one of the worst of his life. He seemed "physically beaten" and unsure if he could go on. White static would have conveyed the cacophony of applause, hollers, and whistles. Above McCarthy, chandeliers swayed, behind him patriotic bunting breathed, and around him spectators clapped over the second-floor balcony railing. Waving around a series of photos with trembling right hand, McCarthy gripped the microphone-spiked lectern with his left hand for balance and his voice glissandoed from guttural barks to tenor whole notes. Slurring slightly, he praised McCarran's work and he promised to put together a "jig-saw puzzle" that would reveal the country's "deliberate planned retreat from victory." He raised the audience's blood asking "Will Communism win or will America win?"

At this historic moment, when McCarthy, speaking live, held the nation's attention more rapt than ever, he attacked Bernard DeVoto. But it revealed much about McCarthy's mind, and the jigsaw puzzle inside it, that he growled to his audience that it needed to be suspicious of "Richard Dee Voto."

Pause during the grim comedy of McCarthy in Chicago flubbing Bernard DeVoto's name and flash to Wyoming and Colorado. There, it had been front-page, top-fold news when Bernard made a name mistake. However, members of the biggest livestock associations cheered McCarthy, never explaining why it was acceptable for him to screw up, but not Bernard.

Rather than draw attention to McCarthy's carelessness, a cattle rancher spokesman rushed a libelous editorial to the *Denver Post* that ran two days later. Using McCarthy-style language, plus his trick of asking incriminating questions without probable cause, the editorial smeared Bernard as corrupt. It alluded to McCarran's lie that the Forest Service was communistic, and it resurrected the Wyoming Stock Growers Association's bit of character assassination that Bernard was taking bribes.

"I do not know whether a clique in the forest service pays Mr. DeVoto," the stock growers' spokesman wrote. "I do know . . . that he plays their party line."

Flash back to McCarthy continuing to attack Bernard DeVoto in Chicago. In the short time he spent on Bernard, McCarthy tried to tell the story of Hilde Eisler, the stranger whose free speech rights Bernard had lectured the mayor of Boston about more than five years earlier. Then, Bernard's free speech advocacy had made him an advisor to a Republican presidential candidate. Now, on behalf of another presidential candidate, McCarthy used it against him.

McCarthy spoke a falsehood that implicates Hoover in the story's origin. The Eisler incident had merited only a few short and quickly forgotten stories in the *Boston Post*. But one somehow made its way to McCarthy. The specific story contained an inaccuracy. It said that Bernard "headed" the civil liberties group fighting for Eisler's free speech rights, rather than that he acted at its request and on its behalf. It was quintessential McCarthy that he twisted the error further and told the nation that Bernard "headed" the group that originally sponsored Eisler's speech (surely McCarran's mind lit up at hearing the words "DeVoto" and "Eisler"). What was most conspicuous about McCarthy's use of that verb is that Bernard's FBI file contained a summary of the "headed" story. In finding the origin and path of the smear, the word acts like a radioactive tracer in blood, giving the appearance that the story went from Hoover through Surine to McCarthy.

Because the text of McCarthy's speech had been printed in advance in newspapers, Bernard already knew that McCarthy would attack him for having written "Due Notice to the FBI," his *Harper's* column against investigatory overreach. It was darkly ironic, considering that damaging details voiced by McCarthy appeared to have been given to him by the FBI. But speaking live, showman McCarthy deviated from his script so he could play to his crowd and improvise for laughs and gasps. What McCarthy said turned out very different than what he said he would say. McCarthy's prepared remarks stated that Bernard "denounces the FBI as nothing but 'college trained flatfeet.'" Live, and punctuated by startled crowd noise, McCarthy charged, "DeVoto denounces the FBI as, quote, 'nothing but . . . college . . . trained . . . flat . . . feet.' Then he says this! 'And I would refuse to cooperate with the FBI.'"

While McCarthy invented falsehoods to impugn Bernard's character, he scrupulously avoided citing Surine, the FBI, or even the *Boston Post* as the source of his information. Instead McCarthy made a show of citing an aggregator also mentioned in Bernard's FBI file: "the Communist *Daily Worker.*" Speaking the words "DeVoto" and "Communist" together let the audience make the connection. What McCarthy did not say about the *Worker* was that at that moment it was preparing to excoriate Bernard as "bourgeoise" and "imperialist." Bernard found himself in the ridiculous position of being simultaneously attacked *as* a Communist and also *by* Communists.

Bernard disembarked from the Stevenson campaign train on October 28 in New York City. Reporters tracked him down in his hotel and asked what he had to say about McCarthy's performance. "I have no desire to call him names. But this is a very evil force he represents." Bernard was asked a barrage of follow-up questions about the bold-face headlines from across America. "M'Carthy Charges Adlai's Advisors Pro-Communists," announced the *New Times* in Philadelphia, Ohio. "Past 'Dealings'

Revealed REDS BACKING ADLAI SEN. McCARTHY SAYS," went the *San Antonio Express*. "Senator McCarthy Tells 1400 Howling Admirers of Stevenson and Communism," echoed the *Commercial-Mail* of Columbia City, Indiana. ("Ike Silent on Salvo by Senator," added the *Minneapolis Star*.)

Reporters asked Bernard's response to McCarthy's specific charges.

"He quoted me as having made in the piece about the F.B.I. statements which in fact I did not make."

He was asked if he was a Communist sympathizer.

"Anyone who knows my writings knows I am one of the most anti-Communist writers in the country."

He was asked to explain why he stood up for Communist spouse Hilde Eisler's right to speak.

"I do believe in civil liberties. I did nothing then I would not do for Joe McCarthy."

His quotes were printed in newspapers across the country. But rather than accept them, McCarthy amplified his attacks. Political observers would wonder whether J. Edgar Hoover prodded McCarthy, or whether he just groveled. After McCarthy rallied five hundred people in Buckhannon, West Virginia, on October 30, the Associated Press reported, "he reviewed much of his Chicago speech, particularly his attacks on Bernard DeVoto." The next night, McCarthy told five hundred more people in Milwaukee, plus a statewide radio audience, that Bernard "failed to answer."

McCarthy's Bernard DeVoto obsession became so obvious that an Ohio newspaper connected the dots. It was because of Bernard's long fight against McCarran handing out public lands to special interests. "The giving gets under way and here is Bernard DeVoto exposing and opposing it. That makes him, as a certain sort of senator is quick to suggest, a subversive character, maybe a Communist."

The night before the election, with pundits calling the race a dead heat, and surrogates for both the Eisenhower and Stevenson campaigns scrambling for every vote, McCarthy went to the Rio Theatre in Appleton,

Wisconsin. The same group that had put on his speech in Chicago fund-raised again for him to repeat it in front of 1,500 more supporters and another nationwide radio audience of millions.

McCarthy waved a *Harper's Magazine* in the air and boasted that he "exposed" Bernard DeVoto. He repeated his lie that Bernard had told his readers "don't tell the great FBI about Communists." McCarthy acknowledged that Bernard refuted his charges. But he said that was all superseded by the opinion of "one of the greatest Americans I know, after Doug MacArthur and Eisenhower, J. Edgar Hoover."

> I suggest before you vote tomorrow, you go to the public library, pick up Har — Harper's, which normally I wouldn't recommend for reading (laughter). Pick up, heh, up Harper's for October 1949 and turn to the article "Due Notice to the FBI," by Stevenson's adviser, and then get the following issue, which contains the letter from J. Edgar Hoover. The Hoover — now, I ask the American people, especially the good loyal Democrats, when you go to the polls tomorrow, to remember Stevenson said, "Judge me by the advisers whom I select." And keep in mind that he selected as a top adviser a man who says, "If you know about Communists, don't tell the FBI." Now, my good friends, what — what will his job be if a calamity does occur tomorrow and if Stevenson were elected — what job would he have? Would he perhaps have the job of head of the FBI — who knows?

Bernard DeVoto listened live on his hissing, crackling home radio as the calumny against him filled the bulk of that broadcast. The *New York Times* would write that he drew down "radio lightning from Senator McCarthy." Bernard angrily paced his floor, realizing how much he had underestimated McCarthy's power and overestimated his character. Avis watched Bernard mutter about the need for good citizens to "make scenes." She had pain in her eyes, and her cheeks were pale and hollow. Her anemia had worsened because the psychosomatic stress knotted her stomach against all entrants except orange juice and coffee. The phone jangled. Another reporter wanted response. Bernard quit the sucker's game of presuming good faith and spoke four straight words: "McCarthy is a liar."

The next day, Eisenhower had a landslide victory. It crushed the DeVotos' hopes of reigning in McCarthyism and stopping the Echo Park Dam. Because the margin was so decisive, and because McCarthy quickly moved on to other antics, political observers spent no time on the revisionist question of how many votes he affected. But five words in a historical Election Day Associated Press story preserved, as if in amber, exactly whom, in the 1952 election's critical last days and hours, Eisenhower's highest-profile campaign surrogate made into a national terror. "McCarthy concentrated mainly on DeVoto."

13

"TO AVIS AND BERNARD"

IT MIGHT HAVE BEEN NOVEMBER 5, 1952, when the DeVotos emerged into the world again and took their stroll to the little shops in Harvard Square. The sky was dreary gray and the temperature lolled in the forties. Even without the election they could not have helped pondering the US presidency. Visible from their backyard (past Buddy Hunt's campus) was the three-story Georgian mansion that George Washington commandeered for his Revolutionary headquarters. As they continued, to their left, was the misty Cambridge Commons where he had taken command of the Continental Army on July 3, 1775. Grand trees and great men were honored along the walk. A stone monument in the Commons marked the location of an elm that it was claimed Washington accepted his troops beneath, and farther, was another marker at the site of a spreading chestnut that inspired a poem by the claimer, Longfellow. It was a small number of steps from there to where Mount Auburn and Brattle Streets unite. Around that intersection, Brattle Square, in Colonial Revival–style buildings, were the family stores the DeVotos had long patronized, their grocer, butcher, tailor, seamstress, banker, haberdasher, and many book-sellers. Avis remembered how queasy she felt when she realized people they had known for years were staring at them, eyes jaundiced, "with that little worm of doubt—always perfectly visible to us," looking for red in their coats.

Her contradictory reactions to McCarthy's "hit-and-run" attacks suggest psychological trauma. Years later she would boast that she "didn't care a bit." But she also remembered the shopping trips when she was scrutinized—an agony for her. What hurt worse were people whom she thought were friends dropping out of her life, fearful of guilt by association. The ones who stayed she adored more than ever. Like loyal literary agent William Sloane, who had the grace to send Bernard a note of understanding. "I can imagine how tired you must be, Richard."

The DeVotos were still depressed over Stevenson's loss when, on December 25, they experienced a Christmas miracle. That afternoon, Avis paused making dinner (turkey with sage and onion stuffing, mashed potatoes, giblet gravy, string beans sautéed in olive oil, homemade cranberry sauce) to send an excited letter to Julia Child. With the campaign over, Julia had sent Avis a draft chapter on sauces. Julia asked for an honest critique. "Please be frank and brutal." Avis thought it was masterful culinary writing, albeit needing some keen editing. "Absolutely convinced that you really have got something here that could be a classic and make your fortune and go on selling forever." Avis decided she had to get Julia a book deal with a major publisher. Avis asked Bernard for his thoughts and relayed back to Julia that his response was that there was "no conceivable doubt" that his publisher would be her best home. "I want to grab this book for Houghton Mifflin. They have published B. since *Across the Wide Missouri* and he is in every way deeply satisfied with them."

The DeVotos conspired beside their decorated tree. Houghton Mifflin's vice president, Lovell Thompson, came over with his traditional gift of bourbon. Avis—colorful lights twinkling in her eyes—began "preparing the way" by bragging about Julia's writing. With Julia's permission, Avis showed the sample chapter to a company editor, Dorothy de

Santillana. Avis reported that it made de Santillana "itch to get into the kitchen and cook like mad. Interesting reaction. Same as me." Julia was astonished that Avis was expending "all this time and devotion and energy to promote something by people you only know through two pieces of cutlery."

In breathtaking time, Avis could write "We are all set, and a contract will be on its way." It was January 22, 1953 — less than a month after she broached the idea to Houghton Mifflin, less than a year after she "met" Julia. The chef she knew only as a pen pal struggled for words. "I can't tell you my emotions of love and gratitude for all your interest and hard work in the behalf of our book; you display the marks of a Great Gourmande."

"I am as pleased as if I had a new baby," Avis replied.

After Christmas, the DeVotos' oldest child, skinny Private Gordon DeVoto, was sent to Fort Leonard Wood in Missouri to train for his spring 1953 deployment to Korea. Mark, thirteen, bawled and hugged him, certain he would never see his brother again.

McCarthy's admirers and emulators in Congress joined in the dogpile on Bernard DeVoto. In April, Pennsylvania representative Carroll Kearns, citing the House Un-American Activities Committee, condemned "the activities of Bernard DeVoto, which speak for themselves." Five months later, his House and party colleague, Oregon Republican Mathew Ellsworth, would draw hearty laughs from a crowd at the American Mining Congress by using a McCarthy speaking trick to achieve a dramatic effect but elide responsibility. "Mr. Bernard DeVoto and his fellow trav . . . I mean writers." Bernard sent Ellsworth an angry letter that earned the reply "I did not at any time refer to you as a 'fellow-traveler.'" A spokeswoman for the Daughters of the American Revolution would make an insinuation similar to Ellsworth's. It prompted Bernard to tell them that he wished he could respond but he did not associate with subversives.

What Bernard feared most were more blacklistings and boycotts, which would destroy his ability to care for Avis and Mark. He would learn that another editor plus a lecture agent were asking whether they would lose money if they hired him. Financially desperate, he signed a contract with an agency that would book him on grueling nationwide lecture tours, mostly done by train, that paid $200 per one-night stand. Because fear of censorship made him take the work, he chose to lecture about the Bill of Rights. The slouchy man in the rumpled topcoat with his fedora pulled low became a lonely, wide-roaming, anti-McCarthy army of one.

Speaking to mixed crowds of fans and antagonists, often in community libraries, with his baritone punctuated with what had become a persistent smoker's cough, his speeches were eerily similar to the ones he delivered during World War II. Instead of Axis propaganda, Bernard rattled that McCarthyism was the new "poison," and that it succeeded in dividing the country like never since the Civil War. His glasses flashed as his head nodded to and from the 3 x 5 notecards shuffling through his fingers. "McCarthy has told us that he is interested in uncovering not Communists but 'Communist thinkers.' That is, anyone who opposes McC, or anyone whom McC may call a Com. thinker because there is a headline in calling him one, or because he can make headway against someone or some cause—or merely because someone has refused to be silenced by him." On a blizzardy trip out to Washington, he would be heckled away from his lectern in the cities of Bellingham and Richland.

As she cheered from afar, Avis could sound like Abigail Adams. "Too few people know what we are guaranteed under the Constitution, or how much torture and death went into winning these freedoms." But she also would say that her husband was her "greatest comfort," so she pined for his company. "We miss the old man. We think it's fine for him to dash around the country . . . But the fact remains that 8 Berkeley is damned dull without him." In her drafty, half-empty house echoing with the sounds of Mark (a music prodigy) practicing Chopin on piano, she called herself a "widow." Julia sympathized from across the ocean. "I cry with you for lack of Benny."

They could take spirit from a story about Bernard in Summit, New Jersey, making a blunt point about manners. A heckler, seated beside his wife, kept interrupting by asking if Bernard was currently or ever had been a member of the Communist Party. Bernard caused the couple to storm out fighting with each other by asking the man if he was currently or ever had been an adulterer.

Knowing the stresses and strains the DeVotos were under, both Childs sent mail to cheer them. Paul added the DeVotos to his exclusive mailing list for special handmade valentines. Paul crafted brilliantly whimsical, funny, loving cards, sometimes photographed, sometimes drawn. The photos could be straightforward (Julia and Paul sit next to each other, eyes touching, big red hearts pinned to their white shirts). They could be theatrical (Paul wears a dark wig and an old-time frock coat; Julia's wig is long and dark, above a white shawl and a choker of pearls; together they clutch a red heart, pinkies held aloft). They could also be risqué (Paul and Julia are naked in the bathtub, shrouded in bubbles). Paul's drawings ranged from simple (a chef toting an oversize ladle full of hearts, a man and a woman plucking hearts off a tree). To Freudian (a Hellenistic nude woman pulls toward her an oversize arrow that a nude man is thrusting through a heart). To elaborately androgynous (a tall figure in a blue robe shares a sensual embrace with a shorter, bearded, longhaired figure in a pink robe as male and female angels lift hearts above them in an image that looks like a stained-glass window). On that Valentine, Paul wrote a sixteen-line poem on the back saluting "Avis, paragon divine of kitchenry" and "Bold Ben the writer." The first letter of each line spelled from top to bottom "TO AVIS AND BERNARD."

Meanwhile, Avis and Julia would lift each other's spirits by swapping jokes seasoned, to their shared taste, with corn and salt. Avis, possibly after some bourbon, wrote a setup that two mice are arguing at a bar over which starlet has the best legs, Marlene Dietrich or Betty Grable. They ask a third mouse to settle it. "'Sorry, fellows,' said the solitary mouse, waving his drink. 'I'm just a titmouse.'"

(Insert a slide-whistle laugh . . .)

". . . And do you know why Santa Claus has a black eye? Because he laid the wrong doll under the Christmas tree."

Julia, in response: "Definition of a wife: a gadget you screw on the head that does all the housework."

Such chemistry, trust, and intimacy grew between the two families —particularly Avis and Julia—that it was cruel that fate had not yet allowed them to so much as shake hands. Imagining how they would someday embrace each other in person brought a happy dream into their lives during a difficult time. Julia told Avis she could not wait for the laughs they would share "when at last the great DeV/Ch meeting takes place."

14

Black Macs and Banned Books

AS BERNARD DEVOTO CONTINUED SPEECHIFYING AND WRITING against the disinformation, division, and demonizing of the McCarthy era, his ideas became a touchstone. One fan from Huntington Woods, Michigan, reached out to tell him that he too felt morally horrified by "the two Black Macs, 'McCarthy and McCarran.'" Author Ray Bradbury, at the time channeling his outrage into his novel *Fahrenheit 451* ("the temperature at which book paper catches fire"), reached out to Bernard in solidarity. "I simply couldn't stand it anymore." Bradbury enclosed an open letter he published in the *Daily Variety* saying that the 1952 election had been decided "on the issue of fear itself, and not on the facts," and that he would "not welcome it from McCarthy *or* McCarran."

Some corners of the media warmed back up to Bernard in the wake of the election. *New York Times* publisher Arthur Hays Sulzberger asked Bernard what he thought about his editorial pages' "consistent opposition to Mr. McCarthy, Mr. McCarran, and all their works?" Bernard's old friend Elmer Davis, now at ABC News, confessed in a letter that his great worry was "McCarthy and McCarran may have some more shining tar-gets." Bernard pleaded with Davis to also cover conservation, but Davis replied that he did not know how much time he could "devote to conser-vation of wood and water, being more primarily involved with conserva-tion of the freedom of the mind."

Out in Nevada, McCarran received loads of mail praising his union with McCarthy. One unintentionally prescient letter from a Reno woman arrived in an envelope addressed "Senator McCarran" with a letter inside that began "Senator McCarthy." Another fan wrote on letterhead with a heroically drawn picture of McCarthy proclaiming love for him "and his methods." One envelope had a sticker that said "I'm For McCarthy" and the writer proudly scribbled next to it a version of the Wyoming Stock Growers Association's marketing campaign, "EAT-MORE-MEAT." Mc-Carthyites embraced McCarran's range war.

Bernard understood the threats to the environment and human free-dom were conjoined, and he slashed his pen at them both as he fought against the Echo Park Dam. Bernard's "Easy Chair"s in the 1950s swung back and forth, one month for conservation, the next month against Mc-Carthyism, always holding his ethical line. He flew into wild fury at sug-gestions that the way to resist the Black Macs was to become like them. A Portland, Oregon, man wrote to condemn "McCarthy, McCarran, et al," but he alleged that they were tools by which America was being at-tacked by the Vatican. Bernard, who had a personal code requiring that everyone who wrote got a reply, fired back. "I cannot distinguish between what McCarthy is doing and what you are endeavoring to do. You are on precisely the same ground as the totalitarian anti-Semites and all similar manipulators of ignorance, bigotry, and falsehood."

A new character scaled into McCarran and McCarthy's orbit. The sena-tors swapped the services of Roy Cohn, a fearsomely brilliant young law-yer whom McCarthy hired as his chief council. Cohn had moved from McCarran to McCarthy as Republicans took control of Congress and McCarthy's Permanent Subcommittee on Investigations rose to prominence alongside the McCarran Committee. Leading up to the 1952 election, Cohn, as an assistant attorney general, had scoured McCarran Committee testimony transcripts to find any witness inconsistencies that could be made into perjury charges. Cohn had impressed McCarran by winning, in 1951, what would turn out to be the final major espionage case of the Second Red Scare. Julius Rosenberg gave atomic secrets to Russia in World War II, and his wife, Ethel, was complicit in the spying. The Rosenbergs would die together by electrocution in June 1953 after Cohn's aggressive overdramatizations of their crimes ensured they received America's only peacetime civilian death sentences for conspiracy. Like the Rosenbergs, Cohn was Jewish, which shielded McCarran and McCarthy against accusations of anti-Semitism. Slightly built and slightly overweight, Cohn had hair the color of squid ink and deep-set eyes with lids that hung at half-mast, conveying calculated malice.

Cohn and McCarran alleged that huge numbers of Communists worked at the United Nations headquarters in New York City. In the leadup to the 1952 election they hounded Abraham Feller, its acting assistant secretary-general. Feller, forty-seven, a balding, gaunt man, had grown severely depressed as he personally fired three dozen of the United Nations' more than two thousand employees to appease McCarran.

Nine days after the election, Feller threw himself out his twelfth-story apartment window, though his wife tried to hold him back. Feller became another in a growing list of suicide victims who all shared antagonistic contact with McCarran, McCarthy, or Cohn. A journalist photographed Feller's twisted corpse lying near Central Park among blowing newspapers. Another journalist tracked down McCarran a few miles away as he waited to embark on a luxury cruise to South America. Remorseless, McCarran said, "If Feller's conscience was clear he had no reason to suffer from what he expected of our committee."

Three months later, former Wisconsin senator Robert LaFollette Jr., fifty-eight, who still blamed himself for losing to McCarthy in 1946, shot a gun into his mouth in his Washington, DC, home. Days later came Robert Kaplan.

The Cohn, McCarthy, McCarran trio accused the Voice of America radio station, for which Kaplan was an engineer, of Communist conspiracy. The harassment Kaplan felt proved too much to bear. On the campus of the Massachusetts Institute of Technology, he pocketed a suicide note to his wife and son that read "If I don't I am afraid you too through absolutely no fault of your own will be continuously hounded for the rest of your lives." Kaplan, forty-two, deliberately stepped in front of a speeding ten-ton tractor trailer and died of his wounds three hours later. Imitating McCarran, McCarthy assured reporters, "Mr. Kaplan had no fear of this committee whatsoever."

The DeVotos tried not to dwell on how the suicides injected horror and hopelessness into the atmosphere. But the fear almost literally rammed through their front door. Kaplan's March 1953 suicide happened 2 miles from their house. It might have caused Avis to remember the fright of being a young bride whose husband also suffered terrifying depressions. So obviously was she shaken that five days later she suddenly typed to Julia: "I must warn you to be careful about what you say about McCarthy. B. and I can say what we damn well please, and we do. But Paul has a job. And he could lose it. The situation is just as bad as that. I'm beginning to realize what it must feel like to live in a police state."

It can be imagined how she felt a month later, in April 1953, when Julia told her that Cohn was in Paris investigating the library Paul helped to build. Cohn was on the hunt for books by authors whom McCarthy wanted censored. Bernard DeVoto's name was on the list, and books in Europe were catching fire again.

Guilelessly, the Childs played with that fire. As McCarran and McCarthy investigated Voice of America, Julia gleefully wrote Avis that the station broadcast a Bernard DeVoto interview all across Europe. Though Avis admonished herself for not mailing it first, the Childs bought a copy of Bernard's just-published *The Course of Empire*. Paul photographed it in Julia's kitchen. Its bold white title and cover painting of westering pioneers cliff-hung contrastingly on a high shelf beside mixing bowls and pitchers, over a horizontal row of wall hooks dangling a lemon juicer, a cheese grater, and a bone saw, above a metal cabinet holding a shiny steel pot and an ivory electric mixer. Enclosed with the photo was a note from Julia purporting to be from a company called "FOREIGN PUBLICITY SERVICE" addressed "Dear Prospective Client:"

"This is just an illustration of what we can do for YOU, in putting YOUR WORKS where they belong in every home in any foreign country of your choosing. Our charge for this service is only 10% of list price."

When the news arrived in early 1953 that *The Course of Empire* won the National Book Award, Julia's whimsey reduced to boiling joy.

"Paul and I are so happy and proud that DeVoto won that award. It is heartwarming and encouraging and just as it should be. He is certainly some one whom we have admired immensely over the years, and for a 'Real American' (how I hate that term when used by a politician) DeVoto's it, for our money. He's a courageous, vigorous, outspoken historian and political observer, and his blood and guts and learning blaze through everything he writes. My God, he's the kind of man that makes America the home of the brave and the land of the free."

Avis, intuiting how bad it might look to McCarran and McCarthy for a couple affiliated with the State Department to promote Bernard DeVoto, responded twelve days later with a warning.

"People either adore DeVoto, or resent him violently."

Books were burned and lives were wrecked as McCarran and McCarthy investigated the overseas libraries. McCarran slashed the budget for the 230 libraries visited by 27 million people so severely that Paul watched monthly book purchases drop from 20,000 to fewer than 1,600. McCarthy, by sending over Cohn as his investigator, frightened librarians into burning, pulping, and locking away classic works. McCarthy claimed the libraries held more than 31,000 "subversive" books. But he did not specify *which* books (with the strange exception of those by mystery novelist Dashiell Hammett). The effect it had on librarians was to make them, out of fear for their own security, book burners.

Meanwhile, back in America, J. Edgar Hoover secretly collected information on people reading and sharing Bernard DeVoto's books. A source let Hoover know that the History Book Club in New York City was distributing *The Year of Decision: 1846*. "I understand that Mr. DeVoto has been cited as a Communist either by you or somebody else," the tip-ster wrote. "You were most thoughtful to bring this matter to my atten-tion," Hoover replied. It was a measure of how much the country had changed that a book which on publication had been nationally hailed for telling stories of westering pioneers that inspired soldiers in World War II was now being tracked. Texas, Illinois, Alabama, and Indiana consid-ered state book bans, as did individual towns stretching from Salinas, Cal-ifornia, to Shrewsbury, Vermont. Bernard's books were in distinguished company. With McCarran and McCarthy inspiring the persecution, themes of environmental care, racial harmony, and liberty of thought were banned: *Walden, The Grapes of Wrath, Moby Dick, The Souls of Black Folk, Huckleberry Finn, The Rights of Man*.

Bernard was proud to have his works counted with them. On his speaking tours he challenged other writers that their courage as truth tellers would be measured by whether McCarthy and McCarran wanted them banned. "Glad to say that I am on this list," he said. "Glad because we have reached the place where one must say like Henri IV to the recre-ant Duke, 'We have fought at Arques. Where were you?'"

Julia could not contain her anger as she was drafted into the book purging. Her handwriting shook as she wrote Avis: "I have never been so <u>infuriated</u> over politics, lately brought to a head by McCarthy & his stu-pid investigation of our libraries." Julia and Paul, who had been trans-ferred at the end of February 1953 to the port city of Marseille, were conscripted into an emergency re-cataloging so the Paris library could "get rid of all the books McCarthy says it should get rid of." Julia wished she could get advice from her hero. "What does DeVoto say about what is the solution? I would like to hear him." Speaking to a crowd in Denver, he could only shout an echo of her outrage: "Never has a State Depart-ment shown such sniveling cowardice as at present—these book burn-ings!"

As Julia took down books from high shelves, she could not stop think-ing about two flavors of totalitarianism. McCarthy was "a Hitler, and he's got a following." But also, she considered, he and McCarran used in-terrogation techniques like the Soviets, whereby "any word you utter you know can be twisted out of context, to mean what they want it to mean." The Childs were forced to cut short a long-planned vacation, which, if thoughts could kill, saved Julia from prison. "If I went home now it would be with a machine gun."

Julia shared a story about Cohn that perfectly encapsulated McCar-thy-era hypocrisies. Cohn was not traveling alone. His constant compan-ion was another man, also in his mid-twenties, who was astonishingly handsome. His name was G. David Schine, and Cohn, a closeted gay man, was infatuated. Schine, who would later marry a woman, loved being adored for his looks. Schine was tall, broad-shouldered, and blue-eyed; he had a coif of swept-back golden hair and his lips were as thick and pouty as a carp's. He was the son of a multimillionaire real estate developer, and Cohn's eyelids would have lifted uncharacteristically high upon first spotting him on a Florida beach. Schine aspired to be an enter-tainer, possibly a singer, however the most noteworthy utterances to come out of his mouth were brutish put-downs, often directed at Cohn. Since graduating from Harvard in 1949, where he was chauffeured in a Cadil-lac and kept a framed photo of himself in his dressing room, Schine had filled his days nominally working for his father and dodging the draft. For the purpose of keeping Schine out of Korea, Cohn got him a position on McCarthy's staff as an unpaid "chief consultant."

Julia reported that Cohn and Schine ordered every employee at the Paris library to arrive for inspection at 10 a.m. on Easter Sunday. Em-ployees with families would have to skip morning Easter egg hunts with their children. The staff arrived as they were told. Cohn and Schine stood them up, only to be discovered later lounging in the same Hôtel de Cril-lon suite. "Everyone waited—turned out 'they' was having breakfast at 4:30 in the afternoon," Julia wrote.

For other Americans like Cohn whose sexuality fell—or was rumored to fall—outside the mainstream but who were not as well connected polit-ically, McCarran and McCarthy ratcheted up persecutions. That month, April 1953, President Eisenhower, under extreme pressure from the Black

Macs, signed Executive Order 10450. The order launched a domestic war against gay Americans known as the Lavender Scare. Historians estimate that at least five thousand gay people—and probably significantly more—lost government jobs under the order.

Roald Peterson, the Forest Service range ecologist whose loyalty investigation almost certainly made Bernard DeVoto write "Due Notice to the FBI," was caught at the nexus of bureaucratic punitiveness and fear. By 1953, the Petersons had spent four years in hell. As Peterson was put through his first loyalty investigation in 1949, his wife suffered a psychotic break. Her friends feared she was hallucinatory, a psychiatrist diagnosed her with manic depression (bipolar disorder), and she received electroshock treatment. In 1950 she took her three young children to her Louisiana hometown and abandoned them. When her father scolded her for bad parenting, she fled to Atlanta and abandoned her children again. Her sister committed her to the East Louisiana State Hospital for the Insane.

As Peterson's wife drifted south and out of sanity, a New Orleans man she allegedly spoke with informed the FBI that he suspected Peterson was gay. Peterson's wife had sued him for divorce, and during the ugly proceedings a Montana judge ordered the children put in foster care, where the oldest daughter was sexually abused. Peterson was still financially responsible for his children, and wife, and he did his duty traveling to the farthest reaches of Montana teaching ranchers rotational grazing to conserve grass. After a year of hard work and woe, Peterson got his children back. He moved them to a quiet, safe ranch in the idyllic Bitterroot Valley. An elderly woman on a neighboring ranch, who had lost a son in World War II, helped him raise the kids. The family was emerging from its ordeal, until McCarthyism hit them again and again.

In 1952, J. Edgar Hoover shared the false rumor about Peterson's sexuality with the Agriculture Department's loyalty board. The sourcing made the rumor wholly untrustworthy, but it made the board call Peterson back to defend himself anew against the two old anonymous claims that he had been a Communist when he helped sharecroppers in 1940. Again, more than twenty Montanans, including ranchers of every political stripe, and the entirety of the state's congressional delegation voiced their support for "Pete." Under the burden of proof set by Truman's loyalty order, Peterson was cleared a second time.

Peterson faced a third loyalty investigation after Eisenhower was elected. He underwent his triple jeopardy not from the Agriculture Department's loyalty board, but from the Civil Service Commission's. Not a shred of new evidence was introduced. The ability of Peterson's family to heal and regain a sense of home, security, and stability depended on him keeping the Forest Service job he loved. Peterson wrote a personal letter to Hoover pleading that the accusations against him be considered critically. On April 27, 1953, the day Eisenhower signed Executive Order 10450, Peterson was judged a threat to his country and was fired. (Before Eisenhower left office, about 2,400 more employees were fired and approximately 12,000 resigned.)

Peterson and his children were left reeling. Bernard DeVoto wanted badly to write about their ordeal. About how they were the human cost of McCarran's attacks on public lands trumpeted to the tune of his big lie. Their suffering could be juxtaposed with the simultaneous high living of Cohn, galivanting with Schine through Europe for McCarthy at taxpayer expense, flouting *and* enforcing the executive order that ended Peterson's career. But Peterson told Bernard no. He feared publicity would only cause additional hurt. Montana representative Lee Metcalf rallied legislators to get Peterson his job back. Eisenhower's agriculture secretary refused. For decades, Peterson's story was tucked away in musty government archives and his oldest daughter's painful memory. Peterson's youngest daughter killed herself when she was twenty. Peterson's son killed himself at age forty-two.

Bernard tried doing all he could by writing "Due Notice to the FBI." In the ensuing years he would keep asking, in vain, if he could write about Peterson by name. Bernard believed that to prove that a tree falling in a forest made a sound, people had to be made to hear it. He believed the same about an injustice befalling an innocent Forest Service employee and his family. Bernard's pleas suggest he was haunted by a guilt that he had not done enough to stop a tragedy.

15

Green River Canyons National Park

MCCARRAN'S MONOPOLISTIC POLICIES made their mark on western water-ways and forests in the 1950s. On 70,000 high-mountain acres in the Gila National Forest above thirsty Arizona and New Mexico cities, old firs, pin-yons, and junipers that collected, shaded, and filtered the regions' water were fast-tracked into the teeth of twenty-nine sawmills to create more pasturage for cattle. In California, the US Army Corps of Engineers was inserted into what had been the Bureau of Reclamation's Central Valley Project, allowing large corporate farms and developers to drink dispro-portionately from the Sacramento, American, and San Joaquin Rivers. The Eisenhower administration gutted the Soil Conservation Service, which arose out of the Dust Bowl and consisted of 2,500 individual dis-tricts managed by neighboring farmers and ranchers, on the Orwellian rationale of "local participation and control." Bernard DeVoto would translate the doublespeak of "local control" to "conflicts between one local interest and all the others." Cronyism replaced a once-cohesive fed-eral conservation policy.

The National Park Service became so underfunded and understaffed that the 28 national parks, 85 national monuments, 5 national historical parks, 785 capital parks, and 56 other units were looted and vandalized. Litterers threw trash into emerald hot springs in Yellowstone in Wyoming. Thieves plundered artifacts from the Grand Canyon in Arizona and from George Washington's birthplace in Virginia. A cannon was stolen from Gettysburg National Battlefield in Pennsylvania, as was first-aid equipment from Rocky Mountain National Park in Colorado, as were mounted binoculars from Vicksburg National Military Park in Mississippi. Vandals scribbled with lipstick on the Statue of Liberty in New York Harbor and painted religious graffiti along Going-to-the-Sun Road in Glacier National Park in Montana. Others ransacked an observation station at Scotts Bluff National Monument in Nebraska and rolled boulders onto outhouses in Zion National Park in Utah, spattering sewage all around. Eisenhower's interior secretary, Douglas McKay, a former Oregon governor and Cadillac salesman whose nickname was "Giveaway McKay," joined in the destruction and reapproved the Echo Park Dam.

But the Eisenhower administration's wish had to get through Congress, which was where Bernard DeVoto saw a shooting star of hope. He had mailed to every member of Congress his February 1953 "Easy Chair," "Billion Dollar Jackpot," which warned of landgrabbers resurgent. "In the twentieth century they have won only one victory, the annihilation of the Grazing Service, expertly perpetrated by Senator McCarran. Senator McCarran's technique is in their minds as they prepare now for what they hope will be the kill." The article nipped the movement in its fresh sprout, and small ranchers sent in thanks. "Keep up the fight, Mr. DeVoto," wrote John Chohlis, a field representative for *Western Livestock Journal.* "Many of us out here will be indebted to you for many years to come."

"He's had a good response," Avis boasted to Julia. "Is there anything we can do to help?" Julia asked.

To counterbalance after Adlai Stevenson's loss, Bernard built new relationships with an impressive number of senators and congressmen, all of them unfazed by McCarthy's posturing. Bernard made a special point to build on his already good relationship with John F. Kennedy, who had been his representative and was now his senator. Bernard never fell under the spell of Kennedy's charisma; he privately derided Kennedy's political ambition, calling him "an expert baby-kisser." But in personal relations, Bernard always found Kennedy respectful, eager to learn, and prompt. Kennedy provided government documents whenever Bernard asked, and Bernard gave Kennedy advice privately and—seemingly—publicly. In *Harper's*, Bernard explained what smart politics it would be for an enterprising non-Westerner to criticize the Bureau of Reclamation and support national parks. Kennedy made an important speech on the Senate floor saying essentially that. Bernard complimented Kennedy afterward: "I can find no part of it with which I do not thoroughly agree."

In March 1953 Bernard sent Kennedy his idea to stop the Echo Park Dam by elevating Dinosaur National Monument. The response jumped back: "That was an excellent letter you wrote me on the Green River Canyons National Park." The same month, Bernard received a somewhat astonished letter from the bill's House sponsor reporting that Kennedy had asked what he could do for it. Kennedy rushed the idea to a Nebraska Republican senator, and the bipartisan, multiregional "conservation bloc" grew in Congress. The idea was to pass the bill and then mount a public campaign for Eisenhower—who surely remembered Adlai Stevenson's October surge while giving Bernard's speeches—to sign the new national park into law or face the electoral consequences in 1956. Kennedy supplied the ambition and enthusiasm; other members of Congress supplied the national bipartisanship. Most important, the idea had critical in-region support from Wyoming senator Lester Hunt, always the strong center of the conservation coalition.

Enshrining Dinosaur National Monument as a national park would bring its sacred and stunning canyons into league with Yellowstone, Yosemite, Sequoia, Glacier, Mount Rainier, Wind Cave, Rocky Mountain, Zion, Olympic, Grand Teton, and the Grand Canyon. It would be an act of care that could begin healing an era of hatred and plunder. The DeVotos decided to travel west again in the summer of 1953 to see for themselves the whitewater rapids at the bottom of what they hoped would be Green River Canyons National Park, and open their hearts and minds for more inspiration of how the soul of the land could yet be saved.

In the buildup to departure, after Avis's stomach unclenched, the family ate delectably. Avis was happily working as Julia's American "guinea pig," advising what ingredients were in the United States, whether they went by different names, if the measuring units matched. She checked Julia by cooking her recipes to ensure they translated. Avis gave Julia credit for her feeling healthy again (and going a pinch above her preferred weight).

Spring 1953 was a bountiful time for Avis, an impassioned meat eater. The beef bubble burst and the market glut made steak abundantly afford-able even for families afraid of the blacklist. The overindulgence was de-licious. But the price collapse was bitter for western ranchers. During the landgrab, the Wyoming Stock Growers Association had propounded that market forces should be the only price setter, and that private ranchers, not public regulators, would ensure that grazing allotments were never overstocked because it would be bad for business. Overgrazing, the asso-ciation claimed, was an "economic impossibility." Until it became physi-cal inevitability as swarms of cows with rib bones pushing through their leather staggered across ranges vacuuming up the last grass. This put Ei-senhower in a twisty position because he had campaigned to cut agricul-ture subsidies. "The cattle-raisers are screaming blue murder over this drop in the market, and I can't think of when I've been more pleased," Avis clucked to Julia. "I hope some of them lose their shirts after what they've put the public through these last ten years. Just plain greedy, plus blithely overgrazing the public lands . . . Meantime, steak twice a week, and a big roast for the week-end."

The land became so abused that the Dust Bowl returned. By 1954, 11 million acres of the Great Plains were blowing. Soil flew off denuded cattle ranges and farms overplowed in compensation for a wheat har-vest that was the biggest in history by 500 million bushels. Crop surplus and crashing prices made two million wheat farmers face bankruptcy.

"Things are as bad or worse than they were in the Thirties," a farmer in Rolla, Kansas, told the *Wall Street Journal*. Would the Eisenhower administration intervene with meat and wheat price supports (subsidies) or keep its free market promises? The answer was the federal government would buy a quarter-billion pounds of beef, disproportionately bailing out the biggest ranchers, while underfunding programs to transport that meat to feed hungry people in cities. Eisenhower's secretary of agriculture also worked with the Wyoming Stock Growers Association, and the government began subsidizing its "Eat More Beef" advertising campaign.

Bernard DeVoto's old antagonist J. Elmer Brock, the landgrab leader and veteran Wyoming Stock Growers Association operative, embraced the contradiction of suddenly being pro-subsidy but still anti-government. Brock proposed a particularly brute solution to the western agriculture crisis: he called for subsidies to be withdrawn only from wheat farmers, so that overstocked ranchers could take over their lands. Grazing range was diminishing across the West. Fossil fuel development was booming, particularly strip mining, which scraped off all earth above coal seams. Wyoming's grasslands receded as its coal exports skyrocketed. A tough old rancher like Brock had to be concerned, despite his decades of accrued power. Calls for subsidies on behalf of the coal industry started to drown out cowboys. They came especially loud from the southwestern mining town of Rock Springs, population eleven thousand, which had seen its fortunes dwindle as more easily accessible coalbeds were peeled open elsewhere. The town's Republican mayor, Edward Crippa, knowing that a road to the Echo Park Dam would be built from his town, began agitating for the dam "to the hilt." The dam would subsidize perhaps three thousand jobs around Rock Springs for as many as five years. Mayor Crippa became a minor threat to Bernard DeVoto's conservation coalition in Congress.

As the Echo Park Dam invited subsidy abuse, Avis made sure that a story illustrating the human toll of agriculture subsidy manipulation became a historical document. It was the subject of choice for the next author she landed a book deal for after Julia Child. His name was Thaddeus Snow, a loquacious, white-haired cotton farmer from the southeastern "booth-eel" corner of Missouri. Snow farmed along the Mississippi River at the fulcrum of Illinois, Kentucky, Tennessee, and Arkansas. Avis met Snow in 1949 when he gave a talk at Harvard about his philosophy that each time a farmer fed a hungry mouth it was an act of love and could be a foundation for world peace. "Talking politics with him is the joy of my life," Avis said. Avis loved Snow's earthy, funny, and wise reminiscences about smart collies, brave mules, cleared debt, saved woodlots, character-building floods, mean preachers, cypress swamps, pretty snakes, red clover, dove hunts, and wormless sheep, and she convulsed with laughter reading his tale about young boys learning the meaning of hemorrhoids. Avis said Snow was "the kind of man Robert Frost would be if he wasn't such a bastard."

Snow revealed the exploitation of sharecroppers. Cotton replaced corn as the main crop in "Swampeast Missouri," and as with wheat, its overproduction decimated prices and contributed to the Great Depression. To stabilize the market by reducing supply, New Deal programs paid farmers subsidies to grow less ("plow up every third row"). Franklin Roosevelt's administration set a rate for subsidies so that a quarter would go to the landowner, a quarter to the owner of harvesting equipment, and half to labor, meaning croppers. But Swampeast farmers learned from southern neighbors how to game the system. Under a provision meant to help small farms, if a large landowner's child so much as lifted a rake he could claim his family as "labor," sometimes doubling or quadrupling his money. Snow did this too, because there was no way he could fairly keep his land with so many neighbors cheating the system. But Snow knew it was morally wrong. "Our sharecroppers went hungry." So he made a scene.

Snow welcomed evicted croppers to his land and they organized a unit of the Southern Tenant Farmers' Union. Most of them were Black, but many were white. In January 1939, in makeshift shanties, all their possessions inside flapping fabric walls staked between rusty cars and piles of rickety furniture, a thousand souls staged the Missouri Sharecropper Roadside Demonstration at the flatland junction of Highways 60 and 61. It was the Depression era's highest-profile integrated protest for the rights of the dispossessed. Union leader Owen Whitfield, a Black preacher, had to flee under cover of darkness after lynching threats. Reporters speculated that Whitfield studied Gandhi, but Snow described their movement, which planted a seed that Martin Luther King Jr. would harvest, as "purely indigenous." Snow kept everybody supplied with firewood and gasoline. In February 1939 Franklin and Eleanor Roosevelt had Whitfield and his wife, Zella, to the White House. Snow followed them and lobbied the administration, and by 1940 the subsidy system was being reformed, new housing was being built, and half the bootheel's croppers had signed with the Farm Security Administration, which invested millions in them directly.

But it took a toll that Avis could relate to. Snow was demonized by his neighbors. People threatened to murder Snow, around the same time that bullets flew into a church that gave croppers shelter from the cold. It gave him insights into mass hysteria. "All the people who were inspired by the madness became able to believe practically anything."

Snow eventually shared a draft of his memoir with Avis alone. "I can't tell you how puffed up I am he sent it to me first." In a role-swap, she conscripted Bernard to edit. With her stock as a literary scout sky-high because of Julia Child, she marched the book to Houghton Mifflin. "I ought to be a horse player — my hunches pay off. You and Thad," she crowed to Julia.

The DeVotos would become caretakers for Snow, now seventy-five, in April 1954 when he returned to Cambridge to finish the book. They put him up a block away at the Commander Hotel and Avis would walk with him, her arm threaded through his, the big hobbled farmer leaning on her for support. "I just adore him," she said. They talked through the greatest tragedy of his life: his wife died and he left his farm in the care of his son-in-law, who murdered the Snows' daughter and two grandchildren before turning the gun on himself. When blood appeared in Snow's urine, Avis made Bernard take him to a doctor. She called him "stubborn as a Missouri mule" for not wanting to know if he had cancer. She fed him, but Bernard nursed him. He "had one of B's martinis and he said it practically raised him from the dead."

From Missouri: An American Farmer Looks Back was published in 1954, less than a year before Snow died. It gave Avis, a literary Swiss Army knife in human form, an overarching theme to her co-productions. With Snow spotlighting the forgotten people who harvest, with Julia teaching home cooks how to turn harvest into communal art, and with Bernard DeVoto defending the healthy land and clean water on which it all depended, Avis was a magnifier of environmental justice. "Wish I had more time to try your sauces," she wrote Julia before heading west. "Maybe when the public lands are safe."

Meanwhile, Joe McCarthy remained fixated on Bernard DeVoto. On April 24, 1953, he led a session of the Senate Permanent Subcommittee on Investigations. Beside him at a mahogany table glowered Roy Cohn, G. David Schine, and Don Surine. McCarthy used what he thought was an expert psychological trick: ask a surprise question, catch the person giving testimony off guard, and in the confusion reveal a hidden truth.

> McCarthy: Do you know any of these Young Communists who are in any Government position as of today?
> *New York Post* editor James Wechsler: No, sir; I do not.
> McCarthy: Do you know Bernard DeVoto?
> Wechsler: I trust this is not a sequitur.
> McCarthy: Pardon?
> Wechsler: I trust this is not a sequitur.
> McCarthy: It is a question.
> Wechsler: I believe I may have met Bernard DeVoto . . . I regret to say he is not a close personal friend of mine.
> McCarthy: You regret to say that?
> Wechsler: Yes, sir.

McCarthy was not amused by Wechsler's defiance. He struggled to comprehend how others did not see DeVoto as a threat. McCarthy's epigones would soon wonder if the same pressure used to end Roald

Peterson's career could also break the center of the coalition to create Green River Canyons National Park.

To prepare for their western trip and keep vogue with the '50s, the DeVotos replaced their trusty old Buick with a modern new Mercury sedan, which quickly led to one point of marital discord. "B tried to teach me about Overdrive and we wound up not speaking," Avis recalled.

The family, a trio now, would be among the more than forty-three million people to visit a national park in 1953. They could see out the big-screen windows how the country had become more vibrant with places to eat and shop, flashier signs bidding for their dollars. On Route 66, a portion of which they would follow, there had in 1946 been a single restaurant known as "McDonalds Bar-B-Que." Now there was a proliferation of similar-style joints named Sonny's Place, Your Pal's Place, Mel's Steakette, Hasty-Meal-a-Minute Eatery, and Flock Inn. The newest menu item was frozen shrimp, available inland because of advancements in refrigerated trucks. A regular meal was a foot-long hot dog paired with Storz, Hamm's, or Miller beer. Bernard DeVoto would judge that the overall quality of the food had declined (even, sadly, in Montana). There were kitschy Old West theaters and roadhouses with live country bands fronted by women singing bawdy Tin Pan Alley cowboy songs. Roadside stores sold fishing tackle, cowboy boots, shotgun shells, fox tails, handmade table linens, hand-worked belts, and trinkets from Alaska, Bulgaria, Navajo lands, and Paterson, New Jersey. Signs hung on barn roofs advertising Mail Pouch tobacco, Burma-Shave, Dr. Pierce's Pleasant Pellets. Graffiti on canyon walls shouted "Christ Died for *You!*"

They drove straight to Denver and stayed for a week while Bernard gave interviews to stock grower journalists and spoke with small cattlemen's associations. "B. quite sure that it is only a handful of the older rich entrenched stockmen who will continue to try to stir up trouble—the younger men are OK," Avis told Julia. They lingered in Colorado, visiting the mountain mining towns of Leadville, Ophir, Telluride, and they slept in a fabulous Victorian hotel suite in Ouray. They fell in love with the jagged Uncompahgre plateau. Trusting Avis as the better driver,

Bernard passed her the wheel before they ascended the twisting, hairpin Million Dollar Highway above sheer cliffs in the San Juan Mountains. "That's where I got all those new gray hairs," Avis said. It wasn't enough for her: at Berthoud Pass, she and Mark rode to 12,000 feet on Colorado's first double-seated chair lift while "B. remained on the ground, looking green."

They dropped down into the wild, weird geological dreamscape of the desert Southwest. Avis marveled at the fantastic shapes of sandstone loops inside Arches National Park in Utah, and of Shiprock rising like a giant shark's fin out of the desert in New Mexico (where nascent environmental writer Edward Abbey, also being watched by the FBI, was studying philosophy at the state university). The DeVotos passed beneath the juniper-furred twin bluffs of the Bears Ears and crossed in a fractured and mysterious landscape over the waving Escalante River. Bernard had never cared for desert country before; now it gripped him with its warm colors, miraged vastness, and fantastical shapes. "Suddenly I thought it was swell and if I were ten years younger I'd go back."

Bernard, fifty-six, and Avis, forty-nine, had a physically difficult time in some of the national park lands. Bernard suffered such vertigo after he belly-crawled to the cliff's edge in Black Canyon of the Gunnison National Monument in Colorado that he promptly "deposited my lunch in the chaparral." Avis contracted an infection on the road, and discrete Park Service rangers connected her with antibiotics. Meanwhile, with overtones of teenage rebellion, Mark, thirteen, spent his time with his nose pressed inside chemistry textbooks, the only field of study besides music for which his father had no talent.

At the Fraser Experimental Forest in Colorado, Avis had met a Forest Service official who collected cookbooks and promised to send him a copy of Julia's. At the Snyder Basin Ranger Station in an 8,000-foot-high meadow beneath broad-shouldered mountains on the edge of the Bridger–Teton National Forest, Avis cooked moose, watched deer and porcupines, and chatted with a "fine old ruffian" cowboy who told Mark that the Seven Cities of Cibola were real. "How these myths do carry over," she observed. They continued into the heart of Oglala Lakota country in Badlands National Monument in South Dakota. On the Crow Reservation in Montana they attended a powwow, the air filled with dust from the stomping feet of dancers dressed in beads and feathers and the sky sounding with thumping drums and high-pitched songs. On the hills, Bernard was happy to note the return of Appaloosa horses.

For a week they lived in a CCC cabin in piney northern Idaho between Priest Lake and Lake Pend Oreille, driving on logging roads so dusty they had to turn their headlights on in daytime, at one point driving under a tree thrown by a wrecked logging truck. The acceleration of cutting alarmed them. "Saw a helluva lot of logging operations," Avis remembered. Bernard learned about Forest Service attempts to map the jet stream, and grapple with the environmental effects of private citizens firing silver iodide at the sky, the newest fad in the old dream of rainmaking. Avis cooked stews as well as salmon beurre blanc using Julia's recipe.

Over the Canadian border they wheeled to Banff National Park. Bernard was surprised that the coffee was better outside America. At Waterton Lakes National Park, Avis delighted in driving through a paddock of shaggy wood bison in a grassy pasture hemmed by snowcapped mountains. They went back to the American portion of the world's first international peace park, Glacier, because it was their favorite. They also revisited Yellowstone because "B continues to love the place to distraction." Avis watched with morbid expectation as an "idiot tourist" put peanuts on his child's head to photograph a bear eating them. On a boat in the middle of Jenny Lake, Bernard photographed Avis looking elegant in a beige wool coat and patterned headscarf beneath the peaks of Grand Teton National Park. The view never failed to make him reconsider his agnosticism.

In "lousy" Ogden, they received their first letter from Private DeVoto, which was such a patriotic scene it was commemorated with a photo of the family opening it on the broad front page of the *Ogden Standard-Examiner*. The story noted "Mrs. DeVoto is a trim looker who announced proudly that she and her distinguished husband are about ready to round out 30 years of marriage." Though Avis was never comfortable with strangers asking about her husband, she made a big and frequent exception that year for kids. "The wildest amusement I get out of life is the approach of the young, who frequently approach me with timidity, almost with awe—I am Mrs. DeVoto, wife of the DeVoto." Often it was Boy Scouts, large of eye and crisp of uniform. All because of a surprise hit book Bernard published in 1953, *The Journals of Lewis and Clark*, which Bernard edited and Avis annotated and proofed. Bernard was pleasantly surprised that the journals earned him monetarily "a hell of a lot more than Lewis and Clark." Avis had answered five Long Island Boy Scouts who wrote on letterhead elaborately drawn with Corps of Discovery scenes and who explained they had heard "that the Communists are spreading lies about American Youth and saying that we are good for nothing." How they proposed to prove their worth: have heroic Bernard DeVoto guide them across the Lewis and Clark Trail. Avis shielded their innocence by gently responding that such a trip requires careful planning.

For a week the DeVotos lived in happy luxury in the Florence Hotel in Missoula. "In many years of going up and down the United States, I have never found a better hotel," Bernard would write. Inside, he quietly sat down with Roald Peterson, about to leave Montana with his shattered family and never return. Though Peterson rebuffed Bernard's entreaty for an on-record interview, he thanked him for "our conversation about my loyalty case." Bernard said he was sorry he had not been able to do more to help. Avis gave them privacy by going to the boxy, brick Missoula Mercantile across the avenue and buying spices—paprika, dill, dried peppers—and mailing them to Julia.

So Avis and Mark could see it, Bernard returned to the special place atop Lolo Pass along the Lewis and Clark Trail where he had wept with joy, the red cedar grove. Bernard would write that he was in his true western home "whenever I go back to the Bitterroots." This homecoming was more about solace than ecstasy, for Bernard would have remembered the mountains as the place of his last adventure with writer Joseph Kinsey Howard, his indispensable western friend. It is possible Bernard was thinking about Howard's spirit in those handsome trees when he wrote immediately afterward that the grove would be a fine place for an afterlife, "if working journalists are rewarded on the far shore." Avis was just as moved by the "wonderful country up around the Lochsa which is

B's favorite mountain river—big tree country." She would return there twice more.

Bernard yearned to see with his own eyes the potential future Green River Canyons National Park; the same landscape that the potential future Echo Park Dam would destroy. He signed his family up to take a guided raft trip through Dinosaur National Monument to get the full effect. Anticipation was so high for the DeVotos' whitewater adventure that Utah representative William Dawson entered into the *Congressional Record* an article from the *Deseret News* headlined "Mr. DeVoto Has a Look." The Republican proponent of the Echo Park Dam bashed Bernard as a "scenic carpetbagger" and cheerfully added, "I am pleased to see that you are intending to visit Dinosaur National Monument and I look forward to reading your report on the trip. I, unfortunately, have never had the time to run the Green River myself."

Bernard's "Shall We Let Them Ruin Our National Parks?" had launched a whitewater navy in Dinosaur National Monument in the three years since its publication. It was a boon for a tall, muscled entrepreneur born and raised in the gateway town of Vernal, Utah, who saw his business grow exponentially thanks to Bernard's writing. Bus Hatch guided thirty clients down the Green River in 1945 and forty in 1947. In 1951 he took more than a hundred and more than two hundred in 1953. His rubber ten-person army surplus rafts with two oarsmen had their sides stenciled with the words "HATCH RIVER EXPEDITIONS." Dam proponents, seeing Hatch's business as a threat to their subsidy, resorted to a strain of vigilantism and boycotted a local filling station that gave him space for an information kiosk. Hatch was evicted. Fortunately for him, the Sierra Club signed up as many people as possible to run the "wilderness river trail" and help build a groundswell. It was Hatch who would show the DeVotos the roiling interior canyons.

But the DeVotos did not go. Bernard did not reveal how, but he a fractured a toe, and the painful inconvenience made him decline to spend a week bucking down dangerous rapids through a wilderness that could only be exited by climbing cliffs. He explained privately how his Forest

Service friends helped him out. "I wasn't disabled: simply took to a jeep, the damndest experience, and had myself bumped up mountainsides."

Based on Bernard's description of a view being the "most beautiful" thing he saw, it is probable that he was bumped to a place called Harpers Corner at the heart of Dinosaur National Monument. There, he would have swallowed hard, gulped a breath of thin juniper-spiced air, and limped out onto a cliff shaped like a giant anvil. From its point he would have seen in panorama the result of two rivers forming during the Laramide orogeny, a Rocky Mountain uplift event 40 to 70 million years ago. The two rivers, today called the Green and the Yampa, set their curving course when Late Cretaceous dinosaurs such as tyrannosaurs, torosaurs, and alamosaurs stalked their banks and crocodiles snapped in their waters. As the rivers cut downward, they hit hard Weber Sandstone and their curves became set. Over millions of years, the softer sediments above eroded away until what was left was a mountain range being sawed in two by twisting rivers. The erosion exposed a red-spectrum rainbow of rock layers going back 1.1 billion years and representing twenty-three of Earth's twenty-six geological periods. In some places tectonic tumult blasted the striations from horizontal to vertical. Hanging 3,000 feet above, Bernard would have looked left and had a red-tailed hawk's view of a broad, dark chasm of quartzite that explorer John Wesley Powell named Whirlpool Canyon for the engorged currents of the Green River swirling purply into Utah. Upstream to the right, all Colorado, was a lighter sandstone landscape, polished by wind and the aquamarine Yampa into balletic curves, swoops, and dives. Farther in the distance leapt blue, snowcapped mountains of the Yampa plateau. Bernard would have been on the top balcony of two mountain benches where friction at faults in Earth's crust left behind cliffs later etched with petroglyphs of bighorn sheep.

Straight below was Echo Park, an amphitheater cupping a meadow edged with cottonwoods and fronted by a thin, mile-long, 1,000-foot-high cliff of beige sandstone. Bernard would have thought about how Echo Park got its name. As his hero, John Wesley Powell, bobbed in a wooden raft around a bend toward the mouth of the Yampa on June 18, 1869, his brother belted out the song "Old Shady," a Civil War ode to the joy of freed slaves, and more than a half-dozen times, it echoed.

The ringing amphitheater was also the origin of the Echo Park Dam's name, and Bernard could see the dam coming. Part of his route through sage-sprigged cattle range would have been a road gouged by the Bureau of Reclamation without so much as informing the National Park Service. Holes were already being bored in Whirlpool Canyon — which should have reminded Bernard of the fait accompli of the Garrison Dam equipment he saw being hauled without permission from the Three Affiliated Tribes in North Dakota in 1946. The Echo Park Dam would make a limp reservoir in the shape of a spanner wrench that would flood out the plants, petroglyphs, river rapids, and geological wonders. The natural echoing would vanish and the soundscape of wind blustering and ravens cawing would be replaced with the exhaust-scented fulminations of motorboats blasting radios and dragging squealing water-skiers beneath buzzing power lines and past tourist trinket shops, just like at other reservoirs. The land's uniqueness, its character, its heritage would be gone, homogenized, commercialized, desecrated.

Bernard came away with renewed patriotic vigor from his "most beautiful" view of what he knew should be Green River Canyons National Park. He told the *San Francisco Chronicle*, for a story headlined "DeVoto Comes Out Fighting for the Dinosaur Monument," "I hate birds, and I don't really like animals, and I'm not sure I like nature much but this I do really wonder: What will happen to this country if our wilderness is destroyed? It can't ever be replaced, and in a hundred years from now how will anyone know at first hand what wonders there were in this America of ours?"

Traveling on, Bernard was able to envision a nightmare future with the Echo Park Dam and a scene of what would happen if anti-conservation efforts succeeded. Bernard saw it firsthand as they turned the Mercury toward southwest Colorado and Mesa Verde National Park.

Mesa Verde preserves the phenomenal cliff architecture of the Ancestral Puebloan people who lived on an 8,572-foot-high tabletop plateau.

The drive to the top was so vertiginous that surely the wheel (and the gray hairs) went to Avis. The buildings in two chasms biting through the plateau would have at first looked to the DeVotos like optical illusions: rectangular windows peering out of sheer faces of cliffs were the first things to alert their eyes that there were, hanging in midair, villages with multistoried buildings, their "sidewalks" being indentations in vertical walls for feet and hands. The site of the most impressive collection of buildings, all made of stone mortared with soil, water, and ash, was named Cliff Palace. It presents a skyline of rosy gold brick towers both round and rectangular, featuring 150 rooms fronted by plazas, all beneath a mountain's sandstone soffit.

The history gripped Bernard more than the scenery. Before Columbus sailed, the Ancestral Puebloans built the largest and tallest buildings in North America until Chicago's steel skyscrapers in the late 1800s. The cliff villages were outposts of an interconnected and complex regional society that, while numbering in the low thousands, was remarkably similar in structure to how tens of millions of people live in the modern West. The ancient people of rural communities such as Mesa Verde grew corn, squash, and beans and traded them for manufactured goods, such as jewelry and pottery, made in urban centers, especially Chaco Canyon. It was a city–state system of settlement, and it depended on the continuation of rural agriculture. The Ancestral Puebloans pioneered terracing their farmlands to reduce erosion. They also built irrigation works—prototypes of the Echo Park Dam—much like those the Ancient Romans built in a similarly dry climate on the other side of the world.

The Ancestral Puebloans at Mesa Verde built bigger homes, developed new technology, and embarked on their grandest architectural project: Sun Temple. Construction of the D-shaped temple on the mesa-top began in the 1200s at the climax of seven hundred years of continuous settlement. It was likely planned to be a community or religious center. But the construction of Sun Temple suddenly stopped around the same time the Ancestral Puebloans abandoned their cliff dwellings. The people disappeared. When Navajo sheepherders in the 1700s came upon empty cities on the Colorado plateau, they named the lost builders the Anasazi, meaning "the Ancient Ones." Around Phoenix, they became known as the Hohokam, meaning approximately "those who have vanished."

Dendrochronologists would ask Douglas firs, surviving witnesses, what happened. The tree rings told the story that Earth had warmed slightly and megadroughts struck, correlating precisely with the abandonment of Mesa Verde. The civilization appeared to have grown too big and too fast to weather the shocks of environmental disruption, when rains did not come and forests were spent, crops failed, and game vanished.

It was historical, homegrown horror, and a fate that befell people far more connected to nature than modern Americans. In 1906 Theodore Roosevelt, always a proponent of finding wisdom in history and the outdoors, established Mesa Verde National Park so future generations could ponder the Ancestral Puebloans. Having lifted his eyes from a chemistry book, Mark remembered his father's stubby fingers scribbling furiously with pencil on one of his big yellow legal pads, seemingly having found a parable he might use to teach a mass audience about the original "Westerners Against Themselves" and illustrate the high stakes of protecting natural resources. His mother, meanwhile, sent a souvenir postcard to Julia that elicited the response "I've never seen Mesa Verde, either — must be breathtaking."

16

His True Name Is Legion

WHEN BERNARD DEVOTO RETURNED TO CAMBRIDGE he wrote an "Easy Chair" assailing the funding crisis in the national parks. DeVoto gave the column another provocative headline, "Let's Close the National Parks." He argued that until Congress (McCarran) appropriated more money to the National Park Service, the marquee tourist attractions such as Yellowstone, Yosemite, and the Grand Canyon should be put on strike.

The column also alluded to vicious blackmailing by McCarthy allies targeted at Wyoming senator Lester Hunt, the center of Congress's conservation coalition and the most important vote to stop the Echo Park Dam by elevating Dinosaur National Monument into Green River Canyons National Park. The only politician DeVoto mentioned by name was Senator Hunt, who, after visiting Yellowstone and being appalled at the condition of its infrastructure, wrote the president pleading for better care for the national parks. DeVoto complimented Hunt for his National Park Service advocacy, which was a morale boost for him. Quietly, Hunt was fighting for his political life as his son's life was under threat.

Lester "Buddy" Hunt Jr., the student body president of the Episcopal Theological School next door to the DeVotos' house, had been arrested in June 1953. He traveled from Cambridge to Washington, DC, to visit his father and at 10:30 p.m. took a walk through Lafayette Park near the White House. Among the fireflies he saw a "swaggering" man "trying to attract my attention." It was an undercover vice squad officer with the morals division of the Metropolitan Police Department patrolling for gay cruising. After Buddy made eye contact, he was collared and charged with "soliciting for a lewd and immoral purpose." Buddy was caught in the Lavender Scare, ensnared by Executive Order 10450. He spent a frightening night in the District of Columbia jail, too ashamed about the misdemeanor to call his parents. Unfortunately for Buddy, because he was arrested in the federal city, the US Congress was the municipal government, and McCarran, as a senior member of the committee that ran the police department, regularly had the head of the vice squad report to him on who was arrested. The news leaked to key senators.

The anti-conservation faction in the Senate smelled blood and began the attack. McCarran and McCarthy's ally, Styles Bridges, Republican from New Hampshire, plotted a way to flip the Senate, which was tied 47–47. If Senator Hunt could be made to resign, Wyoming's Republican governor would pick his replacement. The governor had been elected in 1952 after McCarthy made a speech that drew the largest political crowd in Wyoming history. Hunt was given an ultimatum by Idaho Republican Herman Welker, who so mimicked McCarthy that his nickname was "Little Joe from Idaho." If Hunt did not immediately resign, Buddy's arrest on suspicion of being gay would be publicized everywhere in Wyoming. Coming forty-five years before the brutal murder of gay University of Wyoming student Matthew Shepard, it was effectively a death threat. Little Joe from Idaho clearly implied that big Joe McCarthy would keep the violent promise.

Senator Hunt and his wife went to court in early October as Buddy was convicted of wanting to commit an "unnatural act." A journalist would write that Hunt "looked as if he was dying before men's eyes."

Atop Buddy's ordeal was Hunt's sorrow over his brother in Colorado having recently committed suicide. It was into this atmosphere that Bernard DeVoto's compliment of Hunt's efforts on behalf of national parks appeared in print. Hunt had to have appreciated the small and sincere public show of support. However, another earthquake was coming.

The political ground beneath Senator Hunt cracked and threatened to swallow him as the Colorado River Storage Project, which would build the Echo Park Dam, became sedimented with pork for the purpose of flipping votes.

The Colorado River Storage Project had been held back in large measure thanks to the work of Morris Llewellyn Cooke, Bernard DeVoto's source (and the Childs' job reference). In the Truman years, Cooke had broken down how the Bureau of Reclamation was blowing up the federal debt and wasting water. Because of the high altitudes and short growing seasons in much of the Rocky Mountain West, wheat and alfalfa were the most common crops. However, both were in dangerous national oversupply because they were also being farmed in lower, warmer, and more humid lands. To stabilize the market, the federal government paid subsidies to farmers outside the region to not grow wheat and alfalfa. But western members of Congress fought for government funds to build dams that would grow more. To cover up the financial insanity, the Bureau of Reclamation added hydroelectric generators to dams. Its lobbyists claimed that power sales would compensate the federal government so it could build still more wasteful dams in the West. Bernard commented, "Pork appears to be an acceptable substitute for water."

The architects of the Colorado River Storage Project planned, in addition to the six major dam units, to include at least seventeen, but as many as a hundred, "participating projects," or affiliated irrigation infrastructure. Three divergent versions of the Colorado River Storage Project emerged: one version in the House of Representatives, another in the Senate, a third held by the Eisenhower administration. Each had different spoils. A fiscal hawk with the American Enterprise Institute named

Raymond Moley, who would become a vital Bernard DeVoto ally, called it a "perversion" the way the Colorado River Storage Project was advancing without specific details and dollar amounts that the public could scrutinize. Moley also saw it as a gaudy example of greed. "To attempt a serious discussion of such a bill would be like trying to anticipate the humors of a coquette," he wrote. "You only know that she will be expensive and that she will never be satisfied."

Temptation came to J. Elmer Brock, the old landgrabber who, because he hated big federal bureaucracy, had turned into an unexpected ally of Bernard DeVoto in the crusade against the Echo Park Dam. But Brock learned that a "participating project" would include construction of power lines through Johnson County, where he had grown frustrated that private hydroelectricity development was too slow and too expensive. Brock's stature and power in the state meant that, if he flipped his position, the shock waves would break apart Hunt's conservation coalition, on which rested DeVoto's hopes of saving Dinosaur National Monument.

Brock pondered the future of ranching in Wyoming. It had a romantic past; he spent his life fighting to return to it. But Brock decided the future was not cows but coal. He crunched numbers and figured out that more coal companies would come to Wyoming if they were promised federally subsidized hydropower from Bureau of Reclamation dams— the private utility rates were too high. Brock could rationalize that he was not selling out Wyoming's ranchers in supporting the Colorado River Storage Project. He mulled it over with one of his old landgrab partners and they convinced themselves that the road that would be built from the coal mining town of Rock Springs to the Echo Park Reservoir would create better access for livestock grazing. Of course, new strip mines would destroy immense swaths of Wyoming grazing range. But even the hero of Brock's favorite book, *The Virginian*, prioritized coal above cows in the end. Brock's sudden embrace of the full Colorado River Storage Project caused such whiplash that the *Wyoming Eagle* ran an editorial shaming Republicans like him for embracing "socialism."

Anguished letters addressing the shifting tectonics of the Echo Park Dam poured in to Senator Hunt. A Denver lawyer who supported the dam admonished Hunt that by not supporting it he had "raped" the people of Utah. A Laramie woman who opposed the dam wrote, "We think that a majority of Westerners who are not <u>financially</u> interested feel as we do." Amazingly, considering that he was being blackmailed by his colleagues, Hunt responded with statements of institutional faith. "Feel certain that congress would not underwrite any program which would injure any of our national parks or monuments." As Hunt was squeezed all around and his coalition ruptured, McCarran rescinded his support for saving Dinosaur National Monument. When new letters reached him about the Echo Park Dam, he replied in cold tones that he was powerless to do anything.

In 1954, Brock took his lobbying to the top. He held a nearly hour-long meeting with President Eisenhower and would emerge and whoop to a landgrab partner that he hoped to soon have everything that "you and I have been fighting for over many years." Eisenhower would write into his State of the Union address his support for the Colorado River Storage Project. As DeVoto knew, once Eisenhower signed the bill, among the first projects built would be the Echo Park Dam. Soon, it appeared, Dinosaur National Monument would be extinct.

The DeVotos' dream of elevating Dinosaur National Monument into Green River Canyons National Park died in the spring of 1954 with a tragedy that followed Joe McCarthy's humiliation on national television.

The political soap opera known as the Army–McCarthy Hearings was an event that lasted from April through June and was watched by 80 million Americans. The hearings were launched because of Roy Cohn's machinations on behalf of G. David Schine, the crush with whom he had marauded through Europe scouring libraries. Journalist Drew Pearson, who remembered being physically beaten by McCarthy, had asked in print why Cohn and Schine were not in Korea if they cared so deeply about fighting Communists. After the army reviewed Schine's deferments and drafted him, Cohn terrorized officers into giving him special treatment by threatening McCarthy investigations. Cohn promised, "We'll wreck the Army." When the scandal broke, McCarthy counterclaimed it was the army that threatened Cohn to stop an investigation into a dentist who had allegedly falsified a loyalty document. McCarthy, knowing no other way but to escalate, said that actually the army was blackmailing him to fire Cohn, which would be "the greatest victory the Communists have scored up to now."

In March, CBS news anchor Edward R. Murrow used his national platform to rebuke McCarthy, putting himself, in 1954, on the same ground where Bernard DeVoto had stood since 1949. A more intimate indication for the DeVotos of how public courage against McCarthyism was rising came from Julia Child. She learned that a fellow Smith College alumna, Aloise Buckley Heath,* claimed without evidence that their school was knowingly harboring Communists. Heath implored the community to stop donating until the traitors were drummed out. Julia took a deep breath and sat down at her typewriter to reply from France. *In this very dangerous period of our history, where, through fear and confusion, we are assailed continually by conflicting opinions and strong appeals to the emotions, it is imperative that our young people learn to sift truth from half-truth; demagoguery from democracy; totalitarianism in any form, from liberty.* As biographer Jennet Conant explained: "Taking her cue from Bernard DeVoto, Julia took a strong, principled stand in her letter to Heath."

Julia announced she would double her annual contribution to Smith, and others followed suit; the school received more donations that spring than ever before. Julia sent a copy to her father, who had told her "It's a hard dirty job that has to be done and it takes a rough and ready person like McCarthy to do it." It was what she had wanted to tell him for years. She sent another copy to the DeVotos. Bernard thought it was a "noble effort" and Avis praised her "truly magnificent letter to the Smith idiot."

When the Army–McCarthy Hearings began, Bernard tried shuttering himself in his office to write, only to have Avis shout for him. On television was their old friend Joseph Welch, now the army's attorney. The

---

*Sister of William F. Buckley Jr. and sister-in-law of L. Brent Bozell, who had co-authored a sympathetic book, *McCarthy and His Enemies: The Record and Its Meaning.*

DeVotos got to know Welch when he represented the publisher of *Strange Fruit* at the same time Bernard was arrested for buying it to protest censorship. Avis fell "mad in love" with Welch, whom she described, as befitting a Republican who defended free speech, as "a very salty character using plenty of strong language."

The DeVotos watched the hearings climax with Welch challenging Cohn to give an honest answer after it was revealed that a photo doctored by Don Surine had been presented as evidence. McCarthy tried to distract by interrupting and smearing an innocent young lawyer at Welch's firm. Welch cried out nearly in tears, "Have you no decency, sir?" The gallery applauded and the DeVotos cheered. Within the year, Bernard would run into Welch on a train from Washington, DC, to Boston. The old friends would ride together and Welch would share secret details about Army–McCarthy, like how McCarthy started drinking liquor in the morning and never stopped, and that Cohn was gay. Welch would tell Bernard he loved his *Harper's* column about knives. When Avis found this out, she immediately mailed him some that had originally come from Julia.

The hearings revealed McCarthy to the nation as a sloppy bully play-acting McCarran. As McCarthy's approval rating went into free fall, McCarran went on a nationwide tour to defend his understudy. McCarran told veterans gathered in New Hampshire that "enemies of America" were trying to destroy McCarthy with "continued sittings" in a "petty dispute." To McCarran's chagrin, on June 11, Vermont Republican senator Ralph Flanders introduced what became the motion to censure McCarthy.

Suddenly hemorrhaging relevance and the mass attention that sustained him, McCarthy went back to his and McCarran's usual, tired playbook. They would scapegoat someone, and they would tease reporters that the scoop they were on the verge of unveiling was earthshaking. The day after the hearings wrapped, McCarthy announced to a television interviewer he was about to expose an unnamed Democratic senator for "just plain wrong doing."

The same day, a visitor saw Senator Lester Hunt. He was aghast that

Hunt looked so "pale and depressed." Hunt, sixty-one, was broken and ailing, struggling to hold on to hope. Days earlier, he had announced he would not seek reelection. He refused to allow his son's arrest to be made a campaign issue. But also, Hunt would not resign. Political insiders shackled themselves, expecting that the "wrong doing" McCarthy was about to spatter onto every front page in America boiled down to that Hunt was trying to do the best he could, like he always had done, for his boy.

The next morning, Saturday, June 19, Hunt left his wife sleeping and walked out with his .22 hunting rifle hidden under his topcoat. An elevator operator at the Senate Office Building took him to the third floor at 8:30 a.m. and noticed the protruding barrel. Hunt crossed the marble hall and sighed into his big, leather desk chair. He wrote a note to his assistant on how to distribute his belongings. When the assistant arrived at 9 a.m. he found his boss in the chair, struggling to breathe, hole in his right temple, blood pooling on the floor.

Bernard DeVoto's dream of creating Green River Canyons National Park died with Hunt; among the senator's final political acts was acquiescing to the full Colorado River Storage Project. In a surprise move, Wyoming's governor appointed as Hunt's successor Mayor Crippa, of Rock Springs, where campaigning for the project was fervent. Hunt was dead nine days when Senator Crippa gave a speech in the Capitol demanding immediate construction of the Echo Park Dam.

The day after Hunt's suicide, Bernard DeVoto had a graduation speech to give. He can be imagined thinking that, for the sake of wrecking national parks, and prolonging the reign of McCarthy, a man he admired had been driven to death. (McCarthy allies, without proof, quickly disseminated rumors that Hunt had cancer, and wasn't the mystery wrongdoing Democratic senator anyway—though they never revealed who it was.) Bernard admitted privately that a monstrous thing he called "the conspiratorial mind" came for him; it "infects even me . . . We all smell conspiracy."

He resisted it. He could have written a "jigsaw puzzle" speech telling his audience how their future was being ruined by evil plotters. Instead, his peroration stressed responsibly dealing with "Joe McCarthy" not as an infamous man of any importance, but as someone they each knew personally who was susceptible to the monstrous thing, which dated back in America to Salem Village when neighbors accused neighbors of sorcery to grab their land. Bernard called it a "virus" with a life cycle like spores of anthrax bacteria on cattle range—able to lay dormant for decades until, when the social immunities weaken, it can find a mass infection vector by being stepped in with the right cloven hoof. "This is a sickness in American life that will destroy us if we don't fight it," Avis would write Julia after talking with Bernard. "This is a helluva lot more dangerous than the H bomb."

On Sunday, June 20, with Hunt's suicide on front pages all over the nation, Bernard DeVoto gave the commencement address at Goddard College in Plainfield, Vermont. The Class of 1954 sat silent and wide-eyed as Bernard sounded off about McCarthyism. His sorrow over Hunt's persecution and death rattled in between the lines he spoke.

Bernard told the graduates that they faced "a species of war; the war that is as old as ignorance, obscurantism, and terrorism." All around they could see casualties, "in the form of blasted lives, shattered careers, ruined reputations, the end of hope."

The young men and women heard that it was their generation's fate to fight this war just as it had been his generation's fate to fight in World Wars I and II. Portions of the speech were borrowed from the ones he gave in World War II and on his tours, imploring citizens to not believe divisive propaganda. Always, the country's enemies were powerful leaders who "by the vilest of motives for the most repulsive reasons" spread lies, disinformation, hate, slander, and innuendo to disunite America.

In keeping with the theme of his life's work, Bernard exhorted his listeners to fight back with the Bill of Rights. While the national attacks on decency, fair play, and freedom were loudest and most forceful from McCarran and McCarthy, it was American citizens who had to decide how wide and deep the attacks would spread. It was from American communities—from their zealots, their fearful, and the people too shy to correct them—that the "clowns and yahoos in Congress" derived their power. It was in communities that they had to be resisted. "The honest but misguided citizen of your own home town—he is your first and constant objective. He must be reasoned with, when the need comes he must be opposed, and from there on to whatever extremity it may take. The light must be turned on and kept on."

Shaking with adrenaline and emotion, Bernard hit his grace note.

"Joe McCarthy's true name is Legion and he has a residence in every town."

17

The Western Paradox

HUNT'S SUICIDE and the shattering of the Green River Canyons National Park coalition left Bernard DeVoto discouraged and depressed, scrambling, as spring sweltered into summer 1954, to re-strategize how Dinosaur National Monument might be saved. He was always "eight-fathoms deep" in work, Avis remembered.

In good fortune he would not have chosen, he found his conservation writings suddenly welcome in magazines that had rejected him. *Collier's* paid $5,000 for a big piece on the Missouri River basin; *Holiday* bought one about the Forest Service; *Lincoln-Mercury Times* one about the Wasatch Range. Avis credited McCarthy for raising Bernard's profile. Bernard was also shocked that *Empire* was selling well. "B. got a royalty check for $6,000 yesterday and nearly dropped dead," Avis told Julia. "He's never made much of any money on books before." (Her "share of this loot" was a new gas stove giving her eight total burners and two ovens.) Cady Hewes remained a mainstay in *Woman's Day*. *Harper's*, loyally, continued blasting out Bernard DeVoto's one-two "Easy Chair"'s, one for conservation, two against McCarthyism, and he was preparing another double-length public lands feature. But not for a second did he trust his hot streak. He worked seven days a week, sleeping no more than five hours a night, on the run from the blacklist. Only on Sundays did he take a half-day off for the Tribe of Benny gathering, when he basked in the fellowship of his sacred martini and a small revolving cast of his most intimate friends.

One particular Sunday topped all the others. On July 11, 1954, came a clattering station wagon packed with a large, special collection of pots and pans. It chugged through the dappled shadows of sycamores and elms on Berkeley Street at 5 p.m. and wheezed to a stop in the driveway. After more than two years of Avis and Julia being the most intimate of pen pals, the Childs came to finally meet the DeVotos in person. The Childs were in America on leave in the middle of being transferred from Marseilles to Plittersdorf, Germany. The move to a former fascist nation filled Julia with dread. She wrote to Avis questioning "if here the McCarthy's took over, if much the same thing couldn't happen."

Upon learning that his traditional Sunday rite would be invaded by "strangers," for he had corresponded the least with the Childs, Bernard, in his stress and exhaustion, grumped to Avis, "I don't want to meet those people." He was acknowledged and overruled. "Well, all right, this time we're going to."

There had followed hours of anxiety as Avis worried what would happen if her husband did not like her best friend. In the context of the meeting, she would warn Julia that Bernard "is a man of violent dislikes, he does not suffer fools gladly, when he is bored it sticks out all over him in great big knobs." Julia's stomach was filled with butterflies as she fretted about what kind of impression she would make.

The Childs' first view of Bernard was him slumped in a lawn chair in the unseasonably pleasant 75-degree air, sipping a sweating martini, and blowing Chesterfield smoke rings with a quorum of the Tribe of Benny around him. After Julia's 6-foot, 3-inch frame unfolded from the wagon, Avis watched her walk toward the gathering, "utterly graceful and feminine, like a dancer." Avis, doubtlessly wearing a special cocktail dress (for she so wanted the meeting to be perfect that for days she pruned the flower gardens), flew across her yard straight at Julia's affectionate grin and they coiled their arms around each other. Avis remembered it as "love at first sight."

Then came Bernard's turn. Probably in wrinkled shirt and slacks, he galumphed over and stood in front of the woman who had 6 inches on him pre-slouch. He craned his neck back so that when he addressed her she looked down at his stiff, graying hair parted on the right and his yawning nostrils. All pleasantries were eschewed and he got to the heart of it.

"What will you have to drink?"

With gracious tact she gave a flattering answer.

"Well, I think I'll have one of those martinis I've been reading about."

Later, Julia would tell Avis how affected she was. "DeVoto himself is, to me, even more impressive in the flesh. Besides all that learning and all that devotion to his art and his country, there's that lovely and very human man." Avis would reply, "There is no mistaking his whole-hearted acceptance of the Childs."

This was their tribal initiation: Julia had two or perhaps three DeVoto Dries. Never did she waiver nor wobble, nor in the face of what Julia's biographer Bob Spitz called Bernard's "atomic intensity" did she betray any diminution in wit, intelligence, or charm.

"Benny of course admired that enormously," Avis remembered.

At the end of July 1954 Bernard disappeared for a secret mission in Missoula, Montana. This time the company would be another surprise pleasure: Adlai Stevenson. A lock to run for president again in 1956, Stevenson wanted to learn more about conservation and asked if Bernard might give him a field lesson in his beloved Bitterroot Mountains. Bernard said he would drop whatever he was doing. "I can't imagine anything better than being with you in such circumstances."

Bernard insisted that they rent their own car lest it be "alleged that Adlai Stevenson and that bastard DeVoto used government gasoline." ("There's a gallant little bunch of millionaire cattlemen out West—mostly in Colorado and Wyoming—who would give a lot to pin something on DeVoto," Avis whispered to Julia.) Bernard wanted Stevenson to get a citizen's tour of public lands, receiving nothing from Forest Service officials that any of his fellow countrymen did not also have right to. Rooms at the Florence Hotel were booked under Stevenson's assistant's name and the entire operation might have vanished into history had Bernard not brought along a friend with a color movie camera. Herbert Scheinberg, a brilliant New York City doctor, documented what had to be the most important field meeting of a conservation writer and a candidate for president since John Muir presented Yosemite to Theodore Roosevelt in 1903.

Scheinberg's film on August 3 shows the men driving south from Missoula into the Bitterroot Valley. In a field they find a Forest Service employee in a vest and slouch hat. Stevenson, dressed in a white button-down shirt and drab slacks, watches and learns as the man (and Bernard) drop to the ground, show where the bunchgrass meets the soil, and present the candidate with the most literal lesson in grassroots politics. In the foothills they see litter left behind by a sloppy camper, and an intertitle shows that someone has shouted "Clean it up, you son of a bitch!" They rendezvous with five Forest Service officials on Lewis and Clark's trail west of Lolo and inspect skids for transporting lumber off mountainsides. Stevenson wears wayfarer sunglasses, Bernard wears teashades; no one else wears any.

Away from every prying eye except the camera, Stevenson accepts a shotgun seat in a black Forest Service sedan and Bernard rides behind him as Scheinberg follows in the rental. They take to a dusty logging road that becomes a two-track as they ascend from ponderosas to Douglas firs to Engelmann spruces and subalpine firs. They picnic beside the headwaters of Fish Creek, and Stevenson stands and stares awhile at the teal water polishing multicolored stones (he has a dream of catching a cutthroat trout on a fly). Up twisting dirt roads they wind to the White Mountain fire lookout tower, a 14-square-foot home atop 41 feet of stilts with a vista of the whole rugged borderland of Montana and Idaho. Wind whipping, Bernard gives an impromptu lecture about Lewis and

Clark. Stevenson asks probing questions and looks out with binoculars at pointed mountains tumbling out and fading into blue.

The next day, they visit loggers using a long crane to stack timber into the forked bed of a red-cabbed truck. Another intertitle quotes a shocked ax-wielding man: "I'll be goddamned—I never thought I'd meet Adlai Stevenson here." Bernard wears gray slacks and a white button-down shirt with breast pocket bulging with Chesterfields, and a brick-sized camera he holds by a thin leather strap slaps against his thigh. Stevenson has put on an indigo shirt matching his blue jeans, which Avis—who wishes she could be there—will describe from the video as "the most beat-up, droopy-drawered, faded old denim well I can only call it a boiler-suit."

Stevenson and Bernard watch giant firs already killed by tiny pine beetles chainsawed down by a man in a white hardhat, and the crash nearly comes through the silent film. They inspect a grim, stubbled clear-cut being smoothed by a bulldozer and hike across slash piles. At the remote Powell Ranger Station, they talk to more Forest Service men as Stevenson patiently cradles a wicker creel. Finally Stevenson, in his jeans, wades shakily into the azure Lochsa River over slippery stones and, at a logjam, with a flyrod, fulfills his dream of holding a native westslope cutthroat trout. Bernard just listens to the water, folded into an origami shape on a cabin patio, chain-smoking and chatting in the sunshine with a Forest Service gentleman gnawing a toothpick. They agree Stevenson is a quick student and asks the right questions. Perhaps remembering Joseph Kinsey Howard, they paused en route at Bernard's beloved red cedar grove to soothe their spirits.

Stevenson would tell his conservation advisor it was all "as agreeable and educational a field trip as has fallen to my lot."

"We need bold and imaginative thinking about resources," Bernard wrote Stevenson after they parted. The trip was as inspiring for Bernard as for the candidate; it gave him determination to finish his new book, which he would call *The Western Paradox*. It would be a full-length version of the conservation teachings he gave Stevenson in the Bitterroots. Bernard got a jump on it by promptly following up with Stevenson with a six-page, single-spaced letter reemphasizing the major points. He advised that with conservation policy that safeguarded and built on the Roosevelts' legacy —clean air and water, abundant timber and wildlife, open spaces, parks, protected grasslands, restored landscapes, and public access over private interest—Democrats "could get and hold the West indefinitely."

It was obvious who would write the conservation plank of the Democrats' 1956 platform. Doubtlessly recalling that October 1952 surge when he gave Bernard DeVoto's speeches on conservation, Stevenson planned to make the issue a pillar of his next campaign. (Unspoken was Stevenson's certain appreciation of Bernard for absorbing McCarthy's attacks.) As Bernard insisted that somebody be "a mid-twentieth century Pinchot," more Democratic insiders whispered that in a Stevenson presidency, that person would be Secretary DeVoto.

However, Bernard thought ahead in case Stevenson were not the candidate to get his ideas about fixing the environment into the White House. Promptly, he also shared the secret of his Montana trip with the most ambitious politician representing him—someone who had been part of the Green River Canyons National Park coalition. There are hints and pressures pushing through the words Bernard wrote Senator Kennedy. "I have discussed this problem with Governor Stevenson, with whom I spent several days in the field this summer . . . I should like very much to discuss it with you."

From the emotional, political, and physical high of the Bitterroots, Bernard DeVoto came down as he continued with Scheinberg south through Idaho's Lemhi Valley. At Pocatello they headed due south through the Bear River valley to Bernard's hometown of Ogden, which always brought him low. He was aghast that the ranges along the route were filled with highly flammable invasive cheatgrass, mustards, and snakeweed, the juicy native buffalo grasses pulled away. (Bernard was like a badger in the amount of time he spent crawling on the ground, in the grass.) Bernard estimated that the cowburnt ranges had about a tenth of the forage they once did.

The August 1954 *Harper's* ran his double-length feature, "Conservation: Down and on the Way Out." "Every move in regard to conservation that the Administration has made has been against the public interest—which is to say against the future—and in favor of some special private interest." As energetically as Bernard tried, his explanations about tax-amortization privilege, Schedule C classifications, the "preference clause" of the Federal Power Act, administrative appeal criteria, privatization of grazing lease sales, office centralization, rescission of sustained-yield rules for reclamation-adjacent portions of national forests, and co-op interest rates vis-à-vis private utilities failed to hit like he wanted. Compared with "The West Against Itself," "Sacred Cows and Public Lands," and "Shall We Let Them Ruin Our National Parks?" it was a flop. With the Echo Park Dam in mind, Bernard confided to Avis that he thought the public was "too apathetic about conservation, and the power issue, to amount to much in the way of votes."

In his hometown, Bernard grew melancholy. He took a slow stroll, in slacks and a bow tie, on the Union Pacific tracks. After shuffling aside for one of the last big, black steam locomotives on the line, he looked at his grandfather's old farm at the base of a Wasatch Range slope calicoed with shrubby Gambel oaks. All of Samuel Dye's sweet fruit trees—the blossoms of an immigrant's dream, which Bernard as a boy had faithfully watered at 3 a.m.—were gone. The land was being encroached on by housing subdivisions. Bernard fled to Salt Lake City and met his old compatriot Chet Olsen and they drove to Colorado to inspect giant goldmine dredges high in the mountains at Breckenridge, denuded, dead earth everywhere.

Eventually, Scheinberg and Bernard arrived in vibrant stands of Bernard's favorite tree, the ponderosa pine, deep in the Manitou Experimental Forest under the snowy sentinel of Pike's Peak. In the Forest Service's handsome administrative complex, built by the Works Progress Administration out of local red sandstone in the Colorado style, they met book publisher Alfred Knopf. He was an old friend, a hot-tempered New York City native rarefied by a lifestyle of upper-crust Republicanism, with a big silver handlebar mustache. Knopf saw nothing ridiculous in having gone

from wearing French ties and being served French food by a French butler with his French poodles in his palatial Westchester estate to donning
a mint-condition cowboy hat to greet Bernard DeVoto in the Rockies. In
1948, Knopf had asked Bernard to help him chart an epic western road
trip and he returned magnetized. "I am completely sold on the Parks and
Forest Services, and will always want to do anything I can to help them in
their troubles . . . Any time you have any action to suggest my taking—
letter writing or what not—don't fail to let me hear from you."

Bernard, who served on the National Parks Advisory Board, got
Knopf appointed its chairman. Knopf had a lavish meal waiting for Bernard and friends, over which they would discuss conservation. Only fragments of details about the bacchanalia were written down, such as the
curated wine, and that the food "made their eyes bulge." This connecting of conservation and fine dining linked both of the DeVotos' legacies.
Traveling with Knopf was one of his editors, William Koshland, who
loved cooking and would eventually play a pivotal role in Avis's life. Bernard could not have failed to mention to Knopf and Koshland that their
friend Avis just spent a week in her refurbished Cambridge kitchen mastering the art of haute cuisine with an aspiring author named Julia Child.

Bernard certainly also discussed an upcoming Knopf book titled *This
Is Dinosaur: Echo Park Country and Its Magic Rivers*, the first conservation
book that explicitly sought to steer public opinion toward preservation.
Knopf would have the book sent to every member of Congress. The idea
for it came from David Brower, executive director of the Sierra Club, and
the western sage lassoed to edit it was Wallace Stegner.

Talk of Stegner would have brought a smile to Bernard's wine-stained
lips. He had proudly launched Stegner to prominence in 1943 by writing
a rave review of Stegner's first great novel, *The Big Rock Candy Mountain,*
a semi-autobiographical tale of a peripatetic western youth following his
father around boomtowns and eventually adopting Utah as a home. The
bonds between Stegner and DeVoto only grew stronger. Within a month,
Stegner would publish *Beyond the Hundredth Meridian*, a bracing biography of John Wesley Powell that traced his exploration of the Colorado
River to the birth of the conservation idea. Stegner fought his publishers

to have it both dedicated to Bernard DeVoto *and* have Bernard DeVoto write its introduction (a decision that Stegner would later hear cost him the Pulitzer Prize because one judge held a DeVoto grudge). As Stegner toiled, Bernard urged him to connect the history to the contemporary fight against the Echo Park Dam. Stegner obliged and wrote that his book's antagonist, one of Nevada's original senators, was "born again, with slight modifications, in Senator McCarran." When Stegner expressed his admiration to Bernard for his work on behalf of public lands, he heard back: "If you feel like that, goddamit, get into print with it."

Stegner listened. In *This Is Dinosaur*, he wrote:

> It's a better world with some buffalo left in it, a richer world with some gorgeous canyons unmarred by signboards, hot-dog stands, super highways, or high-tension lines, undrowned by power or irrigation reservoirs. If we preserved as parks only those places that have no economic possibilities, we would have no parks. And in the decades to come, it will not be only the buffalo and the trumpeter swan who need sanctuaries. Our own species is going to need them too.

As the effects of the food, wine, fellowship, and fresh air wore off in the starry Colorado night, Bernard could drift into his few hours of sleep more assured that his conservation philosophy was being taken up by a new generation of talented writers, editors, and activists.

When Bernard got back briefly to Cambridge, he resolved to have a serious talk with Paul Child. But first, there was a gift waiting for him: buffalo steaks. Paul and Julia, who drove their rented wagon to California to visit her father, found them. Avis would cook them in the "barbarian" style Bernard liked: with plenty of red hot sauce.

The Childs circled back for a longer stay with the DeVotos in late August 1954, just before Hurricane Carol slammed into Boston. Paul nailed up boards to protect the DeVotos' windows. Though Avis's favorite sycamore trees stayed standing, power lines did not. Because the DeVotos had a gas stove, their neighbors brought over meats they did not want spoiling in their thawing freezers. Avis and Julia (with help from Mark's vegetable garden) made dinner parties out of it. Avis's standard introduction was: "You will adore J., who is more fun than any woman I ever knew in my life."

The Childs needed no introduction to a number of Cambridge residents because the city had become a sort of refuge for former OSS colleagues who had been forced out of government service either by Executive Order 10450 or by McCarran investigations. One man moved to Cambridge because a New York City landlord refused to rent to him after McCarran's allegations. In letters, Avis and Julia shared news and gossip about acquaintances struggling to get on with their lives after being scapegoated.

Bernard had to leave again in late September. His lecture agency was so slipshod that he found out he was speaking in New Orleans by reading it in a newspaper. "Please do not arrange any further engagements," he pleaded. By the time his letter arrived, he had additional dates in Cleveland and Schenectady and would agree to a pay cut if he could travel by Pullman sleeping car. He could at least look forward to visiting Great Smoky Mountains National Park where he would again see Knopf, this time for a meeting with the National Parks Advisory Board. In his strategizing to save Dinosaur National Monument, Bernard connected the board with Morris Llewellyn Cooke, a resource in letting members of Congress know that the Echo Park Dam was a scam. To further promulgate that argument, Bernard set up meetings with Democratic officials in Washington, DC. Bernard would begin his long, autumn tour by traveling to New York City for dinner with a *Harper's* editor. His saturation of frustrations was evident in his request that he just wanted to meet at a no-frills restaurant to "chaw some steak & drink some redeye . . . I said steak. A Cordon Bleu has been staying at 8 Berkeley & I've had all the exquisite food I can bear."

Just before Bernard left, he had his talk with Paul. The topic was McCarran and McCarthy's continued influence in the State Department.

Was Paul worried that he would be made the target of a loyalty investigation? Because that would put his career, and Julia's cookbook, at risk.

Paul said no—he thought his job was "too small."

The DeVotos would chaw on that a lot in the coming year.

Pat McCarran made resurrecting McCarthyism his singular mission in the summer and fall of 1954. The spectacle of McCarthy viciously floundering on TV had made them both look foolish.

McCarthy was in a dark night of whatever soul he had, suddenly less interesting to the media, and awaiting the fate of his censure vote, but he never appreciated McCarran more. Don Surine wrote a note in red pencil telling McCarran that his backing meant the world to their friend. "Sen. McCarran—Joe continually talked last night about your wonderful support during this fight." Hoover also sent McCarran praise for his investigative leadership. "You are the 'Daddy' of the committee and its accomplishments." But no sooner had Hoover's words arrived than one of McCarran's star witnesses, ex-Communist Harvey Matusow, the Bronx actor, confessed that his testimony had been schtick for hire. McCarran and McCarthy were exposed for operating their committees in concert with a professional perjurer.

As McCarthy's censure motion moved forward without protest from the White House, the "Black Macs" turned on Eisenhower and accused him of having become a sympathizer. McCarran charged that the president had fallen "captive in the hands of one of the most ruthless groups of political masters I have ever seen." McCarthy made the last front-page headline of his life—appropriately—by amplifying McCarran. He said Eisenhower had allied himself with "Communist hoodlums."

On Monday, September 27, McCarran tormented Senate minority leader Lyndon Johnson by announcing he would vote against censuring McCarthy. Johnson needed every vote he could get, because Kennedy went to the hospital for back surgery and would abstain (he explained his ill health in a handwritten note to Bernard DeVoto postponing their conservation talk). McCarran's vote would fracture the Democrats and give cover to wavering Republicans, making it unlikely that a majority of the Senate would vote for censure.

The next day, McCarran was chauffeured 130 miles from Reno to Hawthorne, population 1,500, to give a speech supporting candidates who would prop up his political machine. Riding in a convertible on the way from the Mineral County Courthouse to the civic center, he spotted two Boy Scouts waving American flags and told them they held the greatest thing in the world. He took the platform and told the crowd to be afraid. "At no day in history has the U.S. been in such jeopardy as it is today," he thundered. He assured them that only he could save the country, which was "beset with enemies from within and from abroad in greater numbers than ever before."

The crowd engulfed him when he stepped off the podium at 9 p.m. Suddenly his eyes rolled up and he crashed backward, like an ancient, twisted Great Basin bristlecone. An aide leapt atop a chair and cried out for a doctor and a priest. McCarran, seventy-eight, was dead of a heart attack.

Almost as though in harmony with his comrade, on Monday, December 6 — two months after meeting with Eisenhower — J. Elmer Brock was in Johnson County, Wyoming, for a Natural Resource Board meeting at which, as chief, he promoted mining in a wildlife preserve and lobbied for coal subsidies. At 5:30 p.m. Brock walked into the Buffalo Grocery and Market, had a heart attack, and died at age seventy-two.

In his draft of *The Western Paradox*, Bernard DeVoto eulogized McCarran.

> He was a brilliant man and his piracies were on a truly impressive scale. It is true that no crook was too small for him to form an alliance with, but it is also true that he was in lifetime alliance with the largest-scale crookedness of his region. In my time no other Senator has so constantly worked against the interests of the United States.

18

"On Any Grounds Whatever"

MCCARRAN WAS GONE, but he left an unshakable spirit. It was a spirit he inherited from his predecessor, Nevada senator Francis Newlands. The arc of Newlands's career put in perspective the way McCarran's would live on and continue to shape the DeVotos' fight against the Colorado River Storage Project.

Newlands, a dandy with an aquiline nose who wore the finest English fashions and rarely returned to the Victorian mansion he had built overlooking the Truckee River in Reno, helped Nevada earn the nickname "the Rotten Borough." He was born in Mississippi, moved to San Francisco in 1870, worked as a lawyer for the majority owner of Nevada's billion-dollar Comstock Mine, and married into the fortune. Like many a politician whose pocketbook exceeds his talent, Newlands discovered he could win in the West as he could not in the East. Despite his being allergic to sagebrush, Newlands's deep pockets, in the era before direct election of senators, incentivized Nevada Democrats to send him to Washington to enrich them all by securing price supports for silver. In 1902 Newlands attached his name to the legislation that created the Bureau of Reclamation to spite President Theodore Roosevelt, a Republican, for inviting Booker T. Washington to dine at the White House, a first for a Black man in America. By affixing his name on the act that created it, Newlands veneered the Bureau of Reclamation with his explicit racism.

At his molten core, Newlands was a virulent white supremacist. Relocated in Washington, DC, he became horrified to find, as was reported in *The Souls of Black Folk* in 1903, that the largest per capita Black city in America had a school system of such efficacy that it had exported tens of thousands of educators to the South, where illiteracy among children and grandchildren of former slaves dropped below 50 percent. Newlands insisted he serve on the Senate Committee for Washington, DC, the city's municipal government (setting the stage for McCarran's later service on it). He reworked curricula for Black children from scholarship to servitude. "He believed African-Americans were an inferior race who should be educated to be hewers of wood and drawers of water," explained historians Martin Ridge and Walter Nugent. Newlands said he wanted the capitol city to "furnish a model system to all the southern states for the training of colored children."

Privately, Newlands bought farmland on the edge of Washington and developed the bedroom community of Chevy Chase, a prototype for the twentieth-century American suburb, complete with its barring of Blacks and Jews. Newlands agitated to "write the word white into our constitution" and "confer citizenship upon no one but people of the white race." Even by the low standards of the Woodrow Wilson administration, Newlands distinguished himself as a radical racist by pushing to repeal the Fifteenth Amendment and permanently take away the right of Blacks to vote.

To further propagate a white-dominated hierarchy, he held on to power by shilling for large, out-of-state sheep corporations that demanded control of federal grazing ranges in Nevada, where labor came from immigrants from Europe, Mexico, and South America.

McCarran inherited his predecessor's focus on serving a specific caste. His particular brand of discrimination involved accusing those outside it of being Communists. Newlands's spirit was alive and well at McCarran's funeral, where a strange, bellicose, bipartisan collection of politicians paid their tributes at the Romanesque Saint Thomas Aquinas Cathedral in Reno on October 2, 1954. Mingled with Mississippi Dixiecrat James Eastland, who would next lead the McCarran Committee, was Idahoan Herman "Little Joe from Idaho" Welker, who wept, "The nation has lost its greatest patriot." With them was Republican upstart Barry Goldwater of Arizona, who loudly denounced the federal government while voting for more of its dams. In front of the floral bouquet from Generalissimo Franco, Kentucky Democrat Earle Clements bowed his head with Styles Bridges, the Republican who had helped Welker blackmail Senator Hunt. The platform they represented was that for whites, mainly, the federal government could never spend enough; for everyone else it needed to be kept small enough to drown in a (water subsidized, donor contractor prioritized) bathtub. The only conspicuous absence at McCarran's funeral was McCarthy, who was in a hospital with symptoms of the alcoholism that would kill him within three years.

The spirit of using Bureau of Reclamation irrigation subsidies to primarily help whites and hurt Black, Brown, and Indigenous peoples, which Newlands established and McCarran embraced, flowed out into a 100,000-member group in the West that called themselves the "Aqualantes." The name meant "water vigilantes." Leader Tom Bolack, a businessman, rancher, and mayor of Farmington, New Mexico, proclaimed that members were dedicated to "defending the right to develop the water resources of their states." The Aqualantes' sole purpose was to win passage of the Colorado River Storage Project and immediately start construction of the Echo Park Dam.

The Aqualantes pumped out pro-dam propaganda featuring adorable blue-eyed children, and their efforts culminated in a film whose title was a play on *Birth of a Nation*, the silent film that depicted the Ku Klux Klan as heroes. The Aqualanteses' film, *Birth of a Basin*, was not too much for amateur psychiatrists to unpack. They could plead thoughtlessness but not ignorance in the choosing of their title. After the nation became horrified in the summer of 1955 by the brutal murder of fourteen-year-old Emmett Till in Mississippi by white vigilantes, the Aqualantes quietly renamed their film *A Project for People*.

Bernard DeVoto corresponded about the Aqualantes with his friend, Pennsylvania Republican representative John Saylor, a great conservation ally. Saylor issued a statement that began "HI HO AQUALANTES!" "Some of the psychological elements which influenced and motivated the early day vigilantes apparently have weathered the sociological changes which have taken place." Saylor dressed the group down for using shifty language to secure subsidies. "The 'Aqualantes' are not riding to save the West's water . . . The 'Aqualantes' are riding to raid the Treasury of the United States."

Bernard wanted to paint in the public imagination an image of the Aqualantes that represented their absurdity. In early 1955, he told *Harper's* readers to picture the Aqualantes as "bronzed horsemen of the Old West with swim fins on their feet."

It was another winter of lonely times for Avis, offset by her continuing to work through Julia's pages (in addition to writing her weekly detective novel reviews, answering Bernard's mail, keeping house, etc.). There was a measure of relief in Private First Class DeVoto coming home from Korea, honorably discharged and with a meritorious unit citation, in November 1954, just as his father left for another speaking job (in fourteen months he traveled to or through forty-seven of the forty-eight states). "He has been away so much this year, and is so tired," Avis explained. Avis cooked Gordon steaks, chops, spaghetti, and pies, but his eccentricities, the gruff temper, the deep fixations on cars, cameras, crossword puzzles, and guns absorbed him. Gordon received in-patient psychiatric care at the VA hospital, and Avis worried herself to the point of confessing in a dark moment to Julia that she thought she had let him down. "He fails in school. He fails at jobs. He gets fired. He can't live with us. He can't live without us. He is unable to do anything except his own peculiar way, and can't and won't follow instructions, from us or anyone else. What the psychiatrists call 'a hostile dependent.' He just breaks my heart, and I can't eat, or sleep without dope, and I feel as if I'm carrying around a thirty-pound weight in my stomach. I think Benny is too, but he puts up a good front."

Julia sent gifts to Gordon and Mark and she empathized warmly with Avis. She also sent words of encouragement to Bernard, especially as she knew how increasingly exhausted he was after every trip. A hypochondriac about cancer, Bernard had checked himself into Peter Bent Brigham Hospital in Boston for six days of "God-damn tiresome tests" that "had me rolling around as if I was worshipping God in Georgia." He gave up liquor for a week. "Nothing like that has happened since 1909." Doctors found a spot on his prostate, but diagnosed it as benign. Julia wrote, "Much love to Benny, and thank heaven he is not flattened out by his enemies, the beasts and bitches."

On April 18, 1955, a showdown on the Senate floor over the fate of the Echo Park Dam pitted Pat McCarran's ideas square against words from Bernard DeVoto. Though Bernard had been cripplingly sick with flu all spring, he made an emergency trip to Washington, DC, as Congress debated the Colorado River Storage Project.

In previous testimony, dam opponents had drilled down on points that Bernard raised when he launched the fight with his 1950 article in the *Saturday Evening Post.* Those efforts cracked the Bureau of Reclamation's facade of professionalism, especially testimony by David Brower of the Sierra Club. Brower discovered that the bureau had not corrected mathematical errors regarding alternative designs for the project, which Bernard had alluded to in "Shall We Let Them Ruin Our National Parks?"

"Brower presented himself in the true DeVoto tradition," wrote environmental historian John Thomas, "as a simple amateur with only a layman's knowledge of mathematics." Bernard followed up by writing an "Easy Chair" headlined "And Fractions Drive Me Mad," in which he amplified the mistakes Brower re-caught. Bernard wrote that if the Echo Park Dam was still built, "Dinosaur Monument will have been ruined and the national parks system undermined on the basis of errors in arithmetic too gross to be permitted a schoolboy."

But McCarthyist arguments for the Echo Park Dam kept it alive. Communists could win in the event of a nuclear war with Russia if the United States did not build the full Colorado River Storage Project, the governor of Wyoming told Congress (the Aqualantes heartily agreed). Opponents of the dam were called security risks, disloyal, weak, gay. They were "Nature Boys," a veiled reprisal of the old slander that only "short-haired women and long-haired men" had opposed the Hetch Hetchy dam.

Meanwhile, the conservation coalition Bernard DeVoto galvanized swelled to more than eight million Americans. It included the National Parks Association, the American Planning and Civic Association, the Emergency Committee on Natural Resources, the Outdoor Writers Association of America, the Izaak Walton League, the National Audubon Society, American Alpine Club, Appalachian Mountain Club, the Wilderness Society, the American Nature Association, the American Museum of Natural History, the Conservation Foundation, and the Garden and Gun Club of America. The National Wildlife Federation, a conglomerate of state and county chapters of hunters, anglers, and wildlife advocates representing nearly three million people, voted in March 1955 to "do everything possible to see that our national park system is not needlessly invaded or despoiled." Forty-seven of the forty-eight state organizations of the General Federation of Women's Clubs, representing five million members, supported a resolution to protect Dinosaur National Monument. Eleanor Roosevelt, representing her late husband's legacy, wrote a supportive column. Letters to members of Congress about the Echo Park Dam ran eighty to one against it. And still Bernard judged—based on Hetch Hetchy history, the mechanisms of minority power in government, and the McCarthyist tones of dam proponents—it was not enough.

But Bernard DeVoto had the stature, authority, and the savvy to usher into the conservation coalition a faction of strange bedfellows that he thought could give it a chance to win. He introduced his conservation readers to Raymond Moley, the pedantic deficit hawk from the American Enterprise Institute who was as affected by populist pleas and cowboy myths as a grizzly bear was by a swarm of gnats. Moley was a Republican who cared nothing for natural beauty and who thought Joe McCarthy was a lesser evil than his party's spending habits. Moley and his followers called for ending western subsidies, and when DeVoto fans asked how he could form an alliance with such a man (for forest rangers were a western subsidy too), he explained, "I will oppose those dams and any others which threaten to invade the parks as long as I am capable of opposition, and I will accept the help of anyone who cares to join the opposition on any grounds whatever."

Moley's argument was an economic one. He asked of the Colorado River Storage Project why, of every dollar to be spent on it, an out-of-region taxpayer like himself should pay 98 cents and receive virtually no benefits while a taxpayer in Vernal, Utah, receiving nearly all the benefits, should pay only two pennies? "It is an account of deplorable bureaucratic ambition, blundering, and deceit, together with regional rapacity among politicians," Moley opined. In the same "Easy Chair" in which he gave Brower a bigger platform, Bernard DeVoto bridged in the "brilliant articles that Mr. Raymond Moley has lately been publishing, articles which should notify the West that the long indifference of the East is ending." Bernard was building back the old conservation coalition of environmentalists and fiscal conservatives, but on a bigger scale than Senator Hunt had done.

The showdown on the Senate floor pitted Wyoming's Joseph O'Mahoney against Illinois's Paul Douglas, both Democrats. On the subject of the coalition that wanted to stop the Echo Park Dam, O'Mahoney spoke like a maudlin McCarran. "They want to throw us to the Dinosaurs," he mourned. "Pity us."

When Douglas orated against O'Mahoney, it was in opposition to public wealth going disproportionately to the McCarran caste, the oligarchs and Aqualantes. Douglas spoke on behalf of farmers in Illinois, where land could be bought for $20 an acre, which would grow the same $150 hay crop that the Colorado River Storage Project would charge all federal taxpayers about $2,000 an acre to grow in Utah. There was symbolism in Douglas, the liberal lion, who once tried and dreadfully failed to moderate the McCarran Act, rising against an avatar of his old bogey. Standing with his left arm permanently limp from Okinawa, Douglas prefaced his statement as "something I had hoped I would not be compelled to say." But "already the rest of the country is paying through the nose for the 16 votes which the great Mountain States have in the United States Senate . . . It is too bad that these fine people live in a semi-arid region with a river running through deep canyons. We are sorry for them, but I do not think that creates for them a perpetual claim on the public treasury."

The next day, Douglas wrote Bernard. "You will find some of your ideas repeated in my speech—particularly in the closing sections, but of course with less skill and eloquence." Bernard wheezed through the Capitol hallways after a National Parks Advisory Board meeting to the Senate gallery—the lingering effects of the unshakable flu and decades of chain-smoking slowing him—to hear more Echo Park Dam debate. Bernard never had a face-to-face with McCarran; he had to feel proud that Douglas used his ideas to knock down O'Mahoney in what was a proxy DeVoto versus McCarran match.

All the criticism so buffeted the Colorado River Storage Project that over in the House of Representatives, Bernard's fellow Aqualantes critic, John Saylor, introduced an amendment to eliminate the Echo Park Dam. Saylor and five fellow Pennsylvania Republicans who broke with their national party on conservation had won their 1954 elections despite strong gains nationally for liberal Democrats. Counseled by Bernard, Saylor shrewdly switched his conservation strategy. Previously, Saylor had argued to save national parks to preserve their beauty. Now he argued to save them to preserve the federal budget and economic fairness among the states—the Echo Park Dam was pure pork. Saylor's irrigation subcommittee colleagues, all with fresh copies of *This Is Dinosaur*, passed his amendment. Their votes created one version of the Colorado River Storage Project that would not destroy Dinosaur National Monument. Avis excitedly narrated the action to Julia. "We are pretty well going to stop those boys, B. is quite sure—in the House. With the aid of people like Raymond Moley, for the love of God. Paul Douglas is a tower of strength, the conservation groups are doing a magnificent job, and there are those six wonderful Republicans from Pennsylvania. B. quite sure that Echo Park will be knocked out. I hope. I hope. Never underestimate a nature lover."

Bernard's challenge was grabbing the momentum to make arguments and form strategies that would get the Senate and Eisenhower to agree to the bill in the people's chamber. To work out a plan, he scheduled a meeting in Washington with his old, reliable source and ally in the fight against deadbeat dams, Morris Llewellyn Cooke.

Unbeknownst to Bernard, Paul Child had just been ordered back to Washington from Germany, and was shut in a small room with two men working for a McCarran appointee, and was told to remove his trousers and explain how he knew Cooke.

"Paul . . . was flown back for an <u>investigation</u>—so at last it has come to us," Julia handwrote Avis, with a squiggle underline, on April 19, 1955.

Since his arrival a week earlier, Paul had sent Julia increasingly desperate-sounding letters. "Why the Hell am I here at all? This is curiously fantastic, unreal, frightening, and preposterous: and I couldn't wish more that you were here to give me your invaluable moral support."

Paul was being investigated by Scott McLeod, a former FBI agent whose promotion to chief of security in the State Department had been done to appease McCarran. McLeod was so notorious that when he was appointed, Avis commented to Julia about his friendship with McCarthy. "McLeod is his buddy, leaks all his stuff to him." McLeod was a de facto third "Black Mac" and he boasted the usual ornithological standard of proof. "Show that a man quacks like a duck and walks like a duck—not whether he is actually a duck."

Paul was summoned to the State Department Office of Security. In a stuffy room with a table, two of McLeod's special agents sat facing him. On the desk between them was a 4-inch-thick file of personal details: that Paul played cello, studied judo, read French literature, sculpted, practiced woodcarving, and had lived in France like a bohemian. That when he had been a photography instructor at Avon Old Farms School, the dean thought he had "homosexual tendencies." Like McCarthy, the agents switched questions abruptly. There was much talk about Jane Foster, an old, free-spirited friend from the OSS accused of getting sucked into communism in the 1930s, who, in January 1955, unknowingly spoke Paul's name to an undercover FBI agent on a train to Chicago, prompting J. Edgar Hoover to advise the State Department to investigate Paul under Executive Order 10450. One agent suddenly said he thought Paul was a homosexual. Before he could respond, the other challenged him: "So, how about it?"

Paul sat in stunned silence for a moment before he burst out laughing. He asked from whom the agents had received that information. According to the Constitution he had a right to be faced with his accuser, "so who <u>was</u> he (or she)?" Stonily, the agents responded that they could not reveal their source, but that Paul still had to answer. He told them, incredulously, he was married to Julia. "Male homosexuals often have wives," came the response.

The agents had no reason to think Paul was stepping out—a colleague had interviewed the concierge at the building where they had lived in Paris, and she relayed that Paul and Julia seemed devoted to each other because they were always together. But the agents still made him answer for why he had not married until he was forty-four. He was asked if he had ever seen a psychiatrist and he wondered, "for God's sake what is <u>that</u> supposed to prove?" The response was that it might be evidence of "some little homosexual leanings." Finally, when Paul thought they had exhausted the topic, he was given an order.

"Drop your pants."

Paul, flustered and humiliated, demanded to know if they thought they could tell by "just looking."

The interrogation went on for close to seven hours. Before the agents finished working Paul over, they asked about Morris Lewellyn Cooke—possibly, at that moment, with Bernard DeVoto. The agents battered Paul for more than an hour with questions about Cooke's ideas, projects, and whom he talked to. Paul said the eighty-five-year-old was not "an intimate friend."

Before leaving, Paul raised himself up and told the agents how shoddy they were. He was badly shaken and worried for his and Julia's future as he stayed in purgatory in a Washington hotel room awaiting a ruling on his loyalty. He filled a prescription for little orange sleeping pills he called "goldfish" and washed them down with Budweiser. "I have slept badly since leaving, nervous pressure I suppose," he wrote Julia. His blood pressure shot up, he suffered diarrhea, and he shed weight. He replayed his interrogation in his mind and wrote on hotel stationery that he assumed his investigators thought Cooke was a "socialist." (Julia immediately thought it was because of Cooke's criticism of the Bureau of Reclamation.) Paul wondered what he might have said differently. "If you want to have some verbal fun," he wrote Julia, "try to prove sometime to two FBI guys that you *aren't* a Lesbian. How do you prove it?"

"He is forever a marked man—and we are deeply marked in the soul," Julia fumed to Avis. After some breaths she decided her burden was a badge of honor—the Childs fought at Arques. "I am actually glad that it happened, as we are now active participants." She damned McCarran and McCarthy enablers for being "scared right down to the ends of their dribbling little one-syllable asses."

She sent Paul a very intimate inside reference, which, at that moment, he needed. Paul kept a small collection of pornographic drawings and for it he painted a contribution to symbolize his attraction to Julia. The couple's signature shorthand for the mutual, monogamous attraction that represented was a simple heart pierced with an arrow. Julia drew many for Paul after his curiously timed, psychosexual ordeal, and he thanked her for "those libidinous hearts at the ends of your letters, deeply stabbed by what appears to be a stiff cock."

The strangeness and nastiness of Paul's loyalty investigation left a psychic welt on the DeVotos. It could have seemed as if, just when Bernard DeVoto was inside Congress and progress was being made against the Echo Park Dam, McCarran lashed out from his place in eternity. When Avis learned the details—"M.L. Cooke, and homosexuality. My God"—the monster Bernard called "the conspiratorial mind" came for her too. She wondered if Paul was punished for "being so pally with the DeVotos."

Avis telephoned Paul, apologized she could not connect him with Bernard because he was sick and rushing back, and sent the first international cable of her life to Julia. Avis promised that if Paul lost his job she would "move heaven & earth" to find them a new home. Julia repeated that she wished she could have Bernard's guidance and perspective. Bernard got home and collapsed into bed for days with a relapse of high fever. As Avis nursed him through what he would call his "hexed" health, she told him the story and remembered him being "spellbound." When he read Julia's letter with the Cooke detail, he "nearly choked." It seemed Cooke was suspicious to McCarran's men because he fought against dam proponents, whom Julia called the "power boys." They had served on a new deficit-cutting commission led by Herbert Hoover and argued that federal irrigation costs could be repaid with hydroelectricity sales. "But isn't it infuriating?" Avis wrote.

Avis remembered that after Bernard's fever broke, he explained that if he were Paul, "he would fight it to his last breath and his last penny, and our children, and I, would have to take our chances." The Echo Park Dam and Paul's persecution were two fronts of Bernard's same eternal fight against McCarran-style demonization, division, and plunder. McCarthyism was a guillotine dangling over the national parks and the DeVotos' best friends. Bernard was fighting for them with all his strength, Avis let Julia know she supported him "100 percent," and she was doing everything she could too.

"Nobody has too small a job," Bernard told Avis, who told Julia, who did her part by mailing them authentic Frankfurters.

19

"The West Has Done It Once"

" 'GOOD GOD, DELIVER US,' I cried, 'Can he be retiring?'" wrote Agnes Gray of Binghamton, New York, in early November 1955. "What a profound relief, then, to discover that this is but an anniversary."

As the Echo Park Dam approached its moment of truth in Congress, jolts of panic excited DeVoto Nation when the November 1955 *Harper's* appeared because it contained news of a milestone that was misinterpreted as retirement. It carried Bernard DeVoto's 241st consecutive "Easy Chair"; he had held the position for twenty years, written 800,000 words (about six books' worth), never missed a deadline, and made heroic saves of public lands and civil liberties. "No one has got me to say anything I did not want to say and no one has prevented me from saying anything I wanted to," he concluded. "No one knows better than a journalist that his work is ephemeral . . . it is not important, it is only indispensable."

A relieved and exultant nation poured in hosannas. "Long live Benny!" wrote H. S. Wagner of Akron, Ohio. John Oakes, of the *New York Times*, wrote, "This is a good chance to tell you how much—and how long—I have admired your articles in *Harper's* and elsewhere on the conservation issue." Alice Northrup, seventy-four, of Los Angeles, sent the first fan letter of her life to tell Bernard "what I like most about your writing, besides its humor, is that it is so apparently effortless." Charles Eggert of Barrytown, New York, wrote *Harper's*, "You have on your staff one of the very few voices who cry out in defense of sound conservation, the wilderness, and our National Park System—Bernard DeVoto." Senator Neuberger wrote from Oregon, "I do not see how you keep up the writing pace but we certainly need you at this juncture in history."

Rumors of his demise were not the only Twain allusions that Bernard might have sensed. He was Tom Sawyer at his own funeral at a dinner party thrown for him in New York City on the fourth weekend of October to celebrate his twenty-year anniversary and the release of a book-length anthology of his columns, *The Easy Chair*.

Avis loved dressing up for a night on the town. Loyalty investigators had cleared Paul Child earlier in the month, so she excitedly shared every detail with Julia. Twenty Tribe of Benny members—all editors, writers, and other friends—filled the wine room at The Pierre on Fifth Avenue. Avis wore a Harvey Berin dress made of velvety red wool broadcloth with three-quarter tight sleeves, deep scoop neckline, empire waistline, and tight sheathe skirt. "Very dashing and I have not felt so fashionable in many years." Their friends raised toasts and orated tributes that were probably saltier and more specific versions of what was written on the book jacket: "His attacks on the conspiracy of private interests to usurp the public lands have done much to arouse general concern for our natural resources; his consistent defense of the Bill of Rights has brought him denunciation from some notorious public figures." Guest John Fischer, a *Harper's* editor, wrote in the November issue: "'I suppose,' a reader commented recently, 'that DeVoto is so interested in conservation because he feels that the more he sees of people, the more he wants to preserve the grizzly bear' . . . when something he believes in is threatened, he does resemble a mother grizzly."

To the chuckling and cheering crew, immaculately formal waiters drizzled Beaujolais and dispensed foie gras, truffles, lobster bisque, an entrée of guinea hen in white wine sauce with string beans and wild rice, and a desert of bombe made of cake crust, ice cream, raspberry ice, and chocolate sauce. The only mortifying part for Avis was she was called to make a speech. She rose and spoke in a quiet voice, and no record exists of what she said, but it may have been an update of what Bernard affectionately wrote in 1926: "She studies, besides, and runs our small apartment with the utmost efficiency—and has never been cured of the delusion that I am destined for great things." Avis's recollection of her speech was "I about died and don't know what I said but apparently it was all right." She remembered the way Bernard grinned afterward. "B. was an absolute twit."

Harper's and Houghton Mifflin jointly put them up in a hotel. The last time the DeVotos found themselves in such a romantic situation was July 1955 when they drove to Fort Ticonderoga for research and their car tossed a tire in rural Vermont and gave them the unexpected pleasure of having to wait two days in a country cabin for a replacement brake drum. There were amorous intimations in Avis's report to Julia that they spent their time enjoying each other's private company with "plenty of reading matter <u>and</u> a bottle of whiskey." It can be presumed their New York City night was as nice.

Bernard was far less excited to make a return trip to New York City three weekends later. But a development in the Echo Park Dam made it urgent.

The fate of the dam came to hinge on Utah senator Arthur Watkins. Watkins presided over a miniature version of McCarran's old Western Bloc that met in Denver on November 1 to strategize how to keep the dam. Watkins had always been the dam's most rigid advocate. He had also been in such ideological alignment with McCarran that he loyally served beside him on the McCarran Committee. "We were in opposite parties, of course, but in many ways alike," remembered Watkins, a rancher and a Mormon elder.

But in 1953, Watkins publicly fell out with McCarran and their estrangement only grew. With Eisenhower's support, Watkins had introduced the

Refugee Relief Act to allow 120,000 displaced persons into America. *Time* reported that when McCarran found out, he "showered Watkins with such abuse that Watkins turned pale and finally became ill." Watkins went on to lead the committee that recommended censuring McCarthy, who insulted him as an "unwitting handmaiden" of Communists and a "coward."

Watkins arrived at the Denver meeting aching to keep the Echo Park Dam, but he left understanding that if he did not let it go he risked losing the entire Colorado River Storage Project. Three main environmental lobbying groups agreed to support the Colorado River Storage Project *if* Dinosaur National Monument remained untouched, and they came to represent the bulk of Bernard DeVoto's great conservation coalition. However, Bernard's deficit hawk faction, with Moley at the helm, opposed the *entire* project.

Bernard and the Sierra Club's David Brower cranked up the pressure on Watkins in two distinct but related ways. Brower figured out that another dam in the Colorado River Storage Project was needless. The Glen Canyon Dam did not have to be built because the same amount of water it would store could be saved by simply lining irrigation ditches or having Los Angeles treat its wastewater. Comparable amounts of electricity could be generated at new coal- or nuclear-powered plants. Brower had visited Glen Canyon, and his reaction was like that of artist Georgia O'Keeffe, who would make it her painting muse. To shield it from inundation like Dinosaur National Monument, Brower called to make Glen Canyon a national park. Bernard's corollary was that the entire Colorado River Storage Project ought to be scrapped and every part of it reexamined based on the gross mathematical errors that were found by putting a magnifying glass to just the Echo Park Dam. Watkins realized his side was beaten and needed to cut a deal fast. He feared that if in early 1956 the Senate did not pass the House version of the Colorado River Storage Project—which excluded the Echo Park Dam—Bernard DeVoto would win, and the West would lose additional dams.

But President Eisenhower stood in the way. Through his interior secretary, Douglas "Giveaway" McKay, Eisenhower still supported the Echo Park Dam. A plain reason was that it was in line with what Bernard called the Eisenhower administration's "one-way partnership" governance. McKay had approved Idaho Power ("Idaho" meaning eastern shareholders) to build dams at three easily accessible sites on the Snake River in Hells Canyon. McKay also approved the Bureau of Reclamation building dams on the hard-to-reach Green River in Dinosaur National Monument. Therefore, at public sites where a private company could build dams for profit, the administration gave lands away; at public sites where no private company could build dams for profit, taxpayers would build them. The Eisenhower administration's stance ensured that the flow of wealth went one way.

There was another rumored reason for Eisenhower's reluctance to kill the Echo Park Dam. He wanted to give it to Watkins as a way of saying thank you for standing up against McCarran and McCarthy. Privately, Eisenhower loathed McCarthyism. But when it came to McCarthy himself, Eisenhower believed it would diminish his dignity to speak out. "I will not get in the gutter with that guy." What Eisenhower had wanted was for some other prominent Republican—any other—to show courage in resisting McCarthyism. That person, despite his years of dutiful abetting on the McCarran Committee, turned out to be Watkins. But it meant that McCarthyism put Dinosaur National Monument in a no-win situation. The Echo Park Dam would either be built to appease McCarthy's allies, or it would be built in gratitude to one senator who stood up to him. Publisher Alfred Knopf sent a letter to Bernard expressing his incredulity at the entire national park system being trapped in a catch-22. "This is a lulu."

Bernard devised a secret campaign to fight the palace intrigue keeping the Echo Park Dam alive. Starting in mid-November, he scheduled meetings in Washington, DC, with high-ranking members of the Democratic National Party to discuss his vision for the 1956 presidential election. Bernard wanted Adlai Stevenson to champion the basic idea that American land and its resources belonged to all the people and were not to be funneled by the government into the hands of a politically connected few. Under Eisenhower, subsidizing bankrupt irrigation with private hydropower allowed the Bureau of Reclamation to justify a building spree. Even the appearance of how the Echo Park Dam was approved looked terrible politically; in contrast to Stevenson's grassroots conservation education in Montana, Eisenhower had flown in a plane high over Dinosaur National Monument and agreed to the dam. Bernard wanted the next campaign to be about stopping the giveaways. He wanted Stevenson to run on re-empowering Morris Llewellyn Cooke's old Rural Electrification Administration. He wanted to return its authority to judge dams on the basis of providing lowest-cost hydroelectricity to local residents, rather than to subsidize wasteful irrigation.

In conjunction, Bernard found an opportunity to rise above the political fray. Since visiting Mesa Verde National Park, he had searched for a chance to tell the story of the Ancestral Puebloan people to a mass audience. He believed the parable of a civilization in the American West that vanished when its water ran out would shift public opinion regarding the Colorado River Storage Project toward caution, conservation, and preservation.

On the Sunday before his scheduled meetings in Washington, DC, Bernard was booked to appear at CBS Studios in Manhattan to star on the program "Adventure," a collaboration with the American Museum of Natural History. The subject of that week's show was Mesa Verde National Park, and the producers asked Bernard to tell its story. It was the chance he had been waiting for: to share his message that only with nuclear bombs could humankind hurt itself as terribly as by mistreating the environment. Despite how ill he felt, he would embark on another journey, this one to work a strategy he hoped would finally make Eisenhower take a stand.

Though Bernard had come to hate traveling alone, it was decided that Avis would skip this trip. But they reserved a hotel room in Chicago for the summer of 1956 so they could both attend the Democratic National Convention, where Bernard was expected to write the natural resources plank of the party platform. For the time being, Avis would rest a little from her husband's overwhelming presence and then miss it. "I frequently feel as if I were tied to the tail end of a comet," she had told Julia.

"But I must admit I have never had a dull moment." She would look forward to resuming their thirty-three-year conversation. "He can cast such light into dark places and he is <u>always right</u>. About politics, I hasten to add in a wifely way."

Bernard wrote his feelings for Avis in private, effusive letters that she cherished (variations of his 1923 declaration: "She is courage, faith, certainty. And — God help me — by some miracle I mean the same to her"). His public expressions of love were more generalized, but still heartfelt. Picture Avis in his article "The Life and Wife of a Writer" in the April 1949 *Woman's Day.* "The wives of all the writers I know, let me say right here, are helpmeets, family stabilizers, brighter and pleasanter than their husbands, beautiful, compellingly attractive, dressed with incredible smartness on the pittances allowed them for clothes, the admiration and desire of the world."

Bernard's mail in the buildup to his November 13 television broadcast shows his focus becoming laser-like. His mission is to eliminate the Echo Park Dam and fire conservation back to national prominence in the 1956 presidential election.

Bernard writes senators and urges them to reread their colleague Kennedy's speech about wasteful western dams. He agitates for dedicating a Wounded Knee National Historical Monument in South Dakota, and he ridicules a propagandist for logging in Olympic National Park in Washington State who has threatened to "take the first plane to Boston to punch DeVoto in the nose." ("If you were as familiar as he is with some of the recent assaults on the national parks — particularly Echo Park — I think you would understand his point of view," Bernard's editor at *Harper's* scolds the belligerent.)

On October 27, less than three weeks before the broadcast, the DeVotos host the president of the Dinosaur National Monument Council, Ansel Adams, for dinner. ("I should imagine that Benny is in the thick of things," goes that day's letter to Avis from Julia.) Two days later, Oregon senator Richard Neuberger confidently tells Bernard that when Adlai Stevenson is elected, "You are my candidate for either Secretary of the Interior or Secretary of Agriculture." On November 7, Alfred Knopf anxiously prods for Bernard's take on Colorado River Storage Project developments. "What do you think of Echo Park now?" Two days before the broadcast, Arthur Carhart, one of Bernard's great western sources, writes that New Mexico senator Clinton Anderson "publicly renounced intentions of trying to put through Echo Park dam . . . Have you folks got enough chili rojo?"

On Saturday, November 12, a day after Bernard has left for New York City, Avis writes to Chet Olsen, their longtime Forest Service source in Ogden. Her reflective letter follows two of Bernard's from earlier in the month asking for conservation ideas to bring to Washington, DC. And telling Olsen that he has just drafted an autobiographical chapter for *The Western Paradox* about his conservation awakening: surviving the terrifying Wasatch Range flood with Avis in 1925, on land that Olsen healed with the CCC in the 1930s. Avis muses about the future of her marriage and how her love might grow; she dreams that age will plant Bernard more often beside her garden. "He did admit on a few occasions this summer when we were relaxing after dinner out in the back yard that it had become quite a pleasant place, and once in a while he strolls out and asks what I am doing. So I have hopes, though not to the extent that he will ever pull a weed or lift a spade."

She knows her hopes are for another day. DeVoto, fifty-eight, is the same age as Ahab when he last heaved out, harpoon in hand. But the simile Avis thinks of with her husband and his dam is not a man against a whale. She thinks of him as like the sea itself, unstoppable. "I would sooner try to interfere," Avis tells Julia, "than with the actions of the tides."

The fat *New York Times* that thudded on doorsteps and in newsstands around the nation on Sunday, November 13, 1955, carried a hefty story about the Colorado River Storage Project. It explained the Eisenhower administration's intransigence on the Echo Park Dam and stated, "Conservationists cannot yet be sure of final victory." When Bernard DeVoto would appear on *Adventure* to tell the story of the vanished Ancestral Puebloans, there would be no mistaking his allegory.

At precisely 3:30 p.m. Eastern Standard Time, in pulses of gray light tinted with sepia, his face flashed on television screens across America. With his deep, rattling baritone that was perfect for broadcast journalism, and his black disk eyes holding contact with the camera, he delivered his parable. He spoke of how the Ancestral Puebloans, like modern Western-ers, constructed cities, built dams, irrigated farmland, clear-cut forests, damaged watersheds, grew prosperous, developed trade networks, art, weapons, architecture, new technologies. Then the climate warmed, and the droughts struck. "Several thousand Indians were forced to evacuate the land," Bernard said. "Today, if man is improvident enough to deplete his resources, the price will be catastrophic."

Bernard had rehearsed not only the script but also the choreography required of that early live television broadcast, and he hit all his marks ex-pertly. Onto the screen, as Bernard's voice was heard, flashed video foot-age of Mesa Verde. To further dramatize his words, park archaeologists had built dioramas, and an early television special effect "peopled" them with shadows. A lone actor played an Ancestral Puebloan cliff dweller going about daily life, gathering food, observing religious rites, watching the weather — all before the catastrophe.

A few close viewers detected signs of fatigue in the shadows under Bernard's eyes and sun-spotted skin that hung on his face like a too-large topcoat, and the grind in his throat. But all were impressed by his per-formance. As the show ended, he spoke directly to host Charles Colling-wood about the danger of cancerous overdevelopment of dry country.

"What would we do if the valleys of Southern California, already severely short of water, were parched for twenty four years as the Mesa Verde was parched? Where would we evacuate the millions of people who live there? And it's no fantasy, Charles. The West has done it once. It can do it again."

Inside the studio, after filming wrapped, hearty cheers sounded. The show's producer remembered it was a triumph. "There were many calls of congratulations while we were still in the studio." Bernard joined the CBS crew for a celebratory drink in a bar. The producer noticed that he was happy but tired.

Avis would have been able to turn off her television and rest easy despite her ongoing concern for his health; he had met up with his friend Herbert Scheinberg, the medical doctor and amateur videographer who had accompanied him in Montana with Adlai Stevenson in 1954. Bernard did not intend to stay long at the bar, for he had an interview scheduled in Washington, DC, the next morning for what he promised would be a "controversial" new national parks article. Scheinberg walked Bernard back to his room at the Gotham Hotel as a gesture of friendship and they extended their tipsy reminiscing, surely about their trip to the grove of red cedars in the Bitterroot Mountains.

An attack of nausea suddenly overwhelmed Bernard around 6 p.m., followed by excruciating torso pain. He collapsed on the bed and assumed it was a particularly awful gastrointestinal malady—perhaps from the previous day's lunch at Reuben's Restaurant, followed by the heartburn of watching on TV as Harvard's football team lost to Brown (a "moral victory," he called it). The doctor felt Bernard's pulse change and said, suddenly sober, "I think we'd better get you over to the hospital."

"It's bad, isn't it?"

Bernard was in agony and Scheinberg kept stoic during the ambulance ride. The driver did not flick on the siren to cut through thick midtown traffic, and Bernard was furious that there was nothing onboard to ease his pain. "Why don't you damn docs carry a needle with you?" Finally, when they arrived at Presbyterian Hospital, he was shot with morphine. Laid on a bed in the hospital's bright, antiseptic bowels, Bernard began to fall unconscious. He was fighting for his life against something far more serious than indigestion. Scheinberg had suspected immediately, from the changes in Bernard's pulse, that the symptoms were those of a dissecting aortic aneurysm. The heart's main artery tearing open in 1955, Scheinberg knew, was completely, and in every instance, fatal. Scheinberg lacked the heart to tell Bernard.

It is unknown whether Avis had been alerted when at 8:15 p.m. Scheinberg felt Bernard's blood pressure skyrocket. Bernard demanded to know what it meant, then he gasped and stopped breathing. Doctors stabbed a needle full of adrenaline deep into his chest and restarted his heart. His

EKG began to blip again. Bernard opened his eyes and whirled them around, but immediately he slipped into unconsciousness again. The blips grew faint, then erratic, then stopped. Bernard DeVoto was pronounced dead at 8:30 p.m.

Avis surely shook and wept with Mark and Gordon when she heard the news. The family was devastated. Layered on the pain, Avis felt a terrible guilt that she was not by his side. She felt as if her own heart imploded. Her only scintilla of relief was learning from Scheinberg how Bernard felt when he died. "Far from being panicked or frightened, B. was just tearing mad at the last," Avis understood. It gave her solace to know that he left the world in the throes of the emotion that was most comfortable to him.

Across the country the news spread by wire through chilly darkness, and DeVoto Nation mourned. Inside the *Chicago Sun Times,* hard-bitten newspapermen quit clacking their typewriters and hung their heads in a moment of mourning. "Their guy was gone," a reporter wrote. A woman who heard the news on the radio in Boston remembered, "I reached over to my bed side table picked up my rosary and said one for Benny." Adlai telegraphed Avis, "THIS IS ONE OF THE SADDEST DAYS OF MY LIFE." Julia wrote, "I just can't believe that My Hero, whom I have loved and enjoyed for so many years, is gone." From the biggest stock growers associations in Wyoming—whose leaders once joked about triggering Bernard to burst a blood vessel—there was no reaction. But a rancher from Colorado who had come to love Bernard cried, "HOWL DOGS! A wolf is dead."

On Monday, November 14, 1955, Bernard's "Easy Chair" column arrived in the mail at *Harper's,* the last installment of a twenty-year streak. On November 15, his funeral was held at Christ Church in Cambridge and its pews were packed with hundreds of mourners from Boston, New York, and Washington. Wrapped in black, Avis kept so composed that she heard from a friend "you really have strength beyond strength." Mark DeVoto curated the music, Arthur Schlesinger Jr., Lovell Thompson, and Theodore Morrison served as ushers, and the boxy pews shivered with weeping Tribe of Benny members. There was no casket.

Before cremation, DeVoto's body underwent an autopsy to confirm what killed him. It revealed that the relative swiftness of his burst aorta was a mercy. Prostate cancer had already wreaked a different havoc on his body, so advanced that he would have lived no more than two years, and in agony.

Conservationist, historian, friend, teacher, freethinker, fighter, patriot, partner: Bernard DeVoto left the world at his most himself. Had he lived a few more days he would have learned what became of his last campaign.

"A Victory for Bernard DeVoto," proclaimed headlines eighteen days after the *Adventure* coup de grâce. The United Press article datelined from Washington, DC, on December 1, 1955, explained: "Interior Secretary McKay announced today that he was dropping the controversial $176,400,000 Echo Park Dam from the Upper Colorado River Storage Project. Bernard DeVoto would have liked reading this news."

In the five years since DeVoto wrote "Shall We Let Them Ruin Our National Parks?" he chopped and sliced all meaningful support away from the Echo Park Dam. He hammered home its financial cost, engineering errors, factional tensions, and the way it undermined the National Park Service. The climactic defector in his lifetime was Utah's Senator Watkins. Then, DeVoto Nation, in mourning, impressed itself on the Eisenhower administration. "I, like countless thousands of other readers, have lost a friend and gallant spokesman," wrote a woman in Tigard, Oregon. "Few have had a keener perception of Truth," added a man in Colorado Springs. DeVoto gave "battle to the range robbers, the water wasters, and the land-looters of the West," saluted a Sacramento man. "Most poignant loss many of us who love America have had to sustain in many years," came a voice from Tryon, North Carolina. Amid the groundswell of emotion from the country's grassroots, even Giveaway McKay could no longer justify the Echo Park Dam. The coast-to-coast celebrations of DeVoto's life were the death knell for the dam and a rebirth of the country's commitment to the national parks idea.

"What a pity Benny did not live long enough to enjoy the good news,"

Alfred Knopf wrote Avis. E. B. White of *The New Yorker* observed, "Your husband would be the last man to avoid a good clean fight merely because he happened to be dead."

Though Avis's heart was shattered, she could take great pride in the victory. It meant that the wild Green and Yampa Rivers would keep flowing together unobstructed where their canyons converge at Echo Park in Dinosaur National Monument. It meant that the mission of the National Park Service, to leave landscapes untouched by industrial development, "unimpaired for the enjoyment of future generations," was inviolate. Water would continue to swan-dive freely over the Great Falls of the Yellowstone; a full mile of cliff would continue rising from river to rim in the Grand Canyon; the forested valley by which wolves crossed from Canada to America on the edge of Glacier National Park would never be blocked; Mammoth Cave would not be flooded; nor would Civil War battlefields; nor shining Sierra slopes in Kings Canyon. There would be no clear-cuts in Olympic National Park, no oil drilling in Theodore Roosevelt National Park, no cattle herds stomping through Grand Teton National Park, no sugar plantations in Everglades National Park, no sheep grazing in Yosemite National Park. The decision to keep national parks sacrosanct impacted all other public lands; the wildlife refuges and national monuments and the 230 million acres of forests and grasslands and deserts and canyonlands that the DeVotos saved in the 1940s. They would not be put on sale. Fans wrote Avis that the preservation of the wild was Bernard's true memorial. "I wish he could have had ten or fifteen more years, because he had so much to do that we need," she said. "But he got quite a bit done."

On April 11, 1956, President Eisenhower, tanned, smiling, recovered from a recent heart attack, gave an impromptu morning press conference in the middle of a weeklong golf vacation in Augusta, Georgia, and signed the Colorado River Storage Project. It was far from a perfect bill, pork-laden, wasteful, setting up generations of water wars and over-allocation of the river. But because of Bernard DeVoto, it would build four instead of six large dam units. Howard Zahniser of the Wilderness Society had the honor of writing the clause that stated: "no dam or reservoir constructed under the authorization of the Act shall be within any National Park or Monument."

Zahniser immediately furthered Bernard DeVoto's legacy by launching the campaign that would be the next great crusade for the conservationists who fought the Echo Park Dam. National parks became swarmed as tourist playgrounds, exploited for recreation. Likewise with national forests and grasslands, which were also managed for logging, grazing, and mining. What they all shared in common was they were valued for their *use* to people, there was no official designation for land independent of extractive use by modern humankind. On the same day Eisenhower signed the bill, Zahniser sent a letter to key members of Congress asking them to sponsor legislation creating a system of wilderness areas. It would take nine years of negotiations. Numerous drafts were needed to work around moribund water laws set, naturally, by McCarran. But what began on that day, when the torch of the DeVotos' crusade was passed, became the Wilderness Act of 1964. By the end of the first quarter of the twenty-first century, nearly 110 million acres of land, approximately 5 percent of the nation, were set aside to not be exploited by any industry; the values of openness, remoteness, silence, biodiversity, and nature for nature's sake were given standing under US law.

Avis received an especially touching tribute from Julia Child's in-laws. They recognized that everything Bernard DeVoto accomplished, she accomplished too. "Your personal sorrow must be, and I know will be, mitigated by the thought that the Team—for you were a team—has now done its work."

But Avis was not done. She was convulsed with sorrow, and would have to figure out how to live without Bernard. Her best friend knew how to help.

PART III

After great pain, a formal feeling comes—
The Nerves sit ceremonious, like Tombs

—Emily Dickinson

20

Descent to Earth

IN LATE SPRING 1956 Avis tied on a white apron, pulled her dark hair back in a low bun, and faced Julia Child across a white countertop filled with silver pots and wooden cutting boards inside an airy, sunlit Le Cordon Bleu kitchen in Paris. The Childs had sent Avis tickets to spend therapeutic time cooking with them, to begin forging the next part of her life. "This trip is a present from some friends who live in Europe, and I never heard of a nicer one," Avis explained. "It's going to save my life and I hope to be a new woman when I return."

As soon as she landed in London, Avis had a heartwarming reunion with the Childs. She did not have to worry about her sons, who supported her emotionally and promised to take care of themselves. Avis described the conundrum swamping her in shock and sorrow. "I have to face the fact that the center and reason of my whole life is just not here, and what becomes of me anyway?" Julia sympathized, wondering if perhaps Bernard DeVoto died from being "especially tired." Avis's time with the

Childs so dazzlingly bombarded all of her senses that her shell of misery was pierced.

They visited Westminster Abbey, then shared bread, cheese, ham, and beer at Prospect of Whitby, a pub from the 1600s on a brick terrace overlooking the Thames. Avis smelled lilacs, pansies, tulips, bluebells, and forget-me-nots in the lush gardens at Hampton Court. They listened to a choir at King's Chapel in Cambridge and then indulged their eyes on the Elizabethan grandeur of Burghley House in Stamford. They went south, sharing plenty of wine and laughs, and stood atop the White Cliffs of Dover.

On a ferry they crossed the strait to Calais, France, and climbed in the Childs' automobile marked "Corps Diplomatique." Through blazing yellow fields of colza they drove to Amiens, where Julia picked up duck pâté made by the same family since 1634, and they popped champagne to celebrate Avis's fifty-second birthday. In the city of Rouen, they went to the Hôtel de Dieppe, met Simca (who called Avis "quelle chic mammy"), and had an exquisite meal of pressed duck. "It was a poem," Avis remembered. The company was pure delight. They slept in a country inn with a thatched roof in Vieux-Port, a village on the Seine, after a meal of potato leek soup, roasted chicken, cheese, and apple cider. They picnicked the next afternoon on wine, cheese, French bread, and roasted duck from a charcuterie on a hillside blooming with laburnum overlooking the ruins of an abbey in the medieval town of Jumièges. Avis savored every detail —suppressing the pity she felt that Bernard, who never left the North American continent—could not share this with her.

In Paris they dined at Les Deux Magots, L'Escargot, Le Vert Galant, La Méditerranée, La Truite. They tasted snails, sole Normande, pâté maison, and veal in cream, all while sitting at sidewalk tables where they watched the world go by. They visited the Palace of Versailles, the Gothic Sainte-Chapelle, and the Louvre Museum, with an empty courtyard out front like a blank canvas.

Julia introduced Avis to her favorite Parisian markets, to her co-authors, and to master chef Max Bugnard, whom she called her "guiding spirit." Bugnard, sixty-five, a round man with a silver handlebar mustache, round glasses, and an immaculately white hat shaped like a mushroom, taught at Le Cordon Bleu and had himself been taught by the legendary French chef Auguste Escoffier. Avis was bestowed the role of sous-chef to the two French cooking masters as they catered a luncheon at an event space called Electric Light Company: rougets (red mullet) stuffed with vegetables, cheese, and anchovies, and a main course of duck roasted with cherries. The trio also catered a party inside a modest private apartment, and then another inside an opulent mansion on Rue du Faubourg Saint-Honoré. Avis would watch in awe as Bugnard painted a cake like it would hang on a wall.

Inside the Cordon Bleu kitchen, Bugnard confided in Avis that Julia —stirring sauce in a silver pan and wearing a white short-sleeved blouse with four loops of pearls around her neck—was the most brilliant student he ever had. Avis got a deeper understanding of the educational lineage Julia was bringing to her cookbook and how revolutionary it would be for secrets of French cooking to be taught to the world by an American woman.

With Avis having no more Bernard DeVoto books ever to partner on, Julia's project would take on oversize significance in her life. Bernard had been dead only a few days when Avis, in a rare and prescient moment of crystal clarity as she spiraled through her despair, promised Julia "one thing certain—proof-read the cookbook like mad." Committing herself to helping Julia would be a way for Avis to honor her partnership with Bernard, be part of a new team, and have a lifeline to hold on to as she processed her grief.

Meanwhile, over in America, other people were still processing Bernard's life and death too, often in divergent ways.

Before Avis left for Europe, she went to the Capitol building in Washington, DC, at the invitation of Oregon senators Richard Neuberger and Wayne Morse and Montana representative Lee Metcalf so they could salute her family legacy. "No person in America had done more to help save the vast resources of the Pacific Northwest than Bernard DeVoto," Neuberger said for the *Congressional Record*. "Forests, rivers, meadows, mountains, wildlife—he stood between them and those who would do the looting and exploiting." Neuberger added that "the Western outdoors" was a "monument" and a "living memorial" to both DeVotos. Avis received the politicians' tributes dutifully, though it was exactly the type of spotlight she abhorred, and Neuberger's flowery terms made her "want to upchuck."

Adlai Stevenson asked if Avis would step into Bernard's role and advise him on conservation for his presidential run. Avis said she wanted "no part of public life," and specified "I am no more equipped to be Mrs. Pinchot than I am to be Marilyn Monroe." However, through the chairman of the Democratic Committee, Avis gave Stevenson names of men Bernard thought should work on public power. Neuberger asked Avis about Eisenhower's pending appointment to the Interior Department of Wesley D'Ewart, the former Montana representative whom Bernard had voiced opposition to just days before he died. On Avis's advice, Neuberger blocked the appointment.

The only work with DeVoto's conservation network that gave Avis peace was arranging that his ashes be sent directly from New York City to Chet Olsen in Ogden. "Chet I hope you know that Benny was happier and more at ease and functioned better when he was with the Forest Service, you and all the others, than any other time. You were all his kind of people when sometimes the literary or the political or the academics were not. This is the truth."

Olsen couriered the ashes to Missoula and on April 6, 1956, boarded a small plane donated from Johnson Flying Service. He winged south and west for "Operation Lochsa," inspired by DeVoto's musing that the red cedars would be fine company "if working journalists are rewarded on the far shore." It was the first bluebird-sky day of the year and the snow on the Bitterroot Mountains was immensely white and the silence was awesome. "Not a creature was stirring as the plane flew over the course," Olsen reported. Pilot Bob Fogg placed his hand atop Olsen's on the box of ashes and said, "Before God as captain of this ship I and you return this man to the land he loved." A small cloud flew out over the evergreen immensity and Olsen sent a quiet message to Avis, who had asked, "Just say Mission accomplished because God knows I don't want any hoorah."

In a moment of symbolism, she added to the ash collection by setting ablaze in her home fireplace a pair of letter collections that reflected Bernard's two great loves. One was all of their letters to each other, the other was most of his letters with Forest Service men. The former to protect intimacy, the latter to protect sources.

The excitable Neuberger blew the cover of Operation Lochsa by announcing it on the Senate floor and introducing a bill to rename the federal landscape the "Bernard DeVoto National Forest." It was killed by his devious colleague Herman Welker, whose comment in an article headlined "Idaho Sen. Welker Protests Naming Forest for DeVoto" was "If they are such great conservationists—why don't they join the Idaho Republican delegation and unanimously agree to building dams." It would remain the Clearwater National Forest. For once, Avis agreed with Little Joe from Idaho. "Though DeVoto is a pretty name, as names go, and certainly prettier than Neuberger, still, Clearwater is a perfectly beautiful name for a forest."

Meanwhile, the FBI began collecting Bernard DeVoto death notices as soon as they appeared. J. Edgar Hoover was informed via memo on November 18, 1955. In one instance, Hoover angrily scribbled that an appreciative obituarist "places himself in the same class as DeVoto!" Bernard was taken off the "Do Not Contact List" fifteen days after his death, but the FBI was not finished with him. An agent noted in spring 1956 that Montana representative Lee Metcalf had praised Bernard. In 1959, a sycophantic writer for *True Detective* pre-submitted for FBI approval an article warning of a new generation of "DeVotos at work." They were all, said the writer, "communist." For libel-dodging purposes, Hoover lieutenant Lou Nichols advised it be switched to "apologists of communism."

"Your suggested change was a wise one and I'm glad you noticed it," Hoover said.

• • •

As Avis continued her European travels, riding with the Childs through the Ardennes Forest in Belgium and having a drink in Liège, she tried to keep sorrow out of her mind. They crossed into Germany at Aachen and saw the Marshall Plan in action, rebuilding factories, farms, railroads. Avis listened to Julia say with suspicion exceeding exasperation that she still had yet to meet "one single person who had any use for Hitler! It was always somebody else." The women walked the banks of the Rhine in Bonn and saw rubble everywhere. At a restaurant called Im Stiefel they sampled eight kinds of sausages paired with mashed potatoes, sauerkraut, and beer. The Childs took Avis to the extravagant Petersburg Hotel for a rich lunch of foie gras. Avis bought wooden potato mashers and metal lemon juicers as gifts. In the Childs' apartment, Julia cooked Avis French chicken.

They returned to Paris for one more dinner out, at Le Grand Véfour, decorated in the same French neoclassical style as when it opened in 1784. They sat at a table with pink and pale-yellow roses and Noël Coward was beside them. They ate shrimp and thick chateaubriand steak in béarnaise sauce, drank two wines plus a Sauterne for dessert. They shared one more homemade dinner; over many hours Julia cooked Avis shrimp in Normande sauce served in a big scallop shell with a roasted fillet of beef that had been marinated in truffles. The Childs drove Avis to Dusseldorf and they sat in a bar drinking beer near the airport until it was time to hug and kiss goodbye. "What a wonderful trip. And what wonderful people," Avis wrote her parents. "Don't you think I'm lucky to know them?"

Stormy weather that forced Avis to land in Philadelphia instead of Boston might have served as a reminder that despite how lovingly she had been treated, "it doesn't make my descent to earth any easier."

She had been nonstop busy since Bernard died; she did not even miss a "Thrills and Chills" deadline. He was alive in her mind as she answered every wrought condolence letter. "Benny was more of a father to me than my own father," wrote Robert Lee of Iowa City. New Zealander Edgar Cone said he felt "as if I have lost a close friend." Joseph Kinsey Howard's mother wrote from Great Falls how she recognized Avis's anguish.

"The West and what it stands for has lost a champion," mourned Arthur Carhart. "I felt as if I had walked with him over the countryside," added O. D. Duncan of Stillwater, Oklahoma. Attorney Joseph Welch sent condolences. *Harper's* editor Russell Lynes sympathized about forwarding "a great many letters from people who have said in effect that they didn't know who else to write about Benny's death, had to write somebody."

Avis appreciated empathy from close friends, though it made her pain no easier to bear. "You were always so wonderful to him; how lucky he was to have you," wrote historian Catherine Drinker Bowen. "Oh Avis I bet that was no easy man to live with." "You always seemed to reinforce him, to emphasize him, and make him more than he otherwise would have been," wrote friends from Montreal. "I wish I could put my arms around you and keep this terrible thing away from you," added Helen Everitt, editor of *Ladies' Home Journal.* "Be solaced, dear Avis, by the connection of his great love and admiration for you," Katie Seeber wrote from Houghton, Michigan. "You and Benny were a devoted couple and you were a wonderful wife . . . You made him happy and were a great help to him."

The way Avis kept it together while Bernard's friends broke down was amazing, yet classically in character. His best friend, Garrett Mattingly, told her that he shed the only tears of his adult life not because of the news, but because Avis had the grace to call him personally. "I have never known anyone with a more gallant spirit than you." She understood the compliments but still felt guilty. "All loved Benny so much and transfer that devotion to me," she had cried to Julia. "But I should have been with him."

All Avis wanted to do was tell Benny about her trip, among "about eight thousand things I still wanted to talk to him about." She had been so busy and life was so surreal that she thought he would at any moment walk through their door, like he always had. It was not until she was back from Europe, alone at home, and he still didn't, that the most sorrowful bereavement of her life hit her like an avalanche.

• • •

On the bright 57-degree afternoon of October 12, 1957, Avis trundled past yellowed elms and bronzed oaks to join Mark DeVoto, a city councilwoman, and a gaggle of eager Boy Scouts at an overgrown, trash-strewn lot next to Cambridge Cemetery. One of Bernard DeVoto's last "Easy Chair"s, "Hell's Half Acre, Mass.," had been about a new frontier of conservation: making nature available in urban areas, which meant cleaning and protecting blighted lots. There came a groundswell—including a *Boston Herald* editorial—to save this "Hell's Half Acre" and possibly rename it "The DeVoto Memorial Nature Reservation." Avis conceded that would be "warming to our spirits," and Mark combed the landscape and helpfully made a botanical catalog. "There should be some place in Cambridge where people can go see goldenrod in bloom," Avis said.

The "Mrs. DeVoto wife of the DeVoto" that the Scouts saw that day was beautiful, proud, shy, stylish, opinionated, trim, with more gray in her hair and the same red on her lips, and hurting deliriously. "Great blank spaces inside me," she wrote Julia. She ricocheted around all the stages of grief. She denied Bernard was dead ("I feel he just went off into space"). She bargained for more time with him ("We were so terribly dependent on each other"). She was angry ("I am sick of myself, my house, my children, my life"). She grew so "damn depressed" she said her name should be "Old Mrs. Gloom." Each morning she woke up with her jaw sore from grinding teeth. She took phenobarbital four times a day to calm her stomach and she gobbled Bufferins for backaches until they made her ears ring. For sleep she gulped "the whiskey and the pills." She contemplated how she might overdose, or pass out with a lit cigarette while wrapped inside her electric blanket, one of the presents Bernard gave her for their last Christmas.

Gordon was twenty-six and Avis blamed herself for his struggles: he bounced out of school, between odd jobs and psychiatrists' offices, and always back grumpily to his childhood bedroom where he devoured comics and calculus books. Fortunately he had a wonderful relationship with Mark, an overachiever studying chemistry and music at Harvard. Avis had been surprised to learn that Bernard, all his adult life, quietly socked away every penny he could so that Gordon could get the medical care he needed, Mark could get the education he wanted, and Avis could keep their house. It was more than she imagined, however she would need money for food and bills. "My old man really took care of us, bless him," Avis told Julia. "Perhaps some day I will even learn to enjoy life without him, but it will take time."

To the Scouts' disappointment, Avis refused to take a role in trying to save Hell's Half Acre. She thought it would be improper if she lent the DeVoto name to it, as if that, and not the issue of conservation itself, should be a deciding factor. "Of course it would please me to have it in his name but it is not the important principle here."

Onward she went through her emotional half acre of hell.

Avis had collaborated on one book that won a Pulitzer and another that won a National Book Award, but she found herself, a widow, in her fifties, a single mother with a thin résumé, looking for her first salaried job. "You are so familiar with publishing and magazines and writers," Julia encouraged. Bernard's agent, Carl Brandt, suggested the *Boston Globe*'s "Thrills and Chills" columnist write her own mystery novels. Avis practically screamed. "I regard the writer's life with pure horror." She had loved being part of a writing *team*. She knew her strengths: conceptualizing, editing, proofreading, indexing, fact-checking, scouting.

Alfred Knopf knew them too. In September 1956, he gave Avis a prestigious job as his publishing house's only scout, and its only female employee above the rank of secretary (save for Knopf's wife and co-founder, Blanche). Knopf paid Avis $3,000 a year (which eased her financial worry after she rented three third-floor bedrooms to Harvard Law students for $50 each per month). Knopf provided Avis with health insurance, allowed her to work from home, and gave her an expense account to go winding down northeastern turnpikes, her hair wrapped in silk scarves, on author scouting trips. "It's a nice little boost to my faltering ego." Avis's direct boss became friendly, middle-aged William Koshland, who certainly remembered Bernard from the lavish meal they shared with Knopf in the Forest Service building beneath Pike's Peak. Avis went out for an introductory dinner with Koshland and discovered she felt "easy with him"; they had a lot to talk about because — as fate had it — he loved cooking too. When the meal was over, Avis had a surprising realization: he was the first man she had dined alone with since Bernard.

She scored early in 1957 by finding an author named Leonard Drohan, whose novel sending up civil service bureaucracy, *Come with Me to Macedonia,* had a scene where the hero gets drunk at a party and sings "Hooray, hooray for the first of May, outdoor screwing begins today." "Toots, I never laughed so hard in my life," Avis told Julia. Knopf telephoned and said, "Avis, you've done it again!" She crowed that she knew how to pick "a winnah."

Trusting Avis on cookbooks, Knopf sent them for her proofreading, editing, and assessment. One she liked was *Season to Taste* by Peggy Harvey. One she hated was *The Calorie Counter's Cookbook.* She was so offended she wrote the Kentuckian author a long letter saying it was foolish to substitute chemicals for "honest meat and vegetables and green salads and fruit." She expected she came across as "aggressive, opinionated and a terrible Eastern snob. I can't help it." Avis exhorted Blanche Knopf to sign English culinary star Elizabeth David. To Avis went the job of editing David's *Italian Food,* which was full of "booby traps," such as accounting for the two continents' different sizes of scallops and translating English measurements into cups and spoons. Avis relied on her and Bernard's experience smuggling imperial quarts of whiskey down from Canada during Prohibition to iron out the conversions. She sent David twenty-seven single-spaced pages of edits and explanations. They became good friends.

In early 1957 Avis, with trepidation, accepted an invitation to a dinner party. Adlai Stevenson, fresh from being trounced by Eisenhower again — surely he wondered if it could have been different if Bernard DeVoto had lived — ignored other guests and sought out her opinions, which was unexpectedly touching, and another boost to her confidence. In September 1957 she took a risk: she threw her first solo cocktail party. To her delight, neighbors came and enjoyed themselves: Arthur and Marian Schlesinger, McGeorge and Mary Bundy; all chatting, gossiping, laughing, tippling her old-fashioneds and snacking on her onion sandwiches, chicken liver pâté, and aspic with multicolored tomatoes from her garden. "My dears I felt for the first time that I can give a successful cocktail party without Benny and that people will come because they enjoy being here," she reported to the Childs. "This is sort of a milestone in my life."

She was still bitter at her husband's old enemies, but her wicked sense of humor shone through. Joe McCarthy made his final front-page headlines on May 3, 1957, by dying the day before at age forty-eight. "Hooray, hooray for the third of May, Joe McCarthy expired today," Avis chirped to the Childs. "I felt like running up the flag."

Between scouting for Knopf, writing her detective novel reviews, and proofreading for Houghton Mifflin on a freelance basis for $2 an hour, Avis earned $7,500 her first year—not including $2,500 in royalties from Bernard's books. But for as high as her Knopf job was in prestige and glamour, it was just as high in risk because it hinged on forces outside her control. She could know a book's quality but she could not predetermine its sales. Also, if no best-selling books happened to be written, she would be unable to sign them and—per mutual understanding—Knopf would have to fire her.

From Germany, Julia had asked Avis to read a draft of her chapter on poultry, which was more than a hundred pages long and took more than a year of work. Avis immediately bored down on the task—requiring the sharpest eye for detail, the most granular knowledge of grammar, and the highest emotional intelligence—to bring forth Julia's true literary voice. "You are learning and improving all the time," Avis would encourage, while warning against "turning adjectives into adverbs" because that would make Julia look "illiterate." She suggested Julia use more semicolons because "dashes always look breathless to me." Avis coached Julia on tone, not to use the word "persnickety," because it was a classic book, and should sound formal. But she lovingly sympathized with Julia's great challenge. "My God, I do appreciate your problems of text—how to be clear, lucid, readable and simple, without being dull."

Avis would request that Julia quantify the exact amount of water to use for Carolina Long Grain rice versus Uncle Ben's. She caught that Julia wrote two determiners: "the" and "your." "It sticks out on the page." Avis made other changes for clarity. "For coq au vin—change sentence about skim off fat—to, Skim off fat, and rapidly boil down cooking liquid." She streamlined and beautified the text by pointing out where Julia could save words and lose gangly hyphens. "I don't think you have to say <u>fresh</u> minced parsley, saving one word. And say ahead of time, not ahead-of-time." Avis conceded she was being a "fussy friend," but stood on principle. "Sloppy proofreading offends me."

Julia was overwhelmed but grateful. "My, as you said once, there are so many slips and errors, and dangling references, to be avoided." Avis explained she was just doing for "<u>our book</u>" what came naturally. "It is the kind of proofreading I did for Benny."

A decision Avis had been avoiding forced itself on her in the form of raffishly disheveled writer James Farrell, who sidled up so uncomfortably close the fumes on his breath assaulted her. Slurring and with tortoise-shell glasses crooked above his cleft chin, Farrell informed Avis that he was writing her husband's biography.

It was February 15, 1957, and they were inside the elegant Harmonie Club, a 107-year-old wood-paneled Jewish social club on the Upper East Side of Manhattan where the Knopfs threw a luncheon for eighteen employees and a few aspiring authors. Attentive waiters in crisp uniforms orbited the regal Knopfs, laying out a buffet of smoked salmon and sturgeon, oysters Rockefeller, hot clams and fried shrimp. The main course, Knopf explained, was "Kubialka," a piping puff pastry filled with sturgeon, vegetables, and hard-boiled eggs. "Alfred is absolutely lavish with food," Avis dished to Julia. "The only real palate in publishing."

Farrell was not the first author to seek Avis's blessing. The first would-be Bernard DeVoto biographer had propositioned her when Bernard had been dead barely six months. She knew the biography in the wrong hands would "destroy my peace of mind." Yet she considered it her duty to see to it that Bernard's story was told properly, not as hagiography, but certainly not as amateur or hatchet biography. She would want her own presence in the book to be as diminished as possible, and would insist on next to none for Gordon and Mark, to protect them while they were getting established in life. She exerted her influence by withholding cooperation. But writers of certain scruples could work around that, which is what she smelled on Farrell. He told a story about bedding a mutual friend and waved over the waiter for another drink.

Avis flashed her icy blues and caught Knopf's big browns in a knowing glance, and out flared the boss she called "the terrible tempered Mr. Bang."

"No more for you, Jim!" Knopf blared. "You've had enough. All you're going to get."

"Well, so no Farrell at Knopf's, I'm happy to say," Avis reported. "What a bastard."

It made her cast those blues with predilection on the writer she knew would do the job right, Wallace Stegner.

Avis had a special opportunity to beseech her old, dear friend Wallace Stegner in October 1960 when she was flown to California to preside at the grand opening of the Bernard DeVoto papers at Stanford University. Stegner founded its creative writing program and stage-managed the transfer of Bernard's papers. Avis was nervous; it was the first time she had traveled west since Bernard was alive. To her delight, she looked down and could recognize landmarks they had visited: Scott's Bluff, Boulder, the Great Salt Lake, the Bonneville Salt Flats, Bear Lake, the Sacramento River. "I was excited," she said.

Stegner knew those places too. He was on his way to being called "the Dean of Western Writers." Stegner had made his career by sharing themes, subjects, and insights with Bernard DeVoto. Stegner openly admitted the symbiosis. "We were both Westerners by birth and upbringing, novelists by intention, teachers by necessity, and historians by the sheer compulsion of the region that shaped us . . . The same compulsion that made amateur historians of us made us conservationists as well." But Stegner, though he felt, as Bernard did, that he was never given his due by eastern critics, had usurped his old mentor as the nation's recognized authority on the West. Stegner and Bernard DeVoto were so kindred in thought that whispers on citrusy Palo Alto breezes said Stegner was a Communist too.

Upon learning of Bernard's death, Stegner wrote Avis, "I owed him more than I owed anybody in the literary world." So, down palm tree–lined streets, Avis traveled to the Cecil H. Green Library where on display were nostalgic DeVoto mementos, his National Book Award, his copy of *Huckleberry Finn,* his Sierra Club lifetime membership card, his L'École des Trois Gourmandes lifetime membership card. Avis had given herself confidence by splurging on a $145 amethyst-colored, short-sleeved, satin dress with a scoop neck. ("Plain, but very knowing.") Afterward she joined an overflow crowd of more than two hundred in a Spanish-architecture lecture hall. Onstage she recognized—reading a telegram from Adlai Stevenson—the same hard-eyed, soft-voiced "Wally" whom DeVoto Dry martinis used to make twang his guitar and whoop cowboy songs in her backyard.

His hair was silver now, but still wavy and thick. Avis would remember that Stegner and his wife, Mary, treated her "as a monument." They hosted a dinner party for her at their modest home with big windows in the Los Altos Hills. Avis sat at Stegner's right hand and he toasted her. Avis made her pitch by letting it be known that, for him alone, she would cooperate. To emphasize how serious she was, she presented a gift of Julia-sourced knives.

He declined, in much the same way as he had when Avis asked him to finish *The Western Paradox,* the book Bernard was drafting when he died. Stegner wanted to write novels.

By that time, Avis had tiptoed back into the realm of romance. Arthur Maass was a kind, chivalrous professor with a neatly groomed beard who was thirteen years her junior. He taught government at Harvard and, as an expert on western dams, had been a Bernard DeVoto compatriot and admirer. Avis found his affection flattering and allowed herself on weekends to be taken out to dinners, operas, and the Boston Symphony in Maass's speedy Dauphine. For a time she called him her "sort of beau" and she liked his "good friendship and gentle flirtation" (she told Julia she missed sex). Maass was company, not a companion. Conversationally, he was dull and politically he drove Avis nuts. After he disparaged Adlai Stevenson, they drifted apart.

Of greater hurt was that *Come with Me to Macedonia,* the Leonard Drohan novel she scouted for Knopf, flopped. So did another Avis sign, *Home Is the Place,* a novel about prewar Germany by Stefanie Lauer. The light beside Avis's bed burned into the early hours of each morning as she consumed works by potential new authors, but by late 1957 she was panicking. "I have not read a passably good manuscript in months." By early 1958 she was wondering "why on earth he is employing me." Knopf informed her that he would no longer be. He was firing her, effective September 1.

Most upsetting was that Houghton Mifflin wavered on Julia Child. In early February 1958, Avis went to a party with editor Dorothy de Santillana and Paul Brooks, a company executive whom she found "in vino veritas." Avis proposed hosting a dinner in celebration of Julia and her co-author Simca Beck arriving later that month to hand-deliver their completed sauce and poultry chapters. De Santillana advised postponing "anything that seems like social celebrating." There was none when, in late February, Julia and Simca shivered into Avis's snowbound home after sleighing north in a bus from Washington, DC, cradling their manuscript in their laps in a cardboard box. A month later came the icy news from de Santillana that, though it was obvious that Herculean effort went into *French Cooking for the American Kitchen,* the nearly eight-hundred-page manuscript was not the concise work the company envisioned. Its authors and their duenna were cast into literary purgatory: they would have to complete their book before company executives (to whom they were contracted) would pass final judgment, but Houghton Mifflin executives rescinded their assurance to publish. Julia bared her psychic wounds to Avis. "I am deeply depressed, gnawed by doubts, and feel that all our work may just lay a big rotten egg."

Avis was without a partner, without a job, without a biographer, without an end to her grief, and suddenly without guarantee that the project into which she had put so much of herself would ever see daylight. Desperate for stability, she applied in October 1958 for secretarial work at Harvard. For all she had done in her life, it turned out her most salable skill was an ability to type seventy words per minute. Its value: $246 per month before taxes. At the Harvard personnel office she was interviewed by young men against young women and sensed she was feared for being "older, more worldly." It brought her to the verge of tears. "The more they are afraid of me, the more unloved and unwanted I feel," she confessed. "I keep reminding myself that I am grown up, intelligent, literate, devoted, prompt, hard working, johnny on the spot, not apt to get married or have a baby, and of the lot I'm only sure about the last two."

She was placed at Lowell House, an undergraduate residential college, where, at least once, she excused herself to use the restroom to have a private cry. One morning a few months in, she signed her will and that evening she deeply dented a bourbon bottle and wrote a thought to Julia so searing she could not bring herself to repeat it or reread it. She wrote that she regretted leaving college, and, by implication, everything else.

Meanwhile, Julia's co-author, Simca, became amenable to abridging their manuscript to give Houghton Mifflin what it wanted. Julia agonized over the concept and she broached it when Avis was at her gloomiest. "It is just unthinkable that you should bastardize your book," Avis responded. "Stand by your guns, my lamb."

21

Master Avis

ON WEDNESDAY, NOVEMBER 11, 1959, Avis jockeyed up to her typewriter and whipped out a letter for Julia reporting that Houghton Mifflin had rejected her manuscript for *French Recipes for American Cooks*. Male executives, Dorothy de Santillana reported, judged it too long and complex for a mass market of women. The Childs were crestfallen and fearful that a decade of their (and Simca's) lives had been eaten for an advance — which Julia offered to return and Avis said no — of $250. Julia recalled the moment in her memoir from 2006, *My Life in France*. "Almost immediately I got a morale-boosting letter from Avis, our tireless champion, saying: 'We have only begun to fight.'"

Avis had known that if it came to this it would be her job to save the book, not only because of her love for Julia, but because the project honored her partnership with Bernard. Avis had already prepared for battle. Francophile Knopf — who remained her trusted friend despite firing her — was her obvious target to adopt the orphaned book. But she knew a direct campaign to him would fail because of a complicated and

conjoined personal and professional crisis. Avis had watched the Knopfs'
son, Alfred Jr., against his parents' advice, sign cookbook author June
Pratt. Knopf had been so fearful her book would bomb he had Avis rewrite it. ("A drastic improvement," Avis told Julia. "She can't write for
sour apples.") It bombed anyway, and Alfred Jr. announced he was quitting to launch a competitor company. His mother, Blanche Knopf, tried
recouping company losses by putting out a book in late 1959 called *The
Classic French Cuisine* by Joseph Donon. It bombed too. Pitching another
expensive French cookbook to pimento-cheeked Knopf was off the table.

Avis plotted a corporate insurgency. Her old direct boss, William
Koshland, with whom she stayed so friendly that he mailed her new
Knopf books, visited Cambridge in November 1958 for the Harvard ver-
sus Yale football game. Avis invited him to stay with her, and she cooked
Julia's recipes. "Magnificent," Koshland said, eyes dilated. When Kosh-
land returned in June 1959, Avis let him read a sample of the manuscript.
"Impressed to death," was his reaction. What Avis said in response cer-
tainly made him jealous that such a fine book was to be published by
Houghton Mifflin and not *Knopf.*

Koshland became crazed over the book, writing Avis on Knopf stationery to ask about its progress. Houghton Mifflin *loved* it, was Avis's vul-
pine claim — it was (she said in October 1959) "all in the bag."

During Koshland's next visit for the Harvard versus Princeton game,
Avis might have repeated something she had said back when she worked
for him. "Someday a gamble on me will pay off, maybe big." Four days
later, exactly when Avis wrote Julia that she had "only begun to fight," she
took the risk of ordering Houghton Mifflin to send the rejected manuscript directly to Koshland. As if he were not already drooling, Avis asked
him simply to "live with" it "and cook from it."

"It will, of course, have my attention," he assured her.

Avis's missionary work got Knopf's attention and, unfortunately, it reminded him of his recent French flop. "Has she never heard of Donon?"
Avis urged Koshland to quickly share the manuscript with colleagues. He
showed it to Judith Jones, a cool, industrious blonde in her thirties who

fell so under its spell in the winter when the 1950s became the 1960s that she would go home at lunch to prep what she would cook for dinner. "Could become a classic," Jones said.

At a sales meeting, Koshland pronounced that, with a snappier title, it could sell as many as twenty thousand copies in one year. Knopf still derided it as "that book Avis is interested in." Blanche Knopf added, "I don't think we need this do we?" Editor Angus Cameron, an amateur chef, argued it was "astonishing," and "what these authors have done has never been done before."

Avis could almost taste victory in early 1960 when Koshland called and said that he, Jones, and Cameron intended to "tank right over Alfred and Blanche!"

"At my age, this is what keeps you going," Avis explained to Julia while they waited for Knopf's surrender. "The knowledge that from time to time one will have a brief burst of happiness, the realization that you have after all learned a thing or two, that you've got friends you can reach, that things can be funny, that there's life in the old dame yet."

Great happiness returned to Avis in early 1961 when she read that the House of Knopf would publish the project into which she had channeled her heart and soul through her darkest years. She finally found peace enough to feel happy and remember Bernard DeVoto simultaneously. It was there in the note she wrote to Julia celebrating the end of their long trail. "Ocian in view. Oh the joy!"

Between publication in October 1961 and August 1962, *Mastering the Art of French Cooking* sold 100,000 copies. (In the year when Knopf fired Avis, his most lucrative book sold 15,000 copies.) *Mastering* would go on to sell 2.7 million. "I do owe you thanks for bringing the cookbook our way," Knopf said. "It's the result that counts, and the result is most gratifying."

Despite the public attention that *Mastering*'s scout, agent, editor, tester, and proofreader abhorred, she let stand in the acknowledgments two sentences from the lead author diplomatically serving up the biggest portion of thanks.

"Finally there is Avis DeVoto, our foster-mother, wet-nurse, guide and mentor. She provided encouragement for our first steps, some ten years ago, when we came tottering out of the kitchen with the gleam of authorship lighting our innocent faces."

Avis's loyalty to Julia had buoyed her through the agonizing years following Bernard's death. In September 1962, she returned to the red cedars on the high divide between Montana and Idaho to lay down the last of her grief. Bernard's loyal western source Chet Olsen had arranged for the grove in the Clearwater National Forest to be named for DeVoto. In lieu of a gravestone, an embossed bronze plate announced IN MEMORY OF BERNARD DEVOTO 1897–1955 HISTORIAN AND CONSERVATIONIST OF THE WEST. It was pressed into a boulder beside the stream that chuckled at Bernard while he rested his spirit.

Accompanying Avis was Mark DeVoto, now twenty-two, who had become a symphony conductor. Avis was escorted to the grove on the arm of Lee Metcalf, who grew up on a farm at the base of the mountains in the town of Stevensville. The smiling, big-boned freshman senator and the widow dressed in black had their photograph together on the front of the *Missoulian* newspaper.

The sun was bright as clover honey and filtered by millions of flying cedar needles as a few dozen honored guests sat in folding chairs beside native ferns and titanic nutmeg-colored trunks. Avis wore a charcoal skirt and jacket with a black checkerboard pattern and a pearl necklace. "Mrs. DeVoto holding her breath firmly under control said the occasion was such an emotional one for her that she would only express her thanks to those who had made the memorial possible," reported the *Lewiston Morning Tribune*.

At what looked like a dwarf podium, Olsen and Metcalf made speeches. Then Metcalf read a special message from President Kennedy that began: "I want to send my personal best wishes to Mrs. DeVoto."

Kennedy honored the sense of optimism he took from Bernard DeVoto. From Bernard, he understood that in the West, Americans had faced a choice between destroying the land and losing their freedoms, or learning a better way to live in balance with nature. The conservation revolution showed that they chose right. Bernard's "knowledge of the American past and his faith in individual freedom gave him a deep and quiet confidence in the American future."

"It was his sense of the hope and beauty of the West which made him such a powerful battler in the cause of conservation," Kennedy said. "As long as Americans live in this faith the memory of Bernard DeVoto will not perish."

Kennedy proved he meant what he said. He filled his administration with public servants influenced by Bernard DeVoto, from special assistant Arthur Schlesinger Jr., to interior secretary Stewart Udall, to Udall advisor Wallace Stegner. They all helped win passage of critical environmental laws in the 1960s. Bernard's influence had become part of the zeitgeist. One of Kennedy's assistant interior secretaries, Idahoan John Carver, gave a speech to his department explaining how DeVoto's "The West Against Itself" was foundational to the philosophy Kennedy in his inauguration speech called the "New Frontier." Kennedy believed that America's future depended not on exploitation, but on innovation. "The 'New Frontier' is by no means a mere political allusion," Carver said. "It means we can no longer look to a geographical expanse of unappropriated resources for our values and a higher plane of national character. If our society is to remain dynamic and democratic, we must seek our stimuli within ourselves, within the social body which we comprise, and in new worlds of science which our intelligence creates."

The zenith of the New Frontier arrived with Americans walking on the moon, seven years after Kennedy honored the grieving widow of the man who gave his life for the blue marble those astronauts saw in the distance. Avis was deeply touched by Kennedy's magnanimity and it made her rethink him. She had voted for his Republican rival for Senate in 1952, and she hated that his brother, Robert, worked for Joe McCarthy. Her distaste curdled into cattiness: she had wondered how the president and first lady could photograph so well yet appear so less attractive to the naked eye. All of that washed down the creek at the memorial cedar grove.

"Dear Mr. President," she wrote on September 15, 1962. "I hope that some day you can stop for a few moments in that remote spot. There are more dramatically beautiful places in this country, but I have never seen another at once so peaceful and so majestic. To have it set aside in my husband's name pleases me, and my sons, very much indeed."

It seemed that the DeVotos—certainly conservation—were on Kennedy's mind a year later. In September 1963 he helicoptered to Milford, Pennsylvania, and dedicated an institute at Gifford Pinchot's estate, Grey Towers. He then flew to Montana and spent two days stumping with Senator Metcalf. Logistics did not permit him to visit the memorial cedar grove but he stayed in another place both DeVotos wrote rhapsodically about, Grand Teton National Park.

Avis had much to weep about when she absorbed the news from Dallas on her black-and-white television on November 22, 1963.

In February 1968 Wallace Stegner wrote Avis a question: "Is anybody working on a biography of Benny? Have you authorized anyone to do so? . . . If not, are you still interested in having me do one?"

She had waited for him. He understood when she explained, "I cherish my privacy greatly. I do not want publicity of any kind." Stegner, who called Bernard DeVoto his father figure, and said his own environmental advocacy was "all Benny's doing," would show his deference to Avis. "I salute her," he would write.

It took him six years to finish *The Uneasy Chair: A Biography of Bernard DeVoto*. In accordance with Avis's vision, Stegner put his high-caliber intellect and glistening prose to work expounding on the totality of Bernard's writings, giving his novels, cultural criticism, and literary feuds in-depth consideration along with his western nonfiction and conservation journalism.*

Stegner wrote out of self-conscious admiration for both DeVotos. Hence: "I have tried to re-create Benny DeVoto as he was—flawed, brilliant, provocative, outrageous, running scared all his life, often wrong,

---

*As Stegner began work on *The Uneasy Chair* in 1968, the Stanford University library requested DeVoto's file from the FBI. It was denied and the file stayed classified until the 1980s.

often spectacularly right, always stimulating, sometimes infuriating, and never, never dull." His son, Page Stegner, said it was the closest his father came to autobiography. "When he created DeVoto's life, he created his own." When the biography was published in 1974, there were rumblings about Stegner winning another Pulitzer to match his 1971 novel, *Angle of Repose*. But the award for history went to a book about Thomas Jefferson and the biography winner was Robert Caro for *The Power Broker*. In interviews, Stegner pushed back on a common objection that his DeVoto book cut out Avis.

"I very carefully left out his personal life, his family life," Stegner told an interviewer in July 1974. "That didn't seem to me to be anybody's business."

The reviewer who mattered most to Stegner was pleased. "You wrote the definitive Benny book and I can't see anybody foolish enough to try to top you," Avis said. From their hours of interviews, the standout quote Avis had allowed him to include inside the book was her calling her husband "the bravest damn man I ever knew."

From the mid-1960s through the late 1970s, as Avis carried the legacy of her marriage, she stamped onto it her own environmental triumph. She faced off with the Commonwealth of Massachusetts over plans for a memorial John F. Kennedy Presidential Library and Museum in Cambridge, the construction of which entailed chainsawing a handsome urban forest of grand sycamore* trees along Memorial Drive above the Charles River. Avis thought there could be a better way to honor both the Kennedys *and* the character of the local community. Her principled stance pitted her against another stylish widow of high renown, Jacqueline Kennedy.

To save the trees, Avis joined an elite underground group of Cambridge minutewomen known as the "Sycamore Patrol." The Sycamore Patrol drew inspiration equally from Paul Revere and from a group of women in the 1940s in Boston's Beacon Hill neighborhood who staged a

---

*The trees Avis called "sycamore" are actually London planetrees, which are a sycamore hybrid.

sit-down strike to prevent the mayor from paving over historic brick side-walks. As rumors swirled that the legislature would jump-start its plans by sending in loggers at night, patrolwomen kept round-the-clock watch over the sycamores. The moment a chain saw appeared, the plan was to blow a whistle, signaling the woman who lived closest to telephone all members to rush in and throw their bodies in front of the trees.

Avis co-founded the Harvard Square Defense Fund to fight the pro-posed memorial, a nine-story glass pyramid designed by I. M. Pei, an architect handpicked by Jacqueline Kennedy. The defense fund held a so-phisticated position. They certainly supported honoring Massachusetts's fallen native son, but they thought it could be done in a less ostentatious and disruptive way—one that would not glut Harvard Square with reg-icide-themed gift shops. Avis threw herself deeper into the fight when in 1971 she sold her house at 8 Berkeley Street and bought an elegant apart-ment a few blocks away in a regal brick building on Memorial Drive next to her sycamores. Avis hosted meetings in her apartment, where neighbor and friend Ann Oliver remembered her as a grande dame sitting between stacks of books in her favorite chair with lips painted so red it was "shock-ing." "She was a very forceful person," Oliver said. "No shrinking violet." Pebble Gifford, who co-founded the defense fund, added, "Avis was very instrumental." Whereas she had declined to lend her name to efforts to create the Hells Half Acre wildlife sanctuary just after Bernard's death, Avis now wrote stern letters to newspapers and signed them Avis *DeVoto*.

The defense fund, after years of clashes with developers, Harvard, and the Kennedys, forced a compromise. A garbage dump in South Boston beside a University of Massachusetts campus on the edge of Dorchester Bay was chosen as a more agreeable site for the memorial and museum. Above the reclaimed land, inside the redesigned alcove, visitors would be presented a panoramic view of the Boston skyline, and of the sea, which Kennedy always loved.*

---

*In the 1980s, architect I. M. Pei was hired to design a new entry for the Louvre Museum in Paris. The pyramid he built was similar to his original plan for the John F. Kennedy Presidential Library and Museum.

More pleasing to Avis than saving the grand sycamores in Cambridge was the news that landscape architect Carol Johnson would design John F. Kennedy Memorial Park, an extension of the forest. Where previously there was a grungy, outdated rail yard filled with rats, Johnson planted oaks, maples, pines, and plenty of soft grass on which anyone could sit and gaze at fat, chugging Canada geese and lithe rowers in toothpick boats cutting the languid Charles.

"Harvard Square Defense Fund, my outfit, has had a large part in keeping all this under control and in scale," Avis boasted. For her efforts, the Cambridge City Council voted unanimously in 1984 to commend Avis for being "an ardent advocate of environmental protection." A triangular plaza was built in Harvard Square at the intersection of Brattle Square and Mount Auburn Street. Atop it, seven locust trees were planted along with a sculpture by the late Ann Norton of twin brick spires titled "Gateway to Knowledge." A cement lip in the plaza was inscribed BERNARD AND AVIS DEVOTO FRIENDS OF CAMBRIDGE CONSERVATION. One can now walk toward Harvard Square from Cambridge Commons, past Brattle and Story, and in one-third of a mile see consecutively carved in stone the names of the following great Americans: Washington, Longfellow, DeVoto.

Avis grew elderly and became known throughout her community for her arrestingly crimson lipstick and for having such self-assurance that when she wanted to cross the street she would shake her cane at cars and the traffic would part like she was Moses at the Red Sea. Cambridge was not the only place she became known. Avis traveled the world; Portugal, Greece, Ireland, Yugoslavia, Russia, and France, where she stayed with the Childs in the small, stucco second home they built in the village of Plascassier.

Gordon DeVoto found stability as a taxi driver and eventually settled in an apartment in the neighboring town of Arlington Heights, Massachusetts. He regularly took solo western road trips and he enjoyed calculating down to two decimal points the exact mileage per gallon he could achieve at various speeds. Once, the band on his $15 Timex broke and rather than buy a new one he drove to Arizona then doubled back to the factory in Arkansas to have it repaired. None of his psychiatrists diagnosed what made him so stubbornly and eccentrically fixated. "He was generous and he had a heart of gold," Mark DeVoto remembered. (Gordon died of prostate cancer in 2009.)

Mark earned his PhD in music at Princeton University and taught around the country: Reed College in Oregon, the University of New Hampshire, Harvard, and Tufts University, where he was professor of music from 1981 to 2000. From a brief marriage in the 1960s he gave Avis two granddaughters, Emily and Marya, who made her cherish her family more. "Benny would have been so surprised at the volume of wonderful music that flows through Mark's houses, let alone the pleasure he would have taken in two beautiful granddaughters." Letters to grandma, like all her mail, came addressed to "Mrs. Bernard DeVoto."

She had honored Mr. DeVoto's legacy by continuing his environmental fight on her own terms, by ensuring that his biography was written by Wallace Stegner, and by furthering the spirit of their professional partnership through her work with Julia Child.

In early 1960, Avis found the Childs a house on Irving Street in Cambridge a few blocks from her for when Paul would retire from the State Department (which, with bitterness in mind over his treatment when he was investigated, he did that fall, two years shy of earning his pension). When Julia began her sensational television career with *The French Chef,* which aired on Boston's WGBH from 1963 to 1973, Avis volunteered behind the scenes. After her retirement from Harvard in 1969, she dedicated more time to Julia. As with Bernard DeVoto, Avis was the only person whom Julia Child entrusted with answering her fan mail. Avis called it "doing Julia's office." Russell Morash, founder and executive producer of *The French Chef* and three more Julia cooking series, remembered Avis's tenacity and loyalty. "She was part of the furniture," he said, always "with a grip of important documents in her hand that she was trying to get answers to."

Alfred Knopf rehired Avis on a freelance basis as a sort of literary Renaissance woman. Avis helped edit another renowned food writer,

M. F. K. Fisher (who in letters to Avis conspiratorially called herself "your fellow criminal in research in what is casually called The Aging Process"). Avis helped Julia and co-author Simca conceive *Mastering the Art of French Cooking Volume Two,* published by Knopf in 1970. The acknowledgments hint at Avis's role: "Avis DeVoto, still acting as foster mother, wet nurse, guide, and mentor has also taken on the copy editing for our side as well as the position of indexer-in-chief; our admiration and gratitude can only be expressed by her weight in fresh truffles." Quietly, Julia started a trust fund for Avis, which she greatly appreciated. In 1969 Avis donated to Harvard her long correspondence with Julia. Always protective of her privacy, Avis did it on the condition that her letters stay sealed until after her death. She only erred in the singular by describing the archive as "valuable to future generations as a record of how one very special woman lived at this point in history."

Avis continued "doing Julia's office" through the spring of 1987, when she was diagnosed with pancreatic cancer and given months to live. She nonetheless kept focused on her professional partner. "I really feel quite well, except I get tired easily," she told William Koshland. "Julia's energy seems boundless."

At the beginning of 1953, Julia had written Avis, "you display the true marks of a Great Gourmande . . . which always includes the warmest and most generous of natures." The pair would speak for the last time on March 6, 1989, the day before Avis died at age eighty-four. She lived as a consummate doula to creativity, empathetic, loyal, insightful, critical, mothering, strong, resourceful. It is a fact that because of Avis the most important conservation writer and the most revolutionary French chef of the twentieth century found their audiences. It is the truth that she had within her a life force that transformed her loved ones into forces of nature.

EPILOGUE

Remembering

AVIS RETURNED TO THE RED CEDARS for the last time in May 2003 on what would have been the eve of her ninety-ninth birthday. Mark and his partner, Lois Grossman, spread her ashes in the DeVoto Memorial Cedar Grove, reuniting her with her husband. The sky was as blue as it had been on the day DeVoto's ashes fell from the plane.

All around them spread their family's legacy, public lands. "The Western outdoors is DeVoto's monument," Oregon senator Richard Neuberger had said in the Capitol (as Avis's stomach churned in embarrassment). The assessments ascended from there. Arthur Schlesinger Jr. said DeVoto was America's greatest conservation communicator since Franklin Roosevelt. John F. Kennedy said DeVoto had reminded the nation of "our national patrimony." Wallace Stegner judged DeVoto as important to conservation as Theodore Roosevelt and Gifford Pinchot. Stegner further paid homage to DeVoto's conjoined fight for the Bill of Rights, praising him as "the nation's environmental conscience and liberty's watchdog."

Bernard DeVoto could not have done any of it if he had not married Helen Avis MacVicar. Because of her, he was able to learn his history, find his voice, and earn his journalistic platform. He became a writer whom readers could trust to tell them facts (without typos, thanks to Avis). Bernard bridged the Roosevelts' battles to stop American land destruction by monopolization with the struggle against emissions and pollution, ushered in with the 1962 publication of Rachel Carson's *Silent Spring.* From the DeVotos' environmental movement came the watershed 1960s laws the Wild and Scenic Rivers Act, the Clean Air Act, the Land and Water Conservation Fund, and, in the 1970s, the Endangered Species Act and the Federal Land Policy and Management Act.

The Wilderness Act of 1964, born out of the tumult of Bernard's final fight against the Echo Park Dam, is his pinnacle legacy. The act's founding conception of wildernesses as places void of human imprint is imperfect; it slighted Indigenous peoples, and did not envision the impacts of climate change. But its idea of leaving vast outdoor spaces free of industrial development, as refugia for wildlife, as wilderness for its own sake — never to be tamed — marked a turning point in humankind's treatment of the planet. That turning point will only grow more important. In a world dangerously addicted to fossil fuels, the trees and grasses on public lands are pulling carbon from the atmosphere and storing it as fiber, helping to stabilize the climate. The DeVotos recognized the reciprocity: future generations will not just gain enjoyment from public lands; they will gain life from them, on a level as elemental as the oxygen in their blood.

The DeVotos' commitment to the environment made them fight for the Bill of Rights when it and they were most threatened. Patrick McCarran's demonization and dismissal of public lands advocates during the McCarran Hearings were part and parcel of his yen to lock his ideological enemies in concentration camps. It was the apogee of McCarthyism. McCarran's lies, racism, and hypocrisies — which he justified by propagandizing that Americans had to fear their neighbors and trust demagogues — created the paranoid persona Joe McCarthy put on.

Though McCarran's concentration camps provision was repealed in 1971 after grassroots lobbying by Americans of Japanese heritage who re-

membered such camps in the West, repressive residue remains. Later na-
tivists and nationalists stretched McCarran's statutory targeting of Jews
to people of new disfavored faiths and ethnicities, especially Muslims and
Mexicans, plus writers, like Gabriel García Márquez, who was denied a
visa under the McCarran law. There may never be a full accounting of
the collateral damage done by the "duck" hunts, to people like Roald Peterson. The extent of the FBI's abuse of information, collected under the
pretense of security interests, to score political points and settle personal
vendettas, remains in question.

Though J. Edgar Hoover did McCarran the courtesy of locking away
the Bugsy Siegel investigation, the senator and the mobster seemed to inspire a scene in Francis Ford Coppola's 1974 film *The Godfather, Part II*. A
xenophobic Nevada senator, "Pat Geary," who boasts of leading "my own
committee," demands bribes from mob boss Michael Corleone at Lake
Tahoe.

In a true story too seedy even to have been written by Bernard DeVoto
in his fictional alter ego, John August, the McCarran and McCarthy spirit
found a vector into the twenty-first century. In the 1970s Roy Cohn spotted in a low-lit New York City club the doppelgänger of G. David Schine,
who once set his heart (and books) aflame. Smitten, Cohn became Donald Trump's mentor. Cohn died of AIDS in 1986 and twenty years later
Trump was elected president and immediately issued a flurry of executive orders, two of which were pure McCarran. One, citing McCarran
immigration law, barred migrants to the United States from Iran, Soma-
lia, Sudan, Yemen, Syria, and Libya. The other rescinded great swaths
of two national monuments in Utah under the jurisdiction of the Bureau
of Land Management, Grand Staircase-Escalante and Bears Ears (which
had been established, respectively, by Bill Clinton and Barack Obama,
the presidents who, respectively, replaced and repealed Executive Order
10450).

The monument destruction was cheered by members of the Sagebrush Rebellion, a reactionary group that rose in the West in the late
1970s to oppose public lands conservation laws. Interior secretary Ryan
Zinke, a former Montana congressman fond of wearing a black Stet-

son, propagandized the executive order by holding a new iteration of the McCarran Hearings around the West, promoting cowboy mythology, dismissing dissent. Seeing the landgrab in sequel, Mark DeVoto mailed Zinke a copy of Bernard DeVoto's "The West Against Itself," from 1947, where he pointed out that Senator McCarran and his methods were bad for the West and the people of the United States. Its receipt was never acknowledged. All the while, the Sagebrush Rebels spoke of "freedom" and waved flags and were godchildren of a tyrant, the Sagebrush Caesar.

Bernard DeVoto would grow deeply depressed about that western paradox ("get out and give us more money"). That Bernard was able to pull through was, as always, because of Avis.

Into the third decade of the twenty-first century, if references in popular culture are the metric, Avis is the best remembered DeVoto. Through her extraordinary friendship with Julia Child, Avis helped millions of people around the world learn haute cuisine (and proved they could be taught by women). In 2020, Emmy and Tony award winner Bebe Neuwirth was cast as Avis for an HBO Max drama series titled *Julia*. Avis was played by Tony winner Deborah Rush opposite Meryl Streep in the hit 2009 film *Julie & Julia*. One of the artistic liberties late writer and director Nora Ephron took was depicting Julia and Avis meeting *after* DeVoto died, thus missing what would have been a charming scene of Streep showing she could hold her DeVoto Dry martinis. In 2010 Houghton Mifflin Harcourt published *As Always, Julia*, a collection of the Avis and Julia letters edited by Joan Reardon. The book cover featured a photo only of Julia. In a more accurate mix of the families' legacies, Julia's actual kitchen is now on display in the Smithsonian Institution's National Museum of American History in Washington, DC, on land under the jurisdiction of the National Park Service.

Julia remembered her sly, DeVoto-inspired environmentalism until her death in 2004, a decade after Paul's. In 1998 she filmed an episode of the PBS show *Julia and Jacques Cooking at Home* in which she made a saffron-infused Mediterranean seafood stew. It was to be paired with a wine from Kendall-Jackson, a show sponsor that had representatives in the studio. Julia had learned that the vineyard bulldozed nearly a thousand old oaks in the Santa Ynez Valley. When time came to pour wine, Julia instead pulled out two iced bottles of Sam Adams and said to co-host Jacques Pépin, "We're not having wine. Today we're having beer." Avis's Sycamore Patrol, on behalf of the urban forest they saved in Cambridge, could raise their glasses.

The year before Bernard DeVoto died, his memory seemed so assured that Avis called him a new pet name: "Little Sir Classic." A Heritage Press Books committee picked contemporary authors destined to be considered "classic." They chose Ernest Hemingway, William Faulkner, Carl Sandburg, John Steinbeck, Robert Frost, Rachel Carson, and, as Avis told Julia, "lo and behold there was DeVoto." Out of them all, Bernard was the one who fell most quickly and deeply into obscurity. By 2021 his hometown Ogden *Standard-Examiner*—in a story about an insurgent group trying to get the first Utahn to win a Pulitzer Prize any recognition in his native state—could write the phrase "odds are you've never heard of Bernard DeVoto."

The reasons for his fade-out are as numerous and complex as the dissolution of DeVoto Nation. Stegner (who bitterly related) blamed eastern tastemakers caring too little about the West. Come the Vietnam War, DeVoto's decision to have aimed his histories of Manifest Destiny at mass audiences in the World War II era seemed dated, naïve, imperialistic. Left-leaning academics would call DeVoto's theories of geographic determinism insensitive to people of color and ignorant of racism. Right-leaning academics would challenge his assertions of corporate perniciousness. Civil libertarians took up new fights for civil rights. DeVoto's preferred term "conservationist" became replaced by "environmentalist." Meanwhile, legions of small ranchers, a pillar of DeVoto Nation, vanished under the withering pressure of agricultural consolidation. There was little audience left for a writer so electrically independent he would shock away the embrace of anyone whose politics were polarized.

But the land remembers. Every grove in a national forest where old-growth trees stand and every acre the Bureau of Land Management oversees where deep-rooted native grasses grow remembers that in the 1940s the DeVotos stopped a 230-million-acre landgrab. Every national park with a canyon not stapled by a dam, a forest not pocked with clear-cuts or mines, and grizzly bears or buffalo or peregrine falcons not replaced with cows and oil pumpjacks and power lines remembers the DeVotos' 1950s fight against the Echo Park Dam. DeVoto gave his life, and Avis her husband, defending the National Park Service's original 1916 mandate to protect land "unimpaired for the enjoyment of future generations." Every wild place where no "Keep Out, No Trespassing" signs hang off a fence honors the DeVotos. So does every vista where the land rises clear out to a desert or prairie or mountain horizon, not a strip mall or a strip mine or a subdivision in sight. That land remembers its wealth not being given away to demagogues and plunderers who called their dissenters rustlers and Communists.

That day in the DeVoto Memorial Cedar Grove, when Avis and Bernard came together again, Mark noticed something. Lingering at the base of a burly giant cedar was a tiny, gorgeous, fairy slipper orchid, all white and yellow crowned by tall, sharp petals of bright magenta. There is an easy simile with the DeVotos, and it goes below the surface, to where the roots of the tree and the wildflower intertwine, holding the country together, keeping the waters clear.

ACKNOWLEDGMENTS

Missoula, Montana, is where I was born and raised, and when I learned that Bernard DeVoto wished he could say that too, I granted Avis could be right when she said he was a genius. My mom, Kay Vinci, made sure I was born a Montanan and my dad, Phil Schweber, made sure I was raised one. My stepmother, Gig Schweber, made sure I was rooted in Montana and my stepfather, Bill Innes, made sure I explored it. Being ignorant of Bernard DeVoto until I spotted *Across the Wide Missouri* at the Strand Bookstore in New York City is my own fault.

An immense debt of gratitude goes to Mark DeVoto and his partner, Lois Grossman, who were inviting, kind, and patient as I interviewed them first at their summer cottage in Eastport, Maine (because where else does one find the last surviving son of the greatest historian of the West than in the country's easternmost city?), and later at their home along the Mystic River in Massachusetts. Mark saved me from a few of what his parents called "howlers."

A battery of historians, librarians, and archivists helped also. Deep bows to: Vicki Lynne Glantz, Sarah Kesterson, and Emily Brianne Brophy at the American Heritage Center in Laramie, Wyoming; Catherine Magee and Sheryln Hayes-Zorn at the Nevada Historical Society; Donnelyn Curtis and Kimberly Anderson at the University of Nevada, Reno; Sarah Hutcheon and Jennifer Fauxsmith at the Schlesinger Library at Harvard; Sarah Langsdon and Melissa Johnson at Weber State University; Molly Rose Steed and Elizabeth Rogers at the J. Willard Marriott Library at the University of Utah; Amanda Smith at the University of Wisconsin, Madison; Donna McCrea at the University of Montana; Brandon Wilson at the Missoula County Courthouse; Emily Gonzalez at the Cambridge Historical Society; Tara Craig in the Rare Book and Manuscript Library at Columbia University; Erik Johnson at the Theodore Roosevelt Center at Dickinson State University; and Leif Anderson and (especially) Tim Noakes at the Department of Special Collections at Stanford University. Thank you, Richa Wilson, Regional Heritage Program Leader for the U.S. Forest Service's Intermountain Region, and also Tom Peterson and Dave Stack at the National Museum of Forest Service History. Lauren Salkeld and everyone at the Julia Child Foundation: you are worth your weight in truffles.

Deep thanks to Sarah Shomion for sharing details, both tragic and extraordinary, about her grandfather, Roald Peterson. Appreciation to Brock and Paula Hanson for sharing information about their relative J. Elmer Brock. I am truly grateful to Pebble Gifford, Ann Oliver, and Russel Morash for granting me interviews about their friend Avis. Thank you, Kate Doyle and William Burr at the National Security Archive, also Thomas Mcanear at the National Archives and John F. Fox at the FBI. Hat tip to Gary Coffrin and John L. Moore for Miles City history. Thank-yous to Matthew Pearce for a helpful chat about his 2014 thesis "Discontent on the Range" and to Adam Plunkett for illuminating me about the subject of his upcoming biography, Robert Frost. Thank-you to Scott Greenwell of Ogden, one of the insurgents trying to get Utah to finally honor the first great writer it birthed. An echoing thank-you to the staff at OARS (proprietors of the rafting company Bus Hatch founded in Vernal, Utah) for an awesome, shooting-star-riven canyon tour of Dinosaur National Monument.

As an unreconstructed freelancer, I am indebted to an array of colleagues and gig-givers for everything from valuable assignments to invaluable advice. Courtney Brooks, Meghan Drueding, Pauline Eiferman, Dennis Hockman, Patrick J. Sauer, Sam Sifton, and Joel Whitney are all fine editors who, generously, extended assignments that I parleyed into research for this project. Similarly, I owe great gratitude to the Wilderness Society's Kate Mackay and Michael Reinemer. Christopher Ketcham, who has written some of the best public lands journalism in *Harper's* since DeVoto, was unfailingly generous with inspiration and advice. For infusing this tome with some of the soul of our old mentor, investigative reporter Wayne Barrett, I want to "voice" thanks to fellow intern alums Christopher Heaney, Eileen Markey, and Jessica Wisloski. A double-clasped handshake for my author photo goes to Dave Sanders. Numerous people I admire who have summited Book Mountain gave me encouragement, tips, and, in a few instances, help. Thank you, Douglas Brinkley, Jennet Conant, Gregory Crouch, Michael Downs, Bill German, Jeff Hull, Peter Stark, Bonnie Stepenoff, John Taliaferro, Larry Tye, and Jia Lynn Yang. At an early stage of this project, three of the best editors in the business vouched for me. Massive appreciation (for this and much else) to Mary Ann Giordano, Jayati Vora, and Joe Sexton.

Hosannas to the school of journalism at the University of Montana. Also to the institution's alumni magazine, which assigned me to profile hunter–conservationist Steven Rinella, who introduced me to my agent, Farley Chase, who immediately saw promise in this idea, fortified it with his first-class literary instincts, and negotiated a contract in a way that makes me tremble at what must be his poker skills. My editor, Ivy Givens, graced this project with her wisdom, patience, and encouragement; it was an honor to work with her. Elizabeth Pierson copyedited with magnificent thoroughness and—in the middle—made a pilgrimage to Wallace Stegner's grave for spiritual encouragement. My most sincere appreciation to everyone else at HarperCollins who helped with this book, especially: Heather Tamarkin for her deft production work, Jaya Miceli for the beautiful cover design, and Muriel Jorgensen for the best kind of fussy proofreading.

You never know your true friends until you have a far-out story idea that you need to talk through over many hours. Ben Lightle, Ashley J. Peters, Mark Norquist, and the great Hal Herring spent miles behind windshields helping me figure out my narrative highway. Paul Queneau, of the Outdoor Writers Association of America, helped bring us (and many others) together. Thank you to Kay Ellerhoff, who took time away from editing *Montana Outdoors* to transcribe Julia Child pages for me. Garrett Spitzer, longtime manager of New York City's Harmonie Club, allowed me to research its interior by hiring me to front a blues band there (shout-out to guitarists Eric "Roscoe" Ambel and Pete Smith, bassist Keith Christopher, and drummer Eric Seftel). Two fists raised in the air to the mighty Brooklyn Boyz Book Club—with heavy bourbon pours to Yahdon Israel, John Midgely, and master of ceremonies Lenny Bass—for opening my brain to new ideas and my heart to new friendships.

Whatever writing career I have I owe to John Holl; if you're blessed in life, there is a John Holl in it. Thank you also to John's wife, April Darcy, for recommending, and sometimes gifting, excellent books. Some of my fondest memories are of exploring the West with my best friends, Chris Stetler and Lido Vizzutti, and their exemplary wives, Laura Stetler and Jessica Lowry Vizzutti. Deep bow to maestro John Schuberg—the Curtis to our Blues Brothers—for giving detailed directions to and around the DeVoto Memorial Cedar Grove. Thank you to my friends from Hellgate High School, Tobin Addington and Leif Frederickson, for reading versions of this and making sure I had learned a few things. I joined the staff of our high school newspaper because I wanted to be like editor Chad Dundas, now a fine novelist, who also gave me strong feedback and, with it, the unspoken reminder that nothing has changed.

When I dug through the DeVoto archives at Stanford University I stayed with my late mother-in-law, Janet Couchot, who is dearly missed. When excavating McCarran archives in Reno I stayed with my dad's partner, Tammy Callahan, and my nana, Mavis Schweber. When I visited Cambridge I stayed with my cousins Amanda Goldberg (on holiday leave from studying small mammals on western public lands) and her father, Mark. Thank you, all. Same to both of my brothers, Sam Innes and Andrew Schweber, who catch the larger trout. When I explained this project early on to my sister, Erin Schweber, she set me on a better path by saying about Avis: "Center her! Center her!"

I could not have written about an extraordinary marriage if I was not lucky enough to be in one. For as dauntlessly plunging through Wyoming Stock Growers Association archives in a Laramie library as down the Green River in a rubber raft, thank you, Kristen Couchot, my perfecter of The Hour. Do you have any idea how many DeVoto stories she listened to? Read this book a thousand times and you will.

A NOTE ON SOURCES

Bernard and Avis DeVoto wrote troves of letters in addition to the millions of words they dually published. His are at Stanford University, hers are at Harvard University. The rich details in this book are predominantly from them, supplemented with twenty years' worth of asides in *Harper's* plus other publications. Because the DeVotos were both fine and frequent anecdotalists, episodes they obscured — such as how they sourced the transcript that revealed the landgrab, and their relationship with Roald Peterson — could be pieced together via references in letters strung across many years. Additional important letters from both DeVotos are kept, respectively, in the Wallace Stegner Papers at the University of Utah and the Chester Olsen Collection at Weber State University. The American Heritage Center at the University of Wyoming in Laramie was invaluable for papers pertaining to Wyoming politicians, stock growers associations, and J. Elmer Brock. The Nevada Historical Society and the University of Nevada, Reno, are repositories for Pat McCarran documents. Bernard kept transcripts of the Joe McCarthy speeches attacking him in the lead-up to the 1952 election. Other vital sources for new details were FBI files for Paul Child, William Langer, and Roald Peterson, all obtained via Freedom of Information Act requests. A copy of Bernard DeVoto's FBI file is at Stanford University with papers of journalist Tom Knudson, who acquired it by the Freedom of Information Act. Last, this text is informed by author visits to locations described, plus interviews with heirs and friends of characters.

ABBREVIATIONS

ADV, Avis DeVoto
ADVP, Avis DeVoto Papers
BDV, Bernard DeVoto
BDVP, Bernard DeVoto Papers
FBI, Federal Bureau of Investigation
JC, Julia Child
JCP, Julia Child Papers
PMC, Patrick McCarran Collection
WSP, Wallace Stegner Papers

NOTES

PROLOGUE: MARCH 3–JULY 8, 1948

PAGE

xiii *"What have you got"*: George Horne, "A Curry Mystery," *New York Times*, May 22, 1948; additional details, "Bombing Threat in Crank Letter Causes Police to Guard Key Areas," *New York Times*, March 4, 1948.

xiv *"A Curry Mystery"*: *New York Times*, May 22, 1948.

"courage, faith": BDV to Byron Hurlbut, June 1923 (likely), BDVP.

xv *"He could surprise"*: ADV to Robert E. Lee, February 10, 1956, BDVP.

"overtones of a situation": ADV to JC, February 9, 1953, ADVP.

"this is your land": BDV, "The West Against Itself," *Harper's*, January 1947.

"should have a hammer": Charley Meyers, *Wyoming Eagle*, January 16, 1948.

no idea he was: BDV to Merle Miller, February 25, 1948, BDVP.

"unimpaired for the enjoyment": from An Act to Establish a National Park Service, approved August 25, 1916.

xvi *"on very thin ice"*: Newton Drury, June 10, 1948, from Harvey, *Symbol of Wilderness*, 60.

"One can raise": Patrick McCarran to Margaret McCarran, December 20, 1941, PMC.

"pleases me": BDV to Arthur Carhart, June 3, 1948, BDVP.

xvii *"far from a beauty"*: ADV to JC, February 17, 1953, ADVP.

His advice: see BDV to a Mr. Griffith, March 15, 1946, BDVP.

"such vitality": Hugh and Dorothy MacLennan to ADV, November 1955, BDVP, Box 22.

xviii   *"half sick":* BDV to Frederick Allen, July 15, 1948, BDVP.

      "touchy interview": details from DeVoto FBI file.

1. "DEEP AS THE ROOTS OF THE EARTH"

3   *According to Avis's:* details from BDVP, Box 22, Folder 465.

4   *half the size:* Egan, *Good Rain,* 167.

    History swerved: details from Brinkley, *Wilderness Warrior.*

5   *"I am against the man":* Timothy Egan, *The Big Burn: Teddy Roosevelt and the Fire That Saved America* (Boston: Houghton Mifflin Harcourt, 2009), 56.

    "The forest reserves should": ibid., 42.

6   *The 40 acres:* Samuel Dye details from BDV, "Jonathan Dyer, Frontiersman," *Harper's,* September 1933; and M. DeVoto, *Selected Letters,* 120, n. 29.

    Helen Avis MacVicar: young Avis details from student essays written for BDV, BDVP, Box 83; letters to JC; and author interviews with Mark DeVoto.

    "Little Helen": see BDVP, Box 22.

    "Scotty": Stegner, *Uneasy Chair,* 52.

    "Next in order": ADV, October 5, 1922, BDVP, Box 83.

7   *"This is what":* ADV to JC, August 20, 1954, ADVP.

    "I have always": ADV, October 19, 1922, BDVP, Box 83.

    "the Copper Country": ADV, October 12, 1922, BDVP, Box 83.

8   *"until the other fellow":* ADV to JC, July 25, 1959, ADVP.

    "I didn't take 'em": ADV, October 12, 1922, BDVP, Box 83.

    town of Escanaba: ADV to Paul Child, December 16, 1967, ADVP.

    "steamed up": ADV to JC, March 29, 1957, ADVP.

    "beaux," she called them: ADV to JC, January 3, 1956, ADVP.

    "a newspaper office": ADV, September 30, 1922, BDVP, Box 83.

    "the jelly doughnut": ADV to JC, January 21, 1961, ADVP.

    "iron bound": ADV, October 5, 1922, BDVP, Box 83.

9   *"All I know":* ADV to JC, January 17, 1958, ADVP.

    "How can a man": BDV, "The Co-Ed," *Harper's,* September 1927.

    the snowy spires: young BDV details from his "Easy Chair" columns and letters, and author interviews with Mark DeVoto.

    a beauty contest: Stegner, *Uneasy Chair,* 10.

    "shoot the hell": BDV, "Fossil Remnants of the Frontier," *Harper's,* April 1935.

10   *called "genius":* BDV to Robert Forsythe, October 6, 1927, BDVP.

    "bellowed at me": BDV to Katharine Sterne, August 17, 1940, BDVP.

    "continual stubbornness": Florian DeVoto to BDV, September 6, 1923, BDVP.

    A neighbor: the neighbor was Stanley Tracey, who became an assistant FBI director; DeVoto FBI file.

    "the ugliest": Stegner, *Uneasy Chair,* 7.

    "The Lord says": BDV, "Fossil Remnants of the Frontier."

11   *"to explain America":* BDV to "Art," January 24, 1928, BDVP.

    "a maverick": BDV to Melville Smith, July 8, 1920, BDVP.

"*absolutes mean absolutism*": BDV, "Position Maintained," *Harper's,* July 1940.

"*My mind is*": BDV to Byron Hurlbut, May or June 1923, BDVP.

"*pour that arresting*": BDV to Melville Smith, October 22, 1920, BDVP.

Mormon bishops: Bostonian, November 15, 1944.

"*These people are not*": BDV to Melville Smith, July 8, 1920, BDVP.

12 "*a shavetail*": BDV to Lt. Col. John M. Kemper, October 28, 1943, BDVP.

"*the thought of suicide*": BDV to Byron Hurlbut, May or June 1923, BDVP.

"*suppression of*": Florian DeVoto to BDV, September 6, 1923, BDVP.

"*Art is man*": Stegner, *Uneasy Chair,* 157.

"*His classes were*": *Daily Northwestern,* circa spring 1926, BDVP, Box 154–2.

"*He was supposed*": Paul Driscoll, quoted in *Worcester Telegram,* circa 1950s, BDVP, Box 154-A.

"*I must have been*": BDV to Byron Hurlbut, June 1923 (?), BDVP.

13 "*All this is probably*": BDV to a classmate of ADV's, BDVP, Box 83.

"*You write*": all details and dialogue from ADV's essays from BDVP, Box 83.

"*the subtlest mind*": BDV to Byron Hurlbut, June 1923 (?), BDVP.

"*Too trite*": all details and dialogue from ADV's essays from BDVP, Box 83.

14 "*It was because*": BDV to Byron Hurlbut, June 1923 (?), BDVP.

a salary: Boston Post Magazine, December 9, 1951.

a diamond: WSP, Box 102, Folder 10.

half-furnished bachelor pad: Stegner, *Uneasy Chair,* 45.

"*I never really talked*": ADV to JC, June 19, 1969, ADVP.

"*He was always there*": ADV to Chet Olsen, November 16, 1955, Chester J. Olsen Collection, Stewart Library Special Collections, Weber State University, Ogden, UT.

15 "*Whatever the future*": BDV to Byron Hurlbut, May or June 1923, BDVP.

on June 30: WSP, Box 102, Folder 10.

2. THE SAGEBRUSH CAESAR

16 *Death came:* details in this section from BDV, *Western Paradox;* Andrew M. Honker, "Been Grazed Almost to Extinction," *Utah Historical Quarterly,* Winter 1999; and *Afton Star Valley Independent,* August 1923.

"*Dear Children*": Florian DeVoto to BDV and ADV, 1920s, BDVP.

Bernard's "moods": Florian DeVoto to ADV, September 4, 1923, BDVP.

17 *3.8 million:* BDV, "The Western Land Grab," *Harper's,* June 1947.

"*If Noah's flood*": BDV, "The West," *Harper's,* January 1947.

19 "*It is for God's sake*": BDV, *Western Paradox,* 181.

the Dust Bowl: details from Egan, *Worst Hard Time;* Kevin Baker, "Where Our New World Begins," *Harper's,* May 2019; Stegner, *Hundredth Meridian,* including Senator Gore quote, 356.

freshman from Nevada: biographical details from Edwards, *Pat McCarran,* 73.

"*so long as I have*": *Congressional Record,* June 12, 1934, p. 11155.

20 "*the Rotten Borough*": details from Christopher J. Walker, "The History of School Trust Lands in Nevada," *Nevada Law Journal,* vol. 7, issue 1, 2006.

"*The gang on the corner*": Edwards, *Pat McCarran,* 48.

Norman Biltz ran: details in this section from Ybarra, *Washington Gone Crazy;* Lincoln Freeman,

"Norman Biltz, Duke of Nevada," *Fortune,* September 1954; Sally Denton, *The Money and the Power: The Making of Las Vegas and Its Hold on America* (New York: Vintage Books, 2002).

21 *"I fooled you":* Edwards, *Pat McCarran,* 48.

"I wonder if": Norman Henry Biltz Papers, Special Collections, University of Nevada, Reno.

"I don't know why": Ybarra, *Washington Gone Crazy,* 338.

22 *In the 1930s:* Denton, *The Money,* 44. Citing McCarran's bigotry, in 2021 the seven-member Clark County Commission in Nevada voted unanimously to rename McCarran Airport for one of his successors, Harry Reid.

"Greatest senator": Freeman, "Norman Biltz."

"patronage pigsty": Denton, *The Money,* 44.

"son of a bitch": Ybarra, *Washington Gone Crazy,* 379.

"he is always": ibid., 695.

The conservation measure: history of Taylor Grazing Act from Matthew Allen Pearce, "Discontent on the Range" (PhD diss., University of Oklahoma, 2014); Stegner, *Hundredth Meridian;* BDV, *Western Paradox.*

23 *small ranchers:* see Pearce, "Discontent," ch. 6.

"real investigation": Pearce, "Discontent," 281.

curated a series: details from PMC, Boxes 37–41, "Senate Subcommittee on Public Lands Hearings."

"trafficking in public lands": Mary Whitehall to George Storck, September 1945, ibid.

24 *"the sale of land":* A. Phillip Foremaster to George Storck, August 1945, ibid.

"almost an impossibility": Mrs. Charles Ellis to George Storck, September 1941, ibid.

"an earth-shaking force": Ybarra, *Washington Gone Crazy,* 7.

3. "THE BLUEPRINT PLANS OF CREATION"

25 *Evanston* News-Index: Stegner, *Uneasy Chair,* 60.

"We have arrived": BDV, quoted by John A. Gudmundsen, BDVP, Box 5.

26 *Alone, Avis peeled:* see BDV to "Art," June 20, 1928, BDVP.

a *"con-game":* BDV, "College and the Exceptional Man," *Harper's,* January 1927.

Bernard's face: Northwestern Purple Parrot, BDVP, Box 154-2.

waste good alcohol: see Stegner, *Uneasy Chair,* 49.

"He has strong likes": ADV to JC, February 9, 1953, ADVP.

wrote "tripe": BDV to Katharine Sterne, May 13, 1936, BDVP.

"I'll have my": H. L. Mencken to BDV, March 20, 1926, BDVP.

hurled in anger: Stegner, *Mountain Water,* 250.

27 *"smugness" and "self-righteousness":* see, e.g., "Ogden: The Underwriters of Salvation" in Duncan Aikman, ed., *The Taming of the Frontier* (New York: Minton, Balch & Co., 1925).

"injure the delicate": Ogden Standard, no date (circa 1926), BDVP.

"picked up from DeVoto": ADV to JC, April 28, 1953, ADVP.

checks peeking: Stegner, *Uneasy Chair,* 80.

artistic nudes: BDV to Katharine Sterne, February 11, 1935, BDVP.

running liquor: BDV, "My Career as a Lawbreaker," *Harper's,* January 1954.

"the family bootlegger": Schlesinger, *A Life,* 38.

cynical and "adolescent": New York Times Book Review, October 5, 1924.

was called "overlong": Stegner, *Uneasy Chair*, 57.

"self-conscious manner": New York Herald Tribune, July 29, 1928.

"disappointment of the year": Stegner, *Uneasy Chair*, 160; DeVoto's last printed novel, *Mountain Time* (Boston: Little, Brown, 1946), would earn fair reviews and sell moderately.

he might not have: the teacher was LeBaron Russell Briggs; see Stegner, *Uneasy Chair*, 71, 398.

"young ass": BDV, "Kent Potter Story," in M. DeVoto, *Selected Letters*, Appendix B 4.

28 *"You have put into words"*: Helen O. G. to BDV, August 12, 1948, BDVP, Box 12.

"love for the country": Stegner, *Uneasy Chair*, 75.

"goose bumps of delight": Susan P. Bowling to BDV, August 12, 1948, BDVP, Box 7.

"He was roaring now": L. H. Butterfield, "Discover Our Continental Experience," *New York Times*, February 24, 1974.

29 *threw out 30,000*: Stegner, *Uneasy Chair*, 88.

"Of course I belong": BDV to Katharine Sterne, May 13, 1936, BDVP.

traditional American writers: see, e.g., BDV, "Under Which King, Bezonian," *Harper's*, September 1941, and George C. Homans, *Coming to My Senses* (New Brunswick, NJ: Transaction, 1984), ch. 6.

Avis gave birth: details of the DeVotos' Lincoln residence from Stegner, *Uneasy Chair*, esp. 135, 213.

Avis miscarried: see BDV to Katharine Sterne, January 22, 1940.

"Goodness we had fun!": Stegner, *Uneasy Chair*, 136.

30 *"toothsome young virgins"*: ADV to JC, July 31, 1954, ADVP.

"in the mood": ADV to JC, March 20, 1953, ADVP.

"What do you do": Homans, *Senses*, ch. 6.

Bernard discovered Twain's first: details of BDV and of Twain executorship from Stegner, *Uneasy Chair*, 89.

"Those 20 pages": BDV to Katharine Sterne, April 30, 1938, BDVP.

31 Harper's *was so impressed*: details from BDV "#121," *Harper's*, November 1945, and "Number 241," *Harper's*, November 1955; also Stegner, *Uneasy Chair*, 161–162.

"bellowing from a platform": BDV to Katharine Sterne, July 1935, BDVP.

"subsidizing fascists": BDV to Katharine Sterne, April 25, 1944, BDVP.

"a snake's ass hole": BDV to Katharine Sterne, July 16, 1937, BDVP.

a place he detested: see BDV, "On Moving to New York," *Harper's*, November 1936, and "On Moving from New York," *Harper's*, August 1938.

32 *"Genius Is Not Enough"*: BDV, "The Story of a Novel, by Thomas Wolfe," *Saturday Review of Literature*, April 25, 1936.

"They turned their backs": BDV, "Writers of the Twenties Missed the Real Meaning of the Times," *Saturday Review of Literature*, April 8, 1944.

"imbecile delusion": BDV, "Notes on the American Way," *Harper's*, May 1938.

"monumental credulity": BDV, "The Ex-Communists," BDVP, Box 49.

"settled in advance": BDV, "Notes on the Red Parnassus," *Harper's*, July 1936.

"a prose style so vehement": "Angry Editor," *Time*, March 14, 1938.

a "fascist": see, e.g., BDV to *Nation* editor Carey McWilliams, March 27, 1950; BDV to a Mrs. Field, November 7, 1949.

"spokesman for the literary": Stegner, *Uneasy Chair*, 189.

threats of violence: see BDV to Katharine Sterne, January 25, 1937, BDVP.

being a "snob": New Masses, June 1, 1937.

"the bestial ideology": Russia State House of Foreign Literature retort, January 9, 1948, to BDV's praise of Wilfred E. Binkley's *American Political Parties* (New York: Knopf, 1943), BDVP, Box 154a.

33 *Lewis and Clark expedition:* BDV, "Passage to India," *Saturday Review of Literature,* December 5, 1936.

weasel tails: Stegner, *Uneasy Chair,* 421.

4. A WORLD ON FIRE

34 *Pulitzer Prizes:* Frost won the award in 1924, 1931, 1937, and 1943.

He loved a Harper's*:* BDV, "New England There She Stands," *Harper's,* March 1932.

35 *"I can't get over"*: Stegner, *Uneasy Chair,* 166.

"They would not find": Robert Frost, "Into My Own," in *A Boy's Will* (New York: Henry Holt, 1915).

"You don't know": Stegner, *Uneasy Chair,* 166.

"I go tearful": BDV to Katharine Sterne, January 29, 1936, BDVP.

Avis's term: see ADV to JC, November 19, 1958, ADVP.

36 *physically attractive:* ADV to Stegner, September 27, 1987, WSP, Box 14, Folder 14.

The DeVotos proudly: details from Stegner, *Uneasy Chair,* 167; Kathleen Morrison details from Cambridge Women's Heritage Project (https://www2.cambridgema.gov/Historic/CWHP/bios_m.html#MorrisonK).

"a family of sorts": Jay Parini, *Robert Frost: A Life* (New York: Henry Holt, 1999), 315.

"the monkeys": BDV, "The Critics and Robert Frost," *Saturday Review of Literature,* January 1, 1938.

write his biography: see BDV to Katharine Sterne, September 2 (?), 1938, BDVP, and Stegner, *Uneasy Chair,* 192.

37 *"Avis and I"*: Frost to BDV, October 30, 1938, BDVP.

Frost began an affair: Jeffrey Meyers, in *Robert Frost* (Boston: Houghton Mifflin, 1996), claims that Bernard DeVoto had an affair with Kathleen Morrison and other women. He cited unpublished personal notes from Frost biographer Lawrance Thompson quoting the poet as saying Bernard kept a "harem" of women and that Morrison said her relationship with Bernard had an "innocence" because of his "impotence." Meyers interpreted each word sexually rather than figuratively and platonically. No evidence exists in the DeVotos' correspondence that Bernard ever strayed. Behavior speaks louder. Though the Morrisons and the DeVotos were never as close after Frost's affair, there was no breach to suggest that Avis and Theodore had been betrayed by their respective spouses coupling. Avis stayed friends with Kathleen all her life, and Theodore served as an usher at Bernard's funeral.

"I am too strong": quoted by Stegner, *Uneasy Chair,* 248.

"You're a good poet": ibid., 249.

"He was a devil": ADV to JC, September 2, 1960, ADVP.

38 *"Avis is too tough"*: BDV to Katharine Sterne, September 8, 1941, BDVP, Box 3.

"such a bastard": ADV to JC, November 5, 1953, ADVP.

Her name was: details from M. DeVoto, *Selected Letters.*

"female zombie": Katharine Sterne to BDV, February (likely) 1942, BDVP.

"den of horrors": Katharine Sterne to BDV, July 14, 1940, BDVP.

"a hell of a lot": Katharine Sterne to BDV, January 1941, BDVP.

39   *"Instead of writing":* ADV to JC, February 21, 1956, ADVP.

complimented her book reviews: Katharine Sterne to BDV, after February 21, 1943, BDVP.

Avis agreed: Stegner, *Uneasy Chair,* 222.

"witty, restrained": ADV to JC, February 21, 1956, ADVP.

"She kept her distance": ADV to JC, February 21, 1956, ADVP.

"Sure you're romantic": BDV to Catherine Bowen, in Stegner, *Letters,* 277.

"You shouldn't have": Katharine Sterne to BDV, spring 1942, BDVP.

40   *"wasn't always the most":* ADV to Chet Olsen, "Wednesday" after BDV died, Chester J. Olsen Collection, Stewart Library Special Collections, Weber State University, Ogden, UT.

be too tolerant: When Avis became executive of the Sterne letters after DeVoto's death, she put them under seal until after her own death. Near the end of her life she assisted her son Mark in preparing an edited collection that was published in 2012. Avis said her delay in making the letters public was because others were alive whom DeVoto wrote about with extra vitriol, not because of any complicated questions it would raise about the workings of her marriage.

when Bernard reached: details in this section from BDV, *Western Paradox,* ch. 1; "Easy Chair" columns; Katharine Sterne letters from summer 1940; and Schlesinger, *A Life.*

41   *"That part of Kansas":* BDV to Katharine Sterne, July 14, 1940, BDVP.

"practically pathological": BDV to Katharine Sterne, July 14, 1940, BDVP.

Her tough love response: BDV, *Western Paradox,* 182.

"bring the land back": BDV to Katharine Sterne, July 14, 1940, BDVP.

Schlesinger would remember: Schlesinger, *A Life,* 232.

"Storm coming up": BDV, *Western Paradox,* 183.

42   *The environmental triage:* FDR and CCC details from Brinkley, *Rightful Heritage.*

"A nation that destroys": Brinkley, *Rightful Heritage,* 289.

"We must all dedicate": ibid., 344.

"a better country": BDV to Katharine Sterne, June 15, 1940, BDVP.

Though overwhelmingly male: Sexual integration was not a CCC achievement; auxiliary camps opened for fewer than 10,000 young women, despite Eleanor Roosevelt's agitation. Brinkley, *Rightful Heritage,* 255–256.

"I'm afraid you get": BDV to Katharine Sterne, July 14, 1940, BDVP.

43   *"world is on fire":* BDV, "All Quiet Along the Huron," *Harper's,* November 1940.

"prophets of disaster": BDV to Katharine Sterne, July 14, 1940, BDVP.

upstaged by Pat: McCarran closed the event; see "Lindbergh Urges We 'Cooperate' with Germany if Reich Wins War," *New York Times,* August 5, 1940, and Charles A. Lindbergh, *The Wartime Journals of Charles A. Lindbergh* (San Diego: Harcourt, 1970), 375.

"ready to get into": BDV to Katharine Sterne, June 15, 1940, BDVP.

"those who would not": FDR fireside chat, May 26, 1940.

"I guess maybe": BDV to Katharine Sterne, June 15, 1940, BDVP.

"*Avis dissuaded him*": Schlesinger, *A Life,* 234.

44   "*Always the loveliest*": BDV to Katharine Sterne, June 15, 1940, BDVP.

    Avis could sleep: see January 2, 1941, ADV to Mrs. Eugene Manlove Rhodes, BDVP.

    and never leaving: "I could hardly get her out," BDV to a Dr. Waldrop, April 29, 1946, BDVP.

    "*Buffalo country*": BDV to Katharine Sterne, July 14, 1940, BDVP.

    This "fine trip": BDV to Katharine Sterne, June 15, 1940; for more on DeVoto's sense of geographic, ecologic, geomorphic, and climatologic determinism, see his *Course of Empire* and Kaplan, *Earning the Rockies.*

45   "*We cannot separate*": Abraham Lincoln, first inaugural address, March 4, 1861.

    "*the great arsenal*": Franklin Roosevelt, radio broadcast, December 29, 1940.

5. YEARS OF DECISION

47   *In the stormy spring:* details of the DeVotos' house from letters, recollections of Mark DeVoto, and Stegner, *Uneasy Chair,* 229–230; for financing details and interior descriptions, see BDV to Katharine Sterne, May 28, June 12, and September 8, 1941, BDVP.

    half of all Americans: Goodwin, *No Ordinary Time,* 42.

    $20,000: Stegner, *Uneasy Chair,* 427, n. 9.

    Buick Special: BDV, "Western Trip, Impressions and Experiences," *Harper's,* August 1946.

    oak parquet: BDV, "Les Amis des Deux Fishboulettes," *Harper's,* May 1952.

    "*For the first time*": BDV to Katharine Sterne, June 12, 1940, BDVP.

    framed photos: see ADV to JC, February 9, 1953, ADVP.

48   "*Villa DeVoto*": ADV to JC, February 13, 1955, ADVP.

    "*a happy woman*": recollection of "Betty" to ADV, November 17, 1955, BDVP, Box 22.

    registered for the draft: BDV, "Commencement Address," *Harper's,* July 1942.

    The army put Bernard: see BDV, "Easy Chair," *Harper's,* March 1945.

    studied Nazi propaganda: see BDV, *The Literary Fallacy* (Boston: Little, Brown, 1944), 115–116.

    "*The swagger*": BDV, World War II speech, circa 1942, BDVP, Box 52.1.

    marine brigadier general: see ADV to JC, May 10, 1957, ADVP.

49   *feel "giddy":* BDV to Lt. Col. John M. Kemper, October 28, 1943, BDVP.

    Public lands contributed: details from Brinkley, *Rightful Heritage;* Goodwin, *No Ordinary Time;* and National Park Service, "World War II & The American Home Front" (Washington, DC: US Department of the Interior, 2007).

50   *rancher from Goleta:* see BDV to Katharine Sterne, May 18, 1943, BDVP.

    "*feel proud*": Stephen Ambrose, introduction to the year 2000 edition of BDV's *The Year of Decision* (New York: St. Martin's Press).

    "*gone blind*": ADV to JC, February 9, 1953, ADVP.

51   "*raise merry havoc*": Patrick McCarran to daughter Margaret, December 20, 1941, PMC.

    "*Hah-ha!*": handwritten in margin of October 25, 1940, letter from George Storck to R. F. Camalier, PMC, Box 37.

    "*go to town*": Earl Haskell to H. H. Hening, March 15, 1945, PMC, Box 37 (reference to New Mexico senator Carl Hatch, committee leader).

    made house calls: see Earl Haskell to W. A. Berryhill, April 9, 1942, and to Roderick Beach, August 27, 1943, PMC, Box 9.

interrupt and take over: see A. S. Gillespie to Patrick McCarran, September 29, 1941, PMC, Box 37.

for being "unbiased": Russell Thorpe, secretary, Wyoming Stock Growers Association, to George Storck, October 10, 1941, PMC, Box 37.

"the fairest": J. B. Wilson, secretary, Wyoming Wool Growers Association, to Patrick McCarran, October 11, 1941, PMC, Box 37.

translated only by white men: see Earl Haskell correspondence re: potential Navajo translator at Albuquerque meeting, PMC, Box 9.

highest per capita: "By the Numbers: A Look at Native Enlistment During the Major Wars," Vincent Schilling, *Indian Country Today*, February 6, 2014, https://denix.osd.mil/na/military/.

the only group: according to letters sent during the McCarran Hearings by the Congress of American Indians, Wyoming Stock Growers Association Records, Box 84, American Heritage Center, University of Wyoming, Laramie.

Haskell tipped: see Earl Haskell to Kelsey Presley, August 17, 1942, PMC, Box 9.

"every consideration": Arizona Cattle Growers Association Newsletter, December 9, 1941, PMC, Box 37.

Haskell encouraged: see Earl Haskell to Jim Butler, September 15, 1945, PMC, Box 41.

52 *government targets:* see Earl Haskell to Benjamin F. Casey, March 31, 1943, PMC, Box 37.

protect them against "reprisals": Earl Haskell to Roderick Beach, August 27, 1943, PMC, Box 9; see also Haskell to Walter Sarracino, November 13, 1943, PMC, Box 37.

fury and distrust: see Earl Haskell to Jim Butler, September 15, 1945, PMC, Box 41.

affect the conservation workers: Earl Haskell, letter, January 19, 1945, PMC, Box 41.

Haskell privately called: see Earl Haskell re: Virginia Graham, PMC, Box 9.

more than fifteen million: see BDV, "Easy Chair #134," *Harper's*, December 1946, and "The West," *Harper's*, January 1947; also J. Elmer Brock, "Truth vs. Fiction," *American Cattle Producer*, May 1947.

"The whole business": Paul F. Frieder to BDV, January 4, 1946 (probably 1947), BDVP.

"stockmen were hoarding": J. B. Wilson to *Harper's*, February 20, 1948, BDVP.

"a large percentage": J. Elmer Brock, *American Cattle Producer*, May 1947.

"Nevada stockmen": Walter Gilmer to Patrick McCarran, January 14, 1943, PMC, Box 37.

53 *"We do not want":* H. Stanley Coffin to Patrick McCarran, January 28, 1943, PMC, Box 37.

"We have no chance": "Norman H. Biltz: Memoirs of 'Duke of Nevada,'" interview by Mary Ellen Glass, University of Nevada Oral History Program, Special Collections, University of Nevada, Reno.

Roosevelt received a report: Ybarra, *Washington Gone Crazy*, 362–363.

"Norm, I can't": "Norman H. Biltz: Memoirs of 'Duke of Nevada,'" interview by Glass.

"Patsy told me": ibid.

54 *"The way to get":* BDV to Elmer Davis, March 28, 1944, BDVP.

"intellectual revolutionary": DeVoto FBI file.

barred from reading: see Stegner, *Uneasy Chair*, 233–234.

don't go unless: DeVoto's friend was Sam Morison, an admiral in the US Navy Reserve and a World War II historian; author interview with Mark DeVoto.

55 *"I don't think I'd better"*: BDV to Katharine Sterne, April 25, 1944, BDVP.
   "Well, will you wait": *Boston Daily Globe,* April 12, 1944.
   both arrested: Stegner, *Uneasy Chair,* 261.
   "If they were to": *Boston Traveler,* January 3, 1945.
56 *"The place to fight"*: BDV to Mina Curtiss, October 14, 1946, BDVP.
   They met: see Wendell Willkie to BDV, March 6, 1944, BDVP.
   "DeVoto points out": Wendell Willkie, March 10, 1944, BDVP.
   "To those who believe": *Boston Herald,* March 24, 1944.
   the charges: see BDV, "Literary Censorship," *Harper's,* May 1947, and "For the Record,"
   Harper's, June 1955; also Stegner, *Uneasy Chair,* 299, 349–350.
   "It was perfect": BDV to Katharine Sterne, April 25, 1944, BDVP.
57 *"courageous defense"*: Lillian Smith to BDV, May 24, 1944, BDVP.
   "Dear Avis": undated letter, BDVP, Box 21.
   "I'm tougher": ADV to JC, December 19, 1955, ADVP.

6. THE LANDGRAB

61 *The original Corps:* travelogue in this chapter drawn heavily from BDV's "Easy Chair" columns, August 1946–January 1947; BDV to Garrett Mattingly, June 4, 1946, BDVP; BDV,
   Western Paradox; reminiscences from ADV to JC, ADVP; Stegner, *Uneasy Chair;* and author
   interview with Mark DeVoto, August 2017.
   "I think he's got": ADV to JC, June 11, 1953, ADVP.
   Mark fell carsick: BDV to Garrett Mattingly, June 4, 1946, BDVP.
62 *An estimated one-third:* Stegner, "The Rediscovery of America: 1946," in *Mountain Water,* 44.
   "my old groove": BDV to Walt Dutton, September 23, 1945, BDVP.
63 *The Garrison Dam:* details from Reisner, *Cadillac Desert;* Peter Matthiessen, *In the Spirit of Crazy
   Horse* (New York: Penguin, 1983).
   "a genuine blown": BDV to Garrett Mattingly, June 4, 1946, BDVP.
   "pick up hints": BDV, *Easy Chair,* 352.
64 *not be allowed to fish:* Reisner, *Cadillac Desert,* 200.
   "pan-fried to parfleche": BDV, "Western Trip, Impressions and Experiences," *Harper's,* August
   1946.
   As the DeVotos saw: details from BDV, *Western Paradox,* ch. 6.
65 *J. Elmer Brock:* details from J. Elmer Brock Collection, American Heritage Center, University
   of Wyoming, Laramie.
   Horace Curzon Plunkett: Matthew Allen Pearce, "Discontent on the Range" (PhD diss.,
   University of Oklahoma, 2014), 43.
   "The outlaws": Brock Collection, Folder 6.
66 *"a miserable population"*: BDV, *Western Paradox,* 375.
   "get us what is ours": Pearce, "Discontent," 347
   nearly verbatim: Pearce, "Discontent," 280, n. 1.
   60 percent: BDV, "Sacred Cows and Public Lands," *Harper's,* July 1948, and Ybarra,
   Washington Gone Crazy, 380.

a half-million acres: Salt Lake Tribune, October 3, 1941.

67 *"a classic demonstration":* BDV, *Easy Chair,* 355.

In a move: Pearce, "Discontent," 311; Truman created the Bureau of Land Management on July 16, 1946.

"Beautiful. Ripe wheat": ADV to JC, December 16, 1967, ADVP.

"the romance of my life": Edmund Morris, *The Rise of Theodore Roosevelt* (New York: Random House, 1979), 771.

Above the DeVotos: details about wildlife resurgence during FDR's presidency from Brinkley, *Rightful Heritage,* esp. 594 (map).

68 *"the greatest good":* Gifford Pinchot, *The Fight for Conservation* (New York: Doubleday, 1910), 48.

"to help the small man": ibid.

shook the hand: see BDV, "Gifford Pinchot's *Breaking New Ground,*" *Harper's,* May 1948.

"something important": BDV, *Easy Chair,* 352.

"require you to commit": BDV, "Number 241," *Harper's,* November 1955.

"most articulate spokesman": ADV to JC, February 7, 1953, ADVP.

"The high Montana": BDV to Katharine Sterne, July 14, 1940, BDVP.

"Western roots": BDV, "Western Trip."

69 *"Even the crossroad":* ibid.

"you begin to encounter": BDV, "The Anxious West," *Harper's,* December 1946.

"raw, thriving": from Herman Hagedorn, *Roosevelt in the Badlands* (Boston: Houghton Mifflin, 1921), ch. 23.

Custer County acres: James Allen Muhn, "The Mitzpah-Pumpkin Creek Grazing District" (MA thesis, Montana State University, 1987).

wooden bar: description from November 28, 2018, author interview with Miles City resident John L. Moore.

70 *"I could have avoided":* BDV, *Easy Chair,* 352.

"born fighter": BDV's introduction to Joseph Kinsey Howard's *Strange Empire* (New York: William Morrow, 1952), 3.

71 *"tenderloins and T-bones":* BDV, "Western Trip."

"smile, stranger": BDV, "Wayfarer's Daybook," *Harper's,* December 1951.

"Avis was really": Joseph Kinsey Howard to BDV, July 11, 1946, BDVP.

"bitterly resented": BDV, *Easy Chair,* 352.

western "neurotic": Joseph Kinsey Howard to BDV, March 31, 1949, BDVP.

"You people": Joseph Kinsey Howard to BDV, July 11, 1946, BDVP.

72 *"Gosh, I wish":* BDV, "Marco Polo's Ford," *Woman's Day,* May 1947.

"Echoes of your passage": Joseph Kinsey Howard to BDV, July 11, 1946, BDVP.

"Let it blow": BDV, *Western Paradox,* 245.

73 *"The shabbiest chapter":* BDV, "The Sturdy Corporate Homesteader," *Harper's,* May 1953.

74 *"There has never been":* BDV to Ansel Adams, December 24, 1948, BDVP.

"an emotional presentation": Ansel Adams to Elbert K. Burlew, first assistant secretary, Department of the Interior, December 28, 1941, as quoted by Lauren Johnson in "Reading and Re-Reading Ansel Adams's *My Camera in the National Parks,*" *Panorama,* Fall 2020.

Yosemite Firefall: author interview with Mark DeVoto, August 2017. (The firefall was discontinued in 1968.)

"*Drive it at night*": BDV, "Night Crossing," *Woman's Day*, August 1947.

75 "*stopped above eternity*": BDV, "Roadside Meeting," *Woman's Day*, July 1947.

"*most hair-raising drive*": BDV, "Western Trip."

"*those subterranean notions*": BDV, "Night Crossing."

76 "*It's moonlight*": ibid.

"*We were as exhausted*": BDV, *Western Paradox*, 201.

"*I am an absolutely*": ADV to JC, June 11, 1953, BDVP.

"*I pay due tribute*": BDV, "Night Crossing."

77 *Chester J. "Chet" Olsen:* biography courtesy of Richa Wilson, Regional Heritage Program Leader, US Forest Service, Intermountain Region.

Utah had: details from Kenneth W. Baldridge, *The Civilian Conservation Corps in Utah* (Salt Lake City: University of Utah Press, 2019), and Twila Van Leer, "CCC Camps Changed Utah— and Lives of Workers," *Deseret News*, August 8, 1995.

"*the most spectacular*": BDV, "Restoration of the Wasatch," *Harper's*, October 1949.

78 "*A darling*": ADV to JC, March 20, 1953, ADVP.

After World War II: Ybarra, *Washington Gone Crazy*, 664–669.

79 *twelve million veterans:* ibid., 397. (An estimated 5 million families needed homes; 100,000 vets were homeless in Chicago alone, according to Oshinsky, *A Conspiracy So Immense*, 66–67).

"*said that Senator*": from Bugsy Siegel FBI file (https://vault.fbi.gov/Bugsy%20 Siegel%20), Part 18, p. 50.

"*funds made available*": ibid., 99.

"*They were in the middle*": Ybarra, *Washington Gone Crazy*, 667.

"*in case he was*": Siegel FBI file, Part 18, p. 54.

"*pound the table*": Ybarra, *Washington Gone Crazy*, 668.

80 *McCarran chauffeur:* see William B. Rice telegram of May 14, 1945, PMC, Box 37.

81 "*best thing I ever did*": BDV to Garrett Mattingly, August 1, 1946, BDVP.

"*Thirty-nine miles*": BDV, "Western Trip."

"*I know what*": ADV to JC, February 17, 1953, ADVP.

"*Some of the big*": BDV to Mrs. Hanson, October 5, 1948, BDVP. Added Bernard to Mrs. Hanson: "It was their bragging at Salt Lake City in the summer of 1946, in fact, that gave me the clue I needed to take me to a transcript of the Joint Committee meetings."

"*loud talk*": BDV, "Two-Gun Desmond Is Back," *Harper's*, March 1951.

"*heart of the matter*": BDV, *Easy Chair*, 352.

Rice entrusted it: see BDV to Walt Dutton, October 21, 1946, BDVP: "the transcript which Chet Olsen and Mr. Rice showed me."

"*Every newspaperman*": BDV, *Easy Chair*, 352.

82 "*swivel-chair oligarchy*": quoted in BDV, "The West Against Itself," *Harper's*, January 1947.

nearly 146 million: 145,777,974 million acres of BLM lands in the contiguous US per Arthur Carhardt, "Don't Fence Us In," *Pacific Spectator*, vol. 1, no. 3, Summer 1947.

resurvey the forests: see J. Elmer Brock, *American Cattle Producer*, May 1947.

"*The plan is*": BDV, "The West Against Itself."

83 "*The West committing*": ibid.

85 *"psychic split"*: ibid.

86 *"Senator McCarran has"*: ibid.

"where my dope": BDV to Joseph Kinsey Howard, May 25, 1948, BDVP.

"magnificent job": Frederick Allen to BDV, September 24, 1946, BDVP.

"My article fused": DeVoto, *Easy Chair,* 354.

7. A NEW WORD FOR "RUSTLER"

87 *"Let no man"*: as quoted by Ketcham, *This Land,* 396.

88 *"Faithful Old Cowboy"*: Harry Sever to BDV, July 16, 1953, BDVP.

"You are just as": Horace Albright to BDV, January 17, 1947, BDVP.

"thinking exactly": Leslie Miller to Alys Ritterbrown, cc'ed to BDV, January 28, 1947, BDVP.

"how the West can": Stephen Kaufman to BDV, February 25, 1947, BDVP.

"discussing and cussing": C. F. Latham to BDV, January 9, 1947, BDVP.

"Do fight for us": Virginia Graham to BDV, February 23, 1947, BDVP.

On behalf of: Albert Van S. Pulling to BDV, January 31, 1947, BDVP.

punctuated "Amen!": F. R. Farnsworth to BDV, December 27, 1946, BDVP.

"I believe no": Richard Neuberger to Frederick Allen, January 20, 1947, BDVP.

"pull the teeth": Jack Holmes to BDV, April 24, 1947, BDVP.

"Keep your wrath!": Bennett Weaver to BDV, January 19, 1947, BDVP.

"you deserve": Paul Frieder to BDV, January 4, 1946, BDVP.

89 *"Your last article"*: C. E. Dougherty to BDV, January 24, 1948, BDVP.

"If I have ever": William Vogt to BDV, January 21, 1947, BDVP.

"blew a gratifying": Henry Seidel to BDV, January 13, 1947, BDVP.

"private ownership": quoted in BDV, "The Western Land Grab," *Harper's,* June 1947.

"I have found": L. H. Linford to BDV, January 23, 1947, BDVP.

"You will agree": *Colorado Granger,* January 1947.

"Well, you sure": Joseph Kinsey Howard, December 15, 1946, BDVP.

"I am so proud": ADV to JC, February 17, 1953, ADVP.

"I truly believe": ADV to Chet Olsen, November 16, 1955, Chester J. Olsen Collection, Stewart Library Special Collections, Weber State University, Ogden, UT.

talked to "reds": Rhoda Hanson to BDV, 1948, BDVP.

"Having met you": ibid.

90 *suffered a heart attack:* see December 3, 1946, telegram from McCarran's office ("Urgent you call Betty McCarran immediately"), Eva Adams Papers, Special Collections, University of Nevada, Reno. "In December 1946 McCarran had a heart attack," Ybarra, *Washington Gone Crazy,* 413.

"campaign of vituperation": see McCarran speech to Izaak Walton League, March 28, 1947, PMC, Box 47. McCarran took advantage of the league's invitation to respond: he was reimbursed $110 for expenses and entered his speech in the *Congressional Record;* see McCarran to Kenneth Reid, March 31, 1947, PMC.

"Agents were stunned": Cartha DeLoach, quoted in Ybarra, *Washington Gone Crazy,* 667.

91 *Topics up for discussion:* details from transcript of 1948 Wyoming Stock Growers Association

meeting, American Heritage Center, University of Wyoming, Laramie. (Border fence, p. 333; Brock re: disease prevention, p. 269.)

"*Attacker of*": ibid., 102.

"*Slapped you fellows*": ibid., 109.

"*We have been lambasted*": ibid., 31.

92 "*I want to file*": Barrett Hearings transcripts, BDVP, Box 76.3.

"*firing squad hearings*": BDV, "Sacred Cows and Public Lands," *Harper's,* July 1948.

"*If it wasn't for*": Struthers Burt to BDV, October 15, 1947, BDVP.

he was "boiling": BDV to Struthers Burt, March 2, 1948, BDVP.

93 "*You started your*": from Double J Ranch to BDV, July 4, 1950, BDVP.

"*Honors for*": Katharine Graham, *Washington Post,* July 4, 1948.

"*weighted in favor*": BDV, "Sacred Cows and Public Lands."

"*Stockman Barrett's*": ibid.

"*acquiring ownership*": J. Elmer Brock, *Denver Post,* February 2, 1947.

94 *went to prison:* Representative Thomas was sent to the same prison as two members of the Hollywood Ten.

"*prescriptive publicity*": see Oshinsky, *A Conspiracy,* 93, 339.

"*Extend* every *assistance*": Gentry, *J. Edgar Hoover,* 353.

"*dude ranch historian*": see J. Elmer Brock to Frederick Allen, July 10, 1948, Wyoming Wool Growers Collection, American Heritage Center, Laramie, WY.

"*pink pen pusher*": J. Elmer Brock to Frederick Allen, February 7, 1948, BDVP.

DeVoto's "ilk": Dan Hanson, *Cow Country,* December 18, 1948.

Bernard mused: BDV, "Correct English and Communists in College," *Harper's,* June 1949.

95 "*one of the stock*": ADV to JC, February 27, 1953, ADVP.

"*bedeviling*" *Bernard:* transcript, 1948 Wyoming Stock Growers Association meeting, p. 283.

"*should have a hammer*": Charley Meyers, *Wyoming Eagle,* January 16, 1948.

Brock demanded: see J. Elmer Brock to Frederick Allen, February 7, 1948, BDVP.

"*oily*" *Bernard DeVoto:* see J. Elmer Brock, *American Cattle Producer,* May 1947; the article was similar to the "Stockman's Brief" that Brock sent to Frederick Allen and J. Edgar Hoover.

96 *Brock would claim:* J. Elmer Brock, *Land Letter,* June 1948.

"*involve costs*": J. Elmer Brock, "Whose Home on the Range?," October 1950, BDVP, Box 68, Folder 1045.

"*We are tired*": J. Elmer Brock, *American Cattle Producer,* May 1947.

"*J. Elmer Brock is*": BDV to Alfred Knopf, February 3, 1949, BDVP.

"*Ye blind guides*": J. Elmer Brock to Russell Lynes, March 13, 1948, BDVP.

"*you are in the dilemma*": BDV to Jonathan Forman, July 27, 1948, BDVP.

97 *contacted Ben Hibbs:* see BDV to Ben Hibbs, June 24, 1949, BDVP.

"*Brock is the prize*": BDV to Russell Lynes, March 10, 1948, BDVP.

"*I have been enjoying*": J. Elmer Brock to J. Byron Wilson, July 20, 1948, Wyoming Wool Growers Collection, American Heritage Center, Laramie, WY.

"*Like you I take*": J. Byron Wilson to J. Elmer Brock, July 9, 1948, Wyoming Wool Growers Collection.

"*a little madder*": J. Byron Wilson to J. Elmer Brock, July 29, 1948, Wyoming Wool Growers Collection.

a fabulist and a plagiarist: see BDV to Frederick Allen, March 21, 1948, BDVP, re: Brock's March 13 letter claiming "this malicious propaganda used by Mr. DeVoto originates from some of the most vicious of the 59 land management agencies. It has been pumped out to the public through your Mr. DeVoto."

"I hope he may": BDV to Alfred Knopf, February 3, 1949, BDVP.

"Brace yourself": J. Elmer Brock to J. Byron Wilson, April 3, 1948, Wyoming Wool Growers Collection.

98 *stroke of genius:* see transcript of 1948 Wyoming Stock Growers Association meeting; Colorado Stockgrowers 1948 Resolution #20 RAISING OF PUBLICITY FUNDS, BDVP, Box 68.

by 1947: transcript of 1947 Wyoming Stock Growers Association meeting.

"Eat More Beef": see transcript of 1951 Wyoming Stock Growers Association meeting. Through decades of evolutions of the livestock associations, and advertising mediums, Two-Gun Desmond is still fighting the bull in the twenty-first century using the updated slogan "Beef: It's What's for Dinner."

"every time a factual statement": BDV, "#121," *Harper's,* November 1945.

apologized for the "injustice": BDV to Merle Miller at *Harper's,* February 25, 1948, BDVP.

"If you proof it": ADV to JC, January 9, 1953, ADVP.

99 *"just no books":* ADV to JC, April 30, 1961, ADVP.

suing for libel: see Frank Barrett to attorney Louis Necho, January 7, 1948, BDVP, Box 7.

"Barrett Rips": State Tribune Leader, January 22, 1948.

"Bernard DeVoto, Rancher's Critic": Denver Post, April 29, 1948.

"merely incidental": Russell Thorpe, quoted in *State Tribune Leader,* April 28, 1948.

Bernard invited Scott: see letter to BDV from W. L. Scott, May 17, 1948, BDVP, Box 19.

"I'M AFRAID": telegram, Walter Scott to BDV, BDVP, Box 19.

100 *suggested Bernard "compromise":* see BDV to Walt Dutton, May 21, 1948, BDVP.

"Such intemperate language": Walter Scott to BDV, May 17, 1948, BDVP.

tip from his western network: see BDV to Frederick Allen, May 21, 1948, BDVP.

"There are now": BDV to William Sloane, May 8, 1948, BDVP.

"defeat the bastards": BDV to Walt Dutton, May 21, 1948, BDVP.

"When the Grazing Service": BDV, "Sacred Cows," reprinted in *Western Paradox,* 79.

8. "DUE NOTICE TO THE FBI"

101 *printing "avowed extremists":* BDV to Jonathan Forman, July 27, 1948, BDVP.

"Brock is making": BDV to Morris Llewellyn Cooke, June 28, 1948, BDVP.

102 *"so visibly transformed":* Arthur Schlesinger Jr., "A Man with a Mission," *New York Times,* December 19, 1954.

11 percent: see BDV, "Conservation Down and on the Way Out," *Harper's,* August 1954.

103 *"unimpaired for the enjoyment":* from An Act to Establish a National Park Service, approved August 25, 1916.

104 *"I do recall":* Morris Llewellyn Cooke to BDV, July 19, 1948, BDVP.

105 *$12 billion:* BDV, "One Hundred Year Plan," *Harper's,* August 1950.

McCarran threatened: see letter to Patrick McCarran from Northcutt Ely, February 18, 1949, PMC, Box 1.

a job reference: see Paul Child to Morris Llewellyn Cooke, September 10, 1947, JCP.

106 *"What finally sparked":* BDV to a Mr. Harding, October 19, 1949, BDVP.

"He checked": ADV to W. H. Hutchison, January 11, 1956, BDVP.

107 *"Of course the evaluators":* BDV, "Due Notice to the FBI," *Harper's*, October 1949.

"witch hunt": see https://www.trumanlibrary.gov/education/presidential-inquiries/trumans -loyalty-program.

historians would estimate: Oshinsky, *A Conspiracy*, 91.

108 *"an avalanching danger":* BDV, "Due Notice."

"We are dividing": ibid.

"I like a country": ibid.

Denver Post *headlines:* "Rancher's Target Moved," *Denver Post*, November 29, 1951, re: Earl D. Sandvig, chief of Forest Service Division of Range and Wildlife Management; "U.S. Shifts Second," *Denver Post*, December 16, 1951, re: Roy L. Williams, supervisor, Bighorn National Forest.

109 *"Accusers did not":* Leon Hurtt to BDV, June 5, 1949, BDVP. Peterson's FBI file reveals that neither of his accusers would sign an affidavit or testify to a grand jury.

a "good job": see "1953, J. Edgar Hoover" at https://news.gallup.com/poll/9964/timeline -polling-history-people-shaped-united-states-world.aspx.

110 *anything "sassy":* ADV to JC, October 26, 1955, ADVP.

"our sheep-like acceptance": Ralph Jacobs to BDV, October 3, 1949, BDVP.

"I want to thank you": W. F. Henze to BDV, October 7, 1949, BDVP.

"There are so few": Florence Eldridge to BDV, March 1949, BDVP.

"You are so right": Claire Cochran to BDV, October 18, 1949, BDVP.

"If, in the future": Jack O'Brien to BDV, October 21, 1955, BDVP.

"Best wishes": Chas Sauers to BDV, April 20, 1949, BDVP.

"I am glad": BDV, quoted by Tom Knudson, "FBI Was Out to Get Freethinking DeVoto," *High Country News*, August 8, 1994.

111 *superlatives like "incredible":* Oshinsky, *A Conspiracy*, 78.

"Joe Frump": ibid., 81.

"That's the way": Tye, *Demagogue*, 107–108.

"This plan and this program": Ybarra, *Washington Gone Crazy*, 8.

"A conspiracy on a scale": Oshinsky, *A Conspiracy*, 197.

"McCarthy had made": ibid., 208.

112 *"If I throw":* "Norman H. Biltz: Memoirs of 'Duke of Nevada,'" interview by Mary Ellen Glass, University of Nevada Oral History Program, Special Collections, University of Nevada, Reno.

"If a fowl": Tye, *Demagogue*, 138.

"From now on": BDV, "Due Notice."

"A surprising number": BDV to a Mr. Wilson, November 7, 1949, BDVP.

"rather obscene": special agent in charge, Butte, MT, to J. Edgar Hoover, September 7, 1949, DeVoto FBI file.

113 *"This article reflects":* memo to all FBI headquarters, October 13, 1949, DeVoto FBI file.

"I do not care": J. Edgar Hoover, *Harper's,* December 1949.

"both slightly tight": Fowler Harper to BDV, October 13, 1949, BDVP.

"Like a dog": Diamond, *Compromised Campus,* 42.

114   *"between true Liberalism":* Bureau Bulletin #71, 1947, DeVoto FBI file.

"Have you ever": BDV to Daniel Mebane, October 19, 1949, BDVP.

"don't try to pass": and additional details, from DeVoto FBI file.

Moles inside: ibid. Freelance writer David Jacobson gave the FBI details about *Harper's,* as Harvard history professor William Elliott likewise did about BDV.

115   *"As far as the sentiments":* ibid.

references to the New Republic: ibid.

"Hats Off": Diamond, *Compromised Campus,* ch. 7.

Hoover "blackballed" him: See Fowler Harper to BDV, October 13, 1949, BDVP.

116   *"I learned long ago":* Diamond, *Compromised Campus,* 164.

The agent's mind: proceeding details from William Langer FBI file.

117   *"extreme cordiality":* ibid. William Langer's stepson, Evan Nelson, recounted in 2021 that according to family lore DeVoto dressed down the FBI agent by asking "how low can you sink?" This is not reflected in the agent's report.

"could surprise me": ADV to Robert E. Lee, February 10, 1956, BDVP.

9. "SHALL WE LET THEM RUIN OUR NATIONAL PARKS?"

118   *"Nobody asked":* BDV, "Shall We Let Them Ruin Our National Parks?" *Saturday Evening Post,* July 22, 1950.

"Shall We Let": the headline was flashed in episode six of the 2009 Ken Burns series *The National Parks: America's Best Idea.*

119   *"The parks do not":* BDV, "Shall We Let."

one of "the finest": Horace Albright to BDV, July 21, 1950, BDVP.

"crisis situation": Arthur Carhart to BDV, July 20, 1950, BDVP.

"those who vote": Leslie Miller to BDV, August 8, 1950, BDVP.

"noble": David Brower to BDV, August 7, 1950, BDVP.

said no: see BDV to Mrs. Owen V. Young, August 15, 1950, BDVP.

120   *approved the Echo Park Dam:* Harvey, *Symbol of Wilderness,* 90–91.

"It looks like": Ybarra, *Washington Gone Crazy,* 501.

121   *shocking testimony:* ibid., 489.

"I have here": Oshinsky, *A Conspiracy,* 109.

"card-carrying" Communists: ibid., 110.

"How do you say": ibid., 186.

122   *"inference, allusion":* quoted in Ybarra, *Washington Gone Crazy,* 491.

"Hell, there ain't": Tye, *Demagogue,* 120.

"My forum is": quoted in Oshinsky, *A Conspiracy,* 167.

"a good thing for the country": Oshinksy, *A Conspiracy,* 158.

fourth most admired: Tye, *Demagogue,* 371.

"pals" with Hiss: BDV to Garrett Mattingly, September 27, 1951, BDVP.

a "prig": ADV to JC, March 1, 1967, ADVP.

"the top Russian": Tye, *Demagogue*, 155.

123   *"Pure moonshine"*: Ybarra, *Washington Gone Crazy*, 496.

camel dung: ibid., 574, and BDV to Katharine Sterne, September 6, 1934, BDVP.

"Positive as": ADV to JC, March 20, 1953, ADVP.

"I doubt if": BDV to Dr. Weimer, March 20, 1950, BDVP.

conflating communism: Something Whittaker Chambers dodged by claiming that quitting communism cured him of being gay. See Gentry, *J. Edgar Hoover*, 363.

"communists and queers": Oshinsky, *A Conspiracy*, 529.

"either a Communist": Tye, *Demagogue*, 206.

letter to the editor: see BDV letter to *Boston Herald*, April 4, 1950, BDVP.

124   *"depressed over world"*: "F. O. Matthiessen Plunges to Death from Hotel Window," *Harvard Crimson*, April 1, 1950.

"If I hadn't pulled": Oshinsky, *A Conspiracy*, 180–181.

"publicly discuss": Ybarra, *Washington Gone Crazy*, 591.

"I have been": ibid.

125   *"he fathered"*: *Deseret News*, February 17, 1951.

"We are hoping": Day Edgar to BDV, August 8, 1950, BDVP.

temporarily barring: see ADV to JC, April 28, 1953, ADVP.

"For the first": Ybarra, *Washington Gone Crazy*, 532.

126   *"almost the perfect"*: ibid., 487.

"totalitarian": ibid., 527.

liberalized deportations: ibid., 465. McCarran's nativism was predictably unequal: in July 1949, as J. Elmer Brock agitated for more livestock-industry loopholes in Wyoming, McCarran said there was "no more important bill on the calendar" than one welcoming 250 Basque sheepherders from Spain.

"an evil man": ibid., 7.

"symptoms of paranoia": BDV, "But Sometimes They Vote Right Too," *Harper's*, November 1950.

127   *"a pissant in"*: Patrick McCarran to wife Martha, October 20, 1952, PMC.

"Pat is one of": *New York Herald Tribune*, January 2, 1954.

"of one blood": Ybarra, *Washington Gone Crazy*, 477.

"who writes for": ibid., 626.

"Under the Taylor": Patrick McCarran to daughter Mary, January 29, 1954, PMC.

128   *"I insist"*: ADV to JC, March 20, 1953, ADVP.

"strange dives": ADV to JC, February 9, 1953, ADVP.

"little hole in the wall": ADV to JC, May 30, 1952, ADVP.

"I am perfectly positive": ADV to JC, February 27, 1953, ADVP.

129   *"like a homing pigeon"*: ADV to JC, May 30, 1952, ADVP.

"just like my boys": BDV to Chas Sauers, May 22, 1950, BDVP.

"Say, son": BDV in A. B. Guthrie, *Nieman Reports*, January 1958.

"the Government issue": Oshinsky, *A Conspiracy*, 139.

quarries inspected: ibid., 172.

The beef bubble: details in this section from Davis, *River*.

130 *"To those of you"*: quoted by Cody Newill in "How Kansas City's West Bottoms Went from Vacant to Vibrant," *KCRU*, August 13, 2014.

131 *"It's the worst"*: Louisville *Courier-Journal,* July 18, 1951.

132 *"The Bureau knows"*: Joseph Kinsey Howard to BDV, circa January 3, 1948, BDVP.

"absolutely uncorruptable": BDV to Henry Allen Moe of Guggenheim Foundation, January 12, 1948, BDVP.

"delighted and proud": Joseph Kinsey Howard to BDV, April 10, 1947, BDVP.

"summit of human": BDV to Garrett Mattingly, October 16, 1951, BDVP; DeVoto "spent ten days in the mts with Joe Howard:"

133 *tears of joy:* see Senator Richard Neuberger, *Congressional Record,* January 20, 1956, p. 1005.

"who also appreciated": Ellers Koch to BDV, December 17, 1952, BDVP.

"I temporarily recovered": BDV to Garrett Mattingly, October 16, 1951, BDVP.

Howard's impoverished mother: see Stegner, *Uneasy Chair,* 411.

"God-damndest fool": BDV to Garrett Mattingly, October 28, 1950, BDVP.

134 *"It's a hell"*: ADV to JC, April 28, 1953, ADVP.

"All of us know": Elizabeth Pike to ADV, BDVP, Box 22.

10. NEW FRIENDS

135 *Though Hunt was:* details from McDaniel, *Dying.*

"pimping for": BDV to a Mr. Basso, August 31, 1951, BDVP.

136 *"for the glory"*: ibid.

"hitting below the belt": McDaniel, *Dying,* 183. Ironically, McCarthy's story that the Nazi confessions were coerced was Soviet propaganda.

"a dam which": Patrick McCarran to Edith L. St. Cyr, February 20, 1952, PMC.

137 *"One couldn't have prayed"*: Harvey, *Symbol of Wilderness,* 7.

138 *"considerable correspondence"*: Lester Hunt to BDV, March 24, 1953, BDVP.

"For your information": Arthur Watkins to Lester Hunt, April 16, 1952, Lester Calloway Hunt Papers, American Heritage Center, University of Wyoming, Laramie.

"The great majority": Lester Hunt to Arthur Watkins, April 19, 1952, Hunt Papers.

DeVoto and Lester Hunt: Lester "Buddy" Hunt Jr. details from McDaniel, *Dying.*

139 *April issue of* Fortune: BDV, "Why Professors Are Suspicious of Business," *Fortune,* April 1951.

"as being associated": BDV, "Crusade Resumed," *Harper's,* November 1951.

"talking out": ADV to JC, July 20, 1956, ADVP.

"a magazine that helps": ADV to JC, February 17, 1953, ADVP.

140 *"the only mission"*: BDV, "Crusade Resumed."

"a Communist or fellow": ibid.

"I do all": ADV to JC, May 30, 1952, ADVP.

"Your able diatribe": JC to ADV, March 8, 1952, JCP.

"Dear Mrs. Child": ADV to JC, April 3, 1952, ADVP.

11. POTENT MIXTURES

141 *"the charming DeVoto"*: Jan Donnelly to ADV, BDVP, Box 22.

"*Dear Mrs. DeVoto*": Ethan W. Vars to ADV, December 9, 1951, BDVP.

"*it is very relaxing*": ADV to JC, May 30, 1952, ADVP.

"*sent back recipes*": JC to ADV, May 5, 1952, JCP.

142 "*6 ft. plus*": JC to ADV, February 23, 1953, JCP.

"*well, dear*": ADV to JC, March 20, 1953, ADVP.

"*He really can*": JC to ADV, January 28, 1953, JCP.

"*a rough-hewn*": ADV to JC, February 17, 1953, ADVP.

"*think McCarthy is* ": JC to ADV, May 5, 1952, JCP.

Julia McWilliams: details from Spitz, *Dearie;* Conant, *Covert Affair;* Reardon, *As Always, Julia;* Child, *My Life.*

143 "*pleasantly crazy*": Conant, *Covert Affair,* 80–81.

"*Over the 18 months*": ibid., 197.

only "*exhausted*": ibid., 199.

144 "*I do love*": Spitz, *Dearie,* 154.

"*operational proof*": Conant, *Covert Affair,* 227.

"*We may have passed*": ADV to JC, December 16, 1967, ADVP.

"*rapacious lumber*": Paul Child, diary, July 20, 1946, p. 404, JCP.

"*that high silent*": JC to ADV, August 20, 1953, JCP.

"*deep-seated charm*": Paul Child, diary, July 28, 1946, p. 421, JCP.

it was working well: Spitz, *Dearie,* 148; "and they made love, often and splendidly."

145 "*I love her*": Paul Child, diary, July 28, 1946, p. 422, JCP.

"*I feel it*": Spitz, *Dearie,* 195.

"*If you could see*": ibid., 194.

"*I immodestly think*": JC to ADV, December 15, 1952, JCP.

"*no such thing*": ADV to JC, December 25, 1952, ADVP.

146 "*art's sunburst*": BDV, *The Hour* (Boston: Houghton Mifflin, 1951), 67. BDV recommended Gordon's gin and Old Forester bourbon.

147 "*Heresiarch!*": Paul Child to BDV, May 23, 1953, JCP.

"*Be not so*": BDV to Paul Child, June 7, 1953, JCP.

Patrick Hurley: details from Fenby, *Chiang Kai-shek;* David Halberstam, *The Best and the Brightest* (New York: Random House, 1972); Ybarra, *Washington Gone Crazy;* Conant, *Covert Affair.*

built picture props: OSS leader "Wild" Bill Donovan wrote "to the boys back home" (likely the Office of the Commanding General, United States Forces, China Theatre), quoted in Paul Child, diary, February 11, 1945, pp. 249–250, JCP: "Child has most effectively aided Gen. Wedermeyer and Hurley in getting across to Chiang Kai-shek the kind of points which can be made in no other way."

He blamed "disloyal": Ybarra, *Washington Gone Crazy,* 567.

"*weakness in*": Conant, *Covert Affair,* 242.

148 "*engineered*": Ybarra, *Washington Gone Crazy,* 456.

"*The floodgates*": ibid., 479.

"*Trojan Horse*": ibid., 364.

"We are having": Martha McCarran to daughter Mary, (undated) 1949, PMC.

"It was grand": Patrick McCarran to daughter Mary, October 27, 1949, PMC.

"Ambassador from Nevada": *Reporter*, September 13, 1949.

"A very tolerant": Patrick McCarran to daughter Margaret, November 9, 1949, PMC.

149 *"My investigation"*: Ybarra, *Washington Gone Crazy*, 469.

"a one-man monkey-wrench": *Washington Post*, August 30, 1949.

"We had not realized": Ybarra, *Washington Gone Crazy*, 478.

"I couldn't get over": Spitz, *Dearie*, 172.

"I wouldn't give": Patrick McCarran to daughter Mary, September 25, 1949, PMC.

150 *"Our aim"*: BDV, "Stevenson and the Independent Voter," *Harper's*, April 1952.

151 *"hadn't been a neurotic"*: BDV to Garrett Mattingly, September 30, 1952, BDVP.

The platform the Democrats: see: www.presidency.ucsb.edu/documents/1952-democratic-party-platform.

"opportunity for ownership": www.presidency.ucsb.edu/documents/republican-party-platform-1952.

152 government *"partnerships"*: Harvey, *Symbol of Wilderness*, 150.

153 *"my hero"*: JC to ADV, November 18, 1954, JCP.

"I want to know": JC to ADV, November 10, 1954, JCP.

"What does Benny": JC to ADV, June 8, 1955, JCP.

"the public lands business": JC to ADV, February 23, 1953, JCP.

"Good God no": ADV to JC, February 27, 1953, ADVP.

"less harried": ADV to JC, June 11, 1953, ADVP.

"damn near all": ADV to JC, February 12, 1954, ADVP.

"B. said": ADV to JC, December 15, 1954, ADVP.

"We are going to have": ADV to JC, March 20, 1953, ADVP.

"B says the best": ADV to JC, September 30, 1954, ADVP.

"We've just gotten": JC to ADV, May 20, 1953, JCP.

"What's the country": JC to ADV, November 10, 1953, JCP.

"Maybe the Republicans": JC to ADV, November 23, 1953, JCP.

12. RICHARD DEVOTO'S ORDEAL

154 *"My family thanks"*: ADV to JC, October 3, 1952, ADVP.

"This is a completely": ibid.

"Drive a bulldozer": BDV to Garrett Mattingly, September 30, 1952, BDVP.

155 *"perfectly hysterical"*: ADV to JC, October 3, 1952, ADVP.

"I was elated": Ybarra, *Washington Gone Crazy*, 621.

Greenspun was the only: quotes that follow from ibid., 684–685.

"Greenspun apparently": ADV to JC, February 22, 1954, ADVP.

"a man I love": Ybarra, *Washington Gone Crazy*, 684.

156 *Hoover had fed:* Gentry, *J. Edgar Hoover*, 402; "Hoover was the source of the whispers."

fired for misconduct: Donald Arthur Surine FBI removal document, February 8, 1950, plus additional details from http://archive.org/details/DonaldA.Surine.

"If it walks": Oshinsky, *A Conspiracy*, 398.

157   *"trying to dig":* BDV to Professor Pedrick, December 11, 1952, BDVP.

Details from the top: DeVoto FBI file.

"physically beaten": Oshinsky, *A Conspiracy,* 243.

a *"jig-saw puzzle":* McCarthy's prepared remarks, "Text of Address by McCarthy," *New York Times,* October 28, 1952.

"Richard Dee Voto": transcript and audio of speech McCarthy actually gave at http://americanrhetoric.com/speeches/joemccarthyagainststevenson.htm.

158   *"I do not know":* Denver Post, October 29, 1952. The spokesman was Farrington Carpenter.

159   *through Surine to McCarthy:* details from DeVoto FBI file; BDV to Professor Pedrick, December 11, 1952, BDVP; *Boston Post,* February 12, 1947. In the Pedrick letter, BDV speculates that McCarthy's investigator (surely Surine) was tipped to the *Post* story by a grudgeful worker in a newspaper morgue; if so, DeVoto's FBI file suggests the FBI could have tipped him to go there.

"DeVoto denounces": http://americanrhetoric.com/speeches/joemccarthyagainststevenson.htm.

"bourgeoise" and *"imperialist":* Daily Worker, December 26, 1952.

"I have no desire": Utica Press, November 8, 1952.

160   *"He quoted me":* BDV to Professor Pedrick, December 11, 1952.

"Anyone who knows": United Press, November 4, 1952.

"I do believe in": Associated Press, October 28, 1952.

"he reviewed much of": Houston Chronicle, October 30, 1952.

"failed to answer": United Press, October 31, 1952.

"The giving gets": The News [Dayton, OH], June 20, 1953.

161   *"I suggest before you vote":* Joseph McCarthy, transcript, BDVP, Box 72. McCarthy was wrong when he said it was the "following issue" of *Harper's* that printed Hoover's response to "Due Notice to the FBI." That came two issues later, in December 1949.

"radio lightning": New York Times, November 30, 1952.

162   *"McCarthy is a liar":* Associated Press, November 4, 1952.

"McCarthy concentrated": ibid.

13. "TO AVIS AND BERNARD"

164   *"with that little worm":* ADV to JC, April 28, 1955, ADVP.

"hit-and-run" attacks: ibid.

"didn't care a bit": ADV to JC, April 25, 1955, ADVP.

"I can imagine": William Sloan to BDV, November 12, 1952, BDVP.

"Please be frank": JC to ADV, December 15, 1952, JCP.

some keen editing: see Calvin Tompkins, "Cooking with Julia Child," *The New Yorker,* December 23, 1974.

"Absolutely convinced": ADV to JC, December 25, 1952, ADVP.

"preparing the way": ibid.

165   *"itch to get into":* ADV to JC, January 13, 1953, ADVP.

"all this time": JC to ADV, January 28, 1953, JCP.

"We are all set": ADV to JC, January 22, 1953, ADVP.

"*I can't tell you*": JC to ADV, January 5, 1953, JCP.

"*I am as pleased*": ADV to JC, January 22, 1953, ADVP.

"*the activities of Bernard*": BDV to Carroll Kearns (no date, circa April 1953), BDVP; also *Congressional Record*, April 23, 1953, p. 3742.

"*Bernard DeVoto and his fellow*": Richard Neuberger to BDV, forwarding note about Mathew Ellsworth from industrial consultant Ivan Bloch, September 23, 1953, BDVP.

"*I did not*": Mathew Ellsworth to BDV, November 9, 1953, BDVP.

he did not associate: see August 31, 1955, DAR president Gertrude S. Carraway to John Fischer at *Harper's*; also Stegner, *Uneasy Chair*, 353.

166 *lose money if*: BDV to Professor Pedrick, December 11, 1952, BDVP.

the new "poison": the 3 x 5 notecards are in BDVP, Box 52.2.

"*Too few people know*": ADV to JC, February 27, 1954, ADVP.

"*greatest comfort*": ADV to JC, March 20, 1953, ADVP.

"*We miss*": ADV to JC, July 31, 1954, ADVP.

a "*widow*": ADV to JC, February 3, 1954, ADVP.

"*I cry with you*": JC to ADV, August 4, 1954, JCP.

167 *storm out fighting*: see BDV, "Hazards of the Road," *Harper's*, March 1955, and Betty Zoss to BDV, January 23, 1955, BDVP.

Paul crafted: the valentines are in ADVP.

"'*Sorry, fellows*'": ADV to JC, February 3, 1954, ADVP.

168 "*Definition of a wife*": JC to ADV, April 11, 1954, JCP.

"*when at last*": JC to ADV, February 18, 1953, JCP.

14. BLACK MACS AND BANNED BOOKS

169 "*the two Black Macs*": see letter from Huntington Woods, MI, resident to BDV, January 7, 1953, BDVP, Box 13.

"*I simply couldn't*": Ray Bradbury to BDV, November 15, 1952, BDVP, Box 52.1.

"*consistent opposition*": Arthur Hays Sulzberger to BDV, December 15, 1953, BDVP.

170 "*McCarthy and McCarran may have*": Elmer Davis to BDV, January 10, 1953, BDVP.

One unintentionally prescient: Zuma Baldwin to Patrick McCarran, July 16, 1950, PMC, Box 51.

Another fan wrote: PMC, Box 16.

One envelope had: ibid.

"*McCarthy, McCarran, et al*": Robert H. Ellis to BDV, March 4, 1953, BDVP.

"*I cannot distinguish*": BDV to Robert H. Ellis, March 4, 1953, BDVP.

171 *perjury charges*: Cohn scrutinized testimony by Owen Lattimore, the American advisor in China during World War II who was a constant McCarran and McCarthy scapegoat. Cohn's reading of Lattimore's twelve days of testimony—the longest of anyone's to date before a Senate investigative committee—resulted in seven perjury counts. All were dismissed after Lattimore's reputation was ruined. The DeVotos donated to Lattimore's defense fund.

Cohn and McCarran alleged: details from Ybarra, *Washington Gone Crazy*, ch. 23.

"*If Feller's conscience*": ibid., 656.

172 "*If I don't I am afraid*": Tye, *Demagogue*, 301.

"*Mr. Kaplan had no fear*": Oshinsky, *A Conspiracy*, 271.

"*I must warn you*": ADV to JC, March 11, 1953, ADVP.

173 "*This is just*": JC to ADV, circa early 1953, JCP, A-167, DeVoto folder 65.

"*Paul and I*": JC to ADV, January 28, 1953, JCP.

"*People either adore*": ADV to JC, February 9, 1953, ADVP.

Books were burned: details from Richard H. Rovere, "The Adventures of Cohn and Schine," *Reporter,* July 21, 1953; Conant, *Covert Affair;* Ybarra, *Washington Gone Crazy;* Oshinsky, *A Conspiracy;* Tye, *Demagogue.*

31,000 "subversive" books: Rovere, "Adventures."

174 "*I understand that*": DeVoto FBI file.

"*Glad to say*": from BDV speech "Some American Symbols" (given in numerous locations, circa 1953), BDVP, Box 52.2.

"*I have never been*": JC to ADV, July 16, 1953, JCP.

"*get rid of*": JC to ADV, undated, circa spring 1953, JCP.

"*What does DeVoto*": JC to ADV, April 8, 1953, JCP.

"*Never has a*": *Rocky Mountain News,* June 25, 1953.

"*a Hitler*": JC to ADV, handwritten, undated, circa April 1953, JCP.

175 "*If I went home now*": JC to ADV, July 16, 1953, JCP.

"*chief consultant*": Oshinsky, *A Conspiracy,* 255.

Julia reported: details from JC to ADV, undated, circa April 1953, JCP.

"*Everyone waited*": ibid.

176 *Roald Peterson, the Forest Service:* Peterson details from divorce records in the Missoula County Courthouse, from Sen. Lee Metcalf files at the Montana Historical Society in Helena, from Peterson's FBI file, and from author interviews with Peterson's granddaughter, Sarah Shomion.

the false rumor: At the time Hoover shared the gay rumor with the loyalty board, he knew that its possible originator, Peterson's first wife, was institutionalized. He ordered agents not to speak to her or assess her mental condition. See FBI Director to New Orleans SAC, June 23, 1952, and New Orleans SAC to FBI Director, July 8, 1952, Peterson FBI file.

177 *approximately 12,000:* www.trumanlibrary.gov/education/presidential-inquiries /trumans-loyalty-program.

15. GREEN RIVER CANYONS NATIONAL PARK

178 *McCarran's monopolistic policies:* details from Egan, *Lasso the Wind;* Stegner, *Hundredth Meridian;* BDV, "Conservation: Down and on the Way Out," *Harper's,* August 1954.

"*conflicts between*": BDV, "Conservation."

179 *The National Park Service:* details from BDV's "National Park Service," *Harper's,* March 1949, and "Let's Close the National Parks," *Harper's,* October 1953.

"*In the twentieth century*": BDV, "Billion Dollar Jackpot," *Harper's,* February 1953.

"*Keep up the fight*": John Chohlis to BDV, April 16, 1953, BDVP.

"*He's had a good response*": ADV to JC, February 27, 1953, ADVP.

"*Is there anything*": JC to ADV, February 23, 1953, JCP.

180 "*expert baby-kisser*": BDV to Garrett Mattingly, September 30, 1952, BDVP.

"I can find no part": BDV to JFK, September 15, 1953, BDVP.

"That was an excellent": JFK to BDV, March 6, 1953, BDVP.

Kennedy had asked: see Rep. Leroy Johnson to BDV, March 25, 1953, BDVP.

181 *"guinea pig":* ADV to Judith Jones, November 26, 1969, ADVP; Avis was explaining her donation of letters to the Schlesinger Library.

"The cattle-raisers": ADV to JC, February 27, 1953, ADVP.

182 *"Things are as bad":* Alfred Meyers, quoted in "New Dust Bowl? Drought and Wind Rake 11 Million Acres in West; Crop Losses Top 1930s," *Wall Street Journal,* 1954, BDVP, Box 52.1.

a quarter-billion pounds: "Texts of Three Eisenhower Statements," *New York Times,* December 19, 1953.

the government began subsidizing: see transcript of 1954 Wyoming Stock Growers Association meeting, American Heritage Center, University of Wyoming, Laramie.

only from wheat farmers: see J. Elmer Brock to Frank Barrett, May 4, 1953, Frank A. Barrett Papers, Box 53, American Heritage Center, University of Wyoming, Laramie.

"to the hilt": see O. E. Bertagnolli to Frank Barrett, March 15, 1954, Barrett Papers, Box 53.

183 *"Talking politics":* ADV to JC, February 27, 1954, ADVP.

"the kind of man": ADV to JC, November 5, 1953, ADVP.

Snow revealed: details from Snow, *From Missouri.*

"plow up every third": ibid., 143.

"Our sharecroppers": ibid., 131.

184 *"purely indigenous":* ibid., 215.

"All the people": ibid., 209.

"I can't tell you": ADV to JC, October 23, 1953, ADVP.

"I ought to be": ADV to JC, February 27, 1954, ADVP.

"I just adore": ADV to JC, April 15, 1954, ADVP.

"stubborn as": ADV to JC, undated, circa spring 1954, ADVP.

"had one of B's martinis": ADV to JC, April 15, 1954, ADVP.

185 *"Wish I had":* ADV to JC, February 17, 1953, ADVP.

"Do you know any": *New York Post,* May 8, 1953.

186 *"B tried to teach":* ADV to JC, June 11, 1953, ADVP.

The family: details from BDV, "Motel Town," *Harper's,* September 1953, and "Parks and Pictures," *Harper's,* February 1954.

"B. quite sure": ADV to JC, September 12, 1953, ADVP.

187 *"Suddenly I thought":* BDV to Garrett Mattingly, October 28, 1953, BDVP.

"deposited my lunch": ibid.

"fine old ruffian": ADV to JC, September 12, 1953, ADVP.

188 *"Saw a helluva":* ibid.

"B continues to love": ibid.

"lousy" Ogden: BDV to Garrett Mattingly, October 28, 1953, BDVP.

"a trim looker": *Ogden Standard-Examiner,* July 10, 1953.

"The wildest amusement": ADV to JC, February 9, 1953, ADVP.

189 *"a hell of a lot more":* BDV to Garrett Mattingly, February 21, 1954, BDVP.

"that the Communists": Boy Scouts, Westbury, Long Island, to BDV, February 3, 1953, BDVP.

Avis shielded: see ADV to JC, February 9, 1953, ADVP.

"*In many years*": BDV, "Notes on Western Travel," *Harper's*, November 1953.

"*our conversation about*": Roald Peterson to BDV, February 6, 1954, BDVP.

buying spices: see ADV to JC, June 11, 1953, ADVP.

"*whenever I go back*": BDV, "Notes on Western Travel."

"*wonderful country*": ADV to JC, September 12, 1953, ADVP.

190   "*scenic carpetbagger*": William Dawson to BDV, July 3, 1953, BDVP.

Hatch was evicted: Harvey, *Symbol of Wilderness*, 253.

191   "*I wasn't disabled*": BDV to Garrett Mattingly, October 28, 1953, BDVP.

"*most beautiful*": ibid.

The erosion exposed: https://www.nps.gov/dino/learn/nature/geology.htm.

192   "*DeVoto Comes Out Fighting*": *San Francisco Chronicle,* January 25, 1954.

193   *The history gripped Bernard:* Ancestral Puebloan details from Diamond, *Collapse,* ch. 4.

194   "*I've never seen Mesa Verde*": JC to ADV, July 16, 1953, JCP.

16. HIS TRUE NAME IS LEGION

196   *a "swaggering" man:* McDaniel, *Dying*, 253.

"*soliciting for a lewd*": ibid., 280.

McCarran, as a senior member: Ybarra, *Washington Gone Crazy*, 591.

"*unnatural act*": McDaniel, *Dying*, 289.

"*looked as if*": Drew Pearson, "Washington Merry-Go-Round," June 23, 1954.

197   "*Pork appears*": BDV, "Intramural Giveaway," *Harper's*, March 1954.

"*participating projects*": Raymond Moley, *What Price Federal Reclamation?* (New York: American Enterprise Association, 1955), 51–54.

198   *a "perversion*": Raymond Moley, "Case Against Colorado River Storage Project and Participating Projects," printed in 1956 Economic Report of the President (Washington, DC: Government Printing Office, 1956).

"*To attempt a serious*": ibid.

private utility rates: see J. Elmer Brock to Frank Barrett, March 30, 1954, Frank A. Barrett Papers, Box 53, American Heritage Center, University of Wyoming, Laramie.

for embracing "socialism": *Wyoming Eagle*, March 28, 1954.

199   *he had "raped*": John Geoffrey Will of Upper Colorado River Commission to Lester Hunt, Lester Calloway Hunt Papers, American Heritage Center, University of Wyoming, Laramie.

"*We think that a majority*": Mrs. B. F. Miller to Lester Hunt, January 19, 1954, Hunt Papers.

"*Feel certain that congress*": Lester Hunt to constituent, January 30, 1954, Hunt Papers.

powerless to do anything: see PMC, Box 60.

"*you and I have been*": J. Elmer Brock to J. Byron Wilson, October 6, 1954, Wyoming Wool Growers Collection, American Heritage Center, University of Wyoming, Laramie.

"*We'll wreck the Army*": Tye, *Demagogue*, 411.

200   "*the greatest victory*": Oshinsky, *A Conspiracy*, 401.

In this very dangerous: Helen Lefkowitz Horowitz, "The Politics of Julia Child '34," *Smith Alumnae Quarterly*, Spring 2013.

"Taking her cue": Conant, *Covert Affair*, 250.

"It's a hard dirty": Child, *My Life*, 182–183.

"noble effort": ADV to JC, dated "Sunday," circa summer 1954, ADVP.

201   "mad in love": ADV to JC, April 30, 1954, ADVP.

"very salty character": ADV to JC, June 7, 1955, ADVP.

"Have you no decency": Tye, *Demagogue*, 436.

mailed him some: see ADV to JC, June 7, 1955, ADVP.

McCarran told veterans: "McCarran Praises McCarthy Success," *New Hampshire Sunday News*, May 2, 1954, PMC.

"just plain wrong": "Hunt Takes Life in Senate Office," *New York Times*, June 20, 1954.

202   "pale and depressed": ibid.

The next morning: details from McDaniel, *Dying*.

final political acts: see Lester Hunt, March 17, 1954, Hunt Papers.

Crippa gave a speech: see Crippa to Senate Interior Committee, June 28, 1954, Barrett Papers, Box 53.

"the conspiratorial mind": BDV to Garrett Mattingly, June 28, 1954, BDVP.

203   "This is a helluva": ADV to JC, April 28, 1955, ADVP.

told the graduates: all quotes from BDV's speech "The Recurring Platitude," BDVP and http://mdevotomusic.org/?p=154.

17. THE WESTERN PARADOX

205   "eight-fathoms deep": ADV to JC, April 28, 1955, ADVP.

"got a royalty check": ADV to JC, December 16, 1953, ADVP.

"share of this loot": ADV to JC, February 9, 1953, ADVP.

206   "if here the McCarthy's": JC to ADV, October 1, 1954, JCP.

invaded by "strangers": ADV: Memoir About Julia Child, dictated to Mark DeVoto, October 16, 1988, ADVP.

"is a man of": ADV to JC, July 31, 1954, ADVP.

"utterly graceful": ADV to JC, October 7, 1955, ADVP.

207   "love at first sight": ADV to JC, July 31, 1954, ADVP.

"What will you have": ADV, Memoir About Julia Child.

"DeVoto himself is": JC to ADV, July 1954, JCP.

"There is no mistaking": ADV to JC, July 31, 1954, ADVP.

"atomic intensity": Spitz, *Dearie*, 261.

"Benny of course": ADV, Memoir About Julia Child.

"I can't imagine": BDV to Adlai Stevenson, June 11, 1954, BDVP.

"alleged that Adlai": ibid.

"There's a gallant": ADV to JC, April 28, 1953, ADVP.

209   "the most beat-up": ADV to JC, December 15, 1954, ADVP.

"as agreeable and educational": Adlai Stevenson to BDV, August 19, 1954, BDVP.

"*We need bold*": BDV to Adlai Stevenson, August 29, 1954, BDVP.

210   "*mid-twentieth century Pinchot*": ibid.

"*I have discussed*": BDV to JFK, September 15, 1954, BDVP.

211   "*Every move in regard*": BDV, "Conservation: Down and on the Way Out," *Harper's*, August 1954.

"*too apathetic*": ADV to JC, August 20, 1954, BDVP.

212   "*I am completely sold*": Alfred Knopf to BDV, August 2, 1948, BDVP.

"*made their eyes bulge*": Stegner, *Uneasy Chair*, 369.

William Koshland: see Alfred Knopf to ADV, March 21, 1974, ADVP.

steer public opinion: see Harvey, *Symbol of Wilderness*, 257.

213   "*born again*": Stegner, *Hundredth Meridian*, 366.

"*If you feel like*": Thomas, *A Country in Mind*, 93.

"*It's a better world*": Stegner, *This Is Dinosaur*, 17. In 1983 Stegner would famously write that the national parks are America's best idea.

buffalo steaks: see ADV to JC, September 27, 1954, ADVP.

the "barbarian" style: ADV to JC, January 9, 1953, ADVP.

214   "*You will adore*": ADV to William Raney, February 28, 1958, ADVP.

"*Please do not arrange*": BDV to Colston Leigh, October 6, 1954, BDVP.

connected the board: see WSP, Box 102, Folder 6.

"*chaw some steak*": BDV to Eric [Larrabee], September 20 [1954], BDVP.

215   *his job was "too small"*: ADV to JC, April 28, 1955, ADVP.

"*Sen. McCarran—Joe*": Eva Bertrand Adams Papers, Special Collections, University of Nevada, Reno.

"*You are the 'Daddy'*": J. Edgar Hoover to Patrick McCarran, January 29, 1954, Adams Papers.

"*captive in the hands*": Ybarra, *Washington Gone Crazy*, 750.

"*Communist hoodlums*": Oshinsky, *A Conspiracy*, 493.

216   "*At no day in history*": Ybarra, *Washington Gone Crazy*, 750.

as though in harmony: "Pioneer Cattleman J. Elmer Brock Dies," *Casper Morning Star*, December 7, 1954.

"*He was a brilliant*": BDV, *Western Paradox*, 476.

18. "ON ANY GROUNDS WHATEVER"

217   *senator Francis Newlands:* details from Rowley, *Reclaiming*; Morris, *Theodore Rex*; Brinkley, *Wilderness Warrior.*

218   *below 50 percent:* DuBois, *Souls of Black Folk*, 60.

"*He believed African-Americans*": Rowley, *Reclaiming* forward.

"*furnish a model*": ibid., 140.

"*write the word white*": ibid., 143.

large, out-of-state: ibid., 145, 159.

219   "*The nation has lost*": Ybarra, *Washington Gone Crazy*, 753.

"*defending the right*": Harvey, *Symbol of Wilderness*, 266.

220 A Project for People: see Tom Bolack to Frank Barrett, November 10, 1955, Frank A. Barrett Papers, Box 53, American Heritage Center, University of Wyoming, Laramie.

Saylor issued a statement: John Saylor, January 31, 1955, BDVP.

"bronzed horsemen": BDV, "Current Comic Strips," *Harper's*, May 1955.

"He has been away": ADV to JC, April 15, 1954, ADVP.

"He fails in school": ADV to JC, November 1, 1954, ADVP.

221 *"God-damn tiresome":* BDV to William Sloan, June 24, 1952, BDVP.

"had me rolling around": BDV to Garrett Mattingly, July 30, 1952, BDVP.

spot on his prostate: Stegner, *Uneasy Chair*, 380.

"Much love to Benny": JC to ADV, August 23, 1954, JCP.

Bernard had alluded to: for BDV's citing of the errors, see article section with U. S. Grant III. Brower's House testimony came after the Bureau of Reclamation claimed it could not build the Glen Canyon Dam 35 feet higher and thus compensate for the storage of the Echo Park Dam. The bureau explained that a higher dam would make a wider surface area for the Glen Canyon Reservoir and would expose to evaporation 165,000 additional acre-feet of water. It said it arrived at that figure by subtracting the planned reservoir surface area, 621,000 acre-feet, from the suggested larger reservoir surface area, 691,000 acre-feet. Brower testified that 691,000 minus 621,000 is actually 70,000. It was one of multiple errors he found. See Harvey, *Symbol of Wilderness*, ch. 7.

"Brower presented himself": Thomas, *Country in Mind*, 173.

"Dinosaur Monument will": BDV, "And Fractions Drive Me Mad," *Harper's*, September 1954.

222 *governor of Wyoming:* Harvey, *Symbol of Wilderness*, 350.

"Nature Boys": Echo Park Dam opponents were derided in the *Denver Post* as "Nature Boys"; Harvey, *Symbol of Wilderness*, 147.

"short-haired women": Nash, *Wilderness*, 169.

the conservation coalition: description from Harvey, *Symbol of Wilderness*.

"do everything possible": ibid., 271.

223 *"I will oppose":* BDV to a Mr. Davoren, March 9, 1955, BDVP.

"It is an account": Raymond Moley to BDV, February 4, 1955, BDVP.

"brilliant articles": BDV, "Fractions."

"They want to throw": Legislative History, Public Law 485—84th Congress, Chapter 203, 2nd Session, S. 500.

about $2,000: see *Congressional Record*, April 19, 1955, p. 4637; Harvey, *Symbol of Wilderness*, 288, notes that an early accounting of the Colorado River Storage Plan showed a cost per acre in Utah of $124,000.

"something I had hoped": *Congressional Record*, April 19, 1955, p. 3916.

224 *"You will find":* Paul Douglas to BDV, April 20, 1955, BDVP.

"We are pretty well": ADV to JC, May 6, 1955, ADVP.

225 *"Paul . . . was flown back":* JC to ADV, April 19, 1955, JCP.

"Why the Hell": Conant, *Covert Affair*, 11–12.

"McLeod is his buddy": ADV to JC, January 13, 1954, ADVP.

"Show that a man": McDaniel, *Dying*, 327.

Paul was summoned: details from Conant, *Covert Affair*, ch. 1; JCP; Child, *My Life;* Spitz, *Dearie;* and Paul Child FBI file.

"homosexual tendencies": Conant, *Covert Affair*, 17.

226 *spoke Paul's name:* Paul Child FBI file.

"So, how about": Conant, *Covert Affair*, 13.

"so who <u>was</u>": Paul Child to JC, April 13, 1955, JCP.

"for God's sake": ibid.

at that moment: see BDV to Arthur Schlesinger, January 18, 1955, BDVP.

"an intimate friend": Conant, *Covert Affair*, 13.

227 *"goldfish"*: ibid., 21.

"I have slept": Paul Child to JC, April 17, 1955, JCP.

Cooke was a "socialist": JC to ADV, dated "Tuesday" [April 19, 1955], JCP.

"If you want": Paul Child to JC, April 13, 1955, JCP.

"He is forever": JC to ADV, "Tuesday" [April 19, 1955], JCP.

"those libidinous hearts": Paul Child to JC, April 23, 1955, JCP.

"M.L. Cooke, and homosexuality": ADV to JC, April 28, 1955, ADVP.

"being so pally": ADV to JC, April 25, 1955, ADVP.

228 *"move heaven"*: ADV to JC, April 28, 1955, ADVP.

his "hexed" health: BDV, "For the Record," *Harper's*, June 1955.

being "spellbound": ADV to JC, April 25, 1955, ADVP.

"nearly choked": ADV to JC, April 28, 1955, ADVP.

"power boys": JC to ADV, dated "Tuesday" [April 19, 1955], JCP.

"isn't it infuriating?": ADV to JC, May 6, 1955, ADVP.

"he would fight": ADV to JC, April 28, 1955, ADVP.

"Nobody has too small": ibid.

authentic Frankfurters: see ADV to JC, April 13, 1955, ADVP.

19. "THE WEST HAS DONE IT ONCE"

229 *"'Good God'"*: Agnes Gray to BDV, November 7, 1955, BDVP.

"No one has got": BDV, "Number 241," *Harper's*, November 1955.

"Long live Benny!": H. S. Wagner, November 7, 1955, BDVP.

230 *"This is a good"*: John Oakes, May 13, 1955, BDVP.

"what I like most": Alice Northrup, September 8, 1949, BDVP.

"You have on your staff": Charles Eggert to *Harper's*, August 25, 1955, BDVP.

"I do not see": Richard Neuberger, October 29, 1955, BDVP.

"Very dashing": ADV to JC, October 26, 1955, ADVP.

"His attacks on": BDV, *Easy Chair*, jacket copy.

"'I suppose'": John Fischer, "A Portrait of the Artist as an Old Bear," *Harper's*, November 1955.

231 *"She studies"*: BDV to Byron Hurlbut, December 29, 1926, BDVP.

"B. was an absolute": ADV to JC, October 26, 1955, ADVP.

"plenty of reading matter": ADV to JC, July 17, 1955, ADVP.

"We were in opposite": Ybarra, *Washington Gone Crazy*, 607.

232 *"showered Watkins"*: *Time*, July 13, 1953.

"unwitting handmaiden": Tye, *Demagogue*, 452.

Bernard and the Sierra Club's: details from Harvey, *Symbol of Wilderness*, 198–199.

ought to be scrapped: see BDV to Paul Douglas, April 26, 1955, BDVP.

233 *"I will not get":* Oshinsky, *A Conspiracy*, 352.

"This is a lulu": Alfred Knopf, handwritten note, March 31, 1955, on letter from Fred Smith, director of Council of Conservationists, BDVP.

234 *"I frequently feel":* ADV to JC, February 9, 1953, ADVP.

235 *"He can cast":* ADV to JC, March 20, 1953, ADVP.

"She is courage": BDV to Byron Hurlbut, June 1923 (likely), BDVP.

"The wives of all": BDV (Cady Hewes), "The Life and Wife of a Writer," *Woman's Day*, April 1949.

"take the first plane": a Mr. Henry to Frederick Allen, May 31, 1955, BDVP.

"If you were as familiar": Frederick Allen to a Mr. Henry, June 22, 1955, BDVP.

"I should imagine": JC to ADV, October 27, 1955, ADVP.

"You are my candidate": Richard Neuberger to BDV, October 29, 1955, BDVP.

236 *"What do you think":* Alfred Knopf to BDV, November 7, 1955, BDVP.

"publicly renounced": Arthur Carhart to BDV, November 11, 1955, BDVP.

"He did admit": ADV to Chet Olsen, Chester J. Olsen Collection, Stewart Library Special Collections, Weber State University, Ogden, UT.

"I would sooner try": ADV to JC, February 9, 1953, ADVP.

237 *"Several thousand Indians":* details from transcript of "Adventure," November 13, 1955, BDVP.

"What would we do": ibid.

"There were many calls": Phyllis Gordon to ADV, November 1955, BDVP, Box 22.

238 *a "controversial" new:* BDV to Carl Brandt, November 4, 1955, BDVP. The article was slated for *Holiday*.

"moral victory": Gordon DeVoto to ADV, BDVP, Box 22.

"I think we'd better": details from Stegner, *Uneasy Chair*, 380.

"It's bad": ibid.

"Why don't you damn": ADV to Chet Olsen, "Wednesday" [Nov. 16, 1955], Olsen Collection.

239 *"Far from being":* ibid.

"Their guy was": Paul W. Ferris to ADV, BDVP, Box 22.

"I reached over": Anne Ford to ADV, BDVP, Box 22.

"THIS IS": Adlai Stevenson to ADV, November 15, 1955, BDVP, Box 22.

"I just can't believe": JC to ADV, November 14, 1955, JCP.

"HOWL DOGS!": W. H. Hutchison, (late) 1955, BDVP, Box 13.

"you really have": Henry Reck to ADV, BDVP, Box 22.

240 *"A Victory for":* see, e.g., *Louisville Times*, December 1, 1955.

"Interior Secretary McKay": United Press, December 1, 1955.

"I, like countless": this and next three quotes from Jane Waldo, William Dokken, Francis McVeigh, and Garth Cate, respectively, BDVP, Box 22.

"What a pity": Alfred Knopf to ADV, December 2, 1955, BDVP.

241 *"Your husband would":* E. B. White to ADV, BDVP, Box 22.

"I wish he could": ADV to Chet Olsen, "Wednesday" [Nov. 16, 1955], Olsen Collection.

242 *"no dam or reservoir":* Nash, *Wilderness*, 219.

"Your personal sorrow": Charlie and Freddie Child to ADV, BDVP, Box 22.

20. DESCENT TO EARTH

245 *"This trip is a present":* ADV to W. H. Hutchinson, April 4, 1956, BDVP.

"I have to face": ADV to Chet Olsen, "Wednesday" [Nov. 16, 1955], Chester J. Olsen Collection, Stewart Library Special Collections, Weber State University, Ogden, UT.

"especially tired": JC to ADV, December 6, 1955, JCP.

246 *"quelle chic":* see ADV to JC, February 7, 1957, ADVP.

"It was a poem": details from ADV letter to "Folks" (likely her parents), June 12, 1956, ADVP.

"guiding spirit": Spitz, *Dearie,* 192.

247 *"one thing certain":* ADV to JC, November 27, 1955, ADVP.

"No person": Richard Neuberger to ADV, BDVP, Box 22; also see *Congressional Record,* January 20, 1956, p. 1005.

248 *"want to upchuck":* ADV to JC, February 11, 1956, ADVP.

"no part of ": ADV to JC, December 1, 1955, ADVP.

"I am no more": ADV to Chet Olsen, December 5, 1955, Olsen Collection.

blocked the appointment: re: Wesley D'Ewart, see *Congressional Record,* January 20, 1956, p. 1005.

"Chet I hope": ADV to Chet Olsen, "Wednesday" [Nov. 16, 1955], Olsen Collection.

"Not a creature": Olsen to ADV, April 13, 1956, Olsen Collection.

"Before God": see letter from Forest Service official in Englewood, CO, BDVP, Box 22.

249 *"Just say Mission":* ADV to Chet Olsen, "Wednesday" [Nov. 16, 1955], Olsen Collection.

"If they are such great": *Ogden Standard,* February 15, 1956.

"Though DeVoto is": ADV to JC, February 21, 1956, ADVP.

"places himself in": details from DeVoto FBI file.

"Your suggested change": ibid.

250 *"one single person":* Avis to "Folks," June 12, 1956, ADVP.

"What a wonderful": ibid.

"it doesn't make": ADV to JC, June 8, 1956, ADVP.

"Benny was more of ": Robert Lee to ADV, BDVP, Box 22.

"as if I have lost": Edgar Cone to ADV, BDVP, Box 22.

251 *"The West and what":* Arthur Carhart to ADV, BDVP, Box 22.

"I felt as if ": O. D. Duncan to ADV, BDVP, Box 22.

"a great many letters": Russell Lynes to ADV, December 6, 1955, BDVP, Box 22.

"You were always so": Catherine Bowen to ADV, BDVP, Box 22.

"You always seemed to": BDVP, Box 22.

"I wish I could": Helen Everitt to ADV, BDVP, Box 22.

"Be solaced": Katie Seeber to ADV, BDVP, Box 22.

"I have never known": Garrett Mattingly to ADV, BDVP, Box 22.

"All loved Benny": ADV to JC, December 7, 1955, ADVP.

"about eight thousand things": ADV to Chet Olsen, "Wednesday" [Nov. 16, 1955], Olsen Collection.

252 *"warming to our spirits":* ADV to JC, October 7, 1957, ADVP.

"Great blank spaces": ADV to JC, February 11, 1956, ADVP.

"I feel he just": ADV to JC, December 1, 1955, ADVP.

"We were so terribly": ADV to JC, December 7, 1955, ADVP.

"I am sick": ADV to JC, April 16, 1956, ADVP.

"damn depressed": ADV to JC, January 15, 1958, ADVP.

"Old Mrs. Gloom": ADV to JC, January 1, 1958, ADVP.

"the whiskey": ADV to JC, December 7, 1955, ADVP.

253 *"My old man"*: ADV to JC, June 16, 1956, ADVP.

"Of course it would": ADV to JC, October 30, 1957, ADVP.

"You are so familiar": JC to ADV, February 20, 1956, JCP.

"I regard": ADV to JC, February 11, 1956, ADVP.

"It's a nice little": ADV to JC, February 11, 1956, ADVP.

254 *"easy with him"*: see ADV to JC, November 19, 1958, ADVP.

"hooray for the first of May": ADV to JC, January 17, 1957, ADVP.

"Toots, I never": ibid.

"Avis, you've done": quoted by ADV to JC, January 21, 1957, ADVP.

"honest meat": ADV to JC, June 15, 1957, ADVP.

"booby traps": ADV to JC, January 29, 1958, ADVP.

255 *"My dears"*: ADV to JC, September 26, 1957, ADVP.

"hooray for the third of May": ADV to JC, May 10, 1957, ADVP.

"You are learning": ADV to JC, October 6, 1958, ADVP.

"turning adjectives": ADV to JC, June 14, 1958, ADVP.

"dashes always look": ADV to JC, Friday the 17th (presumably Nov. or Dec.), 1967, ADVP.

the word *"persnickety"*: ADV to JC, November 13, 1957, ADVP.

"My God, I do": ADV to JC, November 13, 1957, ADVP.

256 *"It sticks out"*: ADV to JC, November 30, 1958, ADVP.

"For coq au vin": ADV to JC, April 3, 1958, ADVP.

"I don't think you": ADV to JC, April 3, 1958, ADVP.

"fussy friend": ADV to JC, November 30, 1958, ADVP.

"Sloppy proofreading": ADV to JC, July 31, 1954, ADVP.

"My, as you said": JC to ADV, February 18, 1953, JCP.

"our book": ADV to JC, October 26, 1955, ADVP.

"It is the kind": ADV to JC, December 7, 1955, ADVP.

"Alfred is absolutely": ADV to JC, February 21, 1957, ADVP.

"The only real": ADV to JC, January 29, 1958, ADVP.

"destroy my peace": ADV to Robert E. Lee, December 2, 1962, ADVP.

257 *"the terrible tempered"*: ADV to JC, November 26, 1960, ADVP.

"No more for you": ADV to JC, February 21, 1957, ADVP.

"Well, so no Farrell": ibid.

"I was excited": ADV to JC, October 15, 1960, ADVP.

"We were both": Stegner, *Uneasy Chair*, author's note.

258 Stegner was a Communist: see Edith Mirrielees to BDV, November 24, 1952, BDVP.

"I owed him": Stegner to ADV, November 28, 1955, BDVP.

"Plain, but very": ADV to JC, September 12, 1960, ADVP.

"as a monument": ADV to JC, October 15, 1960, ADVP.

"sort of beau": ADV to JC, November 28, 1959, ADVP.

259 *"good friendship"*: ADV to JC, March 13, 1960, ADVP.

she missed sex: see ADV to JC, March 13, 1960, ADVP.

"I have not read": ADV to JC, November 29, 1957, ADVP.

"why on earth": ADV to JC, March 25, 1958, ADVP.

"in vino veritas": ADV to JC, February 10, 1958, ADVP.

"I am deeply": JC to ADV, January 12, 1958, JCP.

260 *"older, more worldly"*: ADV to JC, September 27, 1958, ADVP.

"I keep reminding": ADV to JC, December 29, 1958, ADVP.

regretted leaving college: see ADV to JC, February 9, 1959, ADVP.

"It is just unthinkable": ADV to JC, January 17, 1958, ADVP.

21. MASTER AVIS

261 *"Almost immediately"*: Child, *My Life*, 217.

262 *"A drastic improvement"*: ADV to JC, January 17, 1958, ADVP.

"Magnificent": ADV to JC, June 9, 1959, ADVP.

"Impressed to death": ADV to JC, December 27, 1959, ADVP.

Houghton Mifflin loved it: see ADV to JC, October 3, 1959, ADVP.

"all in the bag": see ADV to JC, October 3, 1959, ADVP.

"Someday a gamble": ADV to JC, July 2, 1958, ADVP.

directly to Koshland: see ADV to JC, November 11, 1959, ADVP.

"live with" it: ADV to JC, November 19, 1959, ADVP.

"It will, of course": see Koshland to ADV, November 18, 1959, ADVP.

"Has she never": ADV to JC, November 18, 1959, ADVP.

263 *"become a classic"*: ADV to JC, April 9, 1960, ADVP.

"that book Avis": ADV to JC, November 26, 1960, ADVP.

"I don't think we": ADV to JC, February 18, 1960, ADVP.

it was "astonishing": ADV to JC, April 9, 1960, ADVP.

"tank right over": Wednesday (no date, probably January), 1967, ADVP.

"At my age": ADV to JC, April 15, 1959, ADVP.

"Ocian in view": see ADV to JC (no date, probably January), 1961, ADVP.

2.7 million: according to Knopf, as of April 15, 2021.

"I do owe you": Alfred Knopf to ADV, October 30, 1961, ADVP.

"Finally there is": JC and Bertholle Beck, *Mastering the Art of French Cooking* (New York: Knopf, 1961), acknowledgments.

264 *"Mrs. DeVoto holding"*: *Lewistown Morning Tribune*, September 10, 1962.

message from President Kennedy: quotes in this and the next two paragraphs from JFK, September 5, 1962, BDVP.

265 *"The 'New Frontier' is"*: John Carver, BDVP, Box 83.

"Dear Mr. President": ADV to JFK, September 15, 1962, BDVP, Box 83.

266 *"Is anybody working"*: Jackson J. Benson, *Wallace Stegner: His Life and Work* (New York: Viking, 1996), 365.

"I cherish": ADV to Robert E. Lee, December 2, 1962, BDVP.

"all Benny's doing": Benson, *Wallace Stegner*, 160.

"*I salute her*": Stegner, *Uneasy Chair*, author's note.

"*I have tried*": ibid.

267 "*When he created*": Benson, *Wallace Stegner*, 368.

"*I very carefully*": *Courier-Journal & Times*, July 28, 1974.

"*You wrote the definitive*": ADV to Stegner, September 11, 1987, WSP.

"*the bravest damn man*": Stegner, *Uneasy Chair*, 52.

grand sycamore trees: details from www.jfklibrary.org/about-us/about-the-jfk-library/history; Robert Reinhold, "Kennedy Library Plans Are Unveiled," *New York Times*, May 30, 1973; John Kifner, "Cambridge Loses Kennedy Museum," *New York Times*, February 7, 1975.

268 *it was "shocking"*: author interview with Ann Oliver, age ninety, February 2020.

"*Avis was very*": author interview with Pebble Gifford, age eighty-two, February 2020.

269 "*Harvard Square Defense*": ADV to Stegner, December 29, 1984, WSP.

"*an ardent advocate*": civic citation, ADVP.

270 "*He was generous*": Mark DeVoto, interview with author, December 18, 2019.

"*Benny would have been*": ADV to Stegner, June 6, 1987, WSP.

"*doing Julia's office*": ADV to Stegner, December 14, 1980, WSP.

"*part of the furniture*": author interview with Russell Morash, age eighty-four, February 2020.

271 "*your fellow criminal*": M. F. K. Fisher to ADV, November 1, 1974, ADVP.

"*Avis DeVoto, still acting*": JC and Simone Beck, *Mastering the Art of French Cooking*, vol. 2 (New York: Knopf, 1970), acknowledgments.

"*valuable to future generations*": ADV to Judith Jones, November 26, 1969, ADVP.

"*I really feel*": ADV to William Koshland, September 10, 1987, ADVP.

"*you display*": JC to ADV, January 5, 1953, ADVP.

EPILOGUE: REMEMBERING

272 "*The Western outdoors*": Richard Neuberger, *Congressional Record*, January 20, 1956, p. 1005.

"*nation's environmental conscience*": Stegner, *Uneasy Chair*, 381.

274 *people like Roald Peterson:* In late 1957, Montana representative Lee Metcalf succeeded in clearing Peterson's name and he was offered back his Forest Service job. Peterson, who had moved to Uruguay, remarried, and continued working with small farmers and ranchers, thanked Metcalf but declined, based on the way he had been treated during his loyalty investigation.

276 "*We're not having*": Spitz, *Dearie*, 518.

"*lo and behold*": ADV to JC, April 30, 1954, ADVP.

"*odds are you've never*": Mitch Shaw, "Group Forms to Promote Memory of Accomplished but Little-Known Ogdenite," *Ogden Standard-Examiner*, April 2, 2021.

BIBLIOGRAPHY

Brinkley, Douglas. *Rightful Heritage: Franklin D. Roosevelt and the Land of America*. New York: Harper-Collins, 2016.

———. *The Wilderness Warrior: Theodore Roosevelt and the Crusade for America*. New York: HarperCollins, 2009.

Cawley, R. McGreggor. *Federal Land, Western Anger: The Sagebrush Rebellion and Environmental Politics*. Lawrence: University Press of Kansas, 1993.

Child, Julia. Papers. Schlesinger Library on the History of Women in America, Radcliffe Institute for Advanced Study, Harvard University.

———, with Alex Prud'homme. *My Life in France*. New York: Knopf, 2006.

Conant, Jennet. *A Covert Affair: When Julia and Paul Child Joined the OSS*. New York: Simon & Schuster, 2011.

Davis, Kenneth S. *River on the Rampage*. New York: Doubleday, 1953.

DeVoto, Avis. Papers. Schlesinger Library on the History of Women in America, Radcliffe Institute for Advanced Study, Harvard University.

DeVoto, Bernard. *Across the Wide Missouri*. Boston: Houghton Mifflin, 1947.

———. *The Course of Empire*. Boston: Houghton Mifflin, 1952.

———. *The Easy Chair*. Boston: Houghton Mifflin, 1955.

———. Papers. Special Collections, Stanford University Library.

———. *The Western Paradox: A Conservation Reader*. New Haven, CT: Yale University Press, 2001.

———. *The Year of Decision: 1846*. Boston: Little, Brown & Co., 1942.

DeVoto, Mark, ed. *The Selected Letters of Bernard DeVoto and Katharine Sterne*. Salt Lake City: University of Utah Press, 2012.

Diamond, Jared. *Collapse: How Societies Choose to Fail or Succeed*. New York: Penguin, 2005.

Diamond, Sigmund. *Compromised Campus: The Collaboration of Universities with the Intelligence Community, 1945–1955*. Oxford, UK: Oxford University Press, 1992.

DuBois, W. E. B. *The Souls of Black Folk*. Chicago: McClurg, 1903.

Edwards, Jerome E. *Pat McCarran: Political Boss of Nevada*. Reno: University of Nevada Press, 1982.

Egan, Timothy. *The Good Rain: Across Time and Terrain in the Pacific Northwest*. New York: Vintage, 1991.

———. *Lasso the Wind: Away to the New West*. New York: Vintage, 1998.

———. *The Worst Hard Time*. Boston: Houghton Mifflin, 2005.

Federal Bureau of Investigation. Case file 123-192, Paul Cushing Child.

———. Case files 100-354575, 94-3-4-550, 66-33413, and 66-2542-3-5-852, Bernard Augustine DeVoto.

———. Case file 121-24315, William Leonard Langer.

———. Case file 121-7691, Roald Arnold Peterson.

———. Case file 61-81518, Benjamin "Bugsy" Siegel.

Fenby, Jonathan. *Chiang Kai-shek: China's Generalissimo and the Nation He Lost*. New York: Carroll & Graf, 2004.

Gentry, Curt. *J. Edgar Hoover: The Man and His Secrets*. New York: Plume, 1991.

Goodwin, Doris Kearns. *No Ordinary Time: Franklin and Eleanor Roosevelt: The Home Front in World War II*. New York: Simon & Schuster, 1994.

Harvey, Mark W. T. *A Symbol of Wilderness: Echo Park and the American Conservation Movement*. Seattle: University of Washington Press, 1994.

Howard, Joseph Kinsey. *Montana: High, Wide, and Handsome*. New Haven, CT: Yale University Press, 1943.

———. *Strange Empire: The Story of Louis Riel, the Metis People, and Their Struggle for a Homeland on the Plains of the United States–Canada Border*. New York: William Morrow, 1952.

Kaplan, Robert D. *Earning the Rockies: How Geography Shapes America's Role in the World*. New York: Random House, 2017.

Ketcham, Christopher. *This Land: How Cowboys, Capitalism, and Corruption Are Ruining the American West*. New York: Viking, 2019.

Manning, Richard. *Rewilding the West: Restoration in a Prairie Landscape*. Berkeley: University of California Press, 2009.

McCarran, Patrick A. Senator Patrick McCarran Collection. Nevada Historical Society, Reno.

McDaniel, Rodger. *Dying for Joe McCarthy's Sins: The Suicide of Wyoming Senator Lester Hunt*. Cody, WY: WordsWorth, 2013.

Morris, Edmund. *Theodore Rex*. New York: Random House, 2002.

Muller, Edward K., ed. *DeVoto's West: History, Conservation, and the Public Good*. Athens, OH: Swallow Press, 2005.

Nash, Roderick Frazier. *Wilderness and the American Mind*. New Haven, CT: Yale University Press, 1967.

Oshinsky, David M. *A Conspiracy So Immense: The World of Joe McCarthy*. New York: The Free Press, 1983.

Reardon, Joan, ed. *As Always, Julia: The Letters of Julia Child and Avis DeVoto*. Boston: Houghton Mifflin Harcourt, 2010.

Reisner, Marc. *Cadillac Desert: The American West and Its Disappearing Water*. New York: Penguin, 1986.

Rowley, William D. *Reclaiming the Arid West: The Career of Francis G. Newlands*. Bloomington: Indiana University Press, 1996.

Schlesinger, Arthur M., Jr. *A Life in the Twentieth Century*. Boston: Houghton Mifflin, 2000.

Snow, Thad. *From Missouri: An American Farmer Looks Back*. Boston: Houghton Mifflin, 1954.

Spitz, Bob. *Dearie: The Remarkable Life of Julia Child*. New York: Knopf, 2012.

Stegner, Wallace. *Beyond the Hundredth Meridian*. Boston: Houghton Mifflin, 1954.

———, ed. *The Letters of Bernard DeVoto*. New York: Doubleday, 1975.

———. Papers. Special Collections, Marriott Library, University of Utah, Salt Lake City.

———. *The Sound of Mountain Water*. New York: Doubleday, 1969.

———, ed. *This Is Dinosaur: Echo Park Country and Its Magic Rivers*. New York: Knopf, 1955.

———. *The Uneasy Chair: A Biography of Bernard DeVoto*. Garden City, NY: Doubleday, 1974.

Thomas, John L. *A Country in Mind: Wallace Stegner, Bernard DeVoto, History, and the American Land*. London: Routledge, 2002.

Tye, Larry. *Demagogue: The Life and Long Shadow of Senator Joe McCarthy*. Boston: Houghton Mifflin Harcourt, 2020.

Wister, Owen. *The Virginian: A Horseman of the Plains*. New York: Macmillan, 1902.

Yang, Jia Lynn. *One Mighty and Irresistible Tide: The Epic Story of Immigration in America, 1924–1965*. New York: W. W. Norton, 2020.

Ybarra, Michael J. *Washington Gone Crazy: Senator Pat McCarran and the Great American Communist Hunt*. Hanover, NH: Steerforth Press, 2004.

INDEX